# THE EARLY YEARS OF INDU
# ORGANIZATIONAL PSYC

Focusing on the late nineteenth and early twentieth centuries, this book provides a history of the origins of industrial-organizational psychology. Taking an international perspective, *The Early Years of Industrial and Organizational Psychology* examines the context in which industrial psychology emerged and its origins in the measurement of individual differences. Andrew Vinchur covers the initial applications of psychology in advertising, the study of fatigue, and especially employee selection. The role industrial psychology played in World War I and its post-war expansion are discussed, as well as the education of industrial psychologists, their efforts to establish industrial psychology as a profession, and the beginnings of the organizational side of the field.

ANDREW J. VINCHUR is a Professor of Psychology at Lafayette College. Long interested in the history of psychology, his published work has focused on the history of industrial and organizational psychology, especially the history of psychology applied to employee selection.

# THE EARLY YEARS OF INDUSTRIAL AND ORGANIZATIONAL PSYCHOLOGY

ANDREW J. VINCHUR

*Lafayette College*

# CAMBRIDGE
## UNIVERSITY PRESS

University Printing House, Cambridge CB2 8BS, United Kingdom

One Liberty Plaza, 20th Floor, New York, NY 10006, USA

477 Williamstown Road, Port Melbourne, VIC 3207, Australia

314–321, 3rd Floor, Plot 3, Splendor Forum, Jasola District Centre, New Delhi – 110025, India

79 Anson Road, #06–04/06, Singapore 079906

Cambridge University Press is part of the University of Cambridge.

It furthers the University's mission by disseminating knowledge in the pursuit of education, learning, and research at the highest international levels of excellence.

www.cambridge.org
Information on this title: www.cambridge.org/9781107065734
DOI: 10.1017/9781107588608

First published 2018

Printed in the United States of America by Sheridan Books, Inc.

*A catalogue record for this publication is available from the British Library.*

*Library of Congress Cataloging-in-Publication Data*
NAMES: Vinchur, Andrew J. (Andrew John), author.
TITLE: The early years of industrial and organizational psychology /
Andrew J. Vinchur, Lafayette College.
DESCRIPTION: Cambridge, United Kingdom ; New York, NY : Cambridge
University Press, 2018. | Includes bibliographical references.
IDENTIFIERS: LCCN 2018009844 | ISBN 9781107065734 (hbk)
SUBJECTS: LCSH: Psychology, Industrial – History.
CLASSIFICATION: LCC HF5548.8 .V536 2018 | DDC 158.7–dc23
LC record available at https://lccn.loc.gov/2018009844

ISBN 978-1-107-06573-4 Hardback
ISBN 978-1-107-67168-3 Paperback

*For Bianca*

# Contents

# List of Figures and Tables

## Figures

## Tables

# *Preface*

This book is my attempt to develop a comprehensive picture of the origins and early development of industrial-organizational (I-O) psychology. The time period covered is from the late 1800s until the early 1930s, an interval that saw what was then called industrial psychology evolve from the initial efforts of a handful of individuals to an established professional field. Narrowing the focus to the early years allows me to offer a more fine-grained analysis than writing a history of I-O psychology from the beginning to the present day. I view this book as primarily a work of synthesis, using primary and secondary sources to create an overview of the origins and early years of I-O psychology with an appreciation for both context and those individuals important in its development. Much of the historical work in I-O psychology has been justly criticized as overly focusing on developments in the United States.[1] I-O psychology developed in many countries; I have tried to reflect the global nature of its history. The United States does receive proportionally more coverage than other countries, however, because of its central role in the history of I-O psychology and because of my own limitations in accessing non-English relevant materials.

The structure of the book is neither strictly chronological nor strictly topical. I considered both approaches. The former proved too disjointed due to the uneven development of various content areas; the latter required excessive repetition and loss of narrative drive. I compromised with a hybrid approach: roughly chronological, combining coverage of topic areas with biographical sketches of important contributors that present the entire arc of their lives and careers. Psychology applied to employee selection was at the heart of early industrial psychology, and it receives attention appropriate to its importance in this narrative.

---

[1] This includes criticism Salgado, Anderson, and Hülsheger (2010) directed at me (Vinchur, 2007) for a history of personnel selection.

All narrative history tells a story. In shaping that story, I had to decide what is relevant from the large amount of information available. It is impossible to include everything. While all history is told from a particular perspective, one should consciously avoid an unfairly biased perspective. This is easier said than done, as I am enough of a psychologist to realize that we are not always aware of our biases and that it is very difficult to step outside one's cultural and educational experiences. While my intention was to write an accurate, balanced account of the origins and early years of I-O psychology, it is critical to stress that this is *a* history, not *the* history. Other histories, with different perspectives, emphases, and information, are possible, inevitable, and welcome.

In writing this history of the beginning years of I-O psychology, I tried to find a balance between what are sometimes referred to as the "old" and "new" historiographical approaches to the history of psychology. External influences and context are important, but so are the actions and ideas of the participants, including biographical information relevant to their contributions. While this is a critical history in the sense that discontinuities and missteps are discussed, I believe that real progress occurred, and those accomplishments are noted. I used primary sources when possible and secondary sources when it was not or when those secondary sources added nuance or contributed to an understanding of the material. This was particularly true for non-English material. While I tried to write a history sensitive to how the historical actors would have experienced events at that time, I do at times draw connections between past and current research and practice, not to judge necessarily (although there is some of that) but to illustrate similarities and differences.

Deciding how much of a background in I-O psychology I could assume the reader possesses was a difficult question to answer. An earlier draft of this book was geared to a relatively naïve reader with little or no background in I-O psychology, statistics, measurement, or historiography. It even included a primer on I-O psychology, summarizing the content areas that comprise the field. Despite my efforts, reviewers noted that the book was, in fact, more suitable for a reader with some knowledge of I-O psychology, although not necessarily one who is familiar with historiography. While I did excise the primer, I have included explanatory footnotes explaining statistical and I-O psychology procedures and terms that may be unfamiliar, and included a section on historiography to introduce that topic to the reader who may be familiar with I-O psychology but not with historical research. It is my hope that the book can be read profitably by anyone with an interest in the history of I-O psychology.

# Acknowledgments

I have been blessed with a wonderful family and friends, and although they may not have contributed directly to this book, it would have been impossible to write it without having them in my life. Thanks to my colleagues at Lafayette College and to my colleagues and collaborators elsewhere for your kindness and support. I am grateful to Lafayette College for providing material support and a sabbatical leave to work on the book. In particular, I would like to thank the staff at the Lafayette College Skillman Library, who were generous with advice and amazing at procuring needed materials. Diane Shaw, the Director of Special Collections and College Archives, was very supportive and provided a photograph of James McKeen Cattell for the book. The staff at the Cummings Center for the History of Psychology at the University of Akron and at the Carnegie-Mellon University Archives were helpful in locating information and photographs. In addition, I am also grateful to the following archivists for their assistance in locating photographs: Fred Burwell at Beloit College, Leah Loscutoff at the Stevens Institute of Technology, and Anna Towlson at the London School of Economics.

I would like to thank Dave Repetto, my editor at Cambridge University Press, for his patience and faith that the book would actually be completed. Thanks also to content manager Bronte Rawlings, project manager Revathi Thirunavukkarasu, copy editor Karin Kipp, Robert Swanson for the indexes, and everyone at Cambridge Press who worked on the book. I am grateful to a group of anonymous reviewers for their time and thoughtful comments. And special thanks to my wife Bianca Falbo, Associate Professor of English and Director of the College Writing Program at Lafayette College, who helped wrestle my awkward prose into something resembling grammatical English. This book is dedicated to her.

CHAPTER I

# Work, Psychology, and History

This book is a history of the origins and early years of industrial-organizational (I-O) psychology from the late 1800s to the early 1930s. In the early twentieth century, psychology was becoming established in colleges and universities, and the early psychologists were beginning to explore ways of applying their new science to the clinic, courtroom, and classroom. Some of these early scientist-practitioners turned their attention to the problems of industry, initially in the field of advertising and the study of fatigue. Notable was the interest in improving the efficiency of organizations, especially by improving employee selection procedures. From these initial efforts, I-O psychology has evolved into a worldwide enterprise with thousands of researchers and practitioners.

This is not a book of ancient history; this is history just out of reach. Many of the individuals who are central to this history lived well into the second half of the twentieth century. The early years of that century, however, were in many ways a different world. The late nineteenth and early twentieth centuries saw the electrification of cities, the great expansion of railways, and the advent of the internal combustion engine and the automobile. There was the rise of industrialization and of large corporations, with a concurrent emphasis on efficiency and production. Cities were expanding, as people migrated from an agrarian life to an urban one. World War I, the Great War, ushered in the beginning of large-scale mechanized, industrial warfare. There were many advances in science, including popularization of evolution and the establishment of a scientific psychology, central to the history of early industrial psychology. The environment was favorable for a psychology applied to the concerns of industry and business. Before beginning our history of this endeavor, however, a discussion of the terminology used to describe the evolving field is in order, followed by a brief description of present-day I-O psychology.

The use of *industrial-organizational* psychology in the book's title is something of a misnomer, as this term is a relatively recent one that was not in use during the time period covered in this book.[1] During the early part of the twentieth century, psychologists in the United States who worked with business organizations were variously called *economic psychologists, employment psychologists, business psychologists, consulting psychologists, applied psychologists, vocational psychologists,* or *industrial psychologists,* with *consulting psychologists* the preferred term early on and *industrial psychologists* becoming common by the 1920s (Arthur & Benjamin, 1999). *Industrial psychology* was also used in Great Britain, as shown, for example, by its use in the titles of a series of textbooks by the early industrial psychologist Charles S. Myers (Myers, 1925, 1926, 1929). Today in Great Britain the common term is *occupational psychology* (Warr, 2007).[2] In continental Europe, the term used to describe the activities of early psychologists involved in industrial work was a variation of the German *Psychotechniks,* coined by William Stern in 1903 (Allport, 1938).

Psychotechniks was translated into other European languages, including Dutch (*psychotechniek*), French (*psychotechnique*), Italian (*psicotecnica*), Russian (*psikhoteknika*), and Spanish (*psicotecnia*) (Salgado, 2001). Viteles (1932) viewed psychotechnology as akin to applied psychology. He saw the use of the term to describe only industrial applications as mistaken, noting that in Germany, applying psychology to industry was termed *industrielle psychotechnik,* similar to the use of *industrial psychology* in America. Geuter (1992), however, noted that by the 1920s in Germany, *psychotechnics* and *industrial psychology* were synonymous. Hugo Münsterberg (1914), who popularized the term, viewed psychotechnics as a mechanized approach to applied psychology. He viewed psychotechnics' relationship to general psychology as similar to how engineering is related to physics, that is, a technical specialty related to a scientific endeavor (cited in van Strien, 1998a). Viteles (1974), who studied in Europe in 1922 and 1923, preferred the more laboratory- and theory-based approaches to industrial psychology exemplified by the work of Otto Lipmann to the psychotechnology practiced by Walther Moede and Curt Piorkowski. *Psychotechnics* was never the preferred term in English, and in fact American psychologists, such as

---

[1] The American Psychological Association's (APA) division for I-O psychology, Division 14, changed its name from "Industrial Psychology" to "Industrial-Organizational Psychology" in 1973. Seeking a measure of independence from APA, the division incorporated as the Society for Industrial and Organizational Psychology (SIOP) in 1983 (Benjamin, 1997b).

[2] In a 1948 memoir, the British psychologist T. H. Pear noted that although he still used the term industrial psychology, "we . . . tell our students that 'occupational' is a better word" (p. 112).

Kitson (1922b) and Viteles (1932) who used it found it necessary to explain its meaning to readers (Gundlach, 1998). By the late 1930s, even in continental Europe, the term was being replaced by *applied psychology* (Warr, 2007).

In 1912, the term *work psychology* was first used by Leo Engel in two articles in the journal *Zeitschrift für angewandte Psychologie (Journal of Applied Psychology)* (cited in Salgado, 2001), and this term eventually supplanted *psychotechnics* in continental Europe (Warr, 2007). For the most part, in Europe today the field is known as *work and organizational psychology (W/O)* (Salgado, 2007; Warr, 2007), and in Australia and New Zealand as *organizational psychology* (Warr, 2007). *Industrial-organizational psychology (I-O)* or *industrial/organizational psychology (I/O)* is the preferred designation in the United States.[3] Because this is a history of the roots of present-day I-O psychology, use of that term seemed appropriate in the title, though to be consistent with the time period covered, in discussing the early years I will use more time-appropriate terms such as *industrial psychology* or *psychotechnics* and refer to its practitioners for the most part as *industrial psychologists*.

Definitions of industrial psychology and related terms that appeared in contemporary textbooks were variations on the theme of applying psychology to business and industry. Henry C. Link (1919), for example, defined employment psychology "as the application of the scientific method to the mental actions concerned with employment" (p. 13). Early definitions highlighted the usefulness of this application for industry. Hugo Münsterberg (1913) saw applied psychology as an intermediary between psychology and the problems of business: "[T]he psychological experiment is systematically to be placed at the service of commerce and industry" (p. 3). Bernard Muscio (1920) emphasized that the aim of applying psychology to industry is to help industry meet its goals of reducing waste and increasing productivity. Later definitions (e.g., Viteles, 1932) added fostering worker adjustment to the goal of increasing efficiency, making explicit that, in theory at least, industrial psychology should benefit both management and the worker.

Industrial-organizational (I-O) psychology today is the subdiscipline of psychology concerned with the scientific study of work behavior and organizations. The "I" component, *industrial (or personnel) psychology*,

---

[3] Use of a hyphen seems to me to be more inclusive than the use of a slash, which implies more of a separation between the industrial and organizational sides of the field. Therefore, in the interest of disciplinary harmony, I will use the hyphenated I-O throughout the book.

can trace its history to the study of individual differences and associated measurement issues. Industrial psychology has traditionally been concerned with human resource management (HRM) topics such as employee recruitment and selection, performance appraisal, and training. The "O" component, *organizational psychology*, has its roots in employee human relations concerns and covers more broad-based topics such as employee motivation, leadership, organizational power and politics, group processes, and organizational socialization, culture, design, and change. The content of organizational psychology overlaps to some degree with that of social psychology, sociology, political science, and especially its younger, more multidisciplinary sibling, *organizational behavior*. Historically there were other activities associated with I-O psychology. One was *engineering psychology* (aka *human factors* or *human engineering*). While human factors is still occasionally covered in I-O psychology textbooks, the field has become more interdisciplinary, incorporating cognitive psychology, physiology, and other disciplines. In human factors, the emphasis is on fitting the job to the person; that is, designing the job or machinery to best fit the human operator. Examples include designing machine displays commensurate with cognitive and physical abilities and designing a workplace to ensure worker safety. Another topic that was once a prominent part of industrial psychology is *vocational psychology*, finding the best job for an individual based on that person's interests and abilities. This area today is associated more with counseling psychology than I-O psychology. And the study of advertising, an early area of interest for industrial psychologists, is now part of the field of consumer psychology. While the "I" and "O" components of I-O psychology developed somewhat separately, there was overlap among the various topic areas in the early years, and there is much overlap today.[4]

Although I-O psychology today has expanded its focus to organizations in the broad sense, in the early years work organizations were emphasized. Before we begin our exploration of the history of I-O psychology, I would like to first reflect on the nature of work and the central place it holds in our lives. Next is a discussion of the importance of understanding the history of psychology, followed by a section on historiography, the methods used when conducting and writing historical accounts. The chapter closes with an examination of the role of perspective for the historian, illustrating its

---

[4] For the reader interested in more information about I-O psychology, there are a number of excellent introductory textbooks available. Recent examples include Landy and Conte (2016), Levy (2017), Muchinsky and Culbertson (2016), and Spector (2016).

importance by critically examining two classic histories by Edwin G. Boring (1929, revised in 1950) and Loren Baritz (1960).

## The Central Role of Work in Our Lives

On the first day of classes in my I-O psychology course, I often point out to my mostly nineteen- and twenty-year-old students that once they complete their education, they can look forward to working forty to fifty hours a week for about the next forty to fifty years of their lives. My point is not to alarm or depress them but to emphasize just how central work will be in their lives; it will be the primary activity of their waking hours. Forty to fifty years is a long time to be dissatisfied, to be unfulfilled, or simply to be doing something you do not enjoy.

For a field defined as the scientific study of behavior in organizations, primarily work organizations, I-O psychology has surprisingly little to say about the subjective experience of work. Certainly this has been a fertile topic for others, from sociologists and journalists to novelists and poets. Given the history of I-O psychology, this neglect is understandable. I-O psychology came from a functionalist tradition in psychology, a desire to be useful. Usefulness for the early industrial psychologists, for the most part, was based on their ability to increase productivity and efficiency. I-O psychologists today know a great deal about how to do that, through organizational interventions such as improved selection, training, and performance appraisal systems. They also know a great deal about work motivation, leadership, employee satisfaction, group processes, and organizational culture, among many other topics. This is all useful information developed over 100-plus years of research and practice. Yet understanding the *meaning* of work has generally not been seen as an important part of that tradition. I need to be clear here that I am not implying that the early industrial psychologists or their disciplinary descendants were unconcerned with worker welfare or that their research and practice have not benefited workers. Understanding work as a means to something else, such as productivity, however, is not the same as understanding the meaning of work in our lives, although I-O psychologists have in recent years begun to devote more effort in this area (e.g., Ford, Hollenbeck, & Ryan, 2014).

Defining what we mean by the word *work* is not a simple matter. Our common-sense conception is that work is something we do in exchange for compensation and that it is something that, for the most part, we would not do if we were not compensated. But even superficial scrutiny of this definition reveals problems. What about individuals who work without compensation? What about persons who enjoy their work so much that work encroaches on their nonwork time? We get little help from the dictionary. The *Shorter Oxford English Dictionary* (2002) has fourteen separate definitions of work as a noun and an additional twenty-three definitions of work as a verb. In a chapter describing how work is funda-mental to human nature, Weiss (2014) proposed a definition of "working" as "agentic activity done with the purpose of changing the environment" (p. 39). While admitting that this is not *the* definition of work, he saw this definition as a useful starting point for developing a science of the sub-jective experience of working. Whether or not you agree with Weiss's definition, you can agree with him that because work has such an impor-tant place in our lives, it is a worthy subject for scientific inquiry.

So what does work mean to the person engaged in it? There is the obvious: that working provides money and other tangible benefits. These benefits might include health insurance and some sort of retirement benefit. In the late 1800s and early twentieth century when industrial psychology was emerging, compensation was generally viewed as the primary reason one worked. Systems such as Frederick Taylor's scientific management, discussed in Chapter 2, implemented programs to improve employee performance based on a simple transaction: change your beha-vior based on our analysis of how to improve the work process, and your increased production will put more money in your pocket. We will see that things turned out to be not quite that simple.[5]

In addition to compensation, work is also tied to a person's identity. After we learn someone's name, the next question we usually ask is "What do you do?" Our occupation can become an important part of our self-identity. And if the occupational socialization process is strong enough, our career becomes inseparable from who we are. Work can give us the opportunity to learn, to apply our skills in a creative manner, to demon-strate our competence. Our sense of self-esteem can be tied to our job and our ability to do that job well. Work can give structure to our days. While this may appear most applicable to work that allows us some level of self-expression, autonomy, and meaningfulness, work in general can provide an individual with a measure of dignity and self-respect. It is true, however,

---

[5] Things were actually not that simple for Taylor, who had a more nuanced view of work motivation than a simple transaction of money for performance, although that was a major part of his system. Taylor and some of his colleagues were open to collaboration with psychologists and the examination of other motivators, but for the most part managers focused on the link between an individual's pay and output as the key aspect of Taylor's system (Baritz, 1960).

that during the time period covered in this history of I-O psychology, work was increasingly becoming simplified and mechanized, severely limiting its intrinsic value to the individual. In these situations, autonomy was extremely limited. Workers no longer worked for themselves; they now worked for someone else.

It is worth noting that while it is possible to generalize across individuals regarding their responses to work, there is a great deal of variability in how individuals view their jobs. I-O psychology was built on a foundation of the importance of these individual differences. People differ in significant ways in their interests, personalities, abilities, and attitudes, including their attitudes toward work. While we speak in generalities about what holds true for most workers most of the time, there will always be exceptions. Some workers will be perfectly satisfied in what to another person seems like a tremendously tedious job. While most workers desire a safe workplace, some thrive on risk and prefer dangerous environments. The "average worker" is a useful fiction. While the majority of employees will hover around the mean on whatever work-related variable we are measuring, it is important to remember there are others at the tail ends of the distribution, those who by definition differ from that average.

It is also important to emphasize that the meaning of work may differ across different cultures and societies and that the meaning of work has changed over time. Even in the relatively short time span covered in this book, the nature of work changed due to the advent of the second industrial revolution, the move to larger and more complex organizations with increased mechanization, and the beginning of a shift from a manufacturing economy to a service one. These changes, all relevant to the development of I-O psychology, occurred at different times in different cultures. Work has been viewed throughout history as both a blessing and a curse. In antiquity, work was seen as drudgery. Physical labor was viewed as only fit for slaves and the subordinate classes. By the twelfth and thirteenth centuries, theologians in Europe were stressing the moral and social benefits of work; however, they were not claiming that work had inherent value for the individual. Later proponents of the "work ethic" such as the Puritans in England and America saw work as positive, in that it was good for society and good for the character and health of the worker and it kept individuals away from vices such as alcohol, violence, and sex. Little was said, however, of any intrinsic satisfaction that may be derived from working (Thomas, 1999). From a religious perspective, both Catholic and Protestant traditions eventually came to view all work, not just the work performed by the clergy, as noble and necessary for salvation (Hulin, 2014).

The mid-eighteenth-century industrial revolution changed both the nature of work itself and the meaning workers gave to it. Mechanization, the separation of the worker from ownership of the finished product, and the advent of large organizations altered the social philosophy of work. The proto-capitalist Adam Smith (1723–1790) and the socialist Friedrich Engels (1820–1895) both saw human beings as natural idlers, who needed monetary incentives to work (Thomas, 1999).[6] Worth was equated with an individual's level of productivity. But throughout this history of work as necessary drudgery, there have been voices, rare before the late seventeenth century, that work can be meaningful to the individual worker and necessary for both physical and psychological well-being. Separated by more than 200 years, both the English clergyman Robert Burton (1577–1640) and the nurse and hospital reformer Florence Nightingale (1820–1910) wrote of the frustration and misery of voluntary and enforced idleness. Adam Smith's negative view of work was based on manual labor; he believed that other types of work could be inherently rewarding. Karl Marx saw the potential for work to lead to freedom and self-knowledge (Thomas, 1999).

Work is an important activity in our lives, not just an economic necessity but central to our self-identity and psychological well-being. Therefore, the scientific study of the behavior and cognitive processes of workers should have a central role in psychology. This does not seem to be the case, however. I-O psychology, with its focus on psychology applied to a particular setting, rather than examining a particular process, such as cognition or learning, can seem like something of an outlier in psychology.[7]

---

[6] Adam Smith is often caricatured as an uncritical booster for unfettered capitalism (the "invisible hand"). His writings actually demonstrate a great concern for the working poor and a much more nuanced view of capitalism (Smith, 1776/1925).

[7] Evidence for this can be inferred by the paucity of coverage of I-O psychology in the majority of introductory psychology textbooks, which are generally organized around processes. For example, Maynard, Geberth, and Joseph (2002) examined fifty-four introductory psychology textbooks published between 1997 and 2000. They found that only a quarter of them included an overview of I-O psychology and only one text devoted a full chapter to the subject. Less than 2 percent of the total pages contained concepts or examples related to work. In a later survey, Payne and Pariyothorn (2007) looked at fifty-six introductory texts published between 2002 and 2005. Only five contained a chapter on I-O psychology; another three included an I-O psychology appendix. Rozin (2006) found the median number of pages concerned with work across six introductory psychology textbooks was 0.5. On a related note, a 2014 survey of baccalaureate psychology programs in the United States found 66 percent offered a course in I-O psychology/human factors, down from 75 percent in 2005 (Norcross, Hailstorks, Aiken, Pfund, Stamm, & Christidis, 2016).

Paul Rozin (2006) addressed this point. He discussed academic psychology's preference for categorizing its topic areas by process; for example, memory, learning, sensation, and perception. He noted that this propensity dates back to the earliest texts in the field by William James, Edward Titchener, and Wilhelm Wundt, all of whom organized their texts around mental processes. Subsequent textbook authors followed suit. Rozin recorded the median number of pages referred to in the indices of a sample of introductory textbooks for process-related and domain-related words; domain-related words having to do with leisure, food, politics, religion, and, importantly for our discussion, work. He divided up the texts into three time periods, 1890 to 1920, 1922 to 1939, and 1948 to 1958, reviewing five texts per time period. The time period most relevant for our history of early industrial psychology is 1922 to 1939. In that period, he found no entries for "work" in any of the five texts reviewed.[8] Rozin writes that academic psychology has consistently given the highest priority to discovering general laws of behavior and mental processes. It has generally ignored the descriptive phase and moved on to experimental designs to evaluate theory. Basic research was seen as fundamental, and descriptive work and life domains, such as work, were relegated to "applied" research.

As Rozin (2006) implied, in psychology, applied research was seen as less valuable and less challenging than basic research, and basic research was viewed as a prerequisite for applied work. These assertions are open to question. Danziger (1990) could find little evidence for the dependence of applied work on basic research in the early years of the twentieth century. In particular, the industrial psychology topics of personnel selection and advertising developed their own methods and practices that were not dependent on laboratory science. Stokes (1997, cited in Rozin, 2006) demonstrated that many prominent scientists, such as Pasteur, combined basic and applied science. Certainly basic science is dependent on applied work, such as the development of technological advancements (e.g., the MRI for understanding the nervous system). Real-world experimentation can be every bit as challenging as work in the laboratory, where it is easier to control extraneous variables. Rozin's intent is not to place basic and applied research in conflict. It is to show that academic psychology might benefit by spending more time describing and trying to understand life domains, that is, what we actually do, rather than an emphasis on

---

[8] For the 1890–1920 time period, all but one text was published in 1911 or earlier, too early for industrial psychology. The five texts Rozin (2006) reviewed for the 1922–1939 period were Thorndike (1922), McDougall (1928), Woodworth (1929), Fernberger (1936), and Guilford (1939).

process. More than eighty-five years before Rozin's discussion of the importance of applied research, Edward L. Thorndike, well known for his laboratory research, offered his own defense of applied research. Thorndike (1919), in discussing the efforts of applied psychologists in World War I, stated that applying psychology to business, industry, or the military " . . . is harder than making psychology for other psychologists, and intrinsically requires higher talents." He further noted that the lab scientist is to a large extent free to choose the topic, that "[i]t is relatively easy to be scientific when you can direct your talent in any one of ten thousand directions; yourself asking the questions for which you proceed to find the answers!" For Thorndike, applied research was more difficult: "Psychology applied to the complicated problems of personnel work represents scientific research of the most subtle, involved, and laborious type" (p. 60).

The applied versus pure research debate is a reoccurring theme throughout this book. There is little debate, however, about the central place work occupies in our lives. It therefore follows that systematically studying work behavior and its ramifications is a valuable pursuit. I-O psychologists have a long history of doing just that. What are the benefits of studying the history of that undertaking, of examining the history of I-O psychology?

## The Importance of a Historical Approach to Psychology

In 1960, Robert I. Watson published an influential article titled *The History of Psychology: A Neglected Area*. In that article, Watson decried the "provincial" attitude of American psychologists and their lack of interest in the history of their field. As evidence, he surveyed twenty years (1938–57) of the three journals most likely to publish history articles, the *American Journal of Psychology*, the *Journal of General Psychology*, and the *Psychological Bulletin*, and found that only 1 percent of publications in those journals could be classified as primarily historical in orientation. As further evidence, he examined the stated interests of the 1,638 psychologists listed in the 1958 *American Psychological Association Directory* and found that only 0.3 percent of psychologists listed history as an interest area. Watson speculated that the increase in specialization, expansion of the field, and a belief that historical work is somehow unscientific are among the possible reasons for this lack of interest. Nevertheless, as he succinctly put it: "To neglect history does not mean to escape its influence" (p. 255). Roughly half a century later, others (e.g., Benjamin & Baker, 2009; R. Smith, 2007) were still arguing for the relevance of a historical approach to psychology and noting the difficulty in convincing psychologists of that opinion.

What are the arguments for studying the history of psychology? One answer is that understanding the past is a legitimate end in and of itself. There is no need to make history "useful" beyond that goal. In fact, there is a potential danger in trying to write history that is useful, as this can lead to "presentism," viewing the past through the lens of the present. The result can be a biased historical account. While many individuals do find history interesting in and of itself, applied psychology has a long functionalist tradition; considering the usefulness of science is part of its disciplinary DNA. Are there tangible benefits beyond interest for the historian in conducting historical research and for the individual reading this history?

I believe there are multiple benefits for both the historian and the reader. There is an old cliché in academia that you never really understand a topic until you teach it. I would argue it is also true that you cannot truly understand a topic unless you know something about how it developed. Take employee selection, a key activity of I-O psychologists for more than 100 years. Today, we tend to use a limited number of selection tools, such as interviews and psychological tests, which are evaluated using a more or less standard set of statistical procedures. Why those particular tools? Why those procedures? True, we can, and do, answer those questions in an ahistorical manner by citing their effectiveness and usefulness. But a richer understanding is possible by examining the evolution of selection research and practice: what procedures dropped out and why, which ones were retained and why. It is also instructive to note that researchers 100 years ago were struggling with the same questions about selection that we are today. And they approached those questions and problems intelligently and creatively, given the resources they had available to them. This is not to say that from a present-day perspective there were not missteps and wrong turns. It can be useful to learn from those efforts, which obviously we cannot do if we are unaware of them.[9] I am not advocating that history should be written as a litany of progress leading to present-day practice (more on this later in the chapter), only that understanding the history of a topic can increase understanding and appreciation of it.

In addition, I believe it is important to give credit where credit is due. An all-too-common experience for those who take a historical approach is to see a new theory or research finding appear in the literature, or more commonly in the press, with no recognition that this work has deep

---

[9] I am studiously avoiding a "those who ignore history are doomed to repeat it" cliché here.

historical roots and, in fact, has already appeared in a recognizable form in some earlier incarnation.[10] It is perfectly understandable that a working scientist is more interested in making history than studying it. And it is true that virtually all research articles in psychology contain a "literature review" that purports to trace the progress of previous work on a research problem. Nevertheless, it would be gratifying to see more recognition of the accomplishments of those pioneering figures who were there first and whose work is foundational to the development of the field. Critical history should not be just a celebratory record of accomplishments, nor should it be simply an homage to individual achievement. But it can, in context, identify those persons who had a creative idea, developed an insightful solution to a problem, or simply made a contribution through dogged determination and hard work.

As is true of any maturing science, psychology has evolved into a highly specialized discipline. As knowledge expands, researchers narrow their focus and learn more and more about increasingly specific topic areas. While no one would argue against the many benefits of this phenomenon, there are some drawbacks. An important one is that this specialization can result in the fragmentation of a field, as researchers and practitioners increasingly identify with their own particular specialty areas and less with the field as a whole. We have seen this in psychology, for example, when physiologically minded psychologists identify with neuroscience and when the gulf between academic researchers and practitioners continues to widen. At an earlier time, at least in the United States, psychology graduate students had a core set of course requirements that provided a common basis or grounding for their identity as psychologists. As noted by Benjamin and Baker (2009), students in different specialty areas may complete their graduate training and have learned little in common except for research design and statistics.[11] While not vilifying specialization and noting its benefits, Benjamin and Baker, along with other historically minded psychologists, argue that an appreciation of the history of psychology can provide a context to evaluate this specialized knowledge, a sense of continuity in the discipline, and perhaps even a heightened sense of

---

[10] It is, however, important to distinguish "foundations" from "antecedents," as discussed in the next section of this chapter.

[11] While this may be true for programs not accredited by the APA, accreditation guidelines for professional (i.e., clinical, counseling, and school psychology) do require, in addition to statistics and research design, breadth of understanding of biological, cognitive, affective, and social aspects of psychology. An understanding of history and systems of psychology is also required (APA Guidelines and Principles for Accreditation, n.d.).

community for psychologists, whatever their specialized interests might be. History provides a valuable sense of perspective and an understanding of common goals.

While knowledge of the history of the field can make one a better scientist and a better scientist-practitioner, Roger Smith (2007) noted that a problem with these sorts of practical or utilitarian arguments is that they make knowledge of history seem optional. Understanding history is nice perhaps, but not essential, and time spent on history might be more productively spent on more current concerns, i.e., on "real" science. Smith disagreed. He argued that practical justifications do not go far enough, that historical knowledge is critical because of the perspective it provides, perspective that is essential for understanding human behavior. In Smith's view, perspective, or context, provides a framework or coherent story for understanding the statements psychology puts forth. In addition, Smith claimed that knowledge of human nature alters that nature; that is, the subject matter of psychology is constantly evolving. We are reflective; changing our beliefs will change who we are. Therefore, we cannot presuppose that persons in the past are just another version of ourselves without examining their context. Smith's overarching point is that an understanding of history is not optional, it is essential. He echoes Robert Watson (1960) in noting that simply avoiding thinking about history does not negate its effects.

How much progress has been made in uncovering the history of psychology and making that history available since Robert Watson's (1960) call to arms? A great deal. Where Watson found virtually no interest in history in the American Psychological Association (APA), there is now an entire division of that organization, *Division 26: History of Psychology*, devoted to historical research. Where Watson combed general psychology journals, mostly fruitlessly, for historical articles, there are now entire journals, such as the *Journal of the History of the Behavioral Sciences*, *Revista de Historia de la Psicologia*, and the APA's *History of Psychology*, dedicated to scholarly historical research. While interest in the history of psychology, including I-O psychology, is growing, there is still an unfortunate bias against historical scholarship by some empirical researchers. This is one reason why psychologists working in this area will often also maintain a more traditional research program (Zickar, 2015). Given the benefits previously described for a historical approach to psychology, there is hope that one day psychology departments will no longer ask if a psychologist-historian is really needed but rather "Why don't we have one?" (Vaughn-Blount, Rutherford, Baker, & Johnson, 2009, p. 123).

## A Note on Historiography

Historiography is the study of the theory and methods used to conduct and present historical research. While Stocking (1965) wrote that "history itself is in many respects the most undisciplined of disciplines" (p. 211), historians have generated an enormous body of work about how to properly carry out a historical study. Historians of psychology are no exception. They have examined their techniques and, influenced by the larger discussion of general historical methodology, have identified areas of concern. These issues can be conceptualized as competing viewpoints or perspectives about how historical research in psychology should be conducted and what types of phenomena should be emphasized (Hilgard, Leary, & McGuire, 1991). One set of perspectives, the "new" history of psychology, is contrasted with the "old" or traditional history. As described by psychologist-historians and historians of science such as Furumoto (1989, 2003) and Hilgard and colleagues (1991), the old history tended to be presentist in that it viewed past events through the lens of current research and practice. The new history concentrates on understanding the motivations and concerns of historical actors from their own perspectives, striving to view the historical period under study as it appeared during that time. Traditional history emphasized internal accounts, focusing on classic studies and discoveries within the field of psychology, while the new, external histories encompass the social, political, cultural, economic, and other factors that influence that development.

The old history was personalistic, emphasizing the accomplishments of "Great Men" (in the older histories they were usually men); new histories emphasize context and intellectual climate or "Zeitgeist."[12] Traditional histories viewed psychology's history as one of steady, incremental progress and in that sense could be more of a celebration of progress than a critical examination of history. The new histories are more critical, viewing progress as discontinuous and at times nonexistent. Another criticism of traditional histories of psychology is that they rely on so-called "scissors-and-paste" histories, piecing together historical accounts from existing histories (Early & Bringmann, 1997). This use of secondary sources is contrasted with the new historian's emphasis on primary sources. Other problems with old histories are their failure to dig deeply into psychology's roots (Leahey, 2002) and their difficulty of distinguishing *anticipations*,

---

[12] The concept of zeitgeist has been roundly criticized. "It has been rightly characterized as the lazy historian's way of contextualizing events" (Brock, 2017, p. 200). Zeitgeist is revisited in Chapter 2.

isolated ideas that are similar to but are not directly tied to current work, from *foundations*, concepts that have traceable, relatively continuous lines of influence (Sarup, 1978). And finally, new histories tend to be written by trained historians, while the old histories tended to be penned by psychologists without formal training in historiography (Lovett, 2006).

Some of the criticisms of the older, traditional histories are straightforward criticisms of poor historical scholarship. For example, factual information should be accurate and representative, foundational concepts should actually be foundational, and the historian should not begin with preconceived notions and cherry-pick information to support that view. For other criticisms of the old history, there is a danger of exaggerating the differences in the perspectives for effect, that is, setting up a straw person to knock down. While the "old" history is generally viewed as inferior to the "new" history of psychology, not all traditional histories fit the old history template (Lovett, 2006). And salient criticism is more appropriate when a characteristic of the old history is taken to an extreme. Take presentism, understanding the past in service of the present, versus historicism, understanding the past in service of the past. Presentism was characterized by Butterfield (1931/1965) as "Whig" history: history written from the viewpoint and in service of the present. The whiggish historian looks for antecedents for present-day phenomena and presents that history as an inexorable march of progress to a particular end. Whig history "is history with a happy ending" (Kelly, 1981, p. 229). As Stocking (1965) noted, whiggish history, a form of presentism, can be a problem for the scientist-historian who wants that history to be useful to the present-day reader. That historian can fall prey to "the sins of history written for the sake of the present … anachronism, distortion, misinterpretation, misleading analogy, neglect of context, oversimplification of process" (p. 215).

These are clearly bad outcomes. But is it even possible to write history without some reference to the present? And is presentism always a negative in writing history? Like the historical figures we write about, we are also influenced by our social, educational, political, cultural, and other environments. We can try to step outside that framework, but it is difficult to question assumptions we may not be aware of. Earlier in this chapter there was a discussion of the benefits of writing and studying history. Those benefits depend to a degree on a taking a presentist approach. This approach ideally would avoid a distorted, oversimplified history that ignores context. For students to be able to understand the connections between disparate areas of psychology and see how and why these areas eventually grew separate, however, some degree of "the past for the sake of the present" is necessary. What is needed is what Stocking (1965) called "an enlightened presentism"; one that can provide useful information relevant for the present-day reader while avoiding the pitfalls associated with that approach. As Brock (2017) noted, presentism is concerned with answers, not with the questions that are asked. There is nothing wrong with asking questions motivated by current concerns, nor is there a need to suspend current moral values when conducting historical research. The danger is when the past is used simply to justify present-day practice rather than to examine the historical period in all of its contextual richness.

Regarding the criticism that the old history presents the past as a tale of uninterrupted progress, it may be that the history of science is one area where the "progress" portion of "uninterrupted progress" makes sense. This point was made by George Sarton (1936/1957) more than eighty years ago, when he pointed out that scientific growth can be unpredictable and explosive at times. It may be that our common-sense conception of science has more than a little truth to it.[13] It is a feature of the scientific method that hypotheses and theories are tested with empirical data and are supported or disconfirmed. Progress, in the sense of describing, predicting, understanding, and controlling behavior and mental processes, should ideally result. This is not to say that progress is continuous or linear. It is the historian's task to document what actually occurred: the missteps, blind alleys, and, at times, discontinuous nature of the process (albeit all judged from our present-day perspective). But real progress is possible. One need not describe history as an unbroken litany of accomplishment to reflect that.

While advocates of the new historiographical approach to psychology have made valid criticisms of previous histories of psychology, it would appear that there is merit to some aspects of the older approach. The author's goals are a determining factor. For example, a journal article concentrating on a specific past event could profitably rely solely on primary sources, including unpublished ones. The synthesis and scope of a text covering a large swath of the past, however, would necessarily use a mix of primary and secondary sources. While it is true that there is a danger of perpetuating "origin myths" and other misinformation by relying on

---

[13] The classic example of a discontinuous rather than continuous view of the history of science is Thomas Kuhn's (1962) treatise on the paradigmatic nature of science. Normal science operates within a particular paradigm that dictates what questions are worthy of investigation and the proper methods of investigation. Major change occurs not within the paradigm but when the paradigm, the accepted worldview, is overturned. Think classical physics versus relativity or biology before and after evolutionary theory. Kuhn believed that psychology lacks an overarching paradigm; it is therefore pre-paradigmatic.

secondary sources, carefully vetted secondary sources can provide historical summaries in areas where access to primary sources is difficult or impossible. They are useful for identifying primary sources and can help in the interpretation of those sources (Zickar, 2015). At their best, they provide a scholarly commentary, offering different interpretations of data or events.

It is impossible, and may not even be desirable, to completely exclude a presentist orientation, as long as the historian is aware of the pitfalls of that approach. While with the advantage of hindsight it is tempting to concentrate on only those activities that survived and led to current practice, it is important to remember that individuals active during the period under examination did not have that luxury. They did not know how the story ended, and therefore viewing their efforts from their perspectives is essential. Context is important, but so are individual initiative and effort. Along with an appreciation of the historical context should be a recognition of those individuals who made critical contributions to the discipline. In the end, the important distinction may be not between old and new history but between bad and good history.[14]

The question of proper training and preparation for conducting a historical investigation is an important one. Anyone writing history should be familiar with the relevant historiography and be prepared to defend her or his choices.[15] Trained historians of science have an advantage in this, and psychologists interested in historical research need to put in the time and effort to develop the knowledge and expertise to conduct historical research. One contribution the psychologist-historian can bring to historical research is a deep understanding of the subject under investigation based on many years on intensive study. Knowledge of both historiography and the science itself is essential to understanding the history of any scientific enterprise. In the end, it is not credentials that are important but the quality of the historical scholarship that is produced.[16] Weidman

---

[14] Lovett (2006) noted that the difference between traditional and new histories may not be as great as it has been characterized. For example, some "new" history can also be criticized for the perceived sins of the old history, such as focusing on outstanding individuals, albeit not individuals found in traditional histories. Roughly ten years later, Brock (2017) published a point-by-point criticism of Lovett (2006), admonishing him for, among other perceived distortions, claiming that the new historians view presentism in an absolutist sense, that they deny the possibly of progress in psychology, and that they want the history of psychology moved from psychology departments to history departments. Lovett (2017) refuted Brock's critique, also point by point.

[15] See the Preface for a discussion of the choices I made for this book.

[16] Dewsbury (2003) describes three types of psychologist-historians: *dabblers* who view their historical research as an adjunct to other work in psychology, *retreads* who change their primary research area to history and take steps to become proficient in that area, and *straight-liners* who are trained in graduate programs in the history of psychology. In the interest of full disclosure, I best fit the *retread* category.

(2016) argued that while historians of science and psychologist-historians should retain their own orientations, identities, and departments, progress in the history of psychology depends on overcoming their mutual isolation, a scenario "in which communication and mutual understanding broaden and intensify" (p. 248).

In some historical accounts, the perspective of the historian is made explicit; in others, it is not. In either case, that perspective will affect what material is included and how that material is interpreted and presented. I close the chapter with an illustration of how perspective can affect the historical account by describing two histories relevant to our discussion of the history of I-O psychology. Both are, in my opinion, well-written, generally accurate accounts; both are considered classics. Both authors had an agenda, however, that influenced what they included and how that material was presented.

## A Tale of Two Histories

*The Servants of Power: A History of the Use of Social Science in American Industry* (Baritz, 1960) is interesting for what it has to say about the development of I-O psychology. The *History of Experimental Psychology* (Boring, 1929, 1950) is relevant for what it does not say; that is, for its curious lack of virtually any discussion of industrial psychology as a component of the history of scientific psychology. Historian Loren Baritz (1928–2009) examined the sometimes precarious position industrial psychology has held in economic organizations and the managerial orientation he believed industrial psychology adopted as a result. Edwin G. Boring's (1886–1968) lack of coverage of industrial psychology illustrates that discipline's conflicted position within mainstream scientific psychology. While these themes will be expanded on in later chapters, these two histories are a useful introduction to the difficulty industrial psychology has had in establishing a distinctive identity. Psychology has been divided in recent years between a large applied clinical psychology component and an increasingly fragmented scientific component, with academic researchers increasingly self-identifying as neuroscientists, cognitive scientists, and other specialists. I-O psychology, as discussed earlier, has been somewhat marginalized within the overall discipline. I-O psychology has had difficulty establishing an identity distinct from the myriad of other consultants offering their services and finding a balance between management and worker concerns. The roots of these difficulties extend back to the very beginnings of industrial psychology.

Baritz's *Servants of Power* (1960) is not a history of industrial psychology per se, although Baritz did discuss a great deal of the history of American industrial psychology. While he occasionally mentioned European developments for the sake of contrast, his focus was on industrial social science in the United States. Baritz was interested in the relationship between intellectuals and American society. Since he viewed the traditional role of the intellectual as one of societal resistor or critic, Baritz set out to examine those intellectuals who take the contrary position of supporting societal norms and values. As a case study, he used the relationship between social scientists, including psychologists, and industry. Based on his introductory remarks, Baritz seems to have started with the conclusion that industrial psychologists, sociologists, and other professionals working in industry had adopted the values of management; he does provide a great deal of historical evidence to make a compelling case for his thesis.

Baritz saw managers as single-minded in their pursuit of profits. He stated that managers "are in the business to make money. Only to the extent that industrial social scientists can help in the realization of this goal will management make use of them" (p. 196). According to Baritz, industrial psychologists have been only too eager to side with management, compromising their scientific bona fides by adopting an almost exclusively pro-management perspective. He wrote that " . . . most industrial social scientists labored in industry as technicians, not as scientists . . . hemmed in by the very organization charts they helped to contrive" (p. 194). Baritz concluded that industrial psychologists' subservience to the "industrial elite" caused them to abandon their own intellectual obligations as scientists. They were trapped by their own aspirations: "Hired by management to solve specific problems, they had to produce" (p. 195). These conclusions would not have been news to the early industrial psychologists. For example, Arthur Kornhauser and Forrest Kingsbury noted in 1924 that it was management that controlled access to the research setting. If psychologists wanted access to organizations, they needed to play by management's rules. For Baritz, because of this subservience, the goals of industrial psychology research were dictated by management, not by the psychologists who should be pursuing knowledge for its own sake.

*Servants of Power* raises important questions about the relationship between industrial psychology and industry and about the practice and aspirations of industrial psychologists. First, has there been a persistent bias in favor of management by industrial psychologists? Next, if this is true, is this necessarily a bad thing? That is, can a case be made that despite taking a mostly pro-management view, industrial psychologists were still providing a valuable service, not only for their employers but for the advancement of knowledge (the "scientist" portion of the scientist-practitioner model)? These questions have been discussed within the profession since its very beginning and have periodically been debated, sometimes with Baritz's critique as a focal point.[17] The industrial psychologist and historian of psychology Leonard W. Ferguson (1912–1988) was an early critic of Baritz. Ferguson (1962) wrote that Baritz's claim that industrial psychology is virtually always pro-management and seldom pro-labor "places a false emphasis on the true spirit of industrial psychology and can easily be refuted" (p. 7). In this article, Ferguson limited his pro-labor counterexamples to events and individuals associated with the first graduate program in industrial psychology at the Carnegie Institute of Technology.[18] Among his counterexamples to the charge of pro-management bias were the activities of the Division of Applied Psychology at Carnegie Tech, the Personnel Research Federation, and the Scott Company consulting firm, all of which are discussed later in this book. Ferguson describes how these and other organizations actively cooperated with and showed concern for labor.[19]

The early industrial psychologists gave considerable thought to their role in industry. One of the founders of industrial psychology, Hugo Münsterberg (1913), argued that industrial psychologists should take a neutral, scientific stance and not concern themselves with how business uses their expertise. That is, Münsterberg believed psychologists should be impartial, conducting the research in accordance to scientific principles and leaving the application to others. They should concern themselves only with the means, not with the ends, of their efforts. Other psychologists disagreed. Abraham Roback (1917) questioned whether such an impartial stance was even possible. He noted that the applied psychologist works as an agent of whomever is paying the fee, not as a broker who can serve both parties fairly. Others debated the psychologist's role in industry. Bingham (1923) stated: "Applied psychology . . . is *psychology in the service of ends other than its own*" (p. 294, italics in original). In that article, Bingham discusses the confusion as to whether the goal of psychology itself is primarily scientific, practical, or, as he believed, a combination of the two. Kornhauser (1947), a longtime critic (e.g., Kornhauser, 1929–30b) of industrial psychology's focus on the needs of

---

[17] See, for example, the comment by Shore (1982), who was highly critical of industrial psychology's pro-management orientation, and the rejoinder by Stagner (1982).

[18] See Chapter 8 for a discussion of this program and its staff and students.

[19] The relationship between industrial psychology and organized labor is examined in Chapter 9.

management, noted that while industrial psychology has been highly successful as a management technique, as a scientific enterprise, it "remains a puny infant" (p. 224). In a discussion that to an extent foreshadows Baritz's book, Kornhauser discussed the limitations of taking the management viewpoint and argued that industrial psychology should also be concerned with societal, not just managerial, problems.

Adherence to a managerial perspective implies that there is less concern for the welfare of non-management workers. Certainly industrial psychologists were aware of the inherent conflict between the concerns of management and those of employees. The hope was that the work of industrial psychologists would benefit both groups. Improvement in efficiency and productivity would result in benefits for all; for example, scientific selection of applicants would result in employees who were both productive and satisfied in their jobs. Concern for workers was sometimes made explicit in early texts. For example, in his early text on employment psychology, Link (1919) devoted a chapter to "The Applicant's Point of View" and his concerns that applicants be treated fairly and with courtesy. And in his landmark 1932 text *Industrial Psychology*, Morris Viteles wrote that psychologists should be willing to sacrifice economic gains when attaining those gains conflicts with human values.

While we can point to instances of concern for workers, there is no question that to a large extent the early industrial psychologists not only identified with the goals of management for pragmatic reasons but also adopted management's ethic of productivity and efficiency. This view was consistent with early twentieth-century beliefs in continual progress and continuous improvement. As discussed in Chapter 2, psychologists were not alone in this orientation; their contemporaries in the scientific management movement held similar beliefs. The early industrial psychologists wanted to be useful, and for them usefulness involved demonstrating to business and industry that they could help management achieve organizational goals. Psychologists had to overcome management indifference and distrust to do so. In theory, a more efficient, productive, and therefore profitable organization should be good for workers and management alike, in that profitability provided continued employment for both groups. An added benefit for industrial psychologists was that working toward the goal of improved organizational performance permitted them access for research in applied settings, and this did result in scientific progress. The salient question is not whether improved productivity is a legitimate goal but whether, as Baritz implied, industrial psychologists worked to achieve this goal at the expense of the workers.

That question is more difficult to answer. The large industrial organizations that emerged as a result of Industrial Revolution presented new, unique problems for management, and strategies that were successful in small organizations were no longer viable. Large numbers of applicants had to be screened, selected, and trained. Their performance had to be evaluated, their compensation determined, and their productivity maintained. Counterproductive practices, such as nepotism and favoritism in selection, became more difficult for management to justify. The early industrial psychologists believed their scientific approach would contribute to better organizational functioning, and they were prepared to empirically demonstrate the effectiveness of their interventions. As noted previously, the early industrial psychologists believed their procedures could benefit all parties, and they did not see the goals of improved productivity and improved worker satisfaction as necessarily antithetical to one another.

There is a related relevant question, however, that has to do with transparency. Given that the early industrial psychologists often, although not always,[20] worked for management, how aware were the workers of the reasons for the tests, rating forms, and other interventions to which they were subjected? Some procedures were straightforward; for example, a job knowledge test to select workers for a skilled position would appear fair and relevant to an applicant. On the other end of the spectrum would be the use of a questionnaire or counseling program to ostensibly improve working conditions but actually used by management to identify union sympathies.[21] This lack of transparency would be viewed not only by workers but also by industrial psychologists as unethical. A grayer area is the use of interventions by psychologists where workers are subtly manipulated into practices, such as participation, that ostensibly improve their lot but whose unstated purpose is improved productivity. It is my impression that Baritz was more concerned with the subtle thread of subterfuge in these types of interventions than in those instances where the purpose of interventions was straightforward.

Baritz raised a number of important questions about the motives and practices of American industrial psychologists. Edwin G. Boring, on the

---

[20] There were a number of prominent exceptions – for example, Arthur Kornhauser, who appears in a number of places in this text, most prominently in Chapter 9.

[21] The relationship between early industrial psychology and labor unions in the United States was actually more nuanced than our discussion here would suggest. For example, the first industrial psychology consulting firm, the Scott Company, declined to work for companies that were anti-labor (Ferguson, 1962–65), and James McKeen Cattell, who founded the Psychological Corporation in 1921, had a long-standing positive relationship with Samuel Gompers of the American Federation of Labor (Sokal, 1984). See Chapter 9 for a discussion of industrial psychology and organized labor.

other hand, did not raise issues of concern to industrial psychologists; he erased the history of industrial psychology almost entirely. Boring's *History of Experimental Psychology* (1929, revised in 1950) was the standard academic history of psychology for much of the twentieth century. Nance's (1962) survey of history of psychology courses in the United States found that 75 percent of them used Boring's text.[22] Boring's *History* is often put forth as an exemplar of the old approach to the history of psychology, but it is not a perfect fit for that criticism. Boring relied to a great extent on primary sources, was quite critical of theory and theorists, and, at least in the 1950 revision of his book, emphasized the zeitgeist as an important factor in the history of psychology (Lovett, 2006). It is true, however, that the first edition strongly emphasized individual contributions and included a great deal of biographical information and discussion of the personalities of these individuals. Boring has been criticized for his treatment of Wilhelm Wundt, a pioneering figure in scientific psychology. Similar to his teacher and mentor Edward Titchener, Boring stripped Wundt's psychology of its complexity and deprived his readers of Wundt's contributions to social psychology (Cerullo, 1988).[23]

There is another criticism of Boring and his book that is more germane to our history of I-O psychology. O'Donnell (1979) presented evidence that Boring wrote his *History* from a specific perspective with specific goals in mind. During the 1920s, as is still true today, there was tension between the "pure science" and the "applied" orientations in psychology. Boring, the head of the psychological laboratory at Harvard University, was squarely in the pure science camp. An acolyte of Cornell's Edward B. Titchener and his *structuralist* approach to psychology, Boring was a steadfast foe of *functionalist* orientation and of what he considered a premature rush to applied psychology.[24] Based in part of the perceived success of applied psychology in the World War I effort, he was greatly

---

[22] It is interesting that in 1929 two other histories of psychology were published in addition to Boring's text. Neither of the books by Murphy (1929) nor Pillsbury (1929) have had nearly the influence of Boring's book. One plausible explanation for Boring's influence is that his book provided a scientific pedigree for the field greatly in need of one, in a way that was understandable to both psychologists and non-psychologists (see Capshew, 1999).

[23] See also Blumenthal (1975), Danziger (1980), and Leahey (1979); Goodwin (1999) provides a summary of the misconceptions about Wundt's psychology.

[24] *Structuralism* has as its goal the analysis of the mind into its fundamental structural elements (Goodwin, 1999), while *functionalism*, heavily influenced by evolutionary theory, focuses on the usefulness of the mind, that is, what is the mind *for*? These two orientations and their influence on industrial psychology are discussed in Chapter 2.

concerned that by the 1920s a shift was occurring toward the applied approach.[25]

Boring had reason to be concerned. Terman (1921) analyzed the 1920 APA membership data that Boring compiled as secretary of that organization. In that data, 340 of 393 members reported having research fields. Terman classified 167.1 (53 percent) of the 340 as conducting applied research (social and industrial psychology, "Chiefly Education," and psychopathology).[26] The high percentage of psychologists interested in applied work represents a striking realignment from the early days of the field. Terman was unconcerned with the trend toward applied work, noting that other sciences such as biology, chemistry, and physics have benefited from a focus on real-world problems. Boring did not agree. He took a number of actions to counteract this trend, including influencing the APA to suppress membership for applied psychologists (O'Donnell, 1979). He also set out to write a history of psychology whose narrow definition of "experimental" excluded the applied wing of the field altogether. O'Donnell (1979) stated that "[f]or Boring, history was not merely a matter of describing the past but of altering the future" (p. 289). Boring saw the efforts of applied psychologists as opposed to the true purpose of psychology as a laboratory science solely concerned with knowledge for its own sake. Therefore, the history of those applied efforts must be excised from the historical record.

One can make the argument that because Boring's history is explicitly a history of "experimental" psychology, it is entirely appropriate to omit an applied field like industrial psychology.[27] After all, it is not fair to criticize Boring for writing the book he did not set out to write. While this sounds perfectly reasonable on the surface, a closer look reveals some serious difficulties with this argument. The scientific method is as applicable to field research as it is to research conducted in the laboratory. There is no

---

[25] Boring contributed to that success with his service in the US Army Psychological Service (Murchison, 1929). Boring was not always hostile toward testing and applied work. Early in his career he wrote a number of papers (e.g., Boring, 1923) on applied topics. S. S. Stevens (1973), in an appreciation of Boring, wrote that Boring " . . . acquired a high respect for the wisdom and scientific honesty of the mental testers" (p. 45).

[26] Only 7.4 of those 340 members gave industrial psychology as their field of research. Another 10.7 gave "Applied" psychology as their field (Terman, 1921). APA members who reported more than one field of research were counted fractionally into those fields; this accounts for the fractions in Terman's results. While the percentage of industrial psychology researchers is small (2 percent), the applied category conceivably could have included some industrial psychology research.

[27] Boring (1950) saw experimental psychology as having three temporal phases: the first focusing on sensation and perception, followed by a concentration on learning, and the final stage concerned with the problems of conscious and unconscious motivation.

particular reason to say, for example, that a field biologist is not a scientist while one who works in a laboratory is. And while it is true that much of the industrial psychology research in, for example, employee selection was correlational rather than causal in nature, there is nothing inherently unscientific about correlational research. Boring's contemporary Joseph Jastrow (1930) wrote that to examine American psychology without reference to its practical aspect was a serious omission, and Lewis Terman privately admonished Boring for his bias toward experimentalism (O'Donnell, 1979). Boring could have justified including industrial psychology in his history. He chose not to do so.

O'Donnell's case against Boring is based on carefully documented but circumstantial evidence. While he wrote that antipathy toward applied psychology was Boring's primary motivation for writing his history, O'Donnell also noted that other personal, professional, and intellectual reasons are possible. Boring's desire for psychology to disengage from philosophy is one Boring himself mentions.[28] Samelson (1980), while not disagreeing that hostility toward applied psychology could have been a factor, suggested a number of other potential motivators. In addition to Boring's opposition to philosophy's control of psychology at Harvard, Samelson listed concerns Boring had about his expertise in the applied area, pressure on him to publish, and, possibly, his need to separate himself from his mentor Titchener's system of psychology. Samelson also noted that at the time Boring wrote his *History*, the boom in industrial psychology and testing in the early 1920s had passed and industrial psychology was in a period of slow growth and therefore not as large a threat to Boring's conceptualization of pure science as it once was. Regardless of the reasons, the result was that Boring did decide to leave industrial psychology out of his history.

In the first edition of Boring's book, the index has one entry for British industrial psychology and none for industrial psychology in the United States. Industrial psychology did merit a couple of sentences in the text. Boring mentioned the National Institute of Industrial Psychology in Great Britain and claimed that "[a]t the present time industrial psychology has been more successful in Great Britain than in 'practical America'" (Boring, 1929, p. 484).[29] The 1950 revision did not include an index entry for industrial psychology. While Boring did mention a number of

---

[28] By the time Boring revised his *History* in 1950, he saw the split between psychology and philosophy as completed.

[29] This interpretation regarding the relative success of industrial psychology in Great Britain and the United States is questionable; see Chapter 6.

psychologists central to the history of I-O psychology, it was generally in reference to their accomplishments outside of industrial psychology, although their applied work was occasionally mentioned in passing. For example, Hugo Münsterberg "began at the core" of experimental psychology "but was lured to other interests in America" (Boring, 1929, p. 418). Münsterberg's seminal work in industrial psychology merited only a few words in the 1950 revision; his laboratory work was discussed in more detail. Boring (1950) did note that pioneering British industrial psychologist Charles S. Myers left Cambridge University in the early 1920s to direct the National Institute of Industrial Psychology and even referred to Myers's weariness with "academic bigotry" that pushed him toward that decision. Much more space, however, is devoted to Myers's experimental work. Other psychologists who contributed to the development of I-O psychology, such as Pear in Great Britain; Klemm, Poppelreuter, Marbe, Rupp, and Stern in Germany; Matsumoto in Japan; and Bingham, Hollingworth, Poffenberger, Strong, and Thurstone in the United States, appear in the both the original and the revision. If their work in industrial psychology is mentioned at all, it is not the primary reason for their inclusion. Pioneering industrial psychologists Otto Lipmann, Walter Dill Scott, and Morris Viteles, among many others, do not appear at all.

Yet at least in the revised edition, I can sense no hostility to industrial psychology in particular or to applied psychology generally. Boring (1950) did devote a section to one applied field: educational psychology. And Boring seemed to have come around to a position of détente with applied work. He stated that "psychology is gaining self-confidence from the successful application of its facts and principles"; that "[t]he academics now know that psychology is not a mean and narrow subject which they themselves have dreamed up in order to be able to criticize one another"; and finally: "The dire warning of its doubtful parent that it [applied psychology] would come to no good end now seems very long ago" (pp. 742–743). Nevertheless, in Boring's view, industrial psychology was still not a subject for inclusion in his history of experimental psychology. For students in history of psychology courses who used his text, I suspect that the distinction between experimental and nonexperimental psychology was lost and that they emerged from those courses with no appreciation of the history of applied psychology and the impression that Boring's narrowly defined history of experimental psychology was *the* history of psychology.

Two histories, two agendas – one explicit, the other implicit. Both resulted in histories that are incomplete. In the case of Baritz, this resulted in a defensible criticism of industrial psychology as beholden to management, but one that could have recognized that the story was not quite that straightforward and that there are other perspectives worth considering. Despite the occasional polemics, *Servants of Power* generated a great deal of worthwhile reflection on I-O psychology's moral and ethical obligations. As for Boring, he wrote an informative history within the confines of his own definition of what constituted experimental psychology. This was his prerogative; one can make a reasonable case for his decision to exclude applied psychology, just as a plausible case can be made for its inclusion. The practical result of Boring's *History*, however, is that because of its standing as the standard history of psychology, generations of psychology students learned little about the applied aspects of that story, including the history of industrial psychology.

## Chapter Summary

While the topics discussed in this introductory chapter are wide-ranging and may appear only loosely connected, they lay the groundwork for ideas that will be further developed in later chapters. Given the central role of work in our lives, it is worth reflecting on the meaning work has for individuals and on the necessity of studying work behavior. Discussed were the benefits of studying the history of I-O psychologists' efforts to understand work behavior and the use of that knowledge to improve the productivity of organizations and, arguably, the lives of the organizational members. Researching and writing that history involves decisions on what to include and what to leave out and on how to organize and frame the surviving content. The discussion of historiography made explicit the kinds of criteria used in making those decisions, both in general and as specifically applied to the history of the early years of I-O psychology. The perspective one takes when writing history has consequences, as illustrated by the examination of Baritz's (1960) and Boring's (1929, 1950) historical accounts that closed the chapter. In this chapter, it was noted that the context that events occur within is an important aspect of history. In Chapter 2, we will explore the contextual factors that directly and indirectly influenced the emergence of industrial psychology in the late nineteenth and early twentieth centuries.

# Historical Context and Influence

While traditional histories of psychology have emphasized individuals, at least one of the early industrial psychologists was aware of the importance of context. The historical overview in Morris Viteles's landmark 1932 text *Industrial Psychology* includes a discussion of the economic, social, and psychological foundations of industrial psychology. Viteles wrote that to fully understand the scope and current status of industrial psychology, you need to understand the economic, social, and scientific psychology factors that underlie its development. The economic foundations section focused on Frederick Taylor's scientific management movement, with its emphasis on improving worker efficiency and production. Social foundations include increased concern for worker welfare along with the organization of personnel departments in the increasingly large and complex organizations brought about by the rise of industrialization. Scientific psychology, which saw its own rapid rise in the early twentieth century, provided the psychological foundation for industrial psychology. While Viteles was writing about industrial psychology in the United States in the early 1930s, these same factors were influencing the development of industrial psychology in other countries. Kirihara (1959), for example, wrote that the same economic, social, and psychological foundations described by Viteles influenced the development of industrial psychology in Japan during roughly that same time period.

The early industrial psychologists were influenced by the social, cultural, political, economic, and scientific environments of their respective countries and times. Countries varied in the timing and rate of industrialization, in types of political system, and in many other ways. Some of these more specific influences are discussed in later chapters in relation to the development of industrial psychology around the globe. This chapter presents some of the broader influences that can reasonably be inferred to have had a direct or indirect effect on the history of industrial psychology. Two of those broad influences not discussed in this chapter, the measurement of individual differences and the role of World War I in the development of industrial psychology, are important enough to merit their own chapters.

*Zeitgeist* is a term that is sometimes used to describe the context that influences the development of a discipline. Edwin Boring (1950) popularized the use of the concept in the history of psychology. He defined zeitgeist in terms of ideas, " . . . the habits of thought that pertain to the culture of any region and period" (p. 3). Generally conceptualized as the spirit of the times, *zeitgeist* was used by German historians in the late eighteenth and early nineteenth centuries to emphasize that each historical period should be understood in light of the prevailing opinions and tastes of that time. As used by Boring and others, *zeitgeist* has been used as a causal explanation for developments in psychology (Ross, 1969). Ross discussed the following problems with this approach. The term tends to be reified as something separate from the individuals who constitute it; that is, it is not individuals who are responsible for the development of an enterprise, the "zeitgeist" is the controlling factor. In addition, the complexity of the zeitgeist tends to be simplified, with the historian of psychology focusing only on a limited subset of ideas. And by limiting the concept to ideas and attitudes, the zeitgeist ignores institutional, political, social, economic, and other contextual factors that also have an influence. The historian needs to take the entire picture into account, although "[n]o one . . . can do more than approach the total analysis an historical event ideally requires" (Ross, 1969, p. 262). This is not to say that ideas current at the time are not important, nor does it imply that analysis of contextual factors should not be attempted. It is more a recognition of the complexity of these factors and of the difficulty of tying specific influences to individual actors and events.

Many individuals living in the late nineteenth and early twentieth centuries perceived this period as a time of breaking with tradition, a process that came to be called *modernity* (Jarausch, 2015). It was in this environment of change that industrial psychology developed. While the field evolved in different places at different rates, there are some general historical trends that appear relevant. In the United States, Katzell and Austin (1992) identified four cultural forces that contributed to the establishment of industrial psychology in America: advances in science, evolutionary theory and its psychological counterpart *functionalism*, the protestant work ethic and faith in capitalism, and the growth of industrialism. Also important during the formative years of industrial psychology were World War I, the prosperity of the 1920s followed by the worldwide economic depression of the 1930s, and the growth of the field of management. Frederick Taylor's *scientific management* system had an impact, both as a predecessor to industrial psychology and later as a convenient foil for the early industrial psychologists. The new scientific psychology had an influence on how the early industrial psychologists perceived themselves and on their research and practice.

Some events – World War I, for example – were pervasive enough to have a widespread impact on industrial psychology. Other events were specific to the development of industrial psychology in individual countries. Examples of the latter include the 1917 Bolshevik Revolution in Russia, which led to a precipitous decline in industrial psychology in that country by the early 1930s, and the expansion of industrial psychology activity in Germany triggered by the militarization of that country beginning in the 1920s and extending into the following decade.

Demographic trends illustrate worldwide major changes that occurred between 1900 and 1930. The United States provides an example. In 1900, the population of the United States was 76 million, with a total labor force fourteen years and older of 28.5 million. Average life expectancy at birth was 47.3 years. The unemployment rate for the civilian labor force was 5 percent. Female workers comprised 18.3 percent of the workforce, and 6 percent of the workforce were minors age ten to fifteen.[1] Agriculture accounted for 37 percent of workers. Of the remaining non-agriculture workers, 48 percent were in goods-producing occupations such as mining, construction, and manufacturing, while the rest were in service-producing occupations such as transportation, public utilities, trade, finance, insurance, real estate, and government (see Table 2.1 for a more fine-grained analysis of worker distribution). In manufacturing, the average number of hours worked per week was fifty-nine. There were about 12,000 individuals working in personnel and labor relations. Labor union membership stood at 791,000 (US Bureau of the Census, 1976).

By 1930, the US population had increased dramatically to almost 123 million, with a labor force of close to 49 million. Life expectancy at birth had risen to 59.7. The unemployment rate was now 8.7 percent, on its way to an historic high rate of 24.9 percent in 1933. The percentage of female workers had increased to 22 percent. Child workers age ten to fifteen had decreased to 1.2 percent through the efforts of the National Child Labor Committee, founded in 1904, and associated state child labor

[1] Yellowitz (1991) noted that reported percentages for child labor significantly understate the actual number employed. For example, 25 percent of workers in southern cotton mills in 1900 were under age fifteen, with half of those under the age of twelve.

Table 2.1 *Distribution of gainful workers in the United States, 1900 and 1930, in thousands (percentage in each category)*

|  | 1900 | 1930 |
|---|---|---|
| Agriculture | 10,710 (0.37) | 10,480 (0.21) |
| Forestry and Fisheries | 210 (0.01) | 270 (0.01) |
| Mining | 760 (0.03) | 1,150 (0.02) |
| Manufacturing | 6,340 (0.22) | 10,990 (0.22) |
| Construction | 1,660 (0.06) | 3,030 (0.06) |
| Transportation and Public Utilities | 2,100 (0.07) | 4,850 (0.10) |
| Trade, Finance, and Real Estate | 2,760 (0.09) | 7,450 (0.15) |
| Educational Service | 650 (0.02) | 1,650 (0.03) |
| Other Professional Service | 500 (0.02) | 1,760 (0.03) |
| Domestic Service | 1,740 (0.06) | 2,330 (0.05) |
| Personal Service | 970 (0.03) | 2,490 (0.05) |
| Government | 300 (0.01) | 1,050 (0.02) |
| Other | 370 (0.01) | 1,340 (0.03) |
| Total | 29,070 | 48,830 |

From: US Bureau of the Census (1976)

committees (Yellowitz, 1991). The percentage of workers engaged in agriculture had declined steeply to 21 percent; of non-agriculture workers, 41 percent were in goods-producing jobs, while 59 percent were now in service-producing jobs. Average hours worked in manufacturing dropped to 42.1. A total of 73,000 individuals now worked in personnel and labor relations positions. Union membership now stood at 3,632,000 – a large increase from 1900 but down from the 1920 total of 5,034,000 (US Bureau of the Census, 1976).[2]

There are several notable trends reflected in these statistics. From 1900 to 1930, the total population in the United States increased by 47 million, in large part driven by an influx of immigration. Female workforce participation was up, and child labor was down. A trend away from goods-producing toward service occupations was under way, as was the move from rural to urban areas, as shown by the large drop in percentage of farm workers (the 1900 and 1930 totals for number of farmers were virtually identical despite the large increase in population by 1930). The same number of farmers were feeding a much larger number of people due to advances in mechanization and efficiency. Union membership increased.

[2] Except for the unemployment rate, percentages were calculated from the census statistical tables by the author.

Number of hours worked per week in manufacturing decreased, perhaps in part due to the stock market crash and impending Depression. While the workforce increased by 58 percent, the number of workers involved in labor relations and personnel increased sixfold, reflecting the increased viability of these types of occupations in corporate America.

## The Rise of Industrialization

In the nineteenth century, the principle employment sector was agriculture, and well into the early decades of the twentieth century most people around the world worked in this area (Osterhammel, 2014). In 1900, a third of Germany's population worked in agriculture; in France and the United States, the total was slightly over 40 percent. In most of the rest of the world, the percentage of the population engaged in farming was higher than that. The United Kingdom was the exception, where the percentage of workers engaged in agriculture was only 12 percent (Mitchell, 1980; Rodgers, 1998).[3] The shift from an agrarian to an industrial workforce was under way, with the United Kingdom in the forefront. While innovation in technology was continuous, there are two periods where the transformation from an agrarian, rural population to an industrial urban one was so profound it was deemed revolutionary (Chandler, 1991). The first Industrial Revolution occurred between roughly 1750 and 1850, initially centered in Great Britain; from there it gradually spread to other areas of the globe. Influenced by the capitalist philosophy of Adam Smith (1776/1925), powered by the steam engines that James Watt perfected between 1765 and 1776 and by the energy available in coal, and driven by new technologies for spinning cloth and producing iron, the resulting increased level of industrialization dramatically changed the way goods were produced and marketed (Chandler, 1991; Wren & Bedeian, 2009).

More relevant for the development of I-O psychology is the second Industrial Revolution that occurred in the later part of the nineteenth century.[4] There was a shift in industrial dominance from Great Britain to the United States and Germany (Osterhammel, 2014). In the United

[3] Evans (2016) stated that a total of 9 percent of workers in Great Britain were engaged in agriculture in 1900, down from 22 percent in 1850. Percentage of workers engaged in agriculture in 1850 for France was 52 percent and for Germany 60 percent.

[4] Osterhammel (2014), following Werner Abelshauser, prefers to call it the second *economic* revolution, given that its ramifications, such as the modern corporation, were much larger than a narrow focus on technology.

States, by the mid- to late 1800s the manufacture of standardized, interchangeable parts, the American System of Manufactures, was changing the way goods were produced. Samuel F. B. Morse's telegraph led to a nationwide communication system, enhancing train coordination in the nation's first large-scale business: the railroads (Wren & Bedeian, 2009). In addition to advances in communication, improved transportation networks made the high-volume flow of goods possible, and the use of electricity replaced steam as a reliable source of power. There was also the beginning of the use of science to improve industrial processes. Machines were replacing craft workers, and the workforce in general was becoming composed of lesser-skilled workers performing routine tasks with minimal need for training (Chandler, 1991). Most critically, the Industrial Revolution was also an agricultural revolution. Machines like harvesters and tractors replaced animal power. Artificial fertilizers and insecticides increased yields, and refrigeration and rapid transit of food via trains and trucks made transporting food across great distances feasible. Because farms became mechanized and more productive, farmers could produce enough food to support increased urbanization (Harari, 2015).

The development of large corporations that began in the last two decades of the 1800s rapidly changed the face of the global economy. Associated with some of these large corporations were large factories that functioned both as large production facilities and as social activity sites.[5] Especially after 1870, there was increased "bureaucratization" of office work and an increase in the number and influence of white-collar workers (Osterhammel, 2014). Economies of scale allowed large corporations to dominate their respective markets and dramatically reduce costs of their products. The use of scientists, particularly in the electrical and chemical industries, resulted in improved products and processes. These large, technologically advanced corporations drove economic growth, making countries like Germany and the United States into economic powerhouses. By the late 1920s, the United States accounted for more than 40 percent of global industrial output, including 85 percent of the world's production of automobiles. Chemical companies such as Dow and Du Pont, General Electric and Westinghouse in electricity, Remington in typewriters, and Heinz and Campbell in canned goods all achieved dominant market positions. In imperial Russia, for example, the two largest commercial enterprises were the farming machinery manufacturer International Harvester and Singer sewing machines, both American companies (Chandler, 1991).

---

[5] See Chapter 10 for more information on the social functions of large work organizations.

The early years of industrial psychology coincided with this second Industrial Revolution and the dramatic increase in the size and scope of economic firms. Firms attempted to control all aspects of their businesses, from the raw materials to the transporting and sale of the finished product. A steel company, for example, might try to control the companies that extract the iron ore and the railroads that transport both the ore and the finished steel. As these organizations expanded, they became increasingly difficult to manage. Coordination among the disparate parts of the organization became paramount. It was no longer desirable, or even possible, for the organization's founder or owner to micromanage the various parts of the firm. In response to this problem, a professional manager class developed. Managers generally did not have an ownership stake in the companies they managed. They did, however, acquire many of the responsibilities, such as recruitment and hiring, traditionally held both by the owners and by the line supervisors or foremen.[6] These first-line supervisors also saw their decision-making authority diminish due to an increase in government rules and regulations protecting the welfare of workers, the rise of labor unions around the time of World War I, and the efforts of advocates of Progressivism, discussed later, who made one of their primary goals the improvement of employee working and living conditions (Gillespie, 1991; Nelson, 1975).

In the United States, the profession of management began to take shape through the work of individuals such as New York & Erie railroad executive Daniel C. McCallum (1815–78), who developed a set of general management principles in the mid-1800s; and Henry V. Poor (1812–1905), who popularized McCallum's ideas while editor of the *American Railway Journal* (Wren & Bedeian, 2009). By the early 1900s, human resource management functions such as hiring and compensation began to be consolidated into personnel departments, usurping most of the functions traditionally delegated to first-line supervisors. While there were advantages, such as standardization of rates and records, to centralizing employment functions, one disadvantage was the loss of firsthand knowledge about job requirements (Link, 1919). Personnel departments needed systematic approaches to functions such as job analysis and employee selection, opening the door to industrial psychologists and their psychological tests. While not more than 10 percent of companies who were able to support a personnel function did

---

[6] *Line* jobs, such as the line supervisor job, are those jobs directly involved in producing whatever it is the organization produces; for example, the workers who manufacture or sell the product. *Staff* jobs, at least in theory, are there to support the line workers.

so during World War I, by the early 1930s that percentage had increased to about one-third. For firms with more than 5,000 employees, more than half had personnel departments, including all the major automobile manufacturers and their suppliers and more than 75 percent of the iron and steel, food products, and petroleum-refining industries (Baritz, 1960).

The rise of employment testing in the United States was partially the result of rapid population growth, organizations' need to manage a somewhat chaotic labor market, and a desire to make society more democratic by selecting workers based on merit rather than privilege (Hale, 1992). In addition to developing centralized personnel systems, in the United States between 1910 and the mid-1920s, corporations increasingly focused on improving relations with employees. This was driven in part by the external pressures mentioned in the previous paragraph but also by the desire to keep unions from gaining a foothold in organizations. There was also a perception by personnel managers that productivity could be improved by reforming personnel practices to make jobs more attractive and satisfying for the employee. Using these employee-centered practices to reduce employee turnover, for example, could dramatically improve a corporation's financial bottom line (Gillespie, 1991). The new class of managers was open to outside assistance in improving personnel practices, providing an opportunity for the newly minted industrial psychologists, who promised success through a scientific approach to management concerns.

## The Progressive Era

The origins and early years of I-O psychology coincided with the Progressive Era in the United States and Western Europe, which had its most active period from the last decade of the nineteenth century to the early 1920s. While often called the *progressive movement*, the aims and practices of progressives were so diverse that "movement" implies a level of agreement that was not evident; *progressivism* is perhaps a better descriptor. What progressives had in common, as their name implies, was a belief in progress, although there was substantial disagreement in how that could be accomplished. In the United States, progressivism was both political and moral in nature, a reaction to excesses in capitalism, corruption in politics, and a perceived move away from Protestant moral values. Among the national efforts supported by progressives were antitrust legislation, a national income tax, and the direct election of US senators by popular vote. Two other progressive initiatives were women's suffrage and the prohibition of alcoholic beverages. Three US presidents were considered progressive to some degree. Theodore Roosevelt (1858–1919), who served from 1901 to 1909, broke up the large corporate trusts and supported natural resource conservation, pure food and drug laws, and regulation of the railways. In 1912, he ran a second, unsuccessful presidential campaign as a candidate of the Progressive, or Bull Moose, party. William Howard Taft (1857–1930), president from 1909 to 1913, continued to enact a progressive agenda as a trustbuster and as an advocate of the Interstate Commerce Commission. And Woodrow Wilson (1856–1924), who served two terms from 1913 to 1921, took progressive ideals into World War I, characterizing it as a battle for democracy (Crunden, 1991).

While most if not all progressive reforms generated controversy in their time, from a present-day perspective some progressive goals, such as a woman's right to vote and a reduction of political corruption, seem self-evidently positive. Others, such as restrictive immigration policies, are more controversial. Eugenics-based policies such as enforced sterilization of "defective" individuals would receive widespread condemnation today; however, advocates at the time saw such policies as scientifically based and socially necessary. Many of America's leading economists, for example, were strong supporters of eugenics policies (Leonard, 2016). Progressives were strong believers in the power of science to transform society. Science included the new psychology in addition to increasingly professionalized social sciences such as economics, political science, and sociology. Progressives were also strong advocates for workplace reform: a shorter working day, safer working conditions, minimum wage guarantees, and the right of labor to organize.[7] Of particular importance for the history of I-O psychology was the emphasis on efficiency and productivity, the hallmarks of progressivism. Faith in science, including the new science of psychology, and an interest in improving the efficiency of industrial organizations opened the door not only to industrial psychology but also to its predecessor: scientific management.

## Scientific Management

The era's emphasis on efficiency and productivity found a champion in Frederick Taylor (Figure 2.1) and the system of *scientific management* or,

[7] According to Leonard (2016), some advocates of the minimum wage saw it as a method to restrict immigration by forcing companies to be selective by hiring only highly skilled immigrants, thereby reducing the number of unskilled workers who could immigrate and find work.

Figure 2.1  Frederick Taylor. Image courtesy of the Samuel C. Williams Library, Stevens Institute of Technology.

when referring specifically to Taylor's system, *Taylorism*.[8] Frederick Winslow Taylor (1856–1915) was an American engineer who received his degree from the Stevens Institute of Technology in 1883. He attended Stevens at night while working at the Midvale Steel Company in Philadelphia. At Midvale, Taylor began as a laborer and worked his way through a series of jobs including time keeper, machinist gang boss, assistant engineer, and, finally, chief engineer. His experiences there and at Bethlehem Steel led him to develop his system of management. Taylor became an independent consultant in 1893 with a focus on improving the efficiency of the worker (Magnusson, 1990). He explained his system in *Shop Management*, a presentation to the American Society of Mechanical Engineers in 1903, and in his 1911 book: *The Principles of Scientific Management* (Magnusson,

[8] According to Frank Gilbreth (1923/1960) and Harwood Merrill (1960), the term *scientific management* was coined not by Taylor but by a small group of supporters that included Henry Gantt and Louis Brandeis in 1910. They were planning hearings on Taylor's system to be held by the Interstate Commission and decided that scientific management was suitable shorthand for "science applied to management."

1990; Person, 1947/1972). Taylor's approach soon spread beyond the United States to Europe and Asia; for example, his *Principles* was translated into Japanese by Y. Hoshino in 1912 (Kirihara, 1959).[9]

To improve worker efficiency and overall productivity, Taylor (1911) advocated improving machinery and the work process, improving the work habits of the individual worker, and a division of labor between management and workers, in which management had sole responsibility for determining how the worker performs the job. The foundation of his management system was "*high wages* and *low labor cost*," a seeming paradox Taylor maintained could be achieved through application of his management principles (Taylor, 1903/1972, p. 22, italics in original). As an example, at the Bethlehem Steel Corporation Taylor (1911/1972) found that the seventy-five pig-iron handlers were loading into railroad cars on average about 12.5 tons per person per day.[10] Taylor determined that this could be increased to between forty-seven to forty-eight tons per day. He selected one of the workers, who he referred to as "Schmidt," to demonstrate. Based on Taylor's careful analysis of the job, Schmidt's rest periods were scheduled in such a way that he was able to load 47.5 tons. He was able to continue this pace for the three years Taylor was at Bethlehem Steel. For his improved productivity, Schmidt's daily wage increased 60 percent, from $1.15 to $1.85 per day.

This example illustrates the elements of scientific management. Following careful selection of the worker, the worker's performance is improved by analyzing the job into its various components and then determining the optimal, most efficient way to complete the job. Although Taylor was not completely opposed to accepting suggestions from workers, in general he believed that the implementation of scientific management could only be done by an outside expert; the worker her or himself lacked the requisite knowledge. It was up to the expert to determine the "one best way" to perform each job. The worker's reward was increased pay for increased productivity through the use of a piece-rate incentive system. In theory, at least, everyone benefited. The organization was more profitable due to increased productivity, and the worker's pay, tied to individual productivity, should increase.[11]

---

[9] A number of aspects of Taylor's system of scientific management such as profit sharing were anticipated by Charles Babbage (1792–1871), an English mathematician who is remembered today for his designs for a "difference engine" and "analytical engine," calculating machines that foreshadowed modern-day computers (Magnusson, 1990; Wren & Bedeian, 2009).

[10] A "pig" of iron weighs approximately ninety-two pounds (Taylor, 1911/1972).

[11] The concept of paying someone based solely on her or his performance is of recent origin. For most of recorded history, a worker's value depended on social status, and those who were considered inferior were paid less or, in the case of slavery, not paid at all. In the United States, less-paid "inferiors" for the most part included everyone except white males who owned property (Leonard, 2016).

Scientific management's emphasis on efficiency and productivity was in harmony with the goals of the progressivism in the United States. Taylor's promise of increased productivity, improved labor relations, and higher wages through the application of scientific principles to the workplace found many admirers among prominent progressives. Jurist Louis Brandeis, who eventually served on the US Supreme Court, considered Taylor a genius and used his system to criticize the railroads in a 1910 court case. Other supporters included the progressive economist John R. Commons and journalists Ida Tarbell and Walter Lippmann. Tarbell was best known for her critical investigation of the Standard Oil Corporation, while Lippmann was a trenchant critic of intelligence testing.[12] US president Theodore Roosevelt was a proponent of Taylor's ideas. Even Thorstein Veblen, who was highly critical of capitalism and initially had misgivings about scientific management, became an ardent supporter. Scientific management principles were applied beyond private industry to government (e.g., New York City's Bureau of Municipal Research, founded in 1906, and Milwaukee, Wisconsin's Bureau of Economy and Efficiency, founded in 1910), education, charity, and other areas (Leonard, 2016).

To promote the philosophy and procedures of scientific management, the Taylor Society was established in the winter of 1910–11, originally as the Society to Promote the Science of Management. It was later renamed in honor of Frederick Taylor after his death in 1915. The Society favored what it termed an engineering approach to management. This perspective recognized that the worker was a critical factor in management but cautioned that the human element must be studied factually, not emotionally, and that personnel management and operation management must work in tandem. In 1914, the Society began publication of a periodical, the *Bulletin of the Taylor Society* (Brown, 1925).

Taylor had a number of coworkers and admirers who implemented and expanded his scientific management system. Prominent were Frank B. Gilbreth and his wife, psychologist Lillian M. Gilbreth; Harlow S. Person; and Henry Laurence Gantt. The Gilbreths developed "time-and-motion" studies designed to minutely analyze job tasks and determine the time needed to complete them. While generally supportive of Taylor's system, the Gilbreths, particularly Lillian Gilbreth, thought Taylor did not pay sufficient attention to worker rights and needs (Kelly & Kelly, 1990). For example, the Gilbreths were more concerned than Taylor with accidents and fatigue and worked to reduce both (Lane, 2007).

---

[12] See Chapter 5.

*The Gilbreths*

Frank B. Gilbreth (1868–1924) and Lillian Moller Gilbreth (1878–1972) were innovators in what they called "the science of management" and the "one best way." Frank began his career in construction, where he developed his Gilbreth system for improving efficiency in bricklaying. Through reducing the number of motions needed by the bricklayer and other work process changes, Gilbreth was able to almost triple the number of bricks laid in an hour (Viteles, 1932). The Gilbreths' management system included standardization of tools and "tool study," an examination of all tools to be sure workers are using the best tools in the proper condition. In order to determine the one best way to perform the work, three things are needed: *motion study*, which includes investigating the causes of fatigue; *skill study* to determine the optimal method to acquire and transfer skills; and *time study* to determine how much work can be completed in a given time period (Gilbreth, 1923/1960).

Lillian Gilbreth, an outspoken advocate for the application of psychology to business and engineering, was prominent in both scientific management and management generally. Gilbreth received her bachelor's degree in 1900 and her master's degree in 1902, both in English from the University of California. She received her doctorate in psychology from Brown University in 1915. Gilbreth's dissertation, which examined the application of scientific management to classroom teachers, was an early example of an American dissertation on a topic relevant to industrial psychology. While she did not publish in psychology journals, her writings (e.g., Gilbreth, 1925) previewed many modern concepts in I-O psychology. Gilbreth's 1914 *Psychology of Management* is considered to be one of the most influential early texts on industrial relations. The text asserts that the laws of psychology support the laws of management, each chapter presenting an underlying scientific management concept and the elements of that idea that can be subjected to psychological investigation. Gilbreth emphasized the need to consider individual differences and the importance of human relations in industry. After the death of her husband in 1924, Lillian Gilbreth managed Gilbreth, Inc. for an additional forty-five years (Stevens & Gardner, 1982).[13]

---

[13] Lillian Gilbreth had twelve children and managed her household in line with scientific management principles, as chronicled in *Cheaper by the Dozen*, a 1948 memoir by her children Frank B. Gilbreth Jr. and Ernestine Gilbreth Carey. Other sources of biographical information about Lillian Gilbreth include Kelly and Kelly (1990), Koppes (1997), and Perloff and Naman (1996). Lillian Gilbreth was the first and, as of this date, the only psychologist to appear on a US postage stamp (Bartle, 1997).

## Criticism and Influence of Scientific Management

Despite a record of some success and an enduring influence on current business practices (see Kanigel, 1997; Locke, 1982), scientific management was heavily criticized. One major criticism concerned the perceived dehumanizing effect the system had on workers. Understandably, workers resented outside experts who claimed to know more about how to best perform their jobs than the employees themselves. Worker unrest was at times the result, as was dramatically illustrated by the labor turmoil at the Watertown Arsenal in Massachusetts between 1908 and 1915 following the implementation of scientific management procedures (Aitken, 1985; Muscio, 1920). Due to labor disruptions, in 1912 the US House of Representatives investigated scientific management, resulting in riders attached to military appropriation bills banning its use. In addition, the US Commission on Industrial Relations held its own investigation and concluded that there was no basis for the scientific management's claims (Van De Water, 1997).

Scientific management was a lightning rod for criticism from industrial psychologists. Link (1919) saw the perception of scientific management by labor as a hurdle industrial psychologists would need to overcome: "[T]he entire range of schemes and devices for the promotion of efficiency included under the name of scientific management has contributed to a belief on the part of labor that the science of management is a cold-blooded and heartless method that treats human beings as just so many machines from which the last pound of energy is to be extracted" (p. 376). Criticism was particularly acute in Europe, where there was a tradition of greater emphasis on worker well-being than in the United States. Examples of critics include the English psychologists Charles S. Myers (1925) and Tom H. Pear (1948) and the German psychologist Otto Lipmann (1928–29). In Japan, Shigemi H. Kirihara (1959) was one of a number of psychologists at the Institute of Science of Labour in the early 1920s who criticized the Taylor system based on their analysis of the physiological costs of scientific management and because of the system's lack of emphasis on individual worker differences.

Bernard Muscio (1920) examined labor's criticisms of scientific management in detail. He was careful to distinguish scientific management as put forth by Taylor from imitators who did not follow Taylor's tenets. Muscio noted, for example, that "speeding-up" work, a popular criticism of scientific management, was not part of Taylor's system. Muscio found the majority of the charges against scientific management to be unproven.

While it is true that the bulk of profits from the new methods go to the organization instead of labor, he saw this as defensible, given management's investment in the process. Muscio also noted that labor is generally not aware of the actual distribution of profits. To the fear of widespread unemployment that would result from the implementation of Taylorism, he saw the gradual introduction of scientific management as a way to minimize this concern. As for criticism that the result of scientific management was to "make men into mechanisms, fasten them in a relentless routine, and destroy individuality" (p. 244), Muscio noted that this criticism assumes that workers are somehow freer in the current industrial system; he saw this as a questionable assumption. The charge that scientific management is "undemocratic" assumes the workplace is a democracy to begin with. Scientific management provides "rule of law" as a substitute for arbitrary decisions. Muscio did find merit in the criticism that scientific management, by reducing group solidarity, can be detrimental to collective bargaining.

Muscio's (1920) analysis of scientific management is certainly open to debate; other industrial psychologists at the time were far more critical. Despite criticism from psychologists, however, there is a significant amount of overlap between their aims and methods and those of the engineers advocating scientific management. Scientific management and industrial psychology developed at roughly the same time, and the two groups did cooperate to a degree and attempt to understand each other's perspective. Advocates for both approaches knew each other and were aware of each other's work. This is evident by the coverage scientific management received in industrial and applied psychology textbooks (e.g., Hollingworth & Poffenberger, 1917; Münsterberg, 1913; Muscio, 1920; Scott, 1911). Frank Gilbreth (1923/1960) argued that cooperation with psychologists was particularly valuable and noted with approval the introduction of psychology courses in engineering curricula.[14] As president of the Taylor Society, Harlow Person invited notable industrial psychologists such as Walter Van Dyke Bingham (1924, 1928), Elton Mayo (1924), and Clarence Yoakum (1925) to present papers at the annual Taylor Society conference and then had the papers published in the *Bulletin of the Taylor Society*. Just as psychologists had their views of scientific management, advocates of that approach had their opinion regarding industrial

---

[14] Because Frank Gilbreth's wife Lillian was a psychologist, this may not have been a completely unbiased assessment. Frank Gilbreth did work with other psychologists. For example, the industrial psychologist Harold Burtt (1953) remembered Gilbreth working with Hugo Münsterberg at Harvard around the time of World War I.

psychology. For example, in a paper presented at the 1924 meeting of the Taylor Society, Person (1924) gave his evaluation of industrial psychology. He was careful to distinguish the claims of industrial psychologists, which he found appropriately conservative and modest regarding the practical value of their field to industry, "from the utterances of amateur or dilettante psychologists whose enthusiasm has been more noteworthy than their information or their judgments" (p. 164).[15]

In surveying the field of psychology, Person (1924) discussed the diversity of the discipline. While noting that psychology is primarily "behavioristic," he listed four perspectives within psychology: the mechanical reflex group, represented by the behavioral work of John B. Watson; the quantitative measurement group; the group focused on biological explanations; and the psychoanalyst group of Sigmund Freud and Carl Jung. He saw psychology as a laboratory science with little opportunity to conduct empirical, controlled research in industrial settings. Narrowing the focus to industrial psychology, Person viewed its overall contribution thus far as "relatively meager," mostly in the areas of quantitative measurement and selection. In fairness, he pointed out that industrial psychology was in its beginning stages. For Person, industrial psychology had not yet given sufficient attention to what he considered "the real management problem, that of inspiring interest, understanding, initiative, effort, precision, and personal effectiveness in cooperative activity" (p. 167).

Scientific management has been reevaluated periodically over the past 100 years. Locke (1982), for example, provided a spirited defense of Taylor's management philosophy and his techniques, and he attempted to rebut long-standing criticisms point by point. Locke noted that Taylor's system was designed to be based on research and experimentation rather than tradition. In contrast to the view at the time that management and workers were inevitably in conflict, Taylor saw the potential for cooperation between the two. Locke wrote that many of Taylor's techniques, such as standardization and management responsibility for employee training, are now well accepted in business. According to Locke, criticisms of Taylor's ideas are overblown or incorrect. He did not treat "men as machines"; rather, his methods tried to integrate the two. And Taylor did not ignore social factors, such as group processes in the workplace. He discussed restriction of output ("soldiering") and understood that workers make social comparisons and are concerned with fairness.

---

[15] In the 1920s, the term *psychologist* was not restricted to someone who had a doctorate in psychology. Anyone could call himself or herself a psychologist regardless of training (or lack thereof).

In sorting this all out, it is important to distinguish Taylor himself from other practitioners of his method. For example, Taylor warned against rate-cutting, that is, management not keeping up its part of the increased pay for increased performance bargain. Others were not so scrupulous. Taylor, both in his publications and in his testimony before Congress, consistently claimed to have a high degree of respect for workers (Taylor, 1911, 1912/1972). Perhaps consistent with the prejudices of his day, however, he seemed to have a rather low opinion of the mental abilities of laborers. In describing a worker who loads pig iron, Taylor wrote that such a person is "unable to understand the real science of doing this class of work. He is so stupid that the word "percentage" has no meaning to him, and he must consequently be trained by a man more intelligent than himself . . ." (Taylor, 1911/1972, p. 59). Even in his testimony before Congress, Taylor (1912/1972) could not resist unfavorably comparing the pig-iron handler to the shoveler, noting that the pig-iron handler "is too stupid; there is too much mental strain, too much knack required of a shoveler for the pig-iron handler to take kindly to shoveling" (p. 50). While it appears from the transcript that Taylor's analysis got a laugh from Congress, such sentiments were not likely to endear him to workers.

What can we say in summary about the influence of scientific management on industrial psychology? Muscio (1920) saw industrial psychology as operating within the framework of scientific management. In his 1920 revision of a series of industrial psychology lectures he gave in 1916 and 1917 at the University of Sydney, Muscio saw industrial psychology as useful in scientific management primarily for employee selection but also for incentive use and for constructing optimal work methods. He noted the many connections between the two disciplines. Muscio wrote that regarding scientific management, industrial psychology "*must* be used by it if it is to apply *all available relevant* science" (p. 170, italics in original). Viteles (1932) saw the influence of scientific management on industrial psychology as profound in two ways. First was in determining the scope of the field, to some extent guiding what topics are within the purview of industrial psychology. Second was in establishing an economic objective for industrial psychology and for demonstrating to organizations the economic benefit of intervention by outside consultants. Baritz (1960) agreed, stating that scientific management "not only conditioned the industrial climate for the psychologists; it determined to a large degree the direction, scope, and nature of psychological research" (p. 31). Ensuring the financial well-being of the company through increased efficiency became the goal for industrial psychologists, just as it was for practitioners of scientific management. Managers, not psychologists, defined the objectives; industrial psychologists helped managers reach those objectives. While Viteles saw scientific management as providing the foundation or framework for industrial psychology, he also believed that it contributed little directly to industrial psychology theory and practice.

Following the congressional hearings, attempts by Person and other advocates to rehabilitate scientific management's image were ultimately unsuccessful. Those congressional hearings, along with government investigations, strikes and union difficulties, and the death of Taylor and other leading proponents, led to the decline of scientific management as a viable discipline (Van De Water, 1997). While its influence on management is well documented, today there is no longer a "scientific management" approach to organizations.

## Scientific Psychology

The establishment of Wilhelm Wundt's laboratory in 1879 at the University of Leipzig is often taken as a convenient, albeit somewhat arbitrary, starting point for scientific psychology. This laboratory, however, is better viewed as the result of an accumulation of events that moved psychology from philosophy and physiology to an empirically based science of its own (Murphy, 1930; Viteles, 1932). In addition, because industrial psychology had a number of non-psychologists who made important early contributions, it is overly simplistic to view it simply as a direct outgrowth of Wundt and his students (Campbell, 2007). The new scientific psychology did provide an orientation for industrial psychology, particularly scientific psychology's emphasis on empirical verification, that is, the use of the scientific method.[16] Wundt did have an indirect effect on industrial psychology, as a number of important early contributors to industrial psychology, including Hugo Münsterberg, Walter Dill Scott, and James McKeen Cattell, received their doctorates from him.

---

[16] The scientific method is a somewhat variable concept that tends to be defined differently across disciplines. In psychology, the hallmarks of this method are a systematic empiricism that relies on data, verifiable knowledge through the use replication and peer-review, and testable hypotheses, that is, hypotheses that can be empirically tested and that have the potential to be supported or shown to be false. In addition, unobservable concepts or constructs must be linked to observable events, and all conclusions are considered to be probabilistic. The method or procedures are designed to increase objectivity, since the experimenter cannot be relied on to be wholly objective or unbiased. Thurs (2015) viewed the scientific method as rhetoric that has at least three functions that developed more or less in chronological order: It enforces boundaries between what is science and what is not, it allows communication between scientists and non-scientists, and it is a brand that represents science.

This new laboratory-based scientific psychology soon spread beyond Germany. Different countries adopted the new scientific psychology to varying degrees at various times, dependent on their own traditions and circumstances. In Germany, the new empirically based psychology became established not only at Leipzig but also at other university centers, most notably at the University of Berlin's Psychological Institute, founded by Carl Stumpf (1848–1936) in 1900. In France, the development of psychology was influenced by medicine and philosophy and reflected a strong interest in psychopathology and the application of psychology to education and children. Individuals who were central to the development of psychology in France included Théodule Ribot (1839–1916), Alfred Binet (1857–1911), and Binet's successor at the physiological laboratory at the Sorbonne, Henri Piéron (1881–1964). While British empiricism and associationism broadly influenced scientific psychology, the university system in the United Kingdom was surprisingly resistant to the empirical approach to psychology. Work by independent scholars such as Francis Galton in anthropometry, Herbert Spencer in evolution and psychology, and Alexander Bain's founding of the journal *Mind* in 1876 preceded the first chair of psychology, at Cambridge University in 1891 (Carpintero, 1992).[17]

A portion of Wundt's psychology was concerned with determining the structure or contents of conscious thought. General principles were emphasized, not individual difference characteristics.[18] A variation of this approach called *structuralism* was developed by E. B. Titchener (1867–1927) at Cornell University. Using the technique of introspection, structuralism's primary goal was to determine the essential elements of consciousness, as Titchener (1898) put it: "[T]o analyze the structure of mind; to ravel out the elemental processes from the tangle of consciousness" (p. 450). Sensations are examples of the elemental processes Titchener was referring to. Titchener likened structuralism in psychology to morphology or classification in biology and contrasted structuralism with *functionalism*, whose analogue in biology is physiology. If structuralism attempts to "discover, first of all, what is there and in what quantity," functionalism tries to determine "what is it there for" (Titchener, 1898, p. 450). Titchener believed that for psychology a functionalist approach is premature; first the field must determine the

---

[17] Carpintero (1992) provides a history of psychology as an academic discipline in Germany, France, the United Kingdom, Italy, and Russia along with brief descriptions of psychology's development in the Netherlands, Belgium, Denmark, Sweden, Finland, Switzerland, Spain, Portugal, Japan, China, India, Argentina, Mexico, Brazil, and Peru.

[18] One notable exception was the dissertation of James McKeen Cattell. See Chapter 3.

structure of consciousness before it can scientifically examine function. While Titchener did have his supporters, notably his student E. G. Boring, structuralism as a system did not survive him. Functionalism, however, became the foundation not only for industrial psychology but for American psychology in general.

The functionalist approach was heavily influenced by the evolutionary theories of Charles Darwin and Alfred Russel Wallace.[19] This orientation focuses on practical applications and emphasizes individual differences and their consequences. As such, it was an ideal orientation for the practical concerns of industrial psychology. Boring (1950) wrote "that functional psychology *is* American psychology" (p. 559, emphasis in the original). By the mid-1920s, this was also true for France and Great Britain. In the nineteenth century, Herbert Spencer and Francis Galton in Great Britain and the American psychologists James Mark Baldwin, James McKeen Cattell, William James, G. Stanley Hall, and Edward W. Scripture were all essentially functionalists. By the end of that century, a formal school of functional psychology arose at the University of Chicago under the leadership of John Dewey, whose 1896 paper on the reflex arc criticizing elementalism was a key foundational work on functionalism. Dewey's brand of functionalism was continued at Chicago by James Rowland Angell and Harvey A. Carr. The other functionalist stronghold in America was the psychology program at Columbia University under the leadership of James McKeen Cattell and his colleagues Edward L. Thorndike and Robert Sessions Woodworth (Boring, 1950). A number of early industrial psychologists received their graduate training at these two universities. Examples are Walter Van Dyke Bingham, L. L. Thurstone, and Clarence Yoakum at the University of Chicago and Douglas H. Fryer, Harry Hollingworth, Albert T. Poffenberger, Edward K. Strong, Jr., and Herbert A. Toops at Columbia University (Vinchur, 2007).

Dovetailing with the functionalist school of psychology was *scientific pragmatism*, which based the worth of an idea on its utilitarian consequences. As such, prediction was valued over understanding (Austin & Villanova, 1992). This pragmatism was evident in the work of the early

---

[19] Darwin and Wallace developed their evolutionary theories independently. Although their theories were similar, there were differences. Important for psychology, Darwin included humans in evolution; Wallace was unwilling to take that step. Darwin, perhaps influenced by the work of Adam Smith, emphasized individual selection; while Wallace, influenced by the socialist Robert Owen (see Chapter 10), emphasized group selection (Ruse, 2015). An application of evolutionary theory to social relations, termed *social Darwinism* and first advocated by the English philosopher Herbert Spencer (1820–1903), was sometime used, primarily in the late 1800s, as justification for unrestrained capitalism (i.e., the survival of the fittest) (Foner & Garraty, 1991).

industrial psychologists, particularly in their approach to employee selection. Max Freyd, who with Walter Van Dyke Bingham authored a 1926 text on vocational selection, offered an illustration related to testing. Freyd (1923–24) noted that determining the functions that a selection test measures "may be omitted, since the important point to determine is the correlation of the test scores with the criteria of success" (p. 249). That is, in an applied setting, if the test is a good predictor of job performance, determining what exactly it is that the test measures is of secondary importance.

While psychology's orientation in the United States transitioned to a pragmatic, functionalist approach early in the twentieth century, this may not have been the case in Europe. According to van Strien (1998a), European applied psychologists relied for a longer period on laboratory apparatus rather than the psychological tests characteristic in the United States and maintained a theoretical approach van Strien termed *psychological essentialism*. Similar to a structuralist approach, essentialism differentiates among individuals based on basic mental functions, as measured by standard, scientific instrumentation of the laboratory. Unlike the pragmatic, functionalist approach that was focused on problem solving and, eventually, on the accurate prediction of an external criterion such as job performance, the essentialistic approach was theory driven. It viewed the psychologist, not an "outsider" such as a manager, as the expert and ultimate arbiter of success. The atheoretical, practical approach to employee selection described by Freyd in the previous paragraph would be anathema to a psychologist taking an essentialist approach.

Van Strien (1998a) used the example of the industrial psychotechnical movement in Europe to illustrate the essentialistic approach. There was some scattered activity in psychotechnics that occurred prior to Münsterberg's pioneering efforts, which he described in his 1913 text *Psychology and Industrial Efficiency*. But it was Münsterberg who started the industrial psychotechnics movement in continental Europe. Practitioners of industrial psychotechnics adapted laboratory equipment, such as the tachistoscope, the tremometer, and the Hipp chronoscope,[20] that was used for measuring individual differences and applied it to personnel selection and vocational guidance. The goal was to conduct an analysis of the elemental structural mental components for success in a particular

---

[20] The tachistoscope is used to expose participants to brief visual stimuli. The tremometer measures trembling of body parts, generally the finger. The Hipp chronoscope measures time (Voбořil, Květon, & Jelínek, 2014). The use of apparatus for employee selection is examined in Chapter 7.

vocation. While a form of validation was sometime used (comparing rank orders of test scores with rank orders of workers by supervisors), formal test validation as practiced in the United States was not common in continental Europe until after World War II. The judgment of supervisors, moreover, was viewed as unreliable and inferior to that of the psychologist (van Strien, 1998a). Supervisor ratings were commonly used as a criterion of success when validating tests in America.

While pragmatism did make some inroads in Europe in the 1920s, especially in German-speaking Europe, the shift to the American test-criterion model of selection did not occur until the second half of the twentieth century. Given that the change occurred in the United States early in that century, between 1910 and 1920 for the most part, what caused the delay in Europe? Van Strien (1998a) pointed to differences in primary audiences as a plausible explanation. In the United States, the needs of the consumers of psychological services became paramount early on. Relying on expert psychological judgment was not enough. Psychologists had to be able to demonstrate empirically that their tests did, in fact, do what they purported to do. Paper-and-pencil tests, especially group tests, were more practical than cumbersome laboratory apparatus and therefore became the norm. In Europe, the social and institutional context was different. The early psychotechnologists were concerned with their academic standing and with maintaining the respect of their colleagues. The academy invested the professorate with a great deal of authority; they were viewed as objective, impartial experts whose impartiality permitted them license in applied situations. Approaches that focused on the overall character of the individual, particularly in Germany with the rise of National Socialism, extended this authority.[21]

Meskill (2015) took issue with van Strien's (1998a) conclusions and pointed to the example of the Reich Agency for Job Placement and Unemployment Insurance (aka the Labor Administration) in Germany. Established in 1922, the Labor Administration's roughly 1,200 Labor Offices had virtually complete control of the labor market. Both employers seeking workers and individuals looking for work had to make use of the Labor Offices. The Labor Administration and the German Army were the two largest consumers of applied psychology. Meskill noted that while the Labor Administration did make use of academic theory and methods, its approach was eclectic and included the use of standardized work tests, albeit loosely standardized. Vocational psychologists in the Labor

---

[21] The effect of the rise of the Nazi Party on industrial psychology is discussed in Chapter 6.

Administration regarded the character typologies of the academic psychologists as too formal and were concerned that their use would alienate employers, who were important consumers of the psychologists' services. It was this concern for pleasing employers, not concerns over academic standing or the respect of colleagues, that motivated psychologists in the Labor Administration.

Taking a broader view of psychology, by the 1920s there were a number of theoretical systems competing for dominance. Often referred to as "schools" of psychology, they represented not only theory but also practice, and psychology students were socialized into the profession to a large extent based on the theoretical orientation of their mentors (Capshew, 1999). The school approach was evident in early histories of psychology (Boring, 1929; Murphy, 1929; Pillsbury, 1929) and is exemplified by Heidbreder's (1933) *Seven Psychologies.* In addition to Titchener's structuralism and the University of Chicago version of functionalism advocated by Dewey, Angell, and Carr, the other five psychologies were those of William James, the behaviorism of John Watson, the dynamic psychology associated with Columbia University and Robert Woodworth, Gestalt psychology, and Sigmund Freud's psychoanalysis. The lack of a single, unified theory could be viewed positively, as Edna Heidbreder did, as the growing pains of a new discipline that had not yet reached maturity, or negatively, with multiple competing theories indicating a field with a tenuous hold on scientific credibility. Capshew (1999) noted that this "crisis" of identity in psychology was international, with similar concerns expressed in Germany and in the USSR.

## The International Nature of Industrial Psychology

In addition to the contextual influences discussed up to this point, psychologists influenced each other. Given today's instantaneous worldwide communication and high-speed air travel, it would be easy to conclude that interaction among I-O psychologists around the globe is much greater today than in the early years of the twentieth century. This conclusion, however, is not entirely warranted. Although for much of the twentieth century, I-O psychology was centered in the United States (Salgado, Anderson, & Hülsheger, 2010),[22] this was not true of early industrial psychology. Despite slow international communication and travel, to a remarkable degree the

---

[22] In recent years, there has been an increased emphasis on global issues in I-O psychology. See, for example, Volume 4 of the second edition of the *Handbook of Industrial & Organizational Psychology* (Triandis, Dunnette, & Hough, 1994), which is devoted to cross-cultural and international development in I-O psychology.

early industrial psychologists communicated with one another and were aware of each other's work. This was true for science in general. Academic professionalization and the advent of specialization into academic disciplines in the mid-to-late 1800s found scholars eager to communicate with their colleagues in other countries. International organizations and conferences proliferated (Jarausch, 2015). As early as 1920, applied psychologists were meeting at their own international conference.[23]

For industrial psychologists in America, interaction was fostered by the tendency for American psychologists to be educated and to travel abroad at the turn of the last century (Vinchur, 2005). For example, pioneering American psychologists Walter Dill Scott and James McKeen Cattell received their doctorates under Wilhelm Wundt at the University of Leipzig in Germany. This was also true for Hugo Münsterberg, who despite never relinquishing his German citizenship spent the bulk of his career in the United States. Walter Van Dyke Bingham, who among other important contributions founded the first graduate program in industrial psychology, followed his University of Chicago Ph.D. with an extensive European tour. While abroad, Bingham (1952) interacted with German psychologists Wolfgang Köhler, Kurt Koffka, Carl Stumpf, and Hans Rupp; English psychologists Cyril Burt and Charles Spearman; and pioneering industrial psychologist Charles S. Myers. Early American industrial psychologist Morris Viteles met and was strongly influenced by Myers while traveling abroad in the 1920s (Viteles, 1947).

Much more so than in recent history, American applied psychology journals and textbooks covered developments abroad. The *Journal of Applied Psychology, Journal of Personnel Research*, and other journals published reviews of industrial psychology in France (Fryer, 1923–24; Viteles, 1923), Germany (Hartmann, 1931–32; Kornhauser, 1929–30a; Viteles, 1923), Great Britain (Fryer, 1923–24; Kornhauser, 1929–30a; Viteles, 1923), Russia (Hartmann, 1932), and Switzerland (Heller, 1929–30). Reports from international conferences were published (Bingham, 1927–28; Holman, 1927; Kitson, 1922b), and journal reviews of industrial psychology included summaries of developments from abroad (e.g., Link, 1920; Viteles, 1926, 1928b). American textbooks, such as Viteles's 1932 *Industrial Psychology*, included extensive coverage of industrial psychology in other countries.

This is not to say that relationships among psychologists from different countries were always congenial. The period following World War I was a time of great hardship in Europe as the continent tried to

---

[23] These conferences are discussed in Chapter 9.

rebuild. Conflict among scientists did not end with the armistice; there were recriminations, hard feelings, and attempts to limit contact. The International Congress of Psychology was not revived until 1923, when it was held in Oxford, England, under the presidency of Charles S. Myers. In his autobiography, Myers (1936) recalled that some Germans did not participate, possibly due to conflict between Germany and France, along with Belgium, in the Ruhr. Nevertheless, invitations were sent without regard to nationality, and there were some participants at the conference from Belgium, France, and Germany. Earlier in 1920, the Swiss psychologists Édouard Claparède and Pierre Bovet organized the first International Congress of Psychotechnics Applied to Vocational Guidance in neutral Geneva. While there were no participants from Germany or Russia, they were invited, and plausible reasons for their absence other than internecine conflict were the extremely high inflation rate in Germany and the ongoing revolution in Russia (Gundlach, 1998).

## Chapter Summary

The early developmental period of I-O psychology was a time of global change. There were demographic changes that included the beginning of the migration of individuals from rural to urban settings. The second Industrial Revolution saw a dramatic increase in the size and complexity of organizations, along with the advent of a professional manager class and centralized personnel functions. Progressives in the early twentieth century advocated for workplace changes, and their emphasis on productivity and efficiency was taken up by both proponents of scientific management and psychologists making the transition from the laboratory to industry. While scientific management did not survive as a management system, it did influence the early industrial psychologists by giving them an economic rationale for their work and by paving the way for the use of outside experts for improving an organization's human resources. Scientific psychology also influenced the early industrial psychologists, in part by giving them a professional identity and a functionalist orientation that provided a rationale for their interventions. And the early applied psychologists around the world influenced each other, through international conferences and journals and books that included work from many countries. One major influence on the development of I-O psychology not discussed in this chapter was advances in measurement and statistics. This is the topic of the Chapter 3.

# Measurement, Individual Differences, and Psychological Testing

## Psychological Measurement

It is a truism that a science can advance only as far as its measurement techniques permit. Measurement presented particular difficulties for psychology. Much of its subject matter, such as consciousness and memory, were psychological constructs that are not directly observable and can be measured only indirectly through inference.[1] Indeed, the difficulty in measuring psychological processes objectively was one reason for the German philosopher Immanuel Kant's (1724–1804) pessimistic assessment in 1781 that psychology and chemistry could never obtain the status of natural sciences; they were simply descriptive disciplines (Guilford, 1936; Yoakum, 1925).[2] He separated reality into the external (noumenal) world, which when perceived by the human mind becomes the inner (phenomenal) world. Kant believed that because these mental phenomena have no physical existence, they cannot be studied empirically because they are not open to observation or experiment (Pickren & Rutherford, 2010). Kant was overly pessimistic, as psychology has made an enormous amount of progress as an innovator in research design, measurement, and statistics. Accurate measurement was of particular importance to the development of

---

[1] A construct is a concept with scientific value. The personality trait extroversion, for example, is "constructed" based on patterns of behavior consistent the conception of that trait. Constructs can be useful in organizing and predicting, but they do not have an externally verifiable existence in the same way that, for example, this page of text does.

[2] Chemistry is now universally considered to be part of the natural sciences. For psychology, the picture is more complicated. Psychology is variously cataloged as a natural science, a social science, or, in light of its less than perfect fit in either the natural or social sciences, its own category of behavioral science. A field broad enough to encompass, for example, neurophysiology, the treatment of addictive behaviors, the study of early childhood development, and I-O psychology is bound to be difficult to neatly categorize. Given psychology's assumption that behavior and mental philosophy are natural phenomena amenable to understanding through the scientific method, my own bias is to consider it a natural science. Opinions do vary however.

industrial psychology because the field placed a special emphasis on individual difference characteristics such as abilities, attitudes, aptitudes, and interests. These characteristics, however, are of no use to an industrial psychologist unless they can be accurately measured. Progress in the beginning years of industrial psychology was intimately tied to progress in measurement.

Consistent with the approach of other more established sciences, early academic psychologists were primarily interested in developing general laws of behavior and mentality applicable to all individuals. The earliest attempts to objectively and quantitatively measure psychological characteristics have their roots in physiology. Predating Wundt's lab at the University of Leipzig, Ernst Weber (1775–1878) and Gustav Fechner (1801–87) studied the relationship between the physical dimensions of a stimulus and the observer's perceptions of that stimulus, a procedure that became known as *psychophysics*.[3] Weber, who was a professor of anatomy and physiology at Leipzig, mapped relative tactile sensitivity using the perception of when the pressure of two points on the skin is perceived as one point (the *two-point threshold*). Weber also used this threshold concept in determining the *just-noticeable difference (jnd)* between two weights to formulate the equation now known as Weber's Law,[4] which mathematically describes the relationship between the *jnd* and the weights of the two stimuli (Goodwin, 1999).

Among Weber's contributions to psychology was his demonstration that the relationship between the physical world and the psychological perception of that world is not simple. Increasing the weight of a stimulus by a fixed amount does not always result in the perception of an increase of a fixed amount; the perception depends on the absolute weight of the initial stimulus. In a larger sense, Weber demonstrated that mental events could be measured quantitatively, that the measurement of psychological constructs could be tied to observable behavior. This achievement provided the foundation for measurement in psychology (Goodwin, 1999).

Gustav Fechner studied with Weber and extended his work. Fechner earned his M.D. degree in 1822. He was a polymath whose research in physics earned him a professorship at the University of Leipzig in that discipline. Fechner's work on visual afterimages using the sun as the

---

[3] There are antecedents for Weber's work. Boring (1950) noted that in 1760 Pierre Bouguer anticipated Weber's Law.

[4] Weber's Law = $jnd/S = k$; where $jnd$ is the just noticeable difference, $S$ is the smaller of the two weights compared, and $k$ is a constant. In essence, the law demonstrates that the $jnd$ is proportional to the size of $S$ (Goodwin, 1999).

stimulus resulted in severe damage to his vision and eventually led to his resignation from the university and a period of physical and psychological decline. By the early 1840s, he was recovering, and in 1851 he was reappointed to the Leipzig faculty (Goodwin, 1999).

Fechner was interested in the relationship between humans and nature, in particular the relationship between the psychological and physical worlds. Building on Weber's *jnd* concept and using himself as a participant, Fechner lifted a weight in each hand more than 67,000 times, recording whether he perceived a difference and then calculating the relationship between a perceived difference and the actual physical difference in weights. Taking the smallest perceived difference as the zero point and then plotting *jnds* as a function of the physical differences associated with them, Fechner developed a curve that could be described by a logarithmic function. Although Fechner called his equation Weber's Law, eventually it became known as Fechner's Law (Pickren & Rutherford, 2010).[5]

Although not without critics, the work of Weber and Fechner demonstrated that quantitative measurement of psychological processes was possible, and they provided a technology to do so. Boring (1961) and Stigler (1999) date the beginning of probability-based inferential statistics in psychology to Fechner's 1860 work in psychophysics. Statistics were introduced into psychology decades before their use in economics and sociology, although astronomers had been using them for some time (Stigler, 1999).[6] Weber's and Fechner's work provided a foundation for their University of Leipzig colleague, Wilhelm Wundt, and his new scientific psychology. Like Weber and Fechner, Wundt was interested in elucidating generalizable theories and laws. Individual variation in performance was a problem, in that this "error variance" obscured regularities across persons. There were, however, those who found these individual differences, this error, interesting and appropriate for scientific inquiry.

## Individual Differences

In his pioneering 1913 text *Psychology and Industrial Efficiency*, Hugo Münsterberg wrote that the "development of schemes to compare

---

[5] Fechner's Law is a reformulation of Weber's Law, $S = k \log R$, where $S$ is the perceived size of a stimulus in *jnd* units, $k$ is a constant, and $R$ represents the physical measurement of $S$ (Goodwin, 1999).
[6] For the interested reader, Stigler (1999) provides a chapter-length discussion of why psychology predated economics and sociology in the use of statistics.

the differences between individuals by the methods of experimental science was after all the most important advance toward the practical application of psychology. The study of individual differences itself is not applied psychology, but is the presupposition without which applied psychology would have remained a phantom" (p. 10). A few years later, in his 1919 presidential address to the members of the APA, industrial psychologist Walter Dill Scott stated: "Possibly the greatest single achievement of the members of the American Psychological Association is the establishment of the psychology of individual differences" (Scott, 1920, p. 85). This was most likely news to the academic, experimentalist members of the APA, who were invested in discovering general laws of behavior and mental functioning and viewed individual differences as a problem to be controlled, not celebrated. But for industrial psychologists such as Scott, individual differences formed a foundation for much of their science and practice. The existence and measurement of these differences allowed the psychologist to determine which applicant has the best chance of success in a particular job, which vocation is the best fit for an individual, or which type of training is most suitable for an employee. Three individuals who played key roles in the early attempts to understand and accurately measure those differences were Francis Galton, James McKeen Cattell, and William Stern. While Galton and Cattell's anthropometric testing procedures did not prove viable in the long run, they did demonstrate the possibilities for measurement in psychology. They set the stage for more enduring approaches to psychological measurement, such as the cognitive tests of Alfred Binet.

*Francis Galton*

It is possible to trace the beginning of work on individual differences in performance to late eighteenth-century astronomers' discussion of the "personal equation," the existence of consistent differences among astronomers in measuring the same stellar transits (Yoakum, 1925). We will begin our discussion, however, roughly 100 years later with Francis Galton, whose work had a more direct effect on the development of industrial psychology. The English scientist Sir Francis Galton (1822–1911) was not a psychologist; he was a generalist whose innovations included the basis for modern weather maps and a system of fingerprint identification. He was also a noted explorer who made expeditions to North Africa in 1846 and to previously unmapped Southern Africa in 1850 (Magnusson, 1990). It is Galton's later work on individual differences and quantification that is most relevant for the history of industrial psychology. Galton was a cousin of Charles Darwin. After reading Darwin's *Origin of the Species* (1859/1986), Galton became interested in heredity, particularly the heredity of eminence or success. He published his treatment of that subject, *Hereditary Genius*, in 1869 (cited in Zusne, 1984). Galton believed that psychological traits such as intelligence were innate. In the *nature-nurture* debate, a phrase attributed to him, Galton came down squarely on the side of nature: Intellectual ability is due to heredity, not the environment (Zusne, 1984). This emphasis on heredity led him to develop eugenics, improving humans by the manipulation of hereditary factors. Galton needed a way to accurately measure the individual differences he believed reflected those innate psychological traits.

The concept of the modern cognitive ability test can be traced to Galton's 1865 belief that a test could be developed to identify persons of unusual "natural ability" (Fancher, 1997). Galton developed a number of measures to assess physical characteristics and performance, which came to be called *anthropometric measures*. In 1884, he founded his Anthropometric Laboratory at the International Health Exposition and later transferred the laboratory to the South Kensington Museum. In addition to physical measures such as height, weight, and eye color, Galton also assessed characteristics of a more psychological nature, such as visual and auditory reaction time and judgment (number of errors) in dividing a line and estimating an angle (Sokal, 1987). To analyze this data, he extended the work of Laplace, Gauss, and Quételet on the normal law of error. The French astronomer and mathematician Pierre Simon de Laplace (1749–1827) and the German mathematician Karl Friedrich Gauss (1775–1855) pioneered the idea that a plot of individual errors, such as those made when determining the position of a star in astronomy, form a bell-shaped curve. Most errors cluster around the center of that curve, and proportionally fewer errors occur as the distance from the center of the curve increases in either direction. This idea is the basis for the normal distribution that is central to statistical analysis. The Belgian mathematician, statistician, and astronomer Adolphe Quételet (1796–1874) extended this idea to human physical characteristics, and Galton extended it to behavioral measurement (Boring, 1950; Zusne, 1984). In order to measure the degree of relationship between parents and offspring, Galton developed the basis for the correlation coefficient, a major contribution to statistics discussed later in this chapter. Galton also had a significant influence on another researcher with an interest in individual differences, the American psychologist James McKeen Cattell.

*James McKeen Cattell*

James McKeen Cattell (Figure 3.1) was born in Easton, Pennsylvania, in 1860, three years before his father William assumed the presidency of Lafayette College in that city. James McKeen Cattell graduated from Lafayette College in 1880. While an undergraduate, he was greatly influenced by the renowned philologist Francis March,[7] whose emphasis on the inductive principles of Francis Bacon can be found in Cattell's subsequent work in psychology (Sokal, 1987). After graduation, Cattell set off for Europe to study philosophy, where the work of Wilhelm Wundt and

Figure 3.1   James McKeen Cattell. Courtesy of Lafayette College Special Collections and Archives

[7] Francis Andrew March (1825–1911) received his A.B. and M.A. degrees from Amherst College. A self-taught philologist, one who studies the structure and historical development of language, he was a respected scholar with an international reputation who had more than 190 articles to his credit. Appointed Professor of the English Language and Lecturer in Comparative Philology in 1857, March was possibly the first person to hold the title of Professor of English. He taught English in the same manner as the classical languages, one of the earliest, perhaps the first, to do so (Donahue & Falbo, 2007). March was president of the Modern Language Association and the American Philological Association, director of American readers for the *Oxford English Dictionary*, and the author of groundbreaking books in grammar and English usage (Schlueter & Schlueter, 2005).

Rudolf Lotze impressed him. Cattell returned to America to spend a year with G. Stanley Hall at Johns Hopkins University before returning to Wundt at the University of Leipzig. It was at Leipzig that Cattell first demonstrated an interest in the variability of human performance (Woodworth, 1944). He received his doctorate from Wundt's program in 1886.

Upon his return to America in 1887, Cattell lectured at Bryn Mawr and at the University of Pennsylvania (Boring, 1950). He then went back abroad to Cambridge University with the intention of studying neurology. While at Cambridge, Cattell came under the influence of Francis Galton, who encouraged Cattell to apply the experimental procedures he developed in Wundt's laboratory to the quantitative measurement of individual differences. Cattell wrote that his career was shaped by three men named Francis: Francis Bacon with his theory of induction, Francis March with his emphasis on those inductive principles, and Francis Galton with his work on the quantitative measurement of individual differences (Sokal, 1987).

In 1888, Cattell became Professor of Psychology at the University of Pennsylvania, where he established a psychology laboratory. In 1891, he moved to Columbia University to head its psychology program. Cattell's academic career, however, was cut short in 1917 when his employment was terminated by Columbia's president Nicholas Murray Butler. Reasons for the dismissal included Cattell's pacifist opposition to World War I and his numerous run-ins with President Butler (Sokal, 2009; Summerscales, 1970). His academic career at Columbia over, Cattell devoted much time and effort to editorial duties, an area he had been active in since he cofounded the *Psychological Review* with Mark Baldwin in 1894. Cattell purchased and revived the journal *Science*, took a leadership role in the American Association for the Advancement of Science (Coon & Sprenger, 1998), and founded the Psychological Corporation consulting firm in 1921 (Cattell, 1923).[8]

Cattell, who is often credited with coining the term *mental test* in an 1890 paper, followed Galton in using anthropometric tests of sensory and physiological abilities in his measurement of individual differences. He based the accuracy of these tests on their relations to other tests (von Mayrhauser, 1992). Cattell (1890/1947) saw clearly that unless psychology rested on a firm foundation of measurement and experimentation, it could never hope to match the physical sciences in achievement. On a practical level, he hoped that his anthropometric measures would

---

[8] The Psychological Corporation is discussed in Chapter 6.

be predictive of academic performance. His hopes were dashed, however, when his student Clark Wissler used the recently developed correlation coefficient to test this hypothesis. Wissler (1901) found generally low and negative correlations between these tests and academic performance, providing one of the first uses of the correlation coefficient for this purpose (von Mayrhauser, 1992).

Cattell's contributions to industrial psychology are more indirect and subtle than those of other early pioneers such as Hugo Münsterberg and Walter Dill Scott. Cattell, whose own research program lasted only until about 1900, was a noteworthy teacher and editor and psychology's greatest promoter in the first half of the twentieth century. The number of doctoral students educated at Columbia University during and in the five or so years after his tenure there who made important contributions to industrial psychology is impressive. A partial list would include Edward L. Thorndike (Ph.D. 1898), James B. Miner (Ph.D. 1903), Harry Hollingworth (Ph.D. 1909), Edward K. Strong Jr. (Ph.D. 1911), Albert Poffenberger (Ph.D. 1912), Herbert W. Rogers (Ph.D. 1921), Herbert Toops (Ph.D. 1921), Elsie Oschrin Bregman (Ph.D. 1922), Paul Achilles (Ph.D. 1923), and Sadie Shellow (Ph.D. 1923) (Vinchur & Koppes, 2007). Cattell did make a direct contribution to industrial psychology by founding the Psychological Corporation, an early applied psychology consulting firm. The firm, however, was not successful under his direction, and it took others such as Walter V. Bingham and Paul Achilles to place it on firm financial footing (Achilles, 1957; Sokal, 1981).

Cattell's scientific orientation and faith in applied psychology were his greatest contributions to industrial psychology. His emphasis on measurement, quantification, and objectivity had an important early impact on the field despite his own limitations in statistics. This emphasis is illustrated by the perhaps apocryphal remark, attributed to Cornell's Edward B. Titchener, that "Cattell's god is probable error" (Wells, 1944).[9] Despite his own failure to predict meaningful outcomes with anthropometric measures, Cattell provided an orientation that proved prescient for industrial psychology, particularly for employee selection.[10]

---

[9] Probable error is a measure of a distribution's dispersion or variability. In a normal distribution, 50 percent of the measurements fall between +1 and −1 *PE* (Guilford, 1936). Popular in the early part of the twentieth century in psychology, *PE* has been supplanted by the standard deviation.

[10] While there is no book-length biography of Cattell to date, Michael Sokal has published a series of articles on Cattell's life and work (e.g., Sokal, 1971, 1981, 1984, 1987, 1995, 2009). Although Cattell was asked, he never contributed to the *History of Psychology in Autobiography* series. He did begin an autobiography (reproduced in Sokal, 1971), but it was never completed.

## William Stern

Another psychologist who did pioneering work on individual differences was the German psychologist William Stern (1871–1938). Like his contemporary Cattell, (Louis) William Stern was a pioneer in differential psychology,[11] beginning work on that topic before 1900 (Zusne, 1984). In 1900, he published *Über Psychologie der individuellen Differenzen (On the Psychology of Individual Differences)*. Stern expanded and revised this book in 1911 as *Die differentielle Psychologie in ihren methodischen Grundlagen (Methodological Foundations of Differential Psychology)* (cited in Lamiell, 1996). His conception of individual differences was quite distinct from how that concept is generally used in industrial psychology, where specific individual difference characteristics, such as cognitive ability, are used to distinguish among persons for some practical application. Stern's broader *critical personalism* or *personalistic psychology* focuses on the total person who develops due to a combination of physical, mental, hereditary, and environmental influences and can be understood only by using both natural science and cultural science methods (Zusne, 1984). He did not believe that simply studying individual differences themselves would result in an understanding of a person's individuality (Lamiell, 1996; see Lamiell, 2003, for a fuller discussion of Stern's ideas).

Stern, like many of the first generation of scientific psychologists, was a generalist who made significant contributions not only to differential psychology but also to child, forensic, and applied psychology. Today he is probably best remembered as originating the "mental quotient" (later the intelligence quotient or IQ) concept in 1912, a legacy Stern would not have appreciated. He saw his personalistic psychology as a counterpoint to what he termed the "pernicious" influence of the IQ concept (Allport, 1938). Stern's contributions to industrial psychology were significant. By 1900, he had anticipated much of Hugo Münsterberg's better-known work applied efforts (Hale, 1980). Stern used the terms *applied psychology* and *psychotechnics* in a pamphlet as early as 1903 (Zusne, 1984). With the help of his student Otto Lipmann, Stern founded the *Institut für angewandte Psychologie (Institute for Applied Psychology)* in Berlin in 1906 (G. W. Allport, 1938). In 1907, Stern and Lipmann founded the journal *Zeitschrift für angewandte Psychologie (Journal for Applied Psychology)* (Viteles, 1932).

---

[11] Stern introduced the term "differential psychology" in a 1900 paper (Schmidt, 1997). While Stern used differential psychology to refer to his particular conception of the study of individual differences, today the term refers to the study of individual differences in general.

Born in Berlin in 1871, Stern received his doctorate in 1893 under Herman Ebbinghaus at the University of Berlin.[12] Stern held academic positions first at the University of Breslau from 1897 until 1916 and then at the University of Hamburg, a university he played a role in founding. At Hamburg, he established an institute for research on giftedness, *Hamburger Arbeiten zur Begabungsforschung*, which became notable for work in vocational psychology and educational psychology (Allport, 1938). The rise of National Socialism, however, led to Stern's dismissal in 1933 for his Jewish heritage and to the destruction of many of his books, papers, and research records. In addition, that year both his assistant Martha Muchow and his long-time colleague Otto Lipmann committed suicide (Lamiell, 1996). By 1935, Stern had fled Germany, and after a short time in the Netherlands, he accepted an academic position at Duke University in the United States. He spoke little English and had visited the United States only twice before, once to attend the 1909 conference at Clark University where Sigmund Freud and Carl Jung introduced psychoanalysis to an American audience. Nevertheless, with the help of his wife Clara, he soon mastered the language (Allport, 1938). Stern died in March 1938.

## Psychological Testing

Unlike physical objects or characteristics, psychological constructs have to be measured by inference from behavior; they cannot be measured directly. Eventually these constructs were assessed through the use of psychological tests, which can be broadly defined as measures of samples of behavior. Measuring a construct accurately can be difficult and controversial, as illustrated by the history of measures of intelligence or cognitive ability. From the functionalist, pragmatic perspective of industrial psychology, however, a test can still be useful for prediction of job performance even if the underlying construct is assessed imperfectly. Measures should possess two psychometric qualities: They should be reliable, and they should be valid. Measures are reliable if they are consistent or free from random errors of measurement. These errors can be due to the passage of time,

---

[12] Herman Ebbinghaus (1850–1909) is best remembered today for his work on memory. Influenced by Fechner, Ebbinghaus applied the scientific method to the study of memory and developed procedures, such as the use of nonsense syllables, which are still used today. In 1885, he published his results, including his well-known "forgetting curve" that demonstrated memory loss over time. Ebbinghaus later became interested in test development and devised the *Ebbinghaus Completion Test* for assessing cognitive ability in children (Zusne, 1984).

inconsistency of test content, or – in the case of multiple observers – inconsistent ratings across observers.

Validity is now viewed as a unitary concept that is determined by the usefulness, meaningfulness, and appropriateness of inferences made from test scores (Guion, 1976). In short, a test is valid if it does what it is supposed to do. There are three traditional strategies used today for determining the validity of a measure. Using current terminology, criterion-related validation, the strategy of choice in the early years of industrial psychology, is determined by the strength of the relationship between a test and some other measure called a criterion, most often job performance. Content-related validation, or content-related test development, is concerned with the degree to which a test is a representative sample of important behaviors in the domain of interest.[13] The broader strategy of construct validation is concerned with whether a test actually measures the underlying construct, such as cognitive ability, it was designed to measure. Unlike the other two strategies, evidence for construct validity is built up over time using multiple strategies.[14]

### Early Psychological Tests

In an early history of what at the time was called mental testing, Kimball Young (1923) discussed the British, French, German, and American roots of mental measurement. Young traced the interactions and chain of influence among the four traditions. According to Young, the associationism of the philosopher John Stuart Mill and the statistical innovations of Gauss and Quételet influenced Francis Galton, who in turn influenced Karl Pearson.[15] The Germans Franz Brentano, Edmund Husserl, and Oswald Külpe influenced the British psychologists Charles Spearman, Cyril Burt, and Godfrey Thomson. The French medical psychology of Edouard Séquin, Théodule Ribot, Jean-Martin Charcot, and Blin

---

[13] Technically, in content-oriented test development, inferences are made regarding test development, not test scores; however, the implication is if a test accurately represents the greater domain of interest, it should be valid. Content-oriented validity is sometimes confused with *face validity*. Does the test look like it should be valid? Content-valid tests tend to have face validity, but simply because a test appears valid does not mean that it is.

[14] Construct-related validation began to receive attention in the 1950s, for example, Cronbach and Meehl (1955).

[15] Associationism refers to a number of theories that view cognition and learning as constructed as the result of the association of simple ideas and/or sensations. J. S. Mill's four principles of association were similarity, contiguity, frequency, and inseparability (see Boring [1950] for his chapter on British associationism).

influenced Alfred Binet, whose groundbreaking work on intelligence testing in turn influenced the Americans Henry Goddard, Edmund B. Huey, and Lewis Terman. Weber, Fechner, and other early German physiologists influenced Ebbinghaus, who influenced William Stern and Wundt, who influenced American psychologists such as Cattell, Edward Thorndike, and Truman Kelley and Germans such as Emil Kraepelin. Young emphasized that the historical roots of testing are multinational and reflect a number of different, sometimes conflicting viewpoints.

Because the anthropometric tests of Galton and Cattell proved to be poor proxies for psychological characteristics, a better way to measure those traits was needed. Herman Ebbinghaus's 1897 Ebbinghaus Completion Test for assessing children's cognitive ability anticipated the influential work of the French psychologist Alfred Binet. It was Binet, however, who provided the prototype for virtually all cognitive ability tests that were to follow. Beginning in the late 1880s, Alfred Binet (1857–1911) expressed an interest in individual differences and intelligence. He published a book on the subject, *L'Étude expérimentale de l'intelligence* (*The Experimental Study of Intelligence*), in 1902 (cited in Zusne, 1984). In response to a committee appointed by the minister of public instruction to study the problem of cognitively challenged children, Binet and the physician Théodore Simon (1873–1961) developed their intelligence scale in 1905. The test consisted of a series of tasks of increasing difficulty arranged in order of their ability to be completed by "normal" children. Binet revised his test in 1908 and again in 1911. Scoring the test resulted in a mental age for the child, transformed by William Stern's 1912 formula of dividing mental age by chronological age into a *mental quotient*, later formalized as the familiar intelligence quotient (IQ) by Lewis M. Terman (Zusne, 1984).

Binet's test was used in America in 1908 by Henry H. Goddard (1866–1957), who was then at the Vineland Training School for the Feeble-Minded in New Jersey. In 1910, he published a standardization of the 1908 Binet Scale. Lewis M. Terman and H. G. Childs published a tentative translation and revision in four installments in 1912, and in 1916 Terman published his Stanford Revision. Terman's version, which came to be called the Stanford-Binet, included the IQ concept first suggested by Stern (Pintner, 1923). Like Galton, both Goddard and Terman took a hereditarian view of intelligence. This was contrary to Binet's own views. Binet believed his test should be used only for the practical purpose of identifying developmentally delayed children and the use of the tests should be part of special training for improvement (Rogers, 1995). His own research emphasized the fluid nature of intelligence. In addition to work on his mental scale, Binet conducted naturalistic observation of problem-solving using his daughters as subjects, studies of eyewitness testimony, analysis of cognitive strategies in chess players, and laboratory studies of memory (Cunningham, 1997). The use of intelligence tests as the single indicator of cognitive ability and the emphasis on the hereditary aspects of intelligence caused a great deal of controversy following World War I.[16]

Whether or not intelligence is solely or primarily due to heredity or to the environment, there still remains the not inconsequential question of what exactly it is these tests are measuring; that is, are these tests construct valid? One approach to answering this question was to use the statistical procedure *factor analysis*. The purpose of factor analysis is to examine the pattern of correlations in a correlation matrix to extract a set of factors that underlie or "explain" the common variance among the factors. While the procedure is quite sophisticated statistically, a simple hypothetical example can illustrate the procedure. Assume that a 100-item test is administered to a large sample. Fifty questions measure verbal ability, and fifty measure quantitative ability. Although the test has 100 items, it is unlikely to be measuring 100 different constructs. If each item is correlated with every other item to construct a matrix of the inter-item correlations, factor analysis should extract two distinct factors or constructs, verbal ability and quantitative ability, from that matrix. This logic can be extended to measures of any construct. Factor analysis serves the scientific goal of parsimony; sufficient simple explanations are preferred over complex ones.[17]

The roots of factor analysis are in Great Britain. Charles E. Spearman (1863–1945), who received his Ph.D. under Wundt, provided the groundwork for factor analysis in a 1904 paper on the nature of intelligence. Noting that diverse measures of intellectual performance correlate positively with one another, Spearman concluded this was due to the existence of a common factor (termed $g$). Individuals with high scores across these measures were high in $g$; those with low scores had less $g$. This general factor became synonymous with intelligence.[18] Because the positive

---

[16] The intelligence testing controversy is discussed in Chapter 5.

[17] A comprehensive treatment of factor analysis and the related procedure principal components analysis will not be presented here, only a brief historical survey. Factor analysis is best viewed as a family of procedures; there are a number of different methods used to conduct a factor analysis. There are many excellent primers on factor analysis available; two I recommend are the factor analysis chapter in Kerlinger and Lee (2000) and L. L. Thurstone's classic *Multiple Factor Analysis* (1947).

[18] Spearman was careful to note that $g$ is not the same thing as intelligence; it is a factor derived from statistical operations. It is the factor that does not vary from test to test, as opposed to specific factors that do vary (Deary, Lawn, & Bartholomew, 2008).

correlations were not perfect, Spearman also postulated task-specific factors (*s*). This theory became known as the *two-factor theory of intelligence*, with intellectual performance dependent on both a general factor and an ability that is specific to the individual task (Boring, 1950; Rogers, 1995). Spearman's view of intelligence as mostly due to a single, unitary quality (*g*) fit nicely with the dominant hereditarian view of the time and was offered as mathematical support for that perspective. Spearman summarized his ideas on intelligence and the statistics supporting his views in his 1927 book *The Abilities of Man*.

Spearman's two-factor theory of intelligence did not go unchallenged. Godfrey H. Thomson (1881–1955) demonstrated that the two-factor solution was mathematically only one of a number of possible solutions (Thomson, 1916; Drever, 1955). Thomson's (1952) two major criticisms were, first, that Spearman's methods result in large specific factors that are then overlooked. Second, many small influences can result in intercorrelations that mimic a small number of common factors. The implication is not only that *g* is complex but that the factors are mathematical in basis and therefore psychological interpretations are inappropriate. American psychologists such as Edward L. Thorndike and the industrial psychologist Walter Dill Scott viewed intelligence as a complex of diverse capacities (von Mayrhauser, 1992). L. L. Thurstone (1931, 1935, 1947) developed multiple factor analysis, which, like Thomson, he used to illustrate that factor solutions other than two factors were legitimate. Thurstone viewed intelligence as composed of seven primary abilities rather than Spearman's general and specific factors. Those abilities are verbal reasoning, numerical ability, spatial ability, perceptual speed and functioning, memory, inductive reasoning, and word fluency (Thurstone, 1938). Thurstone developed the original equations for multiple factor analysis in 1922 but did not publish until almost ten years later (Thurstone, 1952). Among his innovations were the centroid method for extracting factors from the correlation matrix; the use of common variance ("communalities") rather than total variance in factor analysis; the use of rotation of axes to provide a more interpretable solution; the use of oblique (correlated) rather than orthogonal (uncorrelated) reference axes; and the concept of "simple structure" to develop psychologically meaningful results from the initial arbitrary centroid dimensions (Adkins, 1964; Jones, 1998; Thurstone, 1947).[19]

---

[19]   Godfrey Thomson (1952) wrote that he had great interest in the work of Thurstone. While Thomson admired Thurstone, he remained unconvinced that Thurstone's multiple factors were any more real than other factor solutions. We will return to intelligence testing in Chapter 5.

*Reliability and Validity*

As described by Tim Rogers (1995), in the early 1900s determining whether a test was a good test was the result of extended negotiation among the testing community. Based on Jastrow, Baldwin, and Cattell's (1898) emphasis on simplicity and cost efficiency and the idea that tests offer a faithful representation of the world, tests were evaluated by the somewhat vague concept of test *trustworthiness*. Jastrow, Baldwin, and Cattell offered a list of "desiderata," or needed qualities, for mental tests. For example, tests should measure a single attribute, be simple and intelligible, and be as short as possible. According to von Mayrhauser (1992), Jastrow, Baldwin, and Cattell put forth "the core assumption of modern mental testing . . . the relationship of individual test performance to the performance of large populations on the same test (distributed on a normal curve) is indicative of individual mental inheritance" (p. 247). The authors, however, did not take the next step of linking test performance with an outside criterion.

Next came the notion of test *reliability*, or freedom from errors of measurement, introduced by Charles Spearman. DuBois (1970) pointed out that while Spearman was developing the concept of reliability as early as 1904, he first used the term *reliability coefficient* in a paper with Felix Krueger (1874–1948) in 1907 (cited in DuBois, 1970). The reliability coefficient is a correlation coefficient used to assess measurement consistency. Spearman noted that poor reliability can explain a low correlation between a test and another variable. He developed a *correction for attenuation* to estimate what the "true" correlation would be if both variables could be assessed without errors of measurement (i.e., perfect reliability) (Rogers, 1995). Spearman was not interested in prediction; he was satisfied that his two-factor theory and *g* would be able to bring order to personnel testing (von Mayrhauser, 1992).[20] By the mid-1920s, reliability of a test was being estimated in ways that would be recognizable to a present-day researcher. A test can be given on two separate occasions and the two sets of scores correlated (what today we would call test-retest reliability). Two separate versions of a test can be correlated (alternate or parallel form reliability), or two parts of the test can be correlated, that is, dividing the test into two parts, scoring each half separately, and then correlating the halves (split-half reliability) (Burtt, 1926; Guilford, 1936).

---

[20] Von Mayrhauser argued that Spearman's lack of interest in prediction was based on a distrust of practical concerns. Spearman saw his elucidation of *g* and reliability as preserving the social order and upper-class dominance (see von Mayrhauser, 1992, for details).

While Francis Galton's anthropometric measures were supplemented by Binet's more cognitive ones, Galton did make a lasting contribution to statistics with his work on what became the correlation coefficient. Recall that Galton believed that eminence, determined in part by intellect, was primarily if not solely the result of heredity. It would be very useful to have a method that could quantitatively assess the relationship between individual characteristics to provide support for his theory. For example, if it were possible to demonstrate that there is a stronger relationship on a characteristic between twins than between siblings or unrelated individuals, this would offer support for Galton's ideas. Galton collected anthropometric measures on 9,337 individuals, and he set out to create a means of determining the interrelationships. He used scatterplots to graphically represent the relation between sets of measures (e.g., strength of pull with strength of squeeze). Galton noticed patterns in the scatterplots: the more linear the pattern of points, the stronger the relationship between the measures (Rogers, 1995).

Galton was unable to translate his scatterplots into a mathematical equation. Intrigued by Galton's work, Walter Weldon (1860–1906), a professor of zoology at University College, London, assessed the degree of relationship among organs first in shrimp and then in crabs. More mathematically sophisticated than Galton, he introduced the possibility of negative correlations (Hearnshaw, 1964). It was Galton's student, biographer, and fellow eugenicist Karl Pearson (1857–1936), however, who developed the familiar deviation-score formula for correlation, today called Pearson's $r$, or the product-moment correlation.[21] Pearson built on the 1846 work of Auguste Bravais (1811–63), who was an astronomer, physicist, and naval officer (Cowles, 2001). The deviation-score formula was only one of Pearson's contributions to statistics that proved useful for psychology. He devised the standard deviation, which eventually replaced the then common use of probable error to measure variability. Pearson derived methods for calculating multiple correlation, correlation for qualitative data, the correlation ratio, biserial correlation, nonlinear regression, and the chi-square statistic (Hearnshaw, 1964). The correlation coefficient was adopted early on in psychological research. Guilford (1936) cited an 1892

---

[21] The economist Francis Y. Edgeworth (1845–1926) coined the term *correlation coefficient* in 1892 (Cowles, 2001). Galton simply called his measure the *index* and Weldon, in honor of Galton, *Galton's functions* (Hearnshaw, 1964) Another important innovator in correlational analysis was George Udny Yule (1871–1951), who created the partial correlation, measured association via a 2 x 2 contingency table, and made important contributions to linear regression (Zusne, 1984).

paper on motor learning by W. L. Bryan as the first application of correlation to a psychological problem.

The correlation coefficient provided a statistic to assess reliability; however, consistency was not enough to demonstrate the trustworthiness of a test. A measure could be perfectly consistent, that is, perfectly reliable, and still not measure what it is designed to measure. That is, a test could reliably measure the wrong thing. For American psychologists, simply evaluating tests based on their correlations with other tests or their approximations to a normal distribution of test takers was not enough, a "waste of time" according to Bingham (1923, p. 292). What was needed was a method to determine not only the reliability of a test but whether it did what it was supposed to do. For example, if one claims a test is an accurate predictor of successful job performance, a method for empirically determining the accuracy of that claim is needed. By about 1910, a method was becoming established to do just that (Rogers, 1995).

This *test-criterion* method used a correlation coefficient to determine the strength and magnitude of the relationship between a predictor, generally some sort of test, and a criterion, an independent standard or measure of success.[22] If the test and criterion were measured at approximately the same time, the test's *diagnostic value* could be assessed. If the criterion was measured at some later time after test administration, the *prognostic value* of the test could be determined. By the early 1920s, the term *validity* was becoming common to describe this process, although that term was used in this context as early as 1915 by Daniel Starch. Starch evaluated tests of speed and comprehension of reading in grade-school children. He examined the validity of those tests in a number of ways, including correlating test score ranks with ranks of teachers' ratings of reading performance. In 1921, the Standardization Committee of the National Association of Directors of Educational Research recommended that the term *validity* be reserved for describing what a test measures and that *reliability* be used to describe consistency of measurement. By the middle of the 1920s, the diagnostic value of a test was becoming known by the modern term *concurrent validity*, and *predictive validity* was being used to describe the prognostic value of a test (Rogers, 1995). Both these strategies are subsets of what today is called *criterion-related validity*.

An alternative method for demonstrating that a test is valid is to use some version of a comparison method. Comparison methods match groups of employees at various levels of a criterion such as job performance

---

[22] As discussed in Chapter 7, the term *criterion* was not commonly used until the mid-1920s.

(e.g., good, average, or poor) with average test scores for each group. If the test scores differentiate among the groups of workers, such that high scores are associated with high levels of job performance and low scores with poor performance, the test is considered valid. The *percentage comparison* method was commonly used. This involved determining the percentage of individuals scoring below or above critical scores on the test. For example, for a particular test, one might determine that 80 percent of individuals who score 25 or higher are successful, while only 20 percent of individuals who score 15 or below succeed on the job (Viteles, 1932). Because percentage comparison methods are readily understandable by managers, Kornhauser and Kingsbury (1924) believed they could be more valuable than the use of complicated correlational methods. In any case, they are a useful supplement to the use of correlation for determining validity.[23]

Walter Dill Scott provided an early example of the use of empirical strategies for test validation. Scott (1917) described four procedures for determining the value of a test: The *firm rank* method compares test scores with average supervisor rankings for employees who vary in performance; the *ringers* method, similar to the method used by Münsterberg (1913), embeds experienced employees of known ability (the ringers) with applicants to determine if the test can identify the ringers; the *vocational accomplishments* method compares test performance with subsequent vocational accomplishment; and the *applicants-experts* method determines whether the test can differentiate between successful employees and applicants on the assumption that applicant performance should be poorer than the successful employees. Scott used all four of these methods to test his selection aids and found them useful; however, he concluded that the *vocational accomplishments* method was superior to the others. Hollingworth and Poffenberger (1917) described in general terms a procedure to evaluate tests. Individuals who are categorized as good, average, or poor workers are "given as many forms and varieties of psychological tests as the patience of the worker, the zeal of the experimenter or the interest of the employer makes possible. Ability in each test is then compared with ability in the work" (p. 196). They noted that it may take

---

[23] Correlations can be conceptualized in terms of rank orders; that is, if the ranking of individuals on one variable is similar to the rank order of those individuals on the second variable, a high correlation will result. High ranks on one variable and corresponding low ranks on the other variable results in a negative correlation; no relationship between the ranks results in a zero correlation. From this perspective, comparison methods essentially give the same information as a correlation, in that rank of one variable (the test) is compared with rank order on the other (the criterion).

thirty or forty different test administrations to determine four or five that are good predictors.[24] E. L. Thorndike, also in 1917, correlated the US Army's Alpha intelligence test with officers' intelligence ratings collected by Walter Dill Scott, an early example of empirical validity with an external criterion. Thorndike also set a precedent for separating the reliability or consistency of a test from its validity (cited in von Mayrhauser, 1992).

In the early 1930s, an alternative strategy to criterion-related validation was developed. For academic achievement tests, representative coverage of a particular area was important (Rogers, 1995). Initially termed *curricular validity*, it is now known as content-validity or content-oriented test development. When using this strategy in selection, one attempts to develop a test that is a representative sample of important behaviors on the job. Trade tests, discussed in Chapters 5 and 7, would be an example of a type of test amenable to this approach. The third strategy in the current three-part concept of validity, construct validity, was not formalized until the early 1950s.[25]

To this point, we have been focused on measuring the predictor; that is, the test. Equally important is an accurate assessment of the measure of success: the criterion. There are two basic categories of criteria: objective and subjective. Objective criteria are generally those things one can count and are therefore verifiable more or less objectively. Examples are tons of coal shoveled or the amount of retail items sold. Subjective criteria rely on judgment. During the early years of industrial psychology, this judgment was generally given by the supervisor. Supervisors can rank employees based on overall job performance or on some aspect of performance, or

---

[24] It is probable that by evaluating so many tests, a small subset of them would emerge as good predictors just by chance. This is a particular problem with small sample sizes, common during this time period. In the statistical hypothesis testing model (which Hollingworth and Poffenberger [1917] did not use), this would be analogous to a Type I error, saying there is a relationship between variables when there is not. They did note a way to deal with this potential problem: repeatedly correlating the surviving tests with success or failure to see if the relationship holds up over time. This is an early example of what today is termed *cross-validation*.

[25] The observant reader will note that this chapter does not include a history of the null hypothesis testing model, the ubiquitous statistical procedure in present-day psychology research. While there was work in this area conducted during the time period covered in this book, it did not become standard procedure in psychology until after 1930. Precedents include Charles S. Peirce and Joseph Jastrow (1885) performing what may be the first randomized experiment in psychology in the early 1880s (Stigler, 1999); and William S. Gosset, writing under the pseudonym "Student," describing what became known as Student's *t* distribution in 1908. It was Ronald A. Fisher's work on analysis of variance (Fisher, 1925) and the null hypothesis (Fisher, 1935) that was the major influence on inferential statistical analysis in psychology.

employees can be evaluated using some form of rating scale. Criteria are discussed in Chapter 7.

## Questionnaires and Rating Scales

Psychological testing and employee selection, with their concomitant emphasis on productivity and efficiency, were primary concerns of the early industrial psychologists. In addition, however, there was attention paid to the welfare of individual workers along with associated topics such as employee motivation, leadership, and employee morale. Early on this concern was more prominent in Great Britain (Farmer, 1958; Myers, 1920), Germany (Hausmann, 1930–31; Viteles, 1932), and other European countries than in the United States. But interest and research on these topics were also evident in America, especially following a series of studies conducted the Western Electric plant in Hawthorne, Illinois, beginning in the 1920s.[26] As was true for selection, progress on these topics depended to a great extent on quantification. That is, in order to study topics such as motivation or morale, the researcher had to be able to accurately measure employees' *attitudes* toward their jobs.

Questionnaires have a long history. About 1805, Admiral Sir F. Beaufort of the British Navy introduced a twelve-point scale to estimate wind velocity (Titchener, 1909), and in 1838, in Bristol, England, a questionnaire was used to collect information about strikes (Boring, 1950). Francis Galton pioneered the questionnaire format, creating an early self-report questionnaire in 1883 to measure mental imagery (Rogers, 1995). Prior to World War I, the American psychologist Walter Dill Scott developed his Man-to-Man Rating Scale that was used in that conflict to select officers. It was not until the mid-1920s, however, that standardized employee attitude questionnaires were developed. There were also attempts to measure attitudes via interviews and/or work participation. One notable example was the work of Whiting Williams (1925), who worked as a miner, factory worker, and railroad worker to gauge employees' reactions to their jobs. An early attempt at a standardized attitude survey was undertaken by management consultant J. D. Houser (1927), who developed a standard set of questions and categorized responses based on negative and positive emotions. Houser's scale, however, required one-on-one interviews with employees, limiting its usefulness (Landy, 1989).

---

[26] The Hawthorne Studies are covered in Chapter 10.

The work of L. L. Thurstone on attitude measurement and psychological scaling (e.g., Thurstone, 1927, 1929; Thurstone & Chave, 1929) is notable for its innovation and impact on subsequent scaling efforts. In contrast to psychophysics, which linked a psychological sensation to a physical stimulus, Thurstone developed a psychological measurement technique that was independent of physical measurement. In attitude measurement, he developed the method of paired comparisons and also used a method based on the dispersion of attitude statements made by judges to create equal appearing intervals (Adkins, 1964; Jones, 1998; Thurstone, 1928). Rensis Likert's 1932 doctoral dissertation introduced a simplification of Thurstone's scaling techniques, the now ubiquitous format known today as the *Likert Scale*.

By the early 1930s, Kornhauser (1933) described five methods available to measure attitudes. The first was an informal approach relying on impressions; the work of Whiting Williams described previously provides an example. While Kornhauser did not consider this method scientific, he proposed it as a valuable supplement to the more formal methods. Next was the use of an unguided interview that encourages employees to elaborate on topics important to them. The work of Elton Mayo in the Hawthorne Studies is an example.[27] Third was the use of a more structured, guided interview. Fourth is Houser's (1927) use of attitudinal question blanks. These blanks generally consist of simple yes-or-no questions that assess employees' opinions. Finally, there is the use of psychometrically sophisticated scales exemplified by the work of Thurstone and Likert.[28]

## The Measurement of Jobs: Job Analysis

In addition to the accurate measurement of individual difference characteristics in persons, it is important to accurately measure the requirements of the job itself.[29] Job analysis is an essential foundation for many organizational activities, including test and criterion development, performance appraisal, compensation, and training. While it is possible to find examples of what looked very much like job analysis dating back to antiquity, the

---

[27] Mayo and the Hawthorne Studies are described in Chapter 10.

[28] Rating scales and their use in test validation are covered in Chapter 7 along with a discussion of common rating errors.

[29] Viteles (1932) defined a *job* as "a self-contained unit of work performed by the individual worker" (p. 142). At a broader level is an occupation, covering allied jobs, although *occupation analysis* was used in Great Britain as a general term for employment investigation.

more immediate predecessors to job analysis as used in industrial psychology are work in the United States Civil Service and in scientific management. Shortly after the American Civil War, the Civil Service Reform League was established. The League gathered information about abilities necessary for government jobs using a method devised by Silas Burt, Naval Officer of the Port of New York, which involved supervisors discussing negative and positive aspects of job performance (Primoff & Fine, 1988). And as discussed in the previous chapter, a key aspect of scientific management was breaking down a task into its component parts or elements. The Gilbreths, for example, used motion picture cameras with speed clocks and other devices to determine the various elements that comprise a job.

In an early history of job analysis, Richard Uhrbrock (1922) viewed job analysis as progressing from narrative job descriptions to a more standardized, quantitative form. He credited P. J. Reilly of the Dennison Manufacturing Company as devising in 1914 the first standard form for recording job analysis data. Whether or not it was the first example, recording information across jobs in a standard manner did represent an advance over the essay style of job analysis. Another early attempt at standardization was the questionnaire method developed by the German psychologist Otto Lipmann in 1916 (cited in Viteles, 1932). Lipmann sent his questionnaire, which originally contained eighty-six items but was later expanded to 148, to a sample of work organizations and others interested in vocational placement. His goal was to obtain a classification of worker characteristics across diverse occupations, which he eventually did for 121 occupations. Viteles (1932) praised this method for assessing the actual behaviors and traits important for job performance and for providing a procedure for rating those traits and behaviors. He was skeptical, however, that accurate information could be provided by workers completing questionnaires who are not trained in observational methods (unlike, presumably, the industrial psychologist).

Job analysis procedures were refined at the Carnegie Institute of Technology's (CIT) Division of Applied Psychology and by the Committee on Classification of Personnel in the US Army (CCPA) during World War I.[30] For example, at CIT, Strong and Uhrbrock (1923) conducted a field study that examined executive jobs in the printing industry.

---

[30] The Carnegie Institute of Technology program, the first doctoral program in industrial psychology, is discussed in Chapter 8. The work of the Committee for Classification of Personnel appears in Chapter 5.

In addition to determining the duties of those jobs, they developed job specifications and created a summary record of the job analysis results.

With the massive influx of recruits into the US Army during World War I who needed to be placed in positions best suited for their abilities, there was a great need for a standardized system of personnel classification. The CCPA was created in August 1917, with Walter Dill Scott as Director and E. L. Thorndike as Chairman, to help accomplish that goal. In addition to the classification and placement of close to a million enlisted men, the Committee was involved in activities that included developing trade specifications and an index of occupations, creating trade tests for skilled workers, and defining the duties and qualifications of approximately 500 separate classes of officers. Walter Van Dyke Bingham, who in addition to directing the CIT program was executive secretary of the CCPA, was a strong proponent of job analysis, considering it the most fundamental aspect of personnel work. He believed it formed the foundation for the work of the CCPA (Bingham, 1919). Trade tests provide an example.[31] Designed to be short, objectively scored tests of knowledge and skills in trades as varied as bricklayer, typist, lathe operator, and statistician, the tests needed to be able to distinguish among the four levels of expertise used by the Army: novice, apprentice, journeyman, and expert. Three types of tests were created: oral tests of job knowledge, picture tests of job knowledge, and performance tests that directly measured skill level (Chapman, 1923). Successful construction of these tests depended on an accurate assessment of the duties performed in each trade and the qualifications (i.e., knowledge and skills) necessary to perform those duties.

Following the war, job analysis procedures continued to be refined. Link (1919) wrote about the importance of job analysis, stating it was equal in importance to the analysis of the worker's abilities. He cautioned against describing jobs simply in terms of broad human qualities needed, such as loyalty. Link called this type of superficial analysis "thinly disseminated character analysis" (p. 256). He offered a systematic procedure for conducting job analysis that assessed the physical characteristics of the job, the mental characteristics needed, and miscellaneous factors such earnings, hours worked, and time needed to train. Kitson (1922a) wrote that too much emphasis had been placed on testing and not enough on analyzing the job. Kitson noted that a properly conducted job analysis will provide

---

[31] Trade tests are discussed in Chapter 7. Ferguson (1962–65) provides a detailed history of the work of the Trade Test Division of the CCPA.

information for setting wages, reduce worker fatigue by revealing operational error and waste, make promotion more systematic, and provide essential data for trade test development and for training. Viteles (1922) developed a job analysis procedure called the *job psychograph method* that included a simplified mental trait classification, a standardized rating procedure, and direct observation of job activities by trained observers. For each job analyzed, thirty-two traits such as energy, endurance, persistence, and judgment were rated on a five-point scale ranging from *Negligible* to *Of utmost importance*. For each job rated, the ratings on the traits were displayed graphically, where the peaks of the curve (i.e., the higher ratings) were designated *keystone* specific mental abilities and deemed essential for job success. Viteles (1974) recalled that his motivation for developing the job psychograph was the vagueness of mental requirements in the then current job analyses and the lack of a standard measure of trait importance and of the amount of each trait that was needed for success.

Job analysis then and today is not a single process but a family of techniques that vary in the operations involved and the information produced. Early on, it was recognized that the purpose for which the information would be used determined the type of procedures used in the job analysis (Meine, 1923). Through the 1920s, job analysis was used for multiple purposes. It was used for improving work methods. The time-and-motion studies favored by practitioners of scientific management would be an example. Job analysis was use to ensure the health and safety of employees. Medical and safety departments needed to determine the physical requirements and working conditions needed so they could protect the health and well-being of the workers. It was used for training workers. In addition to determining the most efficient way to perform the job, a job analysis for training also had to determine how to sequentially arrange the job content in such a way that it could most effectively be learned by an employee (Meine, 1923).

Job analysis was also used for what Meine (1923) termed *employment* purposes. This included employee selection, transfer, promotion, and setting wages across jobs. The purpose was to establish performance standards that would result in the most efficient way to do the job. This application received the most attention in the literature, most likely because of the emphasis in industrial psychology on employee selection. This type of job analysis examined the nature of the job, the processes and procedures performed by the person (and the machinery), and the type and amount of qualifications necessary for that person to successfully perform the job. Meine (1923) references a 1920 report by the Industrial Relations

Association in offering suggestions for carrying out the analysis. He suggested starting in a department best known to the analyst; getting the cooperation of supervisors; conducting an initial classification of all the jobs in that department; and then obtaining information about the jobs from observation, supervisors, workers, and staff specialists such as company engineers. The results were drawn up in a *job specification*, which was then reviewed by supervisors and revised as necessary.

The job specification took the raw data of the job analysis and presented it in a manner that was accessible to the organization. Job specifications varied in format but generally included the duties performed on the job, the qualifications necessary for successful performance, and a description of working conditions. Other information might have included wage rates, the number of individuals employed in the job, the rate of promotion, the types of machines operated and tools needed on the job, time needed to train, and a list of jobs related to the one described.

## Chapter Summary

Industrial psychology developed in concert with advances in measurement and statistics. In order to advance, any scientific enterprise must be able to accurately measure its variables of interest. Ernst Weber and Gustav Fechner demonstrated that psychological constructs could be measured objectively through their work in psychophysics. Weber, Fechner, and the initial cohort of scientific psychologists were interested in general laws of behavior and focused their measurement efforts in that area. Variability in performance was considered error, something to be controlled. For others such as Francis Galton, James McKeen Cattell, and William Stern, this variability due to individual differences was interesting and worthy of study in its own right. While the early anthropometric measures of Galton and Cattell did not accurately predict variables such as academic and job performance, the more cognitive approaches exemplified by the work of Alfred Binet were more successful.

Early psychological tests were initially evaluated based on internal characteristics such as simplicity and reliability. Eventually their relationship with external criteria, their validity, became an important additional attribute. A way of empirically demonstrating the relationship between the test and criterion was provided by the correlation coefficient, pioneered by Galton, Karl Pearson, and others. In addition to the use of tests to predict criteria such as job performance, questionnaires and surveys were created to measure attitudes. These questionnaires, developed in the nineteenth century and refined in the early twentieth, notably by L. L. Thurstone, permitted the early industrial psychologists to assess job-relevant attitudes such as work motivation and job satisfaction. And finally, job analysis – a family of methods for assessing the tasks and associated knowledge, skills, and abilities necessary to perform those tasks – was developed by researchers such as Otto Lipmann in Germany and Morris Viteles in the United States. Job analysis provided the essential foundation for many applications of psychology to business and industry.

Over the past two chapters, we examined the environment in which industrial psychology emerged, influences from outside psychology such as scientific management, and advances within the field of psychology, especially in measurement, that contributed to the establishment of an applied psychology that focused on work and work organizations. In Chapter 4, the initial efforts of psychologists and others to improve advertising, understand and reduce work fatigue, and, most notably, select those employees most likely to succeed on the job are examined.

CHAPTER 4

# Initial Forays into Industry

Establishing the exact origin of industrial psychology, that is, conferring that honor on a single individual or designating a specific event, is an exercise in futility. Lohman (1997) compares establishing the origin of an endeavor to "stepping into a stream at a particular point – perhaps where it rounds a bend" and deciding that here will be our starting point (p. 86). Nevertheless, we must begin our narrative at some point. There have been attempts to locate the origin of industrial psychology with the efforts of specific individuals. Both Viteles (1932) and Baritz (1960) credited Hugo Münsterberg with formulating the initial program of industrial psychology with the publication of *Psychologie und Wirtschaftsleben (Psychology and Economic Life)* in 1912 (cited in Viteles, 1932); revised and translated into English a year later as *Psychology and Industrial Efficiency* (1913). Viteles and Baritz also recognized the work of Walter Dill Scott, who published two earlier books on psychology and advertising (Scott, 1903, 1908) and who in 1911 published *Increasing Human Efficiency in Business*, a general treatment of psychology applied to business. They believed, however, that Münsterberg's influence was more lasting than Scott's. Ferguson (1962–65) gave primacy to Scott over Münsterberg. The first of a series of pamphlets he wrote about the early history of industrial psychology is unambiguously titled *Walter Dill Scott: First Industrial Psychologist.* While Ferguson recognized the important contributions Münsterberg made to the field, he argued that Scott deserves the designation "founder" because he preceded Münsterberg and Scott's work had a greater impact. While conceding that the founder designation is somewhat arbitrary, Hilgard (1987) would tend to agree with Ferguson, calling Scott's 1911 book the beginning of serious industrial psychology.[1]

---

[1] Napoli (1981) would agree with Ferguson and Hilgard in giving Scott primacy for industrial psychology. Napoli viewed James McKeen Cattell's "mental test" article in 1890 as the beginning of a more general applied psychology.

While these authors made reasonable arguments in support of Scott and Münsterberg, I am reluctant to designate either as a "founder" of I-O psychology. Both Scott and Münsterberg made critical contributions in the early years of industrial psychology, but they were not alone. There were others active in applying psychology to industrial and business organizations prior to and during this time.

It is possible to find antecedents to the work of pioneering industrial psychologists such as Scott and Münsterberg. Before there was a discipline of scientific psychology, there were efforts, some dating to antiquity, to use psychological principles and techniques in organizations.[2] While it is instructive and interesting to look at how these events anticipated current science and practice, this chapter concentrates on more recent activities that are directly related to the development of industrial psychology as a science and a profession. The story begins in the mid- to late 1800s with investigations of worker fatigue in Europe and the beginnings of a psychology of advertising in America. Critical mass for the new discipline of industrial psychology occurred in the early 1900s with both an interest in psychology by businesspeople and the desire of academic psychologists to branch out and apply their new science to real-world concerns. In this chapter, we will examine industrial psychology in the private sector from its origins in the 1800s until 1920, two years after World War I ended. The role of industrial psychology in that conflict will be discussed in the Chapter 5.

What was the main impetus to move psychology from the academic laboratory to the world of business and industry? In the United States, the dominant functionalist perspective, as noted in the Chapter 3, was oriented toward the practical and lent itself to a focus on application. Although there was stigma attached to applied work, there were academic psychologists willing and able to tackle industrial problems. Viteles (1932) saw the early growth of the field as due to academics wanting to branch out without severing their university connections and the prestige these positions conferred. Motivations for the move varied, but as illustrated by the story of Harry Hollingworth discussed later, for some, money was an important consideration. For other psychologists, it was the lack of opportunity to obtain an academic position that provided the motivation for a career in applied psychology. This was true for a number of female industrial psychologists whose academic opportunities were limited.

[2] Kaiser (1989), for example, provides a chronology of important events in organizational behavior that begins in 2100 BCE.

Ferguson (1961, n.d.) saw the initiative coming primarily from the business side. He noted examples such as the magazine editor Thomas L. Balmer contacting Northwestern University psychologist Walter Dill Scott in 1901 to give a talk about psychology's usefulness in advertising (Ferguson, 1962–65). Other early examples of business reaching out to psychologists include the following: The shoe manufacturer Ivan Bally contacted the University of Zurich psychologist Jules Suter in 1913 to see if Münsterberg's new industrial psychology program could be applied to his company (Heller, 1929–30). In 1910, Barnard College psychologist Harry Hollingworth received an invitation from the Advertising Men's League of New York City to give a series of lectures on applying psychology to advertising, leading to collaboration between Hollingworth and the League (Benjamin, 2004). Pittsburgh businessmen Edward A. Woods and Winslow Russell contacted Walter Van Dyke Bingham in the early years of the applied psychology program at the Carnegie Institute of Technology to explore collaboration between business and psychology (Ferguson, 1962–65). And English businessman H. J. Welch met with University of Cambridge psychologist Charles S. Myers following a 1918 lecture. As a result of that encounter, Welch and Myers founded the National Institute of Industrial Psychology in 1921 (Burt, 1947; Welch & Myers, 1932).

## Studies on Worker Fatigue

The practical problem of how to reduce physical and psychological fatigue was one that interested researchers in Europe. As early as 1878, Étienne-Jules Marey (1830–1904) of France was conducting experimental work on fatigue. In 1888, the Italian physiologist Angelo Mosso (1846–1910) invented the ergograph, a device used to measure the work capacity of a muscle. He used his invention to study muscle fatigue and the associated reduction of work potential (Fryer & Henry, 1950). Mosso showed that as a muscle becomes fatigued, the contraction time of the muscle grows with a corresponding reduction in work potential, demonstrating that a physiological process can have psychological implications (Koppes & Pickren, 2007). In the late 1800s, Mosso, along with his brother Ugolino, studied the psychological and physical functioning of ten Italian mountain units in the Alps (Bäumler, 1997). In Germany, Gustav Fechner, whose work in measurement was discussed in the previous chapter, conducted research using weights to study fatigue (Münsterberg, 1913).

Other examples of nineteenth-century research on the causes and consequences of fatigue are the work done in Germany by the physician Emil Kraepelin (1856–1926) and by Hugo Münsterberg. Kraepelin researched both physical and cognitive fatigue and developed work curves to illustrate the decrease of production over time. He believed the worker should be in harmony with industrial demands. Part of this process was reducing fatigue, including subjective correlates of fatigue such as tiredness. Kraepelin, while conceding that the work curve for each worker was unique, did not emphasize individual differences in worker characteristics. For Hugo Münsterberg, however, these individual differences were of critical importance. His research on fatigue focused on decreasing worker accidents and improving output (Koppes & Pickren, 2007). Münsterberg later immigrated to America where he continued this line of research.

Fatigue was understood to have both a physiological and psychological component. The physiological component was seen as the result of an accumulation of cellular waste products, "fatigue-toxins," while mental fatigue was how the individual felt as a result of that physiological fatigue. This feeling varies in intensity from boredom to total exhaustion (Muscio, 1920). Also discussed was the related concept of monotony, which was seen as due to the division of labor and the resultant simplification and repetitive nature of the work (Münsterberg, 1913). Münsterberg emphasized the subjective nature of monotony. Work that may appear extremely boring to an outside observer may not be experienced that way by the worker, who, for example, might use self-set short-term goals or engage in daydreaming to make the work bearable or even enjoyable.[3] Münsterberg (1913) speculated that differences in tolerance for monotonous work may be more due to the worker's temperament than to the work itself.

Fatigue was viewed as due to factors such as excessive hours worked, the speed of factory machinery, noise, and excessive specialization. Use of work breaks and decreasing the number of hours worked were potential solutions. As to the concern that reducing the number of hours worked would adversely affect output, Münsterberg (1913) gave the example of factory head Ernst Abbé, who "wrote many years ago" that shortening the workday from nine to eight hours actually resulted in an increase in output (p. 213). Münsterberg stated that numerous subsequent studies have shown that a moderate reduction of working hours does not have a detrimental effect on output. The effect of fatigue on accidents was a particular concern of early industrial researchers. Muscio (1920) gave examples of studies done

---

[3] The subject of daydreaming or "revery" is discussed in Chapter 10.

in Germany in 1887; Lancashire, England, in 1908; and Illinois in the United States in 1910. All showed that the number of accidents peaked in the late morning and in the late afternoon. The implication was that workers were most fatigued at these times and, therefore, accidents occurred at an increased rate. Conversely, Hollingworth and Poffenberger (1917) found that the greatest number of accidents did not occur when the worker was most fatigued; rather, an increase in accidents occurred when production speed was highest and workers were performing at peak efficiency.

Research on fatigue continued in America, Germany, and Great Britain. Of particular note is the work done in Great Britain by the Health of Munitions Workers Committee, founded in 1915 as part of the war effort and renamed the Industrial Fatigue Research Committee in 1918 (Hearnshaw, 1964).[4] In Japan, studies on worker fatigue were conducted shortly after 1900 by researchers such as Hiroshi Chiwa (Kirihara, 1959). Notable is Tsuruko Haraguchi (nee Arai) (1886–1915), the first Japanese woman to obtain a Ph.D. in any field. A 1906 graduate of Japan Women's College, she was unable to attend graduate school in Japan, as women were barred from graduate study at that time. Haraguchi enrolled at Teachers College Columbia University, where she conducted research on the effects of mental fatigue under the supervision of Edward L. Thorndike. She received her doctorate in 1912. Haraguchi expanded her dissertation into the volume *Studies on Mental Work and Fatigue* (1914; cited in Takasuna, 2012), written in Japanese. Unfortunately, her academic career was brief as Haraguchi died of tuberculosis at age twenty-nine (Takasuna, 2012).

## Psychology Applied to Advertising

In the United States, psychologists applied their new science to advertising. In an 1895 text, Wundt's student Edward W. Scripture discussed psychology as it related to advertising and business. He did not, however, conduct any empirical research (Schumann & Davidson, 2007). Appearing the same year was the work of another of Wundt's Ph.D. students, Harlow Gale, who used surveys and laboratory studies to study advertising and was the first to rank-order brands based on advertising information, an early example of the "order-of-merit" technique. He was primarily concerned with discovering the reasoning behind customer preferences. In 1898, James McKeen Cattell developed his

---

[4] See Chapter 5 for more on the Health of Munitions Workers Committee.

own version of the order-of-merit method.[5] Cattell was less concerned with the consumer's reasoning process and more interested in ranking the stimuli on effectiveness (Kuna, 1979). Gale's research was conducted in an academic setting; he did not conduct research in the advertising industry. By the early 1900s, psychologists were conducting advertising research outside of academia. Prominent among those individuals were Daniel Starch, Edward K. Strong Jr., Harry Levi Hollingworth, and Walter Dill Scott.

Daniel Starch's first book on the psychology of advertising appeared in 1910; he went on to publish numerous articles and books on the subject. Starch (1883–1979) taught at both Harvard and the University of Wisconsin, eventually leaving academia in 1932 to found his own marketing research firm (Schumann & Davidson, 2007). Edward K. Strong Jr.'s 1911 dissertation evaluated the relative merits of advertisements. This project, conducted at Columbia University under the supervision of James McKeen Cattell, was suggested to him by Harry Hollingworth (Hansen, 1987).[6] Strong went on to be a part of the pioneering graduate program in industrial psychology at the Carnegie Institute of Technology. While there, he developed an interest in the measurement of vocational interests, the work he is best remembered for today (Strong, 1927).[7]

### Harry Levi Hollingworth

Harry Hollingworth (1880–1956) received his undergraduate degree from the University of Nebraska in 1906 and his Ph.D. from Columbia University in 1909. He conducted research examining consumers' responses to characteristics of advertisements. Hollingworth (Figure 4.1) is credited with the first systematic effort to track consumer behavior, using a panel of consumers from New York City (Kuna, 1976; cited in Schumann & Davidson, 2007). While the bulk of his consulting work involved marketing and advertising, Hollingworth's initial applied work, commissioned by the Coca-Cola Company, was a study evaluating the behavioral effects of caffeine (Hollingworth, 1911). The fee for this work supplemented his meager academic salary and permitted his wife Leta to complete her doctorate in 1916

---

[5] Guilford (1936) wrote that while Cattell and the Columbia Psychological Laboratory are often given credit for the method of rank order, the earliest evaluation of stimuli by ranking was done by Lightner Witmer in 1894. This predated both Gale's and Cattell's efforts.

[6] Strong's dissertation may be the first in the United States on an applied topic.

[7] Strong and his work are discussed in Chapter 8.

Figure 4.1 Harry Hollingworth. Library of Congress, Prints & Photographs
Division, LC-DIG-ggbain-28747

(Benjamin, Rogers, & Rosenbaum, 1991).[8] After successfully completing this research, where he demonstrated that the caffeine in Coca-Cola did not have any deleterious behavioral effects, Hollingworth was inundated with consulting opportunities, completing some forty consultant investigation reports between 1914 and 1917 (Benjamin, 1996).

The Coca-Cola research was important for a number of reasons. Hollingworth brought a level of methodological sophistication to the research that was new to applied psychology. It was perhaps the earliest example of a large corporation funding this type of research, in this case, research with no strings attached. Hollingworth specified that he

---

[8] Leta Stetter Hollingworth (1886–1939) received her doctorate from Teacher's College, Columbia University, where she worked with Edward L. Thorndike. She went on to a distinguished research career, and her research results debunked the received wisdom at the time that women were inferior to men perceptually, emotionally, cognitively, and physically (Schultz & Schultz, 2004).

would publish the results regardless of the outcome and that his findings could not be used for advertising purposes. This study was an early example of cooperation between psychology and business and demonstrated that such cooperation could be beneficial to both parties (Arthur & Benjamin, 1999).

Hollingworth was involved in two short-lived, early attempts to commercialize applied psychology: the Economic Psychology Association and the Morningside Press. The Economic Psychology Association was conceived in 1915 as a cooperative venture between business and psychology. Organized by businessman John J. Apatow, the goal of the Association was to offer science-based practical advice to businesses (Kuna, 1976, cited in Van De Water, 1997). As recalled by Hollingworth (2013) in a 1940 memoir, he and two businesspersons founded the Association and, for a fee, invited firms to be members and psychologists to become associates. A half dozen firms and dozen individuals joined. Controversy was quickly generated, however, by Apatow's demand that he receive an immediate salary. There were also concerns about business improprieties in the association raised by prominent psychologists such as Hugo Münsterberg of Harvard University and James Angell of the University of Chicago. Hollingworth resigned from the board of directors and informed the other directors of the reasons for his decision. The other directors also resigned, ending the Association. Hollingworth's other applied venture, the Morningside Press, was created with Albert Poffenberger to market Columbia University's tests and manuals. Hostility from commercial test publishers and practical difficulties such as a lack of office space and clerical assistance quickly ended the enterprise (Hollingworth, 2013).[9]

Hollingworth wrote two early books about industrial psychology: *Vocational Psychology* in 1916 and, with Poffenberger, *Applied Psychology* a year later. According to Hollingworth (2013), *Applied Psychology* "was the first book of its kind" (p. 106). Despite his successful consulting career and his many contributions to industrial psychology, Hollingworth was blunt regarding his motivation for this work. He did it for the money, to provide income for his wife and him and, at least initially, to provide funds for her to finish graduate school. In an autobiography, written in 1940 but not published until 2013, he stated that he preferred theoretical work and found

---

[9] Later applied psychology commercial ventures such as the Scott Company in 1919 and the Psychological Corporation in 1923 proved more successful. See Chapter 6.

giving talks to businesspersons distasteful and that his applied work "was mere pot-boiling activity" (Hollingworth, 2013, p. 53).[10] Reluctant or not, Hollingworth's contributions to industrial psychology were substantial.

## Psychological Approaches to Advertising

Kuna (1979) described three separate approaches taken by psychologists who did early work applying psychology to advertising. The first, the *mentalist* approach, took influencing the minds of consumers as the goal of advertising. Through the use of introspective techniques, mentalists concentrated on mental processes such as perception and decision-making. Gale and later Scott advocated this approach. Both these psychologists studied under Wundt at Leipzig and were therefore influenced by Wundt's introspective methodology. Hollingworth, on the other hand, took a *behavioral* approach to advertising. A student at Columbia University in the early 1900s, he was influenced by the more objective, quantitative approach espoused by faculty members such as Cattell, Edward L. Thorndike, and Robert S. Woodworth. Hollingworth applied this methodology to advertising, focusing on the characteristics of the advertisements themselves rather than the mental reasoning of the consumer. The endpoint of the process, the actual purchase by the customer, was evidence for the effectiveness of the advertisement (Benjamin, 2004). Hollingworth's student Edward K. Strong Jr. took this behavioral approach in his 1911 Columbia University dissertation, where he focused on the stimulus qualities of advertisements. Both Strong and Hollingworth transitioned to the third *dynamic* approach. Influenced indirectly by the need and instinct theories of Sigmund Freud and William McDougall and directly by Columbia University's Edward L. Thorndike and Robert S. Woodworth, this approach concentrated on the needs and wants of the consumer (Kuna, 1979). Advertisements would be successful to the extent that they tapped into these internal needs.

## Walter Dill Scott

Walter Dill Scott (Figure 4.2) was born in Cooksville, Illinois, on May 1, 1869. He received an A.B. degree from Northwestern University in 1895,

---

[10] Benjamin (2006, 2013) found Hollingworth's claims difficult to believe, noting that he had many opportunities to leave applied work and did not take them.

Figure 4.2  Walter Dill Scott. Library of Congress, Prints & Photographs Division,
LC-DIG-ggbain-31962

where he studied psychology with George Albert Coe. Scott chose psychology rather than his previous career path of missionary and, based on Coe's advice, traveled to Germany for postgraduate training. Scott earned his doctorate in 1900 from the University of Leipzig where he studied with Wilhelm Wundt (Ferguson 1962–65). He returned to America and Northwestern University as an instructor; by 1909, Scott obtained the rank of professor.

In 1901, Thomas L. Balmer, advertising manager for *The Delineator*, *The Designer*, and *New Idea Woman's Magazine*, asked Scott if he would be interested in giving a lecture on psychology's usefulness to advertising. Scott was not the first psychologist that Balmer approached; he had already been turned down by prominent psychologists Hugo Münsterberg, Edward L. Thorndike, and Scott's former professor George A. Coe. Mindful of the stigma attached to applied work by academic psychologists, Scott was reluctant. With the support of Coe, Scott did give a talk at the

Agate Club in Chicago and launched his career as an applied psychologist (Ferguson, n.d.).

The Agate Club talk was followed by a series of magazine articles and two books (Scott, 1903, 1908) on advertising and psychology. Ferguson (1962–65) noted that by 1915, Scott had produced six books and more than 100 articles. In addition to his work on advertising, he also pioneered efforts in group assessment of intelligence (von Mayrhauser, 1989). Benjamin (2004) noted that while Scott was engaged in applied research as early as 1905, for the most part his advice to business about advertising was based on his speculative extension of the current state of psychological knowledge. His popularity stemmed from his common-sense prescriptions, his motivational advice, and his public-speaking ability.

Scott's 1911 book *Increasing Human Efficiency in Business* was quite different in format and content from subsequent, more scholarly books on industrial psychology, as illustrated by the table of contents reproduced in Table 4.1. It reads like a forerunner to today's popular business advice books. Scott's book is an amalgam of anecdotes, personal and otherwise; surveys of businesspersons; and summaries of current psychological knowledge, including a heavy emphasis on instinct as an explanation for behavior (e.g., all normal males possess a hunting instinct). Mixed in are generalizations that are questionable today and probably were in 1911; for example, that the needs of American-born workers are greater than those of immigrants. After an introductory first chapter, Scott's book has eight short chapters, each of which examines a strategy for increasing employee efficiency, such as the use of imitation, competition, loyalty, wages, and "the love of the game," or

Table 4.1  Increasing Human Efficiency in Business *(Scott, 1911)*

Table of Contents
The Possibility of Increasing Human Efficiency
Imitation as a Means of Increasing Human Efficiency
Competition as a Means of Increasing Human Efficiency
Loyalty as a Means of Increasing Human Efficiency
Concentration as a Means of Increasing Human Efficiency
Wages as a Means of Increasing Human Efficiency
Pleasure as a Means of Increasing Human Efficiency
The Love of the Game and Efficiency
Relaxation as a Means of Increasing Human Efficiency
The Rate of Improvement in Efficiency
Practice plus Theory
Making Experience an Asset: Judgment Formation
Capitalizing Experience: Habit Formation

enjoyment in the work itself. The book concludes with chapters on the rate of improvement, practice, judgment formation, and habit formation. In contrast to Scott's book, Hugo Münsterberg's more self-consciously scientific *Psychology and Industrial Efficiency*, published in German in 1912 and in English the following year, set the template for subsequent texts in industrial psychology. That text is discussed later in this chapter.

Scott played a pivotal role in a number of watershed events in the history of industrial psychology, including the first graduate program in industrial psychology at the Carnegie Institute of Technology (CIT) in Pittsburgh and the mobilization of psychologists to assist the US Army in World War I. He also founded the first successful industrial psychology consulting firm in 1919. Scott's roles in these events are discussed later in this text. In 1920, Scott returned to Northwestern University as its president and served with distinction until his retirement in 1939 (Jacobson, 1951). Scott died in September 1955.

## Psychology Applied to Employee Selection

The principal activity of industrial psychologists in the first decades of the twentieth century was employee selection, and it remains a core activity today. Applying psychology to selecting employees can be broadly conceptualized two ways. From a managerial or employer perspective, selection involves choosing those applicants with the highest probability of success in a particular job. Selection can also be viewed from a worker or employee perspective: determining which of multiple jobs is best suited for the interests and abilities of an individual (Kornhauser, 1922). The latter approach, sometimes termed *vocational psychology*, will be discussed later in this chapter.

Employee selection, of course, did not originate with applied psychology. Organizations have always needed a method to determine who does and who does not become part of the organization. The advent of the Industrial Revolution and the corresponding increase in size and complexity of economic organizations exacerbated the need for rational selection methods. Selection based on nepotism, favoritism, connections, bribery, the whim of the first-line supervisor, and other nonscientific criteria were seen as increasingly untenable. Frederick Taylor (1911) was aware of the importance of selection, noting the need for selecting the best individuals to apply his "one best way." He described an early selection study by Sanford Thomas, who used reaction time to select ball-bearing inspectors. Selection, however, was not the primary focus of scientific management. The early industrial psychologists offered the promise of a better approach, one grounded in empirical verification and in the accurate measurement of relevant individual difference characteristics through the use of psychological tests and apparatus. They also developed a method to empirically verify the efficacy of their efforts, that is, to demonstrate that their selection procedures were valid. As noted in the previous chapter, demonstrating validity depended on progress in both statistics and measurement procedures.

Selection by industrial psychologists involved the use of a predictor of job performance, generally some kind of *test*, where test can be defined broadly as any sample of behavior. Selection by the use of tests predated industrial psychology. There was documented use of written examinations in China between 200 and 100 BCE during the late Qin and early Han period. The examinations were discontinued for a time and then resurrected during the T'ang dynasty (618–906 CE). By the Ming dynasty, an elaborate system of civil service examinations was in place (Bowman, 1989).[11] The Chinese model influenced civil service reform in Great Britain, where in 1854 the Northcote-Trevlyan report recommended that civil service appointments be made based on open examinations, with merit also as the criterion for promotion (Evans, 2016). The US Army used tests to select surgeons as early as 1814 (DuBois, 1970), and in 1869 Francis Galton used his recently developed statistical procedures to evaluate admissions test scores at the Royal Military Academy at Sandhurst (Stigler, 1999). Also prior to 1900, Thomas Peters of the Washington Life Insurance Company in Atlanta developed his Personal History Inventory, a forerunner of biographical inventories used today (Ferguson, 1961). As noted in the previous chapter, test evaluation began with a focus on the test's *trustworthiness*, that is, how well it represented reality, with an emphasis on simplicity and cost effectiveness (Jastrow, Baldwin, & Cattell, 1898). Progress continued with Spearman's conception of reliability or consistency and, by 1910, with the correlation-based test-criterion method (Rogers, 1995). Industrial psychologists at last had a method to empirically demonstrate the validity of their selection efforts.

There were a few scattered efforts by psychologists to use tests for selection before 1910. In 1901, in Modena, Italy, the physician and psychologist Ugo Pizzoli (1863–1934) used tests to select apprentices (Salgado, 2001). By 1903, the French psychologist Jean Marie Lahy (1872–1943) was performing selection work for the Ministry of Work (Salgado, Anderson,

---

[11] A number of sources date testing in China to an earlier time, roughly 4,000 years before the present day. That figure, however, is based on unreliable sources (see Bowman, 1989).

& Hülsheger, 2010), using tests to select stenographers by 1905 (Viteles, 1923), and to select streetcar drivers by 1908 (Fryer & Henry, 1950). In the United States, J. L. Meriam (1906) applied the test-criterion method in an educational setting, where he correlated elementary school teachers' normal school grades and city examination scores with teaching efficiency estimates by the principal and superintendent, an example of an early validation study. By the end of the first decade of the twentieth century, Hugo Münsterberg was turning his attention to industrial psychology, particularly employee selection.

### Hugo Münsterberg

Hugo Münsterberg (Figure 4.3) was critically important to the development of industrial psychology. At the time of his death in 1916 at age fifty-three, Münsterberg was possibly America's best-known psychologist (Hale, 1980). He was also perhaps the most reviled in the United States,

Figure 4.3 Hugo Münsterberg. The Drs. Nicholas and Dorothy Cummings Center for the History of Psychology, The University of Akron.

due to his unwavering support for Germany in the buildup to World War I. The low esteem he was held in by both his colleagues and the public at large contributed to the relative neglect of his pioneering work not only in industrial psychology but also in other applied areas such as clinical, forensic, and educational psychology. Recent interest in Münsterberg (e.g., Benjamin, 2000, 2006; Hale, 1980; Landy, 1992, 1997; Spillmann & Spillmann, 1993) has done much to restore the reputation of this pioneering psychologist. Münsterberg's influence extended beyond the United States. His contemporary Karl Marbe (1936), for example, credited Münsterberg with introducing industrial psychology to Germany.

Münsterberg was born in Danzig, East Prussia, on June 1, 1863. He earned a doctorate in psychology with Wundt at the University of Leipzig in 1885 and an M.D. degree at the University of Heidelberg two years later. Münsterberg found a position at the University of Freiburg and developed the psychology laboratory there. His work found an admirer in William James, who convinced Münsterberg to move to Harvard University in 1892 to take over the psychology laboratory. Despite many misgivings and the hope of a prestigious academic appointment in Germany, Münsterberg accepted, first on a trial basis and then permanently. By 1898, he was president of the APA (Hale, 1980).

Like the majority of his academic colleagues in the late eighteenth century, Münsterberg was initially quite hostile toward applying psychology to practical concerns outside the laboratory. In 1898, he published an article in the *Atlantic Monthly* that was highly critical of the child study movement, the applied psychology of the time. He also attacked the idea of mental measurement, claiming it was impossible to measure psychological entities. By the early 1900s, however, he reversed course completely, contributing to clinical, forensic, educational, and especially industrial psychology. In 1906, Münsterberg turned his Harvard laboratory over to his assistants; soon after that he established an applied curriculum at Harvard. Possible reasons for this turnaround include Münsterberg's need for the attention his applied work brought him, the status he gained from being America's psychological expert, and a sincere belief in the importance of applied psychology, particularly psychology applied to business (Benjamin, 2006). In 1909, Münsterberg published his initial article on industrial psychology in *McClure's Magazine* (Benjamin, 2000). Münsterberg taught what he claimed as the first college-level course in applied psychology in 1910–11 (Hale, 1980) and in the ten-year period between 1906 and 1916 published

Table 4.2 Psychology and Industrial Efficiency *(Münsterberg, 1913)*

| Contents | |
|---|---|
| I. | Applied Psychology |
| II. | The Demands of Practical Life |
| III. | Means and Ends |
| | I. The Best Possible Man |
| IV. | Vocation and Fitness |
| V. | Scientific Vocational Guidance |
| VI. | Scientific Management |
| VII. | The Methods of Experimental Psychology |
| VIII. | Experiments in the Interest of Electric Railway Service |
| IX. | Experiments in the Interest of Ship Service |
| X. | Experiments in the Interest of Telephone Service |
| XI. | Contributions from Men of Affairs |
| XII. | Individuals and Groups |
| | II. The Best Possible Work |
| XIII. | Learning and Training |
| XIV. | The Adjustment of Technical to Psychological Conditions |
| XV. | The Economy of Movement |
| XVI. | Experiments on the Problem of Monotony |
| XVII. | Attention and Fatigue |
| XVIII. | Physical and Social Influences on the Working Power |
| | III. The Best Possible Effect |
| XIX. | The Satisfaction of Economic Demands |
| XX. | Experiments on the Effects of Advertisements |
| XXI. | The Effect of Display |
| XXII. | Experiments with Reference to Illegal Imitation |
| XXIII. | Buying and Selling |
| XXIV. | The Future Development of Economic Psychology |

twenty books, mostly on applied psychology.[12] Of these books, it was his 1913 classic *Psychology and Industrial Efficiency* (first published in German in 1912) that had the most-lasting influence.

The consulting opportunities that followed Münsterberg's 1909 magazine article formed the basis for *Psychology and Industrial Efficiency* (Benjamin, 2000). As seen in Table 4.2, the book was divided into three sections: "The Best Possible Man," "The Best Possible Work," and "The Best Possible Effect." "The Best Possible Man" focused on employee selection and vocational guidance, with Münsterberg's own selection studies on streetcar motormen, ship officers, and telephone switchboard

---

[12] Landy (1992) pointed out that Münsterberg's published output did tend to be somewhat redundant and that he often wrote in an essay format that denied proper credit to other researchers. Münsterberg was undeniably prolific. For example, he dictated the 400-page book *Psychotherapy* (1909) in approximately a month and a half (cited in Hale, 1980).

operators as examples. Münsterberg was among the first to use selection tests in industry (Hale, 1980). His tests were primarily apparatus-based rather than pencil-and-paper tests. "The Best Possible Work" discussed training, monotony, attention, fatigue, and physical and social influences on work, including the effects of alcohol (Münsterberg was in favor of moderate alcohol use at work).[13] The final section, "The Best Possible Effect," covered advertising, buying, and selling and cited work by Scott, Weber, and Hollingworth.

In April 1912, at the German Congress of Psychology, Münsterberg first presented the study on the selection of streetcar drivers that appeared in his text (Salgado, 2001). In selecting motormen, he focused on accident reduction, developing a laboratory test that he believed duplicated the streetcar operators' attentional processes.[14] To validate the test, Münsterberg reasoned that a successful test should be able to differentiate unreliable (accident-prone) operators from reliable ones and that operators should perceive that the test measures mental functions similar to those used in driving an electric streetcar. He did find support for the usefulness of the test. Older, experienced operators made fewer errors on the test than inexperienced operators with a higher accident rate. Regarding some of Münsterberg's other tests, he did not report any results for the card-sorting task he developed for selecting ship captains.[15] Münsterberg was able to assess the effectiveness of the series of tests, such as digit span, card-sorting, and word association tests, that he used to select telephone operators. Skeptical of the usefulness of these measures, the telephone company embedded experienced operators among the group of trainees who were tested. The experienced operators obtained the highest test scores.

Another notable achievement by Münsterberg was organizing the 1904 International Congress of Arts and Sciences as part of the St. Louis World's Fair. In addition to seeing a number of prominent psychologists from

---

[13] Although a teetotaler himself, Münsterberg believed moderate alcohol use could reduce daily anxiety and that if individuals are denied alcohol, they may turn to more dangerous drugs (Spillmann & Spillmann, 1993).

[14] In 1915, Piorkowski criticized Münsterberg for failing to include motor responses in his test, reasoning that an applicant may be able to attend to a stimulus but be unable to make the proper response (cited in Viteles, 1925–26a).

[15] Richard M. Elliott (1952), who studied with Münsterberg, wrote that while in Berlin he saw his score on the card-sorting task on the front page of the Berliner *Zeitung am Mittag (the Noon Newspaper)*. Harry Hollingworth (2013), in a posthumously published memoir, claimed that Münsterberg's card-sorting task was originally developed to identify less accident-prone streetcar operators, not for selecting ship captains.

around the world, visitors also had the opportunity to experience the psychologists' new physical and mental tests (Brown, 1992).

Münsterberg's final years were characterized by adversity and stress. He had alienated many of his colleagues with his attacks on their work, his championing of applied psychology, and his relentless popularization of psychology (Benjamin, 2006). His support for Germany in the prelude and opening years of World War I drew suspicion from his colleagues and the general public, and he was even suspected of spying for Germany (Hale, 1980). His graduate student Harold Burtt, later a prominent industrial psychologist himself, noted that Münsterberg looked exhausted when he arrived to teach a class at Radcliffe College in December 1916. A few minutes into the lecture, Münsterberg collapsed at the podium. He was dead of a cerebral hemorrhage at age fifty-three (Bjork, 1983). Writing in 1932, Münsterberg's former student Knight Dunlap admitted that Münsterberg did not have "converts to his philosophy. He was not a man to have disciples." Nevertheless, Dunlap wrote, "There was at least one giant in these days ..." and "modern trends in American psychology ... are easily traceable to Münsterberg" (p. 42).[16]

### Early Selection Research and Practice

While Münsterberg's attempts at test validation were rudimentary, his instincts were correct. To demonstrate the superiority of the psychologist's scientific approach to employee selection, empirical evidence of effectiveness is necessary. A series of selection studies that followed Münsterberg's early efforts demonstrated increasing sophistication in achieving this goal. There was increased use of the test-criterion correlation method, and researchers were beginning to pay attention to potential problems with this procedure such as the unreliability of job performance and the use of inappropriate criteria. For example, in 1916, Link used a series of tests measuring characteristics such as visual acuity, reaction time, steadiness of attention, and accuracy of movement to predict the job performance of shell inspectors and gaugers at the Winchester Repeating Arms Company.[17] Realizing that his job performance criterion might give unreliable results if assessed at a single

---

[16]  Robert M. Yerkes, who studied with Münsterberg and, like Dunlap, was elected APA president, remembered Münsterberg warmly, as someone whose "almost paternal interest and solicitude" and "rare generosity" helped Yerkes personally and professionally. Yerkes admitted, however, that he was "never able to admire him as a scientist" (Yerkes, 1932, p. 389).

[17]  Henry C. Link, who spent his industrial psychology career in industry rather than academia, is discussed in Chapter 6.

point in time, Link averaged performance across a four-week period to improve criterion reliability. He was also concerned that his results might be specific to the tested group, and therefore Link replicated the study with other groups, a procedure today called *cross-validation* (Link, 1918). Herbert Rogers (1917) provided an additional example of concern for the reliability of criterion performance. In a study on the effectiveness of tests for selecting typists and stenographers, Rogers measured his typewriting criterion over a six-month period. These two studies illustrate an early concern with what was later termed the *criterion problem* in I-O psychology, the difficulty in identifying and measuring appropriate criteria that are reflective of job success. Viteles (1932) wrote that the Rogers's (1917) study and studies on the use of tests in telephone operators by Henry C. McComas (1914), the use of the interview in selecting salespersons by Walter Dill Scott (1915), and the use of tests in selecting telegraphers by Edward S. Jones (1917) "mark the beginnings of industrial psychology" in the United States (p. 45).

Scott (1916a) described a battery of "quantitative determinations" useful for selecting employees. The first is an employer reference form, the *Previous Record*, which included a checklist for the former employer to rate the candidate on his or her work, conduct, ability, and character. An applicant's *Physical Condition* should be rated by a physician. Next is a series of timed tests that purported to measure *Native Intellectual Ability*, that is, ability that is not due to learning. Test I, for example, required applicants to determine the opposites of words, put words into larger categories, do simple arithmetic problems, and match "English Proverbs" with corresponding "African Proverbs." Scott cautioned that a selection decision should never be based on the result of a single one of these tests. *Technical Ability* was assessed by means of timed arithmetic, transcription, and number-matching tests. There was also a situational test, where an applicant had five minutes to convince a buyer to purchase a product, and an assessment of *Personality* by a group of interviewers.

Scott's *Aids in the Selection of Salesmen* (1916b) provides an example of the kind of work done in the Bureau of Salesmanship Research at the Carnegie Institute of Technology.[18] In *Aids*, Scott and his student-staff associates described an integrated battery of methods for use in sales selection.[19] Components of that battery included a model application

[18] See Chapter 8 for a description of the Carnegie Institute of Technology program.
[19] It is interesting and perhaps ironic that one of the four individuals offered fellowships at the Bureau of Salesmanship Research was Edwin G. Boring. As shown in Chapter 2, he was certainly no fan of applied psychology during this time period. The other three psychologists who declined the offer were William S. Foster, Calvin P. Stone, and Harry Hollingworth (Ferguson, 1962–65).

form, the Personal History Record, for the collection of biographical data and a model letter of reference for former employers to complete. There was also an interviewer's scale and rating sheet that guided the interviewer in the construction of a rating scale that could be used to compare applicants against benchmark salespersons. This scale was the precursor to Scott's Man-to-Man rating system used by the US Army in World War I. The remaining aids were a series of psychological tests: *Test Ia* was a test of mental alertness, an early example of a cognitive ability test. *Test II* was a test of "foresight" that presented the applicant with a number of hypothetical situations and asked her or him to make predictions based on those situations. In essence, this was an early assessment of creativity (Ferguson, n.d.). *Test III*, based on a test developed by E. L. Thorndike, assessed speed and accuracy in understanding instructions. *Test IV* was an incomplete sentences test that was adapted from an earlier test by Marion Trabue. This test provided a sort of clinical assessment of the candidate. The final test, *Test V*, measured an applicant's range of interests on the theory of Edward S. Robinson that a good salesperson can converse with a customer on a wide range of interests. This test was similar to the information portion of later omnibus tests of general intelligence (Ferguson, 1962–65, n.d.).[20]

An example of a test that used apparatus to simulate the job is provided by the engineer K. A. Tramm of the Greater Berlin Tramway Company. In 1919, the company began using a simulated driver's platform to select motormen. As part of the examination, the applicant had to operate a controller and brake levers in response to various stimuli. This test was supplemented with other performance tests, assessment of night vision, a hand steadiness test, and an intelligence test. The company reported a reduction of 40 to 50 percent in accidents for those motormen who were hired using the examination and a decrease in training time for these individuals of 120 hours (cited in Viteles, 1925–26a).

## Vocational Psychology

The various selection methods discussed thus far in this chapter view the process from the perspective of the organization or manager. Given that there are generally more applicants than there are job openings, how can the organization select those individuals with the greatest chance of job success? Selection can also be viewed from the perspective of the individual

---

[20] As discussed earlier in Chapter 3, Scott (1917) also did some of the earliest work on criterion-related validation.

applicant; that is, of all the potential jobs available, which best fit the abilities and interests of the applicant? This process of selecting jobs for individuals came to be known as *vocational psychology*.[21] In the United States, by the 1930s, a division was evident between those applied psychologists interested in selection and those interested in vocational psychology. The latter began an exodus from industrial psychology, and in recent years those psychologists have been primarily identified with counseling psychology, although individuals interested vocational interests do maintain a presence in I-O psychology (Savickas & Baker, 2005). In the early years of industrial psychology, however, many of the same individuals involved in employee selection were also involved in vocational psychology.

In their history of vocational psychology, Savickas and Baker (2005) distinguished between vocational psychology, which has a foundation in science, and vocational guidance, which predated vocational psychology and in its initial manifestation incorporated pseudoscientific methods such as using appearance to assess character. In the United States, vocational guidance has its roots in the post–Civil War efforts of the Young Men's Christian Association (YMCA) to open employment bureaus. By the turn of the twentieth century, these efforts expanded to trade schools, which in addition to employment bureaus provided vocational guidance to young people. Similar to selection, vocational guidance was associated with the emergence of the factory system, the proliferation of occupational specialties, and the increased interest in individual differences that characterized the late nineteenth and early twentieth centuries.

Frank Parsons (1854–1908), a law professor at Boston University, is generally credited with developing the basic model of vocational adjustment. That model, discussed in his 1909 book *Choosing a Vocation*, emphasized a proper fit between an individual's capabilities and characteristics and the requirements of the job. In an effort to put vocational guidance on a more scientific basis, Parsons and his colleagues enlisted the help of Hugo Münsterberg. While supportive of the concept, Münsterberg was critical of Parsons' reliance on self-reports, advocating instead a laboratory approach to identifying individual capabilities. He called for psychological laboratories to be established in vocational bureaus. The first was in Cincinnati, Ohio, in 1911, directed by Helen Bradford Thompson Woolley (1874–1947), who did her doctoral work with James Angell at the University of Chicago (Savickas & Baker, 2005).

---

[21] In the early years of industrial psychology, *vocational psychology* was also used as a synonym for industrial psychology and employment psychology. For example, the 1924 text *Fundamentals of Vocational Psychology* by Charles Griffitts devoted only one chapter to choosing a vocation; the rest of the book was about employee selection.

Münsterberg attempted to incorporate the vocational guidance movement into psychology. His influence in Europe was a factor in Germany and neighboring countries affiliating vocational guidance with psychological testing, especially vocational aptitude testing and psychotechnics in general. Early activity in vocational guidance in Europe included the Centre for Vocational Guidance, established by Arthur Guillaume Christiaens in Brussels in 1910, and the Bureau of Vocational Guidance, founded as part of the Rousseau Institute in Geneva in 1918 by Julien Fontègne. In 1920, the International Congress of Psychotechnics Applied to Vocational Guidance, a conference whose focus was on vocational psychology, was held in Geneva (Gundlach, 1998).[22]

The first psychologist to take a self-consciously scientific approach to vocational psychology, and therefore arguably the first vocational psychologist, was Harry Hollingworth, who we met earlier in our discussion of psychology and advertising (Savickas & Baker, 2005). Hollingworth published *Vocational Psychology: Its Problems and Methods* in 1916. The text included coverage of selection both from the perspective of an individual making the best occupational choice and from the perspective of selecting the best applicant from a pool of candidates. Hollingworth addresses three questions for vocational psychology. First, how can an individual know her or his own aptitudes, interests, and abilities, and how do those characteristics compare with those of other individuals? This is a vocational psychology question. Next, how can information about the abilities needed in various jobs be acquired to aid an individual in choosing an occupation? This question is concerned with job analysis. And finally, how do employers choose the candidate with the best chance of success from multiple applicants, a traditional employee selection question (Savickas & Baker, 2005)? Central to Hollingworth's first question of vocational choice was the development of occupational interest inventories.[23]

### Early Work in Other Areas

*Performance Appraisal*

As was true for selection, the evaluation of employee performance was becoming increasingly systematic during the early years of the twentieth

---

[22] This conference is discussed in Chapter 9.
[23] The early work on interest inventories conducted at CIT and subsequent work by Edward K. Strong Jr. are discussed in Chapter 8.

century. Measures of performance were of two general types: objective and subjective. Objective standards were measures of output that could be counted. Examples include the number of castings produced in a foundry or the dollar value of items sold in a retail establishment. Subjective evaluation of an employee's performance was generally based on a supervisor's rating or ranking of that worker using some type of scale. The development of rating scales, discussed in the previous chapter, is relevant for performance measurement, as the primary technique used in performance appraisal was some type of rating scale.

Walter Dill Scott's Man-to-Man Rating Scale is an example of a pre–World War I performance rating scale. It was a successor to the Interviewer Scale and Interviewer Rating Sheet he and his students developed in 1916 at the Carnegie Institute of Technology (Ferguson, 1961). The interviewer scale was initially developed as one of Scott's aids for selecting salespersons. The interviewer using the scale was instructed to name at least twenty-five salespersons who varied on five traits: appearance, convincingness, industry, character, and value to the company. The interviewer then had to indicate which of the chosen salespersons were highest, lowest, and intermediate on each of the five traits. For each trait, five names were selected and rank-ordered from highest to lowest and entered on the Interviewer Rating Sheet. This sheet was used during interviews; applicants were compared to the rank-ordered salespersons on each trait and given a numerical value corresponding to the salesperson he or she most resembled (Ferguson, 1962–65). This person-to-person rating system, later termed the Man-to-Man Rating Scale, was used for evaluating performance as well as for selection. Scott adapted it for the US Army in World War I, and later it was modified for use in industry.

## Training

Once on the job, workers need to acquire specific knowledge and skills necessary for success on the job; that is, they need to be trained. Before 1900, for the most part formal training took place in apprenticeship programs, with some training conducted in technical or trade schools (Kraiger & Ford, 2007). Practitioners of scientific management were particularly scornful of the apprenticeship system. In 1910, Frank Gilbreth (1923/1960) stated that "the present apprenticeship system is pitiful and criminal from the apprentice's standpoint, ridiculous from a modern system standpoint, and there is no word that describes its wastefulness from an economic standpoint" (p. 280). Psychologists also found fault in the unsystematic apprenticeship approach and believed that laboratory work in learning could be used to increase training success. For example, Münsterberg (1913) pointed to studies on reading acquisition, typewriting, and telegraphy as examples of an experimental approach to learning.

In the first twenty-five years or so of the twentieth century, standardization and simplicity in training were the focus, as exemplified by scientific management approach. As business organizations grew larger and more complex, they began instituting their own factory schools (Kraiger & Ford, 2007). In 1912, the American Steel and Wire Company started one of the first formal training programs in the United States (Baritz, 1960). As described by Sturdevant (1918), the training course was not intended for beginning employees but for experienced salespersons and "semi-executives." The six-and-a-half-week course took place at three locations: Pittsburgh, Pennsylvania; Cleveland, Ohio; and Worchester, Massachusetts. Trained in groups of twelve, the employees received first-hand experience in how steel and steel products were made. The training used multiple methods of instruction and evaluation: discussion, lectures, quizzes, and exams. The program had three goals: teaching the trainees the fundamentals of the steel business, training participants in their specific job area, and giving the trainees an understanding of how the components of the organization operate as a whole.

An early formal training approach was the use of vestibule schools. Unlike apprenticeships where the new employees are immediately placed on the job, vestibule schools were separate areas where training took place under supervision using duplicate factory or office machinery. The new employee was detained in the vestibule area until she or he was adjusted to the new environment and ready to perform in the new job. Link (1919) saw the vestibule school as serving multiple purposes. In addition to bringing the new employee up to standard, it provided an opportunity for supervisors to observe the "moral qualities" the worker developed, and it allowed the new employee the opportunity to determine whether the job was a good fit. Potential advantages of the vestibule method included better worker placement, detailed records of each worker's progress, and, because the focus was on instruction rather than productivity, enhanced learning (Burtt, 1929).

## Human Factors

The goal of employee selection is to find the person with the best chance of success for a particular job. Once the important tasks that make up a particular job are determined though job analysis, the job can be viewed as fixed. It is then up to the psychologist to capitalize on the relevant individual differences among the applicants to decide which of those candidates has the aptitude, interest, or personality that best matches the demands of the position. A complementary perspective is to view the person as fixed, in the sense that the average individual has certain cognitive and physical abilities and limitations, and one can then design job tasks, the machinery, or the workplace itself to best fit the capabilities of that worker.[24] This approach has gone by a number of names: older terms such as *applied experimental psychology* and *engineering psychology* and later ones representing a more interdisciplinary approach such as *ergonomics*[25], *human engineering, human factors engineering,* and *human factors.* Zionchenko and Munipov (2005) noted that the term *ergonomy* was suggested by the Polish scientist W. B. Jastrzebowski in 1857 in an article that tried to construct a model of work that conformed to what was known about the laws of natural science. While some date the beginning of engineering psychology to the World War II era (e.g., Grether, 1968), attempts to fit work to the human operator have a much longer history. Applied psychologists have been involved in human factors research and practice since the early twentieth century.

There is no bright-line distinction between I-O psychology and human factors, and this was particularly true in the beginning decades of industrial psychology. Psychologists involved in human factors before World War II often considered themselves both industrial and engineering psychologists. Along with other interested parties such as engineers, they tried to obtain an optimal fit between the worker and the workplace. While human factors is now considered to be a field separate from I-O psychology, both share an emphasis on worker productivity and satisfaction. Both have a number of areas of interest that overlap, such as training and organizational stress. Because of this close relationship, both I-O psychology and the present-day human factors share a common set of antecedents. As it was for industrial psychology, scientific or experimental psychology influenced the development of human factors, as did the functionalist tradition in the United States. Scientific management also was a major influence because of its

---

[24] The early German psychotechnician Fritz Giese made a similar distinction between the psychotechnics of the subject, adapting the worker's psychological traits to the objective requirements of the job, and the psychotechnics of the object: adapting the requirements of the job to the psychological characteristics of the worker (Zionchenko & Munipov, 2005). See the Germany section in Chapter 6 for more details.

[25] The Ergonomics Research Society was established by British scientists in 1949, who decided on the term *ergonomics* to describe their field (Zionchenko & Munipov, 2005).

emphasis on the importance of equipment and workplace design. Münsterberg (1913) not only set the agenda for industrial psychology, he also discussed topics central to the human factors approach, including the design of displays (Lane, 2007). The work on fatigue, discussed earlier in this chapter, was relevant when determining human capabilities and limits. Early studies by psychologists on the effects of illumination and on accident prevention took what was recognizably a human factors perspective. Histories of human factors reference other landmarks shared with the history of I-O psychology, such as the establishment of the Industrial Fatigue Research Board and the National Institute of Industrial Psychology in Great Britain (Cumming & Corkindale, 1969) and the Hawthorne Studies in the United States (Zionchenko & Munipov, 2005). Just as it did for psychological testing and selection, World War I provided an opportunity for psychologists to demonstrate their usefulness in fitting the machine to the human operator. This was most evident in aviation psychology, a topic included in the discussion of industrial psychology and World War I in Chapter 5.

## Chapter Summary

Establishing the exact origin of any scientific enterprise is difficult under the best circumstances, and no attempt will be made to do so for I-O psychology. The early years of the discipline were characterized both by a desire by academic psychologists to explore industrial applications of their new science and by businesspersons interested in using that science for the benefit of their firms. The early work of Walter Dill Scott and Hugo Münsterberg was critical to the development of that effort. In Europe, early work relevant for industrial psychology focused on the physiological and psychological aspects of fatigue, along with an interest in the causes and prevention of industrial accidents. While similar work was also being conducted in the United States, there it was the application of psychology to advertising that was most prominent around the turn of the twentieth century. Work by Scott, Harry Hollingworth, Daniel Starch, and others provided psychologists a chance to demonstrate that their new science could be useful in a business setting. That early work on the psychology of advertising began with a focus on the mental processes of the consumer and progressed to an examination of the behavioral properties of the advertisements and the psychological needs of the consumer.

It was psychology applied to employee selection, however, that became the primary activity for industrial psychologists. Both Scott and Münsterberg conducted early research on test validation for selection. By the second decade of the twentieth century, validation studies were demonstrating increasing sophistication by, for example, recognizing the importance of considering the reliability of criteria used in the validation process. In addition to selection, the early 1900s saw psychology applied to other business-related areas. The vocational guidance work of the 1800s provided the basis for what eventually became known as vocational psychology, determining which job is the best fit for an individual. Advancements in performance appraisal mirrored advances in rating scale construction. In training, organizational apprenticeship programs were criticized by psychologists, and other methods of training employees, such as factory schools and vestibule training, were developed. Human factors, designing the task to fit the capabilities of the human operator, also received attention from industrial psychologists. How the needs of a vastly expanded military machine in World War I spurred further development in employee selection, performance appraisal, training, and human factors is the subject of Chapter 5.

# Industrial Psychology and the Great War

World War I began in July 1914 with a declaration of war against Serbia by Austria-Hungary and ended in November 1918. The Allies, which included France, Russia, the United Kingdom, Italy, and the eventually the United States, were victorious over the Central Powers of Germany, Austria-Hungary, the Ottoman Empire, and Bulgaria. The widespread conflict required an unprecedented level of mobilization and organization by the combatants. Applied psychologists were eager to offer their services to the war effort, with varying degrees of influence and success. By no means were all of these volunteers applied or industrial psychologists. Many were academic researchers who took on an applied role for the war's duration and then went back to their laboratories and classrooms after the war.

## Europe

Industrial psychologists contributed to the war effort on both sides of the conflict. Following the lead of Münsterberg, in continental Europe, selection was largely based on the use of apparatus and manual procedures, although the paper-and-pencil tests favored by the Americans were also used. The first of the Allies to conduct substantial research into the aptitude for flying was Italy (Dockeray & Issacs, 1921). As early as 1915, the Italian psychologist Agostino Gemelli used psychological tests for pilot selection for the Italian Army (Gemelli, 1952; Salgado, 2001). Early work on aviation psychology was conducted in laboratories in Turin, Naples, and Rome under the general direction of Giuseppe Gradenigo. In addition to medical tests, the procedures used in the selection of pilots eventually included the following: measures of simple reaction times, emotional reactions, attention, perception of muscular movement, and equilibrium. Simple reaction times to both visual and auditory stimuli were assessed using a Hipp chronoscope, the standard laboratory instrument for measuring time. Following the procedures described by Gradenigo and Gemelli, emotional reactions in pilot candidates were assessed by circulation changes, respiration changes, and hand tremors in response to an "emotive stimulus." The emotive stimulus was a firecracker, automobile horn, or pistol shot. A number of different tests were tried to assess attention or speed of perception. For example, a cancellation test was scored for both time to complete and number of errors. Simple figures were flashed briefly to the applicant, and the time it took to recognize each figure was measured (Dockeray & Issacs, 1921).

Reasoning that pilots need to be able to recognize the amount of pressure placed on the controls and the amount of pressure necessary to change their position a given amount, various types of apparatus to measure perception of muscular effort were developed. For example, the procedure designed by Galeotti required a blindfolded candidate to hold a lever steady while weights varying from two to twelve kilograms were placed on it. To test equilibrium, the Italian researchers used the Barany test and specially designed apparatus.[1] In an early example of the use of simulation, Malan designed a cockpit that could be tilted laterally, backward, or forward. A blindfolded applicant was required to place a rod in a vertical position and report his position while the cockpit was tilted. Disqualification of a candidate did not depend on performance on any single test; rather, the overall profile was important. Results of this work suggested that successful pursuit pilots had excellent position perception, low visual reaction times, but not necessarily strong resistance to emotive stimuli, while Caproni (a type of bomber) pilots showed a great deal of resistance to emotive stimuli (Dockeray & Issacs, 1921).

In France, Jean Marie Lahy, who first began his work in selection more than ten years before the start of the war, used tests to select gunners (Salgado, Anderson, & Hülsheger, 2010). In 1910, Binet and Simon discussed the use of psychological tests for screening out mentally unsuitable military recruits, anticipating their use for that purpose by the US Army. Binet and Simon were unable, however, to convince French medical officers of the tests' potential (Pintner, 1923). Tests of reaction time and emotional stability were favored for pilot selection.[2] The French Air Force used a kymographion, an apparatus that assessed physiological measures such as trembling, heart rate, and respiration. The potential pilot was

[1] The Barany chair is rotated to create a sense of vertigo. The applicant could then be given a series of tasks to test performance in that state.

[2] In contrast to its use today to describe a personality characteristic, *emotional stability* in this context is the same as emotional reaction described in the previous section on Italy. It described an individual's reaction to a startling stimulus (Koonce, 1984).

assessed on these measures following the unexpected sound of a gunshot (van Drunen, 1997). Candidates who had a wide range in their reaction times and those who had exaggerated emotional responses were not accepted to flight school (Dockeray & Issacs, 1921).

In Germany, as the war approached, there was an acceleration of personnel selection work by psychologists. Aptitude testing for pilots, radio operators, and drivers was conducted (Sprung & Sprung, 2001). Otto Klemm, for example, worked on testing individuals for ability to locate sound, and also on aptitude tests for selection in the German artillery service (Klemm, 1936). Walther Moede and Curt Piorkowski constructed a driving simulator to select motorcar drivers for the German Army. Applicants' responses to various driving dilemmas were assessed. This type of procedure was transferred in 1917 by Moede, Piorkowski, and Max Brahn to the selection of locomotive engineers for the Royal Saxon Railroads. In addition to the driving test, they constructed tests of sorting, memory, and willpower (Gundlach, 1997). A major expansion of German military psychology occurred after the war in the 1920s, a subject discussed in the Chapter 6.

According to Hearnshaw (1964), "Applied psychology was brought to birth, as far as Great Britain was concerned, in the 1914–1918 war" (p. 245). It arose in response to three problems: the treatment of the psychological disorder "shell-shock" that was due to battlefield trauma, concern for the health of munitions workers, and selection for highly specialized military tasks. While it is the latter two problems that are directly relevant for the history of industrial psychology, it is interesting that C. S. Myers, a medical doctor soon to be the leading industrial psychologist in Great Britain, treated shell-shocked soldiers and, in fact, may have coined the term (Hearnshaw, 1964).

Due to an extremely heavy demand for munitions, working hours for British munitions workers were dramatically increased. Where in 1914 workers averaged forty-eight to fifty-five hours per week, a year later seventy to ninety hours per week was the norm, and it was not uncommon for workers to exceed that total. Concern for the health of munitions workers and concern that any worker health problems could reduce the flow of munitions led to the establishment of the Health of Munitions Workers Committee in 1915. This Committee studied factors that affected the health and efficiency of workers, such as fatigue and length of time working (Hearnshaw, 1964). One of the principal investigators for the Committee, former Oxford Fellow H. M. Vernon (1870–1951), was arguably Great Britain's first industrial psychologist (McCollom, 1968). While conceding that work in industrial psychology in the United States and Germany preceded the work of this Committee, Hearnshaw (1964) viewed its thorough field investigations as "perhaps the most important of all the pioneer studies of the human factor under modern industrial conditions" (p. 247). He also noted that in addition to its continuing work, the Committee contributed to the establishment of the Industrial Welfare Society in 1919 and the National Institute of Industrial Psychology in 1921, discussed in the next chapter.[3]

Selection research in Great Britain was modest in comparison to the massive program carried out in the United States. Psychologists such as Myers and Tom H. Pear were part of a team that conducted research into the selection of pilots and of submarine detection (hydrophone) operators. Hydrophone operator applicants were tested for memory and appreciation of sound pitch and rhythm, sound localization accuracy, sound intensity discrimination, and ability to separate sounds from background noise. Trainers reported being very satisfied with the candidates selected (Myers, 1925). Charles E. Spearman carried out an independent laboratory investigation on sound localization and was part of a group that investigated night vision and training navy gun layers (Hearnshaw, 1964).

Unlike their counterparts in Italy and France, the British researchers on pilot selection did not rely on measuring reaction times. The Air Medical Investigation Committee was chaired by the neurologist Henry Head, and among its members were the psychologists W. H. R. Rivers and Charles Spearman. While much of the research conducted was physiological in nature, some of it did involve a psychological dimension. In addition to measuring pulse rate, blood pressure, and the amount of time one's breath could be held, researchers examining oxygen need used the MacDougall test, where the subject must spot the center of each circle with a pencil on a tape that passes by with increasing speed. Tests of simple motor coordination, such as standing on one foot for fifteen seconds with eyes closed or open, were also used. Attempts were made to discover the causes of fainting, giddiness, and nausea in flight. Severity of hand tremor and a "line drawing and noise" test were used in applicant evaluation. In that test, the candidate was asked to draw a pencil line lightly across a large piece of paper to determine hand tremor. Asked to draw a second line, while the applicant does so a loud sound is made close to his ear to see the effect on his line, and then a third line is drawn with a warning that the noise will

---

[3] The Health of Munitions Workers Committee became the Industrial Fatigue Research Board in 1918 and was renamed the Industrial Health Research Board in 1928 (Hearnshaw, 1964).

reoccur. The quality of the lines was used to assess ability to control nervousness (Dockeray & Issacs, 1921).

## The United States

The sinking of the British passenger liner *Lusitania* by a German submarine on May 7, 1915, with the loss of 128 American lives, greatly angered the American public. Germany initially suspended its policy of unrestricted submarine warfare in the face of warnings from President Woodrow Wilson. In January 1917, however, in a desperate bid to end the war, Germany resumed open warfare on all ships, including American ships, who could potentially help the Allies. The United States declared war on Germany on April 6, 1917 (Jarausch, 2015). Psychologists had already been discussing ways they could assist the military. At the December 1916 meeting of the APA, G. Stanley Hall discussed the war's potential effect on psychology.[4] He speculated on how it might expedite the United States' independence from European science and on the importance of applied psychology for the war effort. Hall also gave examples of German and French use of psychology in their war efforts (Hall, 1917).

On the day that President Woodrow Wilson signed the Act of Congress declaring war between Germany and the United States, APA President Robert M. Yerkes (1876–1956) was attending a meeting of experimental psychologists at Harvard University. He formed a committee consisting of Raymond S. Dodge, Walter V. Bingham (replaced at this first and only meeting of the committee by Robert M. Ogden), and himself. Yerkes informed the governing APA Council by letter of his intention to appoint a number of additional committees to coordinate the war efforts of the APA. On April 21, he convened a meeting of the Council in Philadelphia, where a nine-person Committee for Psychology was appointed. Among the members of that committee were Guy M. Whipple of the University of Illinois, John B. Watson of Johns Hopkins University, G. Stanley Hall of Clark University, James McKeen Cattell, Edward L. Thorndike of Columbia University, and, eventually, Walter Dill Scott.[5] Twelve additional committees were appointed to address specific areas where psychologists might be useful, such as selecting aviators, treating psychological problems, motivating soldiers, and the psychological examining of

---

[4] See Chapter 9 for biographical information about Hall.
[5] Cattell, whose pacifist leanings were discussed in Chapter 4, later resigned from the Committee (Ferguson, 1962–65).

recruits.[6] These committees varied in their contributions to the war effort (Ferguson, 1962–65). One committee, however, the Committee on the Psychological Examining of Recruits chaired by Yerkes, was to have a major influence not only on the US Army but on the perception of psychology in the general public following the conflict.

Yerkes was a comparative psychologist who is best known today for his work with primates, initially as director of the first primate laboratory in America at Yale University (which eventually became the Yerkes Regional Primate Center of Emory University) (Zusne, 1984). Yerkes did have an interest in human abilities. Before the war, he developed the Point Scale for Measuring Mental Ability, a test he believed was an improvement over the Binet tests.[7] Yerkes viewed mental testing from a purely scientific rather than an applied perspective. As he was interested in the evolutionary development of the mind, Yerkes preferred the term *human engineering* to *applied psychology* in describing his work (von Mayrhauser, 1987). In some ways, he was the antithesis of Walter Dill Scott, who had been involved in applied work for close to two decades, was comfortable identifying as an industrial psychologist, and believed that applied psychology was just as scientific as "pure science" research.[8]

Scott took issue with Yerkes's desire to have psychology under the auspices of the Army Surgeon General. Yerkes viewed psychology as a branch of biology and believed that by having psychological examiners commissioned as officers, the field could capitalize on an association with the established professions of medicine and the military. Scott, on the other hand, wanted psychologists seen not as subservient to physicians but rather as equal to them. He saw the psychologist in the role of a civilian managerial consultant, free to advise the military without officially joining it (von Mayrhauser, 1987). Scott left the Council meeting and, as discussed later in this chapter, went his own way.[9] Yerkes was eventually commissioned as a major in the Sanitary Corps, and a Division of Psychology was established in the Surgeon General's Office (Ferguson, 1962–65).

---

[6] For a complete list of the committees and committee members, see Ferguson (1962–65).

[7] Yerkes's point-scale, developed with James Bridges and Rose Hardwick, used the Binet tests but changed the scoring to a point scale (Pintner, 1923).

[8] Yerkes (1932) subtitled his autobiographical chapter "Psychobiologist," a clear indication of how he viewed himself as a psychologist.

[9] There is some disagreement as to whether Scott "stormed" out of the meeting and whether Bingham also left, as Scott related to Ferguson (1962–65). Ferguson assumed that Scott meant he did not attend the next day, not that he left the April 21 session.

*Army Alpha and Beta*

Members of the Committee on the Examining of Recruits were Robert M. Yerkes (chair), Walter V. Bingham, Henry H. Goddard, Thomas H. Haines, Lewis M. Terman, Frederic L. Wells, and Guy M. Whipple. While Yerkes initially preferred the use of individually administered intelligence tests, Bingham and Terman convinced him that group intelligence tests were the more practical solution for identifying recruits who were cognitively deficient or otherwise unsuitable for service and for the identification of recruits of special ability. The resulting group test was a hodgepodge with ten individual components. Some were adapted from prior tests by Arthur S. Otis, Frederic Wells, Alfred Binet, and others, and some were suggested by work done by the Bureau of Salesmanship Research at the Carnegie Institute of Technology. This test, called "test a," went through a number of field trials and was later revised into two versions, the Army Alpha for literate recruits and the Army Beta for recruits who were unable to read English. Two teams were formed to complete the revisions: The first team were Captain Clarence S. Yoakum, Carl C. Brigham, Margaret V. Cobb, Edward S. Jones, Lewis M. Terman, and Guy M. Whipple. The second team consisted of Lieutenant William S. Foster, C. R. Brown, Arthur S. Otis, Karl T. Waugh, and Raymond H. Wheeler (Ferguson, 1962–65).

The Alpha eliminated two subscales from the *test a* exam: memory for digits and number comparison. The remaining eight subscales were oral directions, disarranged sentences, arithmetical reasoning, information, synonym-antonym, practical judgment, number series completion, and analogies. The Beta test was divided into seven components: maze test, cube analysis, x-o (cross-out) series, digit-symbol test, number checking, pictorial completion, and geometrical construction. Psychological examiners were trained at Camp Greenleaf in Georgia; 354 examiners were then deployed to thirty-five army camps. By the war's end, more than 1,700,000 recruits were tested at a cost of fifty cents per recruit (Ferguson, 1962–65).

How useful was the testing program to the Army: Did it significantly help the war effort? Certainly the Army had a need for the classification of recruits, and the testing of almost 1.75 million individuals is an impressive feat. The success of the program for the Army, however, would have to be characterized as mixed at best. Samelson (1977) noted that Yerkes's published statements relied on testimonials from high-ranking officers and discussed the potential, not actual, usefulness of the tests. Kevles (1968) recounted that many Army officers were suspicious of the tests, considering them impractical and referring to the examiners as "pests." And more seriously, the testing program was viewed as undermining the officers' authority by taking decision-making out of their hands. To be fair to Yerkes, the Army was at times less than completely supportive. It failed to provide Yerkes with the level of authority and staffing that he believed necessary for the program to succeed. Despite a suggestion by the Surgeon General that the peacetime Army continue the program, it was abolished in January 1919.

## The Committee on Classification of Personnel in the Army

Walter Dill Scott believed that the best way for psychologists to assist the Army would be to use the procedures and business model developed at the Carnegie Institute of Technology (CIT). He reasoned that applied psychologists already knew a great deal about how to effectively select and place employees; these techniques could be modified and applied to the military. Scott also saw no need for psychologists to align themselves with the medical profession and inevitably come to play a supporting role to it. In the same way that business owners and managers cooperated with psychologists at CIT, psychologists could best serve the military by operating as civilian consultants, not as commissioned officers.[10] He believed that there was already a highly trained cohort of psychologists capable of this task: the staff and students from the Division of Applied Psychology program at CIT. Many of those individuals did contribute to the war effort, a number working directly with Scott (Ferguson, 1962–65).

Scott first set out to convince the military that his ideas had merit. Along with his students at CIT, Scott modified his Man-to-Man Rating Scale into a *Rating Scale for Selecting Captains*. He then presented his scale to a series of officers, many who were initially skeptical. Through dogged determination and, befitting the director of the Bureau of Salesmanship Research at CIT, an impressive amount of sales ability, Scott was able to convince the Army to give his scale a try (Ferguson, 1962–65). On August 5, 1917, the Secretary of War created the Committee on Classification of Personnel in the Army (CCPA) under the Adjutant General's jurisdiction. The CCPA would operate in a manner similar to CIT's Bureau of Salesmanship Research in that it would be a civilian body providing the Army with advice

---

[10] Nevertheless, the members of the committee and their associates did eventually receive commissions (Thorndike, 1919).

on personnel issues and also conducting research on personnel problems (Strong, 1918).

Bingham (1919) and Strong (1918) provided contemporary accounts of the work of the CCPA that included a list of committee members; Thorndike (1919) also offered a brief summary of the committee's efforts. Members were a mixture of psychologists and businesspersons. Scott served as the Committee's Director; Walter Van Dyke Bingham was Executive Secretary, and Edward. L. Thorndike was Chairman. In addition to these three, the original committee members were businesspersons Robert C. Clothier of the A. M. Collins Manufacturing Company and Horace L. Gardner of the Du Pont Powder Company, along with the psychologists James R. Angell of the University of Chicago, Raymond Dodge of Wesleyan University, J. F. Shepard of the University of Michigan, Edward K. Strong Jr. of George Peabody College for Teachers, Lewis S. Terman of Stanford University, John B. Watson of Johns Hopkins University, and Robert M. Yerkes of the University of Minnesota (Ferguson, 1962–65). While Yerkes became a member of the CCPA, he did not want his work on intelligence testing to come under Scott's control. Yerkes, as previously noted, requested a commission as an officer and was appointed a major in the Sanitary Corps under the Surgeon General. Cooperation between the CCPA and Yerkes' Committee on the Psychological Examining of Recruits was minimal (von Mayrhauser, 1987). In addition to the CCPA members, psychologists and others served as civilian associates of the Committee, military associates, supervisors in military camps, civilian associates in the Division of War Service Exchange, and civilian associates in the Division of Trade Tests (Strong, 1918).

The wartime work of the CCPA was wide-ranging and included a comprehensive personnel program for the Army. Thorndike (1919) likened the work to that of "an enormous and glorified employment agency," albeit one whose "work was a continuous study of human nature and the application of scientific management" (p. 56). Among the accomplishments of the Committee were the classification and placement of close to a million recruits, the development of trade specifications for approximately 600 trades, an index of occupations, tables of occupational needs of personnel specifications for Army units, trade tests for selecting skilled workers that were administered to approximately 130,000 recruits, and a rating system for evaluating officers. In addition, the Committee investigated procedures for selecting aviators, assisted the Navy and Marine Corps in developing a personnel system similar to the Army system, and conducted a study of the personnel system used by the British (Bingham, 1919; Strong, 1918). The work of the CCPA also did foundational work in person analysis and job analysis (Katzell & Austin, 1992). Unlike the intelligence testing work championed by Yerkes, the CCPA was incorporated into the Army in 1918, and many of its procedures were retained (Kevles, 1968). As evidence of Scott's influence and standing, he was the only psychologist awarded a Distinguished Service Medal in World War I, and he was elected president of the APA in 1919.

## Other Contributions to the War Effort

While the personnel selection and placement work of the CCPA and the widespread testing of recruits via the Army Alpha and Beta tests represented a large part of the activities of American psychologists in World War I, there were efforts in other areas that deserve mention. For the first time, morale officers, initially psychologists, were assigned to camps to provide "psychological stimulation of troops"; that is, to keep the troops contented, disciplined, and enthusiastic and eventually to assist soldiers in deployment (Foster, 1919, p. 47). Raymond Dodge, working under the Subcommittee on the Psychology of Special Abilities, developed a simulation that was used both to test applicants for shipboard gun-pointers and to train gun-trainers and gun-pointers. The Navy built sixty of these instruments to be used at its shore-training stations (Thorndike, 1919).

### Aviation Psychology in the United States

As in European countries, there was considerable effort devoted to applying psychology to aviation in America. The need to obtain qualified pilots was acute. By April 1917, the Aviation Section of the Signal Corps had fifty-two trained pilots. By war's end, an Air Service with approximately 16,000 pilots was in place (Henmon, 1919). A systematic method of selecting pilots was needed, as the cost of trial-and-error selection and training would be enormous in personal injury and damaged aircraft. According to Thorndike (1919), to be a successful aviator in the US Army, a candidate must have the ability to complete a ground course in a School of Military Aeronautics; be able to learn to fly in a reasonable amount of time in Aviation School; have the "mental and moral make-up qualifying him for a commission in the army"; and be competent in actual service as a pursuit pilot, observation pilot, bomber pilot, or flight instructor (p. 58).

In June 1917, the National Research Council Committee on Aviation evaluated tests used by the Italians and the French. About forty tests were assessed by Harold E. Burtt, Walter R. Miles, and Leonard T. Troland at the Massachusetts Institute of Technology Ground School; however, no strong conclusions about the efficacy of the tests were drawn (Henmon, 1919). George M. Stratton conducted a similar tryout of tests in San Diego. In April 1918, Stratton, V. A. C. Henmon, and, from the CCPA, Edward L. Thorndike began a systematic evaluation of predictors used in selecting aviators (Thorndike, 1919).[11] Using a sample of cadets and flying instructors from two airfields, the following ten tests were evaluated: Emotional Stability was assessed in a manner similar to that done in Europe. Hand tremor, pulse rate, respiration rate, and ability to solve addition problems were measured in response to a pistol discharge. A tilting chair was used to evaluate Perception of Tilt, while the subject's ability to stand steadily assessed Swaying. Quickness of response to a stimulus was used to measure Visual Reaction and Auditory Reaction, and Equilibrium Reaction was determined by measuring quickness of response to sudden changes of body position using a tilting table. The visual and auditory reaction times were summed, and then the equilibrium reaction time was subtracted from that total to obtain the Equilibrium Differential. The Extension of Curves test simulated distance judgment necessary to land aircraft, Thorndike's Mental Alertness Test was used as a general intelligence test, and, finally, an application blank was developed to assess a candidate's Athletic Achievement and Interest (Henmon, 1919).

While athletic achievement had the highest correlation with the criterion of flying ability, that correlation was discounted for unspecified reasons. Tests showing high individual correlations with the criterion were emotional stability, perception of tilt, and mental alertness. The multiple correlation for those predictors was estimated to be 0.70. The researchers recommended the use of partial correlation coefficients and regression to determine optimal weighting of those predictors. The tests were deemed successful enough at differentiating good pilots from poor pilots that the Air Service authorized their introduction; however, the "all too familiar vexatious delays in securing necessary personnel and equipment" prevented their full implementation before the armistice ending the war was signed (Henmon, 1919, p. 109).[12]

---

[11]  Henmon (1919) reported the starting month as March.

[12]  There was other testing of aviators conducted during the war, some of it overseas. The interested reader can find summaries in Dockeray and Issacs (1921) and Thorndike (1919).

Knight Dunlap (1932) recalled his work with John Watson in the Medical Research Board of the Air Service. They investigated candidates' endurance in low oxygen conditions. Dunlap remembered his wartime experiences as frustrating not because of the work but because of poor decisions made by "a small group of medical officers of no scientific ability . . . interested only in building a large organization and elevating themselves" (p. 48). He noted that the use of rotation tests to assess candidate's equilibrium that was promoted by these medical officers had become a "scandal." Top pilots failed the tests, and applicants who failed the tests later become successful pilots for foreign forces. Dunlap investigated the validity of the tests using trained acrobats and found that even the acrobats failed for "their lack of equilibrium" (p. 49). Despite their lack of validity, the tests continued to be used, although the extent to which examining boards used them is open to question.

### Personality Testing

In addition to the cognitive ability tests, trade tests, rating scales, and other tests, perhaps the earliest example of the modern self-report personality test came out of World War I. Created by Robert S. Woodworth, the purpose of what later came to be called the *Personal Data Sheet* was to predict which recruits were susceptible to shell shock. Giving extensive individual psychiatric exams to recruits was impractical. Therefore, Woodworth developed a group test to measure symptoms of emotional stability or neuroticism. Emotional stability here was defined much as it is today as freedom from neurotic tendencies or behavior, distinct from the emotional reaction or emotional stability construct described in the previous summary of aviation psychology. Woodworth scanned case studies in the psychiatric literature for symptoms of neurotic behavior and wrote questions based on those symptoms. Examples are "Do you ever feel an awful pressure in and about the head?" and "Do you know of anybody who is trying to do you harm?" While conceding that any one symptom could easily occur in the "normal" population, Woodworth believed an accumulation of symptoms represented the potential for difficulty in combat situations. The original inventory had "about 100" items; the subsequent *Personal Data Sheet* had 116. When evaluating the original inventory, Woodworth found that the college students averaged about ten symptoms, while soldiers being treated for shell shock averaged about thirty symptoms. Woodworth reported that A. T. Poffenberger collaborated in the first draft preparation, E. G. Boring helped in obtaining sample results from the Army, and H. L. Hollingworth used the inventory on soldiers who had been sent home due to shell shock (Woodworth, 1919, 1932).

A more impressionistic attempt to understand the personality and temperament of soldiers – in this case, pilots – was undertaken by Floyd C. Dockeray. Dockeray underwent flight training and was commissioned as a captain on active duty. While doing so, he was able to meet with hundreds of pilots, whom he found were much more likely to speak freely to him as a fellow officer and pilot than would be likely if he were an experimenter in a laboratory setting. Among Dockeray's conclusions were that more than in other branches of service, flying requires "individualism"; cadets proceed at their own individual pace when learning to fly and at times do not "feel" ready to fly. Regarding their personalities, Dockeray was unable to draw any generalizations other than successful pilots need intelligence, good judgment, and the ability to adapt quickly to new situations. He believed quiet, methodical individuals were generally good pilots and warned that while "nervous, high strung individuals, or those bordering on the temperamental" can become good pilots, they are also the ones who would be most likely to experience adverse effects from stress (Dockeray & Issacs, 1921, p. 147).

## Performance Appraisal and Training

The prototype of the rating scale used to evaluate more than 180,000 US Army officers was developed by Walter Dill Scott and his colleagues at the Carnegie Institute of Technology in 1917 for use in selecting salespersons (Ferguson, 1961). Later called the Man-to-Man Rating Scale, Scott modified it for rating officers and, as noted previously, through a determined effort on his part eventually convinced the initially reluctant Army hierarchy of the scale's usefulness (Ferguson, 1962–65). Despite its popularity, the scale did have some drawbacks. Each rater had to construct his individual master scale. This process proved difficult, took a great deal of time, and further, because each master scale was unique, did not allow comparison across raters (Farr & Levy, 2007).

In addition to successfully selecting, placing, and evaluating the performance of a large number of recruits, the military was faced with the task of training roughly half a million soldiers for close to 100 trade jobs. There was a need for standardization in training methods. The result was the "show, tell, do, check" method developed by the Energy Fleet Corporation of the US Shipping Board. Among the common-sense training principles posited were that workers should be trained on the job, that supervisors should conduct the training, and that these supervisors should receive instruction on how best to train (Kraiger & Ford, 2007).

## Scientific Management and World War I

Industrial psychology was not the only professional group that contributed to management practices in World War I. Practitioners of Taylor's scientific management system also offered their services to the US military. The Taylor Society suspended its activities for the duration of the war, as half of its members were involved in wartime activities (Brown, 1925). Harlow S. Person, commissioned as a major, organized the administration of a number of war bureaus, and the Gilbreths used time-and-motion techniques to assist disabled soldiers. The practitioner of scientific management who had the greatest impact on the military, however, was Henry L. Gantt (Van De Water, 1997).

Gantt, who befriended Frederick Taylor when they both worked at Midvale Steel, was a mechanical engineer who focused on the worker, not the machine. Among his extensions of Taylor's system was a task and bonus system (Gantt, 1901). Gantt was highly critical of American industry's inefficient management and its lack of readiness for a wartime conflict. With the outbreak of war, he set out to improve weapon and ship production. Gantt developed a bar chart, the Gantt chart, to coordinate munitions production for the Army's Ordnance Bureau by permitting enhanced maintenance and control of production. He advised the Emergency Fleet Corporation and Shipping Board to use his procedures for organizing harbors, repairing ships, and shipbuilding. The production of new ships was critical, as German submarines were sinking ships faster than they could be built. In 1918, more ships were produced in the United States than were built worldwide in 1917, and the time needed to repair and load ships was cut in half from four to two weeks (Alford, 1934; Van De Water, 1997).

Gantt did not seek recognition for his efforts. He resigned his consulting practice, was not commissioned as an officer, and accepted no payment for his services. Like Scott, he was awarded the Congressional Distinguished Service Medal for his contribution to the war effort. Unlike the psychologists discussed later, he did not set out to publicize his wartime work or that of his colleagues. His charts were influential however. Wallace Clark's (1922) *The Gantt Chart: A Working Tool of Management* popularized the technique. It was translated into many languages, including Russian. The *Gantt Chart* sold more than 100,000 copies in Russia and may have been an integral component of the five-year plans there (Alford, 1934; Van De Water, 1997).

### The Afterlife of the Army Alpha and Beta Testing Program

While the military's response to the Alpha and Beta testing was ambiguous at best, the general public perceived the testing program to be a great success. This perception was helped by positive summaries presented by the testing program principals. As discussed in the Chapter 6, this perception fueled a boom in psychological testing and the use of industrial psychologists in industry in the early 1920s. How the results of the Army testing program were interpreted, however, led to a great deal of controversy. Consistent with the Darwinian emphasis on the role of heredity in shaping organisms, some psychologists took a hereditarian view of human behavior and mental processes. This was true for many of the individuals responsible for developing and administering the Army Alpha and Beta tests. They set out to develop tests that measured innate ability. For some of the psychologists associated with the testing program, such as Yerkes, Lewis Terman, and Carl C. Brigham, the focus after the war became the scientific value of the results of that program. They analyzed the enormous amount of data that resulted from testing nearly 2 million recruits (Samelson, 1977). Yerkes (1921) oversaw the analysis, and he coauthored *Army Mental Tests* with Clarence Yoakum describing the program (Yoakum & Yerkes, 1920). Brigham, who served with Yerkes and later became a professor at Princeton University, published his own book, *A Study of American Intelligence* (1923). Other contemporary books about intelligence testing (e.g., Pintner, 1923) made heavy use of the Army data and results.

The conclusions drawn by these researchers were contentious then and now. They provided fodder for the heredity versus environment controversy in intelligence that has flared up periodically over the past century.[13] Because industrial psychologists made use of these types of tests after the war, it is worth examining how the concept of intelligence, or what today we would call cognitive ability, was perceived in the 1920s. There were

---

[13] The World War I Army Alpha and Beta testing program was introduced to a whole new generation of readers with the publication of Stephen Jay Gould's *The Mismeasure of Man* in 1981. Gould attacked the hereditarian view of intelligence through a discussion of craniometry (the measurement of brain size), factor analysis, and the Army Alpha and Beta. The book itself has been quite controversial. It was well received by some but heavily criticized by others, including psychologists, for its alleged polemical viewpoint, cherry-picking of quotations and examples, faulty analyses, and misrepresentation of the motives of people and events (e.g., Humphreys, 1983).

multiple definitions of intelligence available during that time. Pintner (1923) in his text on intelligence testing gives a least a dozen definitions, some of them contradictory. He concluded, following Stern, that the most commonly accepted and most apt definition was that "[g]eneral intelligence is the ability of the organism to adjust itself adequately to new situations" (p. 55, italics omitted). While this definition said nothing about how this adaptive ability was acquired, many psychologists assumed it was primarily due to heredity.

Yerkes (1921) made several assumptions in his interpretation of the results of the Army group testing program: that the tests measured innate intelligence, that intelligence was primarily due to heredity, and that the Army samples were representative of the American population (Sokal, 1984). Among the major findings were that white Americans had an average mental age of 13.08 years, that African Americans had a mental age that was significantly lower at 10.41 years, and that immigrant groups could be rank-ordered based on their average mental age, with immigrants from northern and western Europe ranking higher than those from eastern and southern Europe (Yerkes, 1921). Yerkes (1921) and Brigham (1923) explained these differences from a hereditarian perspective, that the lower-scoring groups were innately inferior in intelligence than the higher-scoring groups. Downplayed or dismissed were explanations that explained the differences as due to environmental factors, such as years of schooling, familiarity with the English language, or familiarity with American culture.

From a present-day perspective, it is obvious that the hereditarian explanations for the group score differences were not supported by the evidence. At best, the appropriate conclusion regarding the reasons for group differences should have been that the researchers did not know. Problems were manifold. For one, given the lack of support for the testing program by the Army command structure, there was great variability in how the tests were administered. Testing conditions at times were chaotic, instructions could be difficult to understand or even hear, particularly for the Beta exam, and promised follow-up testing was not given. Many of the recipients of the Beta test had never before taken an exam. The tests included questions that were clearly dependent on a knowledge of American culture, something recent immigrants generally lacked (Kevles, 1968).

Racism was the norm in the US Army during World War I.[14] African American recruits were segregated into jobs requiring manual labor,

---

[14] In their summary of 100 years of research on discrimination that was published in the *Journal of Applied Psychology*, Colella, Hebl, and King (2017) cited research studies conducted during the 1920s

butchery, or grave digging. Some were placed into the segregated Pioneer infantry (Scott, 1919; cited in Guthrie, 1998). African Americans overwhelmingly were given the difficult-to-administer Beta exam regardless of their level of literacy. Some psychologists involved in the testing program believed African Americans were innately inferior in intelligence. One example was the chief examiner at Camp Lee in Virginia, Lt. George O. Ferguson, the author of the prewar *Psychology of the Negro* (cited in Guthrie, 1998). More than 5,000 African American recruits were tested at Camp Lee. While it is true that no African American had yet be awarded a Ph.D. in psychology in the United States, no African Americans were permitted to participate at any level in the administration of the Army testing centers (Guthrie, 1998).[15]

At the time, a number of psychologists spoke out against Yerkes and Brigham's interpretations. Edwin Boring, for example, questioned Brigham's assumption that the tests measured innate ability and thought Brigham's conclusions were premature given other alternative explanations. The overall reaction from the psychology community to Brigham's book in particular was negative (Minton, 1997). Psychologists questioned the underlying hereditarian assumptions of the mental testers. William C. Bagley's (1874–1946) critique is representative. He examined the implications of assuming intelligence is innate and relatively fixed. Bagley was a 1900 Cornell University Ph.D. who was a professor of education at Teachers College, Columbia University, from 1917 to 1940. Bagley (1922) was careful to insist he had a great deal of admiration and respect for psychologists working on mental measurements. Given the limited understanding of intelligence, however, he was troubled by the belief that a child's potential could be determined early on and, if found deficient, no amount of education could make up the deficiency. In this view, school was "much more of a certifying agency than an educating agency" (p. 375). Bagley stated that the assumption that native intelligence can be inferred by measuring acquired ability is flawed; it assumes that the experience, education, and environment of those being tested are identical. He is, in essence,

and 1930s that assumed the inferiority of women and various racial and ethnic groups to white males. These studies looked for differences in intelligence, temperament, and ability between majority group members and other groups such as African Americans, Native Americans, and Asians.

[15] The first African American to earn a Ph.D. in psychology in the United States was Francis Cecil Sumner (1895–1954), who received his doctorate at Clark University in 1920. Drafted out of graduate school in 1918, Sumner had hoped to be considered for officer training but instead was transferred to the Pioneer Infantry and sent to combat in France. Sumner survived the war and went on to a long academic career, most notably at Howard University (Guthrie, 1998).

making the "nurture" argument in the nature-nurture controversy over cognitive ability.

Bagley wrote that while the determinist is skeptical that education can lift individuals beyond their innate limitations, for the determinist "one lesson can be effectively and universally taught. Every man, he nonchalantly assumes, can be taught to know his own place, appreciate his own limitations, and mind his own business" (p. 379). Bagley did not deny that there are innate differences in intellectual ability, but he believed the assumption that these differences are controlling was undemocratic. Not surprisingly, Lewis Terman disagreed. In a somewhat sarcastic editorial responding to Bagley's attack, Terman (1922) accused Bagley of being a sentimentalist who preferred to believe in "miracles" rather than scientific evidence. In Terman's view, because accepting the reality of significant inborn differences would mean abandonment of the democratic ideal, Bagley dismissed them as practically nonexistent. Terman claimed that Bagley put the burden of proof entirely on the "determinist" to essentially prove a universal negative: to prove beyond any doubt that heredity sets the limits for achievement. This is unfair, according to Terman, who thought the standard should be the preponderance of evidence, not total certainty. Further, Terman accused Bagley of waging a fight against a straw person. There was no intention to limit secondary education to high-IQ students nor to limit the vocational possibilities of the lower-IQ ones. There was simply a desire to develop an educational curriculum tailored to the intellectual capacity of the student to make the most of each child's future regardless of his or her intellectual capacity. For Terman, the existence of native differences in mentality had been amply supported. As for democracy: "Certainly any definition to be acceptable will have to square with the demonstrable facts of biological and psychological science" (p. 62).

The industrial psychologist Henry C. Link, like Bagley, took issue with the hereditarian interpretation of intelligence test scores. Link included a chapter on general intelligence in his 1919 text *Employment Psychology*, written in the form of an imaginary dialogue among a manager, employment division head, psychological section head, and psychological examiner.[16] The manager and employment division head start with the belief that general intelligence is the most important attribute for worker success but then through a series of questions and answers are led by the

---

[16] It is interesting and reflective of the importance applied psychology had for women, who were often closed out of traditional academic positions, that both the head of the psychological section and the psychological examiner are portrayed as women in Link's set piece.

psychological section head and psychological examiner to a more useful and nuanced view of multiple kinds of intelligences rather than a single, monolithic intelligence for the purpose of selecting employees. Link made it clear in this chapter that he questioned the existence of general intelligence and that he viewed performance on tests of general intelligence as primarily due to education, not heredity.

Writing later in *The Atlantic Monthly*, Link (1923b) noted that psychology is an immature science, barely a quarter century old. He wrote that while popular interest moves quickly, science does not. Taking direct aim at the group difference results of the Army tests, Link stated that the conclusions drawn by Yerkes, Brigham, and the other Army psychologists are unsupported by the evidence. He did not have an issue with the tests themselves and called intelligence tests the greatest contribution to education at the time. Link, however, did not see as reasonable the conclusion that these tests measure only innate ability. Common sense "compels" an admission that education and the environment would also have an effect. Until those factors can be held constant, no interpretation that intelligence tests measure innate ability is possible. Link saw these tests as measuring attainment, not intelligence. Before making an inference that any race or group is inferior to another, one must be certain that individuals in those groups have equally favorable social, economic, and educational environments. Link (1923b) concluded that "*[t]here is absolutely nothing in the technique of intelligence tests as applied so far, which warrants any comparison whatsoever between the inherent intelligence of various groups or races*" (p. 381, italics in original). For Link, the only conclusion that can be drawn is that the scores are different, and these differences can be due to any one of multiple factors.

Another prominent industrial psychologist who urged caution in the use and interpretation of tests of general intelligence was Morris Viteles. While not discounting their potential usefulness if properly validated, Viteles (1921) questioned whether grouping diverse occupations by general intelligence is as valid as the use of specific job requirements.[17] He advocated using selection tests that assess specific abilities that are critical for job

---

[17] In the analysis of the Army test data, occupations were grouped based on the median score of recruits in that occupation. So, for example, farmers, laborers, miners, and teamsters were in the lowest score group (scores of 45–49), while Army chaplains and engineer officers were in the highest score group (125 and over). E. L. Thorndike (1919) reproduced seventeen occupational groupings. Even a cursory examination of the groupings show that jobs requiring the most formal education have the highest median scores. Thorndike also noted that the intelligence test he developed for the selection of pilots was found to be useful as a substitute for years of schooling as a predictor, surely an indication that test scores and educational level are related.

success rather than the use of general measures of intelligence (Viteles, 1974). Based on his own research (Viteles, 1928a) and on other studies available at the time, Viteles (1974) found the assertion that differences between African Americans and Whites in intelligence test scores were due to innate rather than social or educational opportunities to be completely unsupported.

There were also critics of the nativist position from outside psychology. The Columbia University anthropologist Franz Boas and his students conducted studies demonstrating the importance of cultural factors in testing. In the popular press, Walter Lippmann wrote a series of articles in the *New Republic* singling out Lewis Terman and attacking the scientific assumptions behind the tests, in particular the assumption that the tests measured innate ability. Terman defended himself in the *New Republic*; however he was evasive regarding a number of Lippmann's assertions and unfairly criticized Lippmann's expertise on technical issues (Minton, 1997).

Did the emphasis on innate group differences by the Army testers have an effect beyond the confines of psychology? It is true that during the time of this debate, the US Congress passed the Immigration Restriction Act of 1924, which limited immigration in a way proportionally similar to the rank-ordering of immigrant groups by mental age in the Army data. It is also true that some psychologists – Yerkes, for example – made the Army testing data available to Congress. There is some disagreement over that impact of the information, with some chroniclers (e.g., Gould, 1981; Kamin, 1975) arguing the effect was significant and others (e.g., Samelson, 1977; Sokal, 1984) arguing that the influence was relatively minor. It is safe to say that given the mood of the country and the Congress, immigration would have been restricted with or without the help of the results of the Army group intelligence testing program.

By the end of the 1920s, psychology was moving toward a greater emphasis on environmental causes, as exemplified by the rise of the behaviorist orientation. Even some of the strongest advocates for the innate nature of differences in intelligence began to rethink their assumptions. Carl Brigham (1930), for example, published a *mea culpa* titled *Intelligence Tests of Immigrant Groups*, where he discussed other possible explanations for the Army group differences. While most of the article focuses on technical issues such as the inadvisability of adding together subtests that measure different abilities, in the penultimate paragraph, he states: "For purposes of comparing individuals or groups, it is apparent that tests in the vernacular must be used only with individuals having equal opportunities to acquire the vernacular of the test" (p. 165). In other words, it is unfair to compare individuals or groups unless they have equal familiarity with the language and culture of the test. Brigham therefore concludes that his own 1923 comparative study "was without foundation" (p. 165).

Despite disagreement at the time as to what the tests were actually measuring, following the war there was a great deal of interest in using intelligence tests in education and industry. E. L. Thorndike (1919), for example, advocated assessing every child starting at age ten and continuing at four-year intervals until age twenty-two. This "census of intellect ... would give superintendents of schools, commissioners of charity, mayors of cities and governors of states facts which they really need every day in their business" (p. 56). In the early 1920s, these tests were taken up by American industry with mixed results, as discussed in Chapter 6.

## Chapter Summary

World War I provided an unprecedented opportunity for psychologists to apply their theories and procedures to large military samples. In continental Europe, the emphasis was on apparatus-based testing and the use of physiological criteria. While some selection activity took place in Great Britain, a more significant volume of work focused on the analysis and reduction of fatigue in workers involved in the war effort. This is illustrated by the work of the Health of Munitions Workers Committee, established in 1915. In the United States, two major efforts in applying industrial psychology were the work of the Committee on the Psychological Examining of Recruits under the leadership of Robert Yerkes and the Committee on Classification of Personnel in the Army under the leadership of Walter Dill Scott. The former, part of the Sanitary Corps in the Surgeon General's Office, developed the Army Alpha and Beta tests. These intelligence tests were used to classify approximately 1,700,000 recruits. The Committee on Classification of Personnel in the Army, on the other hand, operated under a consulting model, with civilian contractors developing a comprehensive personnel program for the Army. While this model arguably proved more successful and had a greater influence on the military and on industrial psychology, the Army Alpha and Beta testing was perceived by the public as successful, contributing to an increase in testing activity in the private sector after the war ended. The Army Alpha and Beta tests and the interpretation of their results generated a fair amount of controversy after the war. Yerkes and other who worked on the tests rank-ordered groups of individuals based on their test scores, resulting in hierarchies of racial and ethnic groups. The testers interpreted these differences in average group test performance as due to differences in heredity. There was pushback by psychologists and others, who argued that the tests were not culture-neutral and that average score differences could just as easily be due to environmental factors rather than hereditary ones.

The efforts of psychologists in World War I did demonstrate that the new science of psychology could have potential usefulness for business, particularly in the area of employee selection. This contributed to the expansion of industrial psychology, both in number of practitioners where it was already established and in the migration of the field to countries were it had yet to appear. Chapter 6 describes that expansion of industrial psychology though the 1920s.

# The Postwar Expansion of Industrial Psychology

After World War I, industrial psychology expanded in those countries where it was already established and was exported to many countries where it was yet to be found. This chapter covers that expansion and migration from the end of World War I to the early 1930s, organized by geographical region. This is a representative sample, not a comprehensive accounting of global industrial psychology during the fifteen or so years following the war. Not every country can be discussed. In some countries, industrial psychology developed for the most part after the 1920s; some of that history appears in the Appendix.[1] This chapter is focused on traditional industrial psychology topics. In Chapter 7, psychology applied to employee selection is examined in more detail. Organizational psychology topics such as leadership and motivation are discussed in Chapter 10.

## Asia

### China

China has a very long history of assessing talent for government positions, dating to the Wei (220–265 CE) and Jin (265–402 CE) dynasties. Interest in modern industrial psychology, however, dates to the 1920s. The American psychologist and philosopher John Dewey, an early advocate of functionalism, gave a lecture tour between 1919 and 1921 and exposed Chinese intellectuals to this orientation. In addition, a number of Chinese nationals studied under Dewey and other functionalists in the United States. It was not until the mid-1930s, however, that China had its first industrial psychologist. Chen Li (1902–2004) studied psychology in

---

[1] Canada, India, and many countries in Africa and South America would be examples of places where I-O psychology developed for the most part after the 1920s (McCollom, 1968). In addition to countries that adopted I-O psychology after the time period covered in this book, there were others where information about the development of I-O was too fragmented and incomplete to include.

Europe, initially at the University College, London, with Charles Spearman. When Spearman retired in 1931, Chen was left without a mentor. He spent a term at Cambridge University working with Frederic C. Bartlett and then returned to University College to complete his doctorate under John C. Flugel. Chen then decided to study with Charles S. Myers at the National Institute of Industrial Psychology, where he became proficient in statistics and psychological testing. He also worked with the Gestalt psychologist Wolfgang Köhler in Germany before returning to China in 1935 amid concerns for his safety under the increasingly powerful Nazi regime. In China, Chen received a joint appointment at Qinghua University in Beijing and at the Institute of Psychology. He taught a course in industrial psychology, conducted research on fatigue, consulted with railway factories, and wrote the first industrial psychology textbook in China: *General Introduction to Industrial Psychology* (1935; cited in Hsueh & Guo, 2012). Later Chen focused on the study of intelligence. Although respectful of his first mentor Spearman's two-factor theory, he corresponded with L. L. Thurstone and broadened his view of intelligence beyond Spearman's two-factor approach (Blowers, 1998; Hsueh & Guo, 2012).

## Japan

In Japan, there were some pre–World War I attempts at applying psychology in the areas of advertising and efficiency (Takasuna, 2012). In the early years of the twentieth century, research on fatigue was conducted by Hiroshi Chiwa and Tsuruko Haraguchi (Kirihara, 1959; Takasuna, 2012). The scientific management approach was also popular during that time period. Works on scientific management and industrial psychology appeared, including translations of Frederick Taylor's *Principles of Scientific Management* by Y. Hoshino in 1912, Hugo Münsterberg's *Psychology and Industrial Efficiency* by K. Suzuki in 1915, and Bernard Muscio's *Lectures on Industrial Psychology* by Riichi Tokiguchi in 1919. Also notable was Yôichi Ueno's (1883–1957) *Lectures on Increasing Efficiency*, published in 1912 (cited in Kirihara, 1959).[2] Japanese psychologists also traveled abroad to observe industrial psychology practice and research. In 1916, research into employee performance, fatigue, and hours of work were begun in telegraph and post offices (Kirihara, 1959).

---

[2] Yôichi Ueno's name also appeared as Uyeno in, for example, the News Notes section of the *Journal of Personnel Research* (1922–23).

The military's interest in industrial psychology began in World War I, which led to industrial psychology work at the Institute of Aeronautics, the Japanese Imperial Navy, and the Japanese Imperial Army. The Institute of Aeronautics was founded in 1918 at Tokyo Imperial University. Two years later, it established an aeronautic psychology department to conduct research on physical and psychological factors involved in aviation. Matataro Matsumoto (1865–1943) served as a consultant in establishing that department. An important figure in the development of psychology in Japan, Matsumoto attended lectures given by Wilhelm Wundt at the University of Leipzig and in 1899 received his doctorate from Yale University, where he worked with Edward W. Scripture. In 1927, Matsumoto was elected the first president of the Japanese Psychological Association (Takasuna, 2012). He established an experimental psychology laboratory at the University of Kyoto in 1908 and from early on demonstrated an interest in applying psychology to industry (Kirihara, 1959).

Appointed as an advisor to the Investigating Committee on the Navy's Application of Experimental Psychology in 1918, Matsumoto observed the use of psychology in the US military in 1918 and 1919. His report on the intelligence tests used by the US military led to the use of similar tests in Japan. An aptitude test division was established at the Naval Institute of Technology, and aptitude tests for telegraphers, artillery operators, pilots, and machinists were developed in 1925 and 1926. The Army also conducted some limited research on intelligence tests in 1924 (Awaji, 1927, 1928, cited in Takasuna, 2012). On the civilian side, the president of the Kurashiki Cotton Mill Company, Magosaburô Ohara, founded the Ohara Institute for Social Research in 1919 to investigate social problems using economic tools. In 1921, Ohara established a sister organization, the Institute for Science and Labour, which took a biological perspective on worker behavior and labor problems. There was also work being done around this time on vocational guidance, some of it involving psychologists (Kirihara, 1959).

Shigemi H. Kirihara (1959) dates the beginning of industrial psychology as a discipline to 1920, following the translation of Muscio's (1917) text in 1919. In 1920, Kirihara (1892–1968) himself conducted a study on fatigue in women day-shift and night-shift workers at the Kurashiki Spinning Mill. He claimed this study to be the first in Japan to apply experimental research methods in an industrial factory setting. Also relevant to the development of industrial psychology, Gito Teruoka organized the Institute for Science and Labour in 1921. On the academic side, in 1924, Yukiyoshi Koga began a course in industrial psychology at Nagoya Commercial College (Kirihara, 1959).

In the early 1920s, Yôichi Ueno visited the Division of Applied Psychology at the Carnegie Institute of Technology in Pittsburgh. While in America, he prepared an account of the current state of Japanese industrial psychology for the *Journal of Personnel Research*. According to Ueno, in 1917, a Japanese association for the promotion of industrial relations was founded by the government. In 1921, the Department of Industrial Psychology was established as part of that association. Goals of the department included providing equipment and staff to conduct research on the scientific basis of management, providing managerial training, promoting efficiency in factories, and maintaining an industrial psychology library. Ueno noted that he had been applying scientific management methods to factories in Tokyo and Osaka since 1920. He had also conducted research on advertising effectiveness for a tonic drink company in Tokyo (News Notes, 1922–23).

## Europe

### Belgium

Initial work relevant to industrial psychology in Belgium involved vocational guidance. The Belgian Military Institute provided vocational guidance to veterans following World War I. In addition, Joseph Cardijn (1882–1967), a Catholic priest, founded the Young Christian Workers movement in 1925. This movement opened centers that provided professional guidance. While employers did use psychological tests for employee selection in Belgium, academic industrial psychology was slow to develop due to objections to empirical research by philosophers (Warr, 2007).

### Czechoslovakia (Currently the Czech Republic and Slovakia)

Shortly after Czechoslovakia's formation in 1918, the Psychotechnical Institute was established in Prague in 1920 as a component of President Tomáš Masaryk's Academy of Work. Among outside specialists who assisted in the early activities of the Institute were the German psychotechnicians Walter Blumenfeld and Ewald Sachsenberg and the American advocate of scientific management Frank Gilbreth. A vocational guidance center was established as part of the Institute from 1921 to 1924. In 1929, an extension of the Institute was established in Bratislava in present-day Slovakia, initially overseen by Josef Stavěl (1901–86). Stavěl also assisted in the establishment of a network of counseling centers. Psychotechnic activity was similar to the work being conducted in the United States and in Germany at the time. For example, in 1925, tests were used to select tram drivers and train drivers (Paulík, 2004), and Vilém Forster (1882–1932) developed selection tests for pilots and drivers (Forster, 1928–29). Psychotechnics laboratories were established in industries such as the Prague electric companies in 1925 (Paulík, 2004), and guidance centers were established at the Vítkovice steelworks (Hoskovec, 2012). By 1926, there were eleven psychotechnical institutes in the country (Viteles, 1932).

## France

Kitson (1921b) noted that the strong influence of the Taylor system of scientific management ("le taylorisme") had "developed into a veritable cult among French engineers" (p. 287). In addition to scientific management, there was activity in selection and in vocational guidance. Jean-Marie Lahy, who pioneered selection test use in the first decade of the twentieth century, was still very much active in 1920s industrial psychology. Using an approach based on differential psychology and a forerunner of ergonomics (Warr, 2007), Lahy's primary focus was on the proper place of each worker in a scientifically designed workplace (Parot, 2012). His work encompassed topics such as personnel selection and vocational guidance (Fryer, 1923–24). Also active in vocational guidance was Henri Piéron (1881–1964), who in 1928 established the Institut National d'Orientation Professionnelle (National Institute of Vocational Guidance) for that purpose (Parot, 2012). Piéron was also responsible for the Psychological Institute at Sorbonne University. Founded in 1920, the Institute's purpose was to train psychologists in clinical, school, and work psychology (Warr, 2007).

## Germany

In the aftermath of its defeat in World War I, Germany was on the verge of bankruptcy. Money was not forthcoming for establishing new psychological laboratories in universities, and the education ministries preferred supporting the psychologists' old rivals, the less expensive philosophers. Growth in psychology was in the applied arena. The military remembered the services of wartime psychologists and wanted that work to continue (Gundlach, 2012). In 1920, the German War Ministry issued an order for the development of psychology. The Commission for Questions of Army Psychotechnic was founded in 1925, and around that same time a psychological examining center was established in Stuttgart and the German Army began using group situation tests (Fitts, 1946). Johann Baptist Rieffert (1883–1956) was the director of German military psychology. Along with Hans Friedländer, Johannes Rudert, and Philipp Lersch, Rieffert developed one of the first examples of the leaderless group technique, the *Kolloquium* (Ansbacher, 1951). By 1927, Army officer candidates were required to complete psychological examinations; a year later, the Navy did the same (Fitts, 1946).

While psychotechnics had been used in the private sector before World War I, its use greatly expanded after that conflict. Viteles (1923) counted twenty-two large business concerns that in 1922 had their own psychological laboratories. Psychotechnical testing took place in 170 testing stations in 1922, and 110 firms were conducting psychotechnical testing in 1926 (Chestnut, 1972; Jaeger & Straeuble, 1981; both cited in Geuter, 1992). Unique to Germany, production engineers applied psychotechnical methods developed by psychologists such as Walther Moede, which led to criticism that perhaps this application was more technological than psychological. This led to tension between the two professions, along with attempts to delineate a separate niche for each group (Geuter, 1992). While in the 1920s psychotechnics was dominated by engineers, in the 1930s psychologists became more prominent (McCollom, 1968).

Industry viewed the use of psychology in personnel selection as a viable strategy (Stern, 1923). This use, successful in the war effort, was seen as a way to help deal with the current economic trouble and as a means to refute pseudo-psychology. The Prussian Ministry for Science, Arts, and Education, for example, held a meeting in May 1920 where psychology was represented by Carl Stumpf, director of the Berlin Psychological Institute, and by the applied psychologists Hans Rupp of the Berlin Institute and Otto Lipmann of the Institute for Applied Psychology. Stumpf recommended that the Ministry create applied psychology departments and associate professorships at all institutes under their control (Geuter, 1992).

The railroads provide an example of the use of psychology in employee selection. After Germany's defeat in World War I, the railroad companies were merged in a new corporation under foreign control, the *Reichsbahn*. Under pressure to maximize profits for reparation payments, the corporation created a committee of physicians, engineers, attorneys, and psychologists, of whom the leading psychologist was Walther Moede (1888–1958). Under Moede's supervision, the test for train engineers was improved, and tests were developed for apprentices, clerks, brakemen, conductors, station masters, and others.[3] In the early 1920s, rather than continue to situate the laboratories in cities, the *Reichsbahn* constructed a psychological testing laboratory in a railway car, allowing the testing of applicants wherever there was rail access (Gundlach, 1997). Unlike in the United States, where the perceived success of paper-and-pencil tests of intelligence triggered a boom in their use in industry, in Germany and in continental Europe generally there was a much greater emphasis on the use of apparatus in vocational testing (van Drunen, 1997).

A number of applied psychology institutes were established in the 1920s, some of which had university affiliations. In 1918, the Institute for Industrial Psychotechnology at the Technical College in Berlin-Charlottenberg was founded by Walther Moede and the engineer Georg Schlesinger (1874–1949) to conduct workplace analyses, ergonomic research, and investigations in aptitude testing (Sprung & Sprung, 2001). The Institute for Vocational and Business Psychology was established in Berlin in 1920 (Tagg, 1925). Founded by Curt Piorkowski (1888–1939) and Otto Lipmann (1880–1933), the Institute focused on developing psychological career aptitude tests and on career counseling (Sprung & Sprung, 2001). Recall that Lipmann, along with William Stern, founded the first applied psychological institute in Germany in 1906. In 1921, Hans Rupp (1880–1954) and Carl Stumpf (1848–1936) founded the Division of Applied Psychology at Berlin University. The Division conducted psychotechnical and industrial psychology research in cooperation with industrial firms (Sprung & Sprung, 2001). Geuter (1992) listed additional lectureships and chairs that were established at technical colleges such as Aachen, Braunschweig, Danzig, Darmstadt, Dresden, Hannover, Karlsruhe, Munich, and Stuttgart.[4] Geuter noted that the first budgeted associate professorship in applied psychology was established for Otto Klemm at Leipzig in 1923.

Lipmann (1926–27) surveyed the chief investigators of industrial psychology topics in mid-1920s Germany, providing us with a snapshot of the variety of settings and the range of work being done there at that time.[5] He mentioned Rupp's work in vocational selection and in evaluation techniques at the Division of Applied Psychology. In addition, Lipmann discussed the following researchers: M. Atzler at the Kaiser Wilhelm Institute

---

[3] Other countries followed Germany's example in applying psychology to the management of their railroads. Examples are Austria, France, Italy, the Netherlands, the Soviet Union, Sweden, Switzerland, and the United States (Gundlach, 1997).

[4] Details can be found in Geuter (1992, Table 3, p. 46).

[5] This article was translated by the American industrial psychologist Morris Viteles.

for the Physiology of Work in Berlin investigated work fatigue. Walter Georg Blumenfeld (1882–1967) conducted research on the measurement of vocational fitness and on advertising displays at the Psychological Institute of the Technical High School of Dresden.[6] Hellmuth Bogen (b.1893) of the Vocational Testing Office of the Berlin Bureau of Investigations focused on vocational guidance research. At the Technical High School of Karlsruhe, the engineer Adolph M. Friedrich worked on the psychology of training. Fritz W. O. Giese (1890–1935) of the Psychological Institute of the Technical High School of Stuttgart investigated a range of topics including industrial psychology theory, the application of psychoanalytic methods to personality assessment, and the improvement of working methods. Willy Hellpach (1877–1955) at the Institute of Applied Psychology at the University of Heidelberg conducted research on increasing worker satisfaction. Hellpach received his Ph.D. under Wundt in 1900 and his M.D. degree, also at the University of Leipzig, in 1903. In 1918, he was appointed a lecturer in psychology at the technical college at Karlsruhe, where in 1920 Hellpach was appointed as the budgeted associate professor of applied psychology (Geuter, 1992). According to Zusne (1984), Hellpach was the first psychologist in Germany to present industrial psychology academic lectures.

Gustav Otto Klemm (1884–1939) worked on machine construction and worker energy consumption at the Section of Applied Psychology of the Psychological Institute of the University of Leipzig. Klemm wrote an early history of psychology, *Geschichte der Psychologie (History of Psychology)* in 1911, that was translated into English in 1912. This was the only German language history of psychology for several decades (cited in Zusne, 1984). At the Institute of Psychiatric Investigation in Munich, Emil Kraepelin (1856–1926) conducted lab research on the distribution of work and on work length. Kraepelin was a medical doctor (University of Leipzig, 1878) who was heavily influenced by the teaching of Wundt (Zusne, 1984). Karl Marbe (1869–1953) at the Psychological Institute of the University of Würzberg worked on accident prevention. Marbe (1936) was one of the first psychologists to testify at a criminal trial. He testified at a sexual assault trial in 1911.[7] More germane to industrial psychology, in 1912 Marbe testified at a civil trial as an expert witness on reaction times related to

[6] Karl Marbe (1936) noted that, in his opinion, commercial high schools were more amenable to industrial psychology topics than the universities.

[7] A number of psychologists involved in early industrial psychology were also pioneers in the use of psychology in courtroom testimony. In addition to Marbe, William Stern, Otto Lipmann, Hugo Münsterberg, and Eduoard Claparède testified in court (Sporer, 1997).

a train wreck near Müllheim (Bartol & Bartol, 2013). In 1913, Marbe founded the applied psychology journal *Fortschritte der Psychologie und ihre Anwendungen (Progress of Psychology and Its Applications)* (Zusne, 1984). According to Marbe (1936), the first book on the psychology of advertising to appear in Germany was the 1924 text by his student Theodor König. Walther Moede researched selection tests, the effectiveness of advertising and accident prevention posters, and the organization of work at the Laboratory of Industrial Psychology of the Technical High School of Charlottenberg and at the Institute of Economic Psychology of the Commercial High School of Berlin. Moede, a 1911 University of Leipzig Ph.D., published a number of texts on industrial psychology and was founder and editor of industrial psychology journals.

Other applied psychologists and engineers mentioned by Lipmann were Wilhelm Peters (1880–1963) of the Psychological Institute of the University of Jena, who worked on vocational aptitudes, and Walther Poppelreuter (1886–1939) of the Institute of Clinical Psychology and Vocational Guidance at Bonn, who worked on trade tests. Poppelreuter held both Ph.D. and M.D. degrees. The engineer Ewald Sachsenberg (1877–1946) of the Technical High School of Dresden investigated work rhythm and work pauses, while the production engineer Georg Schlesinger (1874–1949) of the Department of Scientific Investigation of Machine Tools in the Technical High School of Charlottenberg looked at the organization of plant management. And Lipmann's mentor and colleague, William Stern,[8] was at the Psychological Laboratory of the University of Hamburg working on tests of vocational aptitude.

Lipmann's survey demonstrated a wide range of interests and research conducted by engineers and psychologists. In addition to selection and testing, there was research conducted in vocational guidance, personality assessment, advertising, job satisfaction, training, fatigue, accident prevention, machine construction, and management organization. In *Methoden der Wirtschaftspsychologie (Methods of Economic Psychology)*, Fritz Giese (1927) distinguished between *subject psychotechnics* and *object psychotechnics* (cited in Geuter, 1992). Subject psychotechnics involved adapting individuals to their working conditions and included vocational guidance, employee selection, training, and personnel advising. Object psychotechnics involved adapting working conditions to the psychological nature of the worker. Topics here included advertising; time, motion, and fatigue studies; factory illumination; and accident prevention. Both subject and

---

[8] Stern's contributions to psychology were described in Chapter 3.

object psychotechnics are well represented in Lipmann's survey. In the 1920s, the work of psychometricians centered, as it did in the United States, on methods for determining individual differences (Geuter, 1992).

## Otto Lipmann

At the time Lipmann conducted his overview of psychotechnics in Germany, he was still at his Institute of Applied Psychology in Berlin. Otto Lipmann was born in Breslau, Germany, in 1880. He remained in Breslau for his graduate education, studying with William Stern and Hermann Ebbinghaus at the University of Breslau and earning a doctorate from that institution in 1904. Two years later, Stern and Lipmann founded the Institute for Applied Psychology in Berlin (Stern, 1934). In 1907, along with Stern, Lipmann founded the journal *Zeitschrift für angewandte Psychologie* (*Journal for Applied Psychology*) (Viteles, 1932) and acted as editor until 1933. Of some financial means, he was able not only to provide support for his Institute but also to work as a scholar independent of a university affiliation. Lipmann, like many of the early psychologists, was a generalist who contributed to a number of areas of psychology. For example, he published work on psychodiagnostic methods for physicians, published a psychology outline for jurists, and performed some of the earliest research on sex differences in cognition. Lipmann found that mental traits did not show differences in degree between men and women nor are any mental characteristics exclusive to one or the other sex, a finding that was cited in early feminist literature (Baumgarten, 1933–34).

In industrial psychology, Lipmann constructed some of the first selection tests for aviators in Germany as well as selection tests for industrial apprentices, telegraphers, and typesetters. He was also a pioneer in vocational guidance (Baumgarten, 1933–34). In the early 1920s, he developed a scheme for classifying occupations based on their cognitive demands. Lipmann claimed that occupations differed both in the type of mental functions required and in the intensity that the mental functions are applied. Occupations can be divided into three groups according to whether this mental activity is applied to things (e.g., carpentry), people (e.g., law), or concepts (e.g., mathematics) (Salgado, 2007). A critic of scientific management, Lipmann (1928–29) was concerned that the link between the work and the worker was being severed by technical advances and innovations. He noted that any gains in efficiency made possible by scientific management could be lost by lack of worker interest. Lipmann's *Arbeitswissenschaft* (science of work) made a distinction between a worker's maximal performance under ideal conditions ("capacity-to-work") from "preparedness-to-work," which in turn leads to a "willingness-to-work." The latter includes worker satisfaction and motivation and can be fostered by management policies such as fair promotion, fair compensation, reduced dissatisfaction, and a feeling of community between management and workers. He was concerned that too much emphasis was placed on work capacity through efficient selection and too little emphasis on willingness-to-work (Hausmann, 1931).

*The Rise of National Socialism*
The rise of National Socialism did create opportunities for some industrial psychologists. In particular, work in employee selection expanded in the 1930s with the continuing buildup of the German military, the *Wehrmacht* (Ansbacher, 1941). The Nazi regime, which took power in 1933, was supportive of psychology when it met its purposes. While psychology as a profession benefited because of additional academic positions, research funds, and applied work, the effect on free inquiry in the renowned German university system and on a number of individual psychologists was devastating. The implementation of the Law for the Reconstruction of the Civil Service in 1933 resulted in the removal of at least one-third of college or university psychologists for political or religious reasons, with 14 percent of the membership of the German Psychological Association emigrating in 1933 alone (Sprung & Sprung, 2001). Jewish psychologists prominent in the history of industrial psychology were included in the dismissals and emigration. Wilhelm Peters was dismissed from his position at the University of Jena, and Walter Blumenfeld immigrated to Peru (Geuter, 1992). William Stern and Kurt Lewin were dismissed from their positions and immigrated to the United States.[9] For Otto Lipmann, the consequences of Nazi bigotry were more tragic.

Forced to seek a university appointment due to his declining finances, Lipmann was prevented from taking an offer from the University of Berlin by the 1933 decree (Stern, 1934). He was also discharged from the editorship of the journal he cofounded, the *Journal of Applied Psychology*,

[9] Other psychologists dismissed from their academic positions included Adhemar Gelb, David Katz, Martha Muchow, Otto Selz, and Max Wertheimer. Although not directly affected by the civil service law himself, pioneering Gestalt psychologist Wolfgang Köhler spoke out against the law, tried to protect his colleagues, and in 1935 immigrated to the United States. Although not Jewish herself, Muchow was ostracized and persecuted for her association with Stern and dismissed from her university position in 1933. She committed suicide two days after that dismissal (Miller, 1997). Ten years after his 1933 dismissal, Otto Selz was murdered in Auschwitz (Geuter, 1992; Sprung & Sprung, 2001).

on October 1, 1933. Six days later, Lipmann was dead. While contemporary tributes delicately referred to cause of death as heart failure (e.g., Baumgarten, 1933–34), it is highly likely that Lipmann committed suicide (Lamiell, 1996; Sprung & Sprung, 2001; Viteles, 1974).

Those psychologists not affected negatively by the National Socialist policies found opportunities in the expansion of the military and of academia, where they were involved with the Nazi regime to varying degrees. In a scathing indictment of the activities of a number of German psychologists from World War I to the Second World War, the Swiss industrial psychologist Franziska Baumgarten-Tramer (1948) described the activities during the National Socialist period of industrial psychologists such as Poppelreuter, Giese, Lersch, and Klemm. For example, she noted that as early as 1932, Poppelreuter was teaching a political psychology course based on Adolf Hitler's *Mein Kampf*. Giese informed his publisher that he did not want his name to appear on the same page as Otto Lipmann's, who had always been supportive of Giese's career. When Lersch and Klemm became editors of the *Journal of Applied Psychology*, they removed the names of the journal founders Stern and Lipmann from the title page. Baumgarten-Tramer did note that there were a few counterexamples, such as Hellmuth Bogen, who gave up the practice of psychology rather than work in military psychology.

## Great Britain

The growth of academic psychology in Great Britain was hampered by hostility from philosophers and by challenging economic conditions in the 1920s. It was the medical, educational, and industrial applications of psychology, not academia, that helped establish it as a viable enterprise (Hearnshaw, 1964). The Industrial Fatigue Research Board, mentioned in Chapter 5, continued to conduct research on a wide range of topics relevant to industrial psychology, such as vocational selection and guidance, working conditions, work hours, labor turnover, job design, accident prevention, and task variety. Eric Farmer, one of the first investigators at the Board, recalled how the work done there was in direct philosophical contrast to the scientific management approaches of Taylor and the Gilbreths. The focus was on reducing the effort made by the worker to make the job more pleasant (Farmer, 1958). While observers such as Kornhauser (1929–30a) noted the importance of the work conducted there, the impact of this work outside the discipline was somewhat limited (Warr, 2007).

According to Hearnshaw (1964), the introduction of industrial psychology to Great Britain as a separate, applied branch of psychology was due to the work of the Australian psychologist Bernard Muscio. In 1917, Muscio published *Lectures on Industrial Psychology*, based on a series of lectures he delivered at Sydney University. The British psychologist Tom Pear recommended *Lectures* to C. S. Myers, who was to become Britain's premier industrial psychologist (Rodger, 1971). Myers cofounded the National Institute of Industrial Psychology, the primary source of industrial psychology in 1920s Great Britain.

### Charles S. Myers and the National Institute of Industrial Psychology

Charles Samuel Myers (Figure 6.1) was born in London on March 13, 1873. He was educated at Cambridge University, earning an A.B. degree in 1895, an A.M. in 1900, and a Sc.D. in 1909 from Gonville and Caius College of that university. Myers earned a medical degree from Cambridge in 1901 and qualified as a doctor one year later. He is widely regarded as the most

Figure 6.1  Charles Myers. London School of Economics Library

important British psychologist in the first half of the twentieth century. Myers's career can be divided into two stages: academic and applied. Myers's academic career took place at King's College and Cambridge University, focusing on experimental psychology in the laboratory. In 1909, while at Cambridge he published his *Textbook of Experimental Psychology*, which soon became the standard experimental psychology text in Great Britain (Burt, 1947). In 1912, Myers founded and became director of Cambridge's Psychological Laboratory. In 1915, he became a fellow of the Royal Society.

While Myers's *An Introduction to Experimental Psychology* (1911) did contain two chapters on mental tests, it was during his service in World War I that he first applied psychology to practical problems. In this way, Myers's career path was similar to a number of fellow academic psychologists in the United States. As a psychiatrist and consultant psychologist to the British armies in France, his primary responsibility was treating soldiers for shell shock. However, it was the research Myers conducted on selecting men for hydrophone duty, detecting enemy submarines, which foreshadowed his later career in applied psychology (Myers, 1936).

Returning to academia after the war, Myers found Cambridge University unsupportive of his new interest in applied psychology. In 1918, after giving two lectures on applied psychology, he was approached by businessman H. J. Welch, who was interested in determining if Hugo Münsterberg's methods could be applied to British industry (Burt, 1947). Severing his connection to Cambridge (Bartlett, 1946), in 1921 Myers and Welch cofounded the National Institute of Industrial Psychology (NIIP; Myers, 1936).[10] Welch and Myers began with only two staff members and two rooms, but by 1930 the staff numbered fifty.[11] In the 1920s, the NIIP was the principle employer of psychologists in Great Britain (Bunn, 2001). Myers's staff included Bernard Muscio, G. H. Miles, Cyril Burt, Winifred Spielman, Eric Farmer, May Smith, and Tom Hatherley Pear. The Institute was supported by grants from the Carnegie United Kingdom Trust and from individuals and firms and by fees for investigations. The NIIP engaged in a variety of applied work, teaching, and research. Research topics included improving human welfare in factories, fatigue, productivity, test construction, employee selection,

---

[10] The early history of the Institute can be found in *Ten Years of Industrial Psychology* (1932) by Welch and Myers.

[11] Pear (1948) noted that Myers seemed to have the ideal temperament for running a complex organization such as the NIIP. Myers was "a keen psychologist" and "a good mixer" who "suffered fools gladly" and was "the most sociable psychologist of his age" (p. 115).

vocational guidance, training, and factors involved in product sales (Myers, 1925; Viteles, 1947). Myers directed the NIIP from 1921 to 1930 and after that was employed as a principal until 1938. During that time, he also published the influential textbooks *Industrial Psychology* (1925) and *Industrial Psychology in Great Britain* (1926).

The NIIP was founded on the principle that it should be commercially neutral, a tenet it violated in the early 1930s by using attitude and values research to develop a successful candy for Rowntree's. Seebohm Rowntree was a member of the executive board and a strong supporter of the NIIP. Rowntree's chief rival, Cadbury's, was also a financial supporter of the NIIP. Despite the financial potential of this type of activity, in response to the conflict of interest, the NIIP leadership prohibited additional commercially sensitive research. The timing was unfortunate, as the Institute's grant monies were exhausted by the mid-1930s and it was running a financial deficit. A reorganization, based on a report by Rowntree, questioned Myers administrative skills. Myers belief that the NIIP should be impartial and benefit both the employer and employee was a difficult position to maintain in practice. He was forced out in 1938 (Bunn, 2001). Myers died on October 12, 1946.

Perennial tensions in the field, between basic and applied science and between the practice and the laboratory, were illustrated by the contrast between Myers and his former student Frederic Bartlett. A strong advocate for psychology as a university-based laboratory science, Bartlett took issue with Myers's approach to psychology and questioned his move from the laboratory to industrial psychology (Bartlett, 1948). Bartlett, who succeeded Myers as Great Britain's premier psychologist, preferred a human factors laboratory approach to applied psychology, exemplified by Applied Psychology Unit he established at Cambridge University in 1944. As Bunn (2001) succinctly observed: "Charles Myers had taken psychology out of the laboratory and into the factory. Frederic Bartlett, rejecting his mentor's vision, took it back" (p. 579).

Most of professional activity in industrial psychology in Great Britain in the 1920s was carried out by the NIIP and the Industrial Fatigue Research Board (later called the Industrial Health Research Board) (Kornhauser, 1929–30a). Hearnshaw (1964) called them "the twin pillars of industrial psychology in Great Britain between the wars" (p. 280). Myers (1925) called relations between the two bodies "intimate and harmonious"; they shared investigators and collaborated on projects (p. 17). Outside of the NIIP and the Research Board, there was some mostly small-scale activity in well-established university psychology departments. And while some private firms would occasionally use the services of the NIIP or individuals with psychological training, Rowntree's of York was the only firm to set up a psychological department of its own. Chairman and Director Seebohm Rowntree was an early advocate of improving work conditions and of worker well-being. In 1922, a psychologist was hired to provide selection and training services; from this beginning, a full-scale psychological department grew (Hearnshaw, 1964).

Although industrial psychology in Great Britain started from a scientific management perspective with a focus on fatigue and selection, during the 1920s the field transcended that narrow focus. Fryer (1923–24) pointed out that the use of the term *industrial psychology* in Great Britain was more akin to how *applied psychology* was used in the United States: that is, a broad term that encompasses more than just industrial applications. As exemplified by Myers (1929), increasing efficiency and output was important but not the sole or even the primary concern for industrial psychology. Increasing the well-being, the "ease," of the worker was paramount. In many respects his outlook was ahead of its time with its emphasis on topics such as employee attitudes and satisfaction. For example, Myers (1925) stated that "sometimes the mere presence of the Institute's investigators and the interest they have shown in the employees' work have served to send up output before any actual changes have been introduced" (p. 28). This idea was later popularized by the results of the Hawthorne Studies in the United States and came to be known as the *Hawthorne effect*.

Myers (1925) was a particularly trenchant critic of the scientific management approach. He bluntly stated, "There *is* no 'one best way'" (p. 27, italics in original). Myers was concerned that scientific management would discourage employee initiative. He preferred an approach that gained the confidence of the worker by removing obstacles that prevent workers from obtaining optimal performance. Myers's colleague Tom H. Pear (1948) conceded tongue in cheek that at least Frank Gilbreth "injected some milk of human kindness" into an "inhuman doctrine," emphasizing just how inhumane he considered Taylor's system to be (p. 112). Like the American psychologist Morris Viteles and the German psychologist Otto Lipmann, Myers and Pear were critical of scientific management's rigidity and perceived lack of emphasis on the well-being of the worker.

### Italy

One of the first to use selection tests was Ugo Pizzoli in 1901, who used them to select apprentices (Salgado, 2001). Others involved in the development of psychotechnics in Italy included the physiologist Mariano Luigi Patrizi (1866–1938), who founded the Laboratory of Work Psychology in Modena in 1889 (deWolff & Shimmin, 1976); Zaccaria Treves (1869–1911); and Guido Della Valle (1884–1962), who introduced the term *psychotechnics* into Italy in 1910. Applied psychology, including work psychology or psychotechnics, was a part of scientific psychology from the beginning in Italy. Industrial psychology in 1920s Italy to a great extent involved work in personnel selection and vocational guidance. Agostino Gemelli (1878–1959) founded the Institute of Psychology at Catholic University in Milan in 1923. Some of the work of the Institute involved industrial psychology topics (McCollom, 1968). In addition to his role as rector of Catholic University, Gemelli was a Franciscan monk, a psychologist who was also trained in medicine, and an officer in the Italian Air Force in World War I. Like many psychologists of his generation, Gemelli had a wide range of interests, including psychotechnics (Foschi, Giannone, & Giuliani, 2013). Gemelli (1952) wrote that his use of aptitude tests for pilots in 1915 was the first use of such tests in Italy. He advocated for the use of aptitude tests for all military positions and in 1917 published a book on military psychology: *L'anima del nostro soldato (The Soul of Our Soldier)* (cited in Gemelli, 1952).

During the rise of Fascism, interest in general psychology was almost completely replaced by a focus on psychotechnics (Foschi, Giannone, & Giuliani, 2013). Psychotechnics was encouraged because it was viewed as an aid to more efficient social, economic, and industrial policies (Cimino & Foschi, 2012). In this way, the development of industrial psychology in Fascist Italy was similar to that of Nazi Germany. Gemelli was suspected of collaboration with the Fascist regime; however, his cooperation can be viewed as an opportunistic attempt to keep psychology alive during this period and also a reflection of his conservative Catholic beliefs (Foschi, Giannone, & Giuliani, 2013).

## The Netherlands

As in much of Europe, psychotechnics in the Netherlands in the first half of the twentieth century was mostly concerned with personnel selection and vocational guidance. The Netherlands was late to industrialization and a noncombatant in World War I. Psychotechnics did not develop until after that war. In 1918, the linguist and Jesuit priest Jacques van Ginneken (1877–1945) founded the Centraal Zielkundig Beroepskantoor (Central Psychological Occupation Office), which tested the vocational fitness of hundreds of laborers. This was followed by the Social Pedagogical Dr. D. Bos Institute in 1920, a private center of psychotechnical research affiliated with the Heymans Laboratory at the University of Groningen. A year later, a psychotechnical laboratory was established as part of the municipal health service of the city of Amsterdam. In 1922, the Philips Light Bulb Company founded the first psychotechnical laboratory in a private company in the Netherlands. The Nederlandse Stichting voor Psychotechniek (Dutch Foundation for Psychotechnics), the first private testing company in the Netherlands, was founded in 1927 at Utrecht (van Strien, 1998b).

Psychologists in the Netherlands used a variety of instruments for testing individual difference characteristics. Laboratory equipment designed for determining general laws of psychology were repurposed to measure individual differences. Specially designed psychotechnical apparatus was used. They were of two types: instruments designed to measure a characteristic germane to the job and those designed to simulate part or all of the job.[12] Paper-and-pencil tests and simple performance tests were also used, both individually administered tests and group tests. Finally, measures of personality, including observational methods, were in use (van Strien, 1998b).[13]

## Poland

Poland once again became an independent state in 1918. A year prior to this, Józefa Joteyko (1866–1928) published a critique of scientific management. Joteyko was critical of scientific management's emphasis on efficiency and its focus on the managerial perspective. She stated that workers' interests, as well as managers' interests, should be considered and that workers should be placed in creative jobs that are well suited to their abilities. The Institute of Psychotechnics was established in Cracow in 1920, and in 1926, the Polish Psychotechnical Society was founded. The Society published the journal *Psychotechnika*, organized annual congresses, and set up a series of psychotechnical centers in industry and vocational schools. The principal activities of the Society were psychological testing using adaptations of American and French tests, vocational guidance, and improving work conditions. An example of industrial

---

[12] Myers (1925) termed the first type, where elementary functions were measured, as *analytic* tests; job simulations he called *analogous* tests. The latter were also called the *synthetic* approach (van Strien, 1998b).

[13] For examples of these tests and their use, see van Strien (1998b).

psychology test use was a 1920 study conducted by Bronisław Biegeleisen-Zelazowski in the wood industry. Biegeleisen-Zelazowski constructed apparatus for testing the individual abilities of workers for the purpose of assigning them to jobs (cited in Dobrzyński, 1981).

## Russia (Union of the Soviet Socialist Republics)

The 1917 revolution had a dramatic impact on Russian psychology, including industrial psychology. Initially the early Bolsheviks seemed favorably inclined toward science. Three years prior to the revolution, the Moscow Institute of Psychology at Moscow University was founded by Georgii Ivanovich Chelpanov (1862–1936), a professor of philosophy who had studied with Wundt and who established a psychology laboratory at the university. In 1918, the new Soviet Ministry of Education recognized the Institute, and in 1920, Chelpanov added a section of applied and work psychology. The Central Institute of Work was directed by the poet Aleksei K. Gastev (1882–1941) and employed Isaak N. Shpil'rein (1891–c1930s), who concentrated on psychotechnics and test development.[14] In the early 1920s, Chelpanov was removed in a coup engineered by his former student Konstantin N. Kornilov (1879–1957). Chelpanov was found to be insufficiently Marxist. In 1924, the Moscow Institute of Psychology became the Moscow State Institute of Experimental Psychology. In addition to Shpil'rein, the Institute employed S. G. Gellershtein (1896–1967), who specialized in psychotechnics (Sirotkina & Smith, 2012).

What did industrial psychology look like in the Soviet Union in the 1920s? Max Tagg (1925) reviewed a pamphlet outlining the work the Central Institute of Work and the annual report of the Industrial Psychotechnical Laboratory of the People's Commissariat of Labour. Tagg noted that the work of the Central Institute was focused solely on increasing production. The methods used to accomplish this were based on the scientific management philosophy of Taylor and the Gilbreths, assisted by visits by German psychologists and engineers. Tagg was highly critical of the narrowness of this approach. Tagg wrote: "They tend to 'out-Taylor' Taylorism!" (p. 364). The Institute was divided into a series of laboratories, one that concentrated on motion studies, one that focused on fatigue, another that assessed the aptitude of apprentices, and a fourth that studied and standardized working tools. A fifth laboratory, the Industrial Psychotechnical Laboratory, was created to examine the psychological processes

---

[14] Shpil'rein also appears as Spielrein in some non-Russian language accounts (e.g., Viteles, 1932).

involved in work. Tagg reported that the activities of the Industrial Psycho-technical Laboratory were varied. They included the standardization of tests for selecting tramway conductors and drivers, what we would describe today as human factors investigations of problems such as the optimal type of seat for telephone operators, studies of fatigue in operators and printing compositors, and intelligence testing in the Red Army.

Viteles (1932) was somewhat more positive in his assessment of the Central Institute and the state of Russian industrial psychology in general, although quite critical of the political atmosphere. He saw the focus on the use of tools, in this case only the hammer and the file, as an original approach and viewed the concentration on scientific management as one that attempted to avoid the difficulties encountered with that approach in the United States. Viteles also noted that in 1927 there were more than sixty centers conducting research on production in Russia and that in 1931 the Central Institute alone had 1,000 branches (Weber, 1927; Tramm, 1931; both cited in Viteles, 1932). He toured the country in 1934–35 and "had many opportunities to observe the pernicious effects of political and social ideology upon science and scientists (Viteles, 1967, p. 435). While admiring of individual psychologists, Viteles was scornful of the intolerance of the political system toward intellectual freedom. He wrote that while his *Industrial Psychology* (1932) text was available in a mimeographed translation during his year there, two chapters on individual differences were missing. Viteles was asked to cooperate in a formal translation; however, those two chapters would have to be revised to reflect Communist ideology. Viteles refused to participate (Viteles, 1974).

George W. Hartmann (1931–32) was also critical. While conceding the enthusiasm in Russia for industrial psychology, he saw the methods only superficially similar to those in the United States, Germany, and elsewhere. Although a large literature had been generated, Hartmann stated: "[M]uch of it comes from untrained and incompetent authors as one may see a common lack of precision and specificity in reports and useless duplication of elementary research" (p. 354). He took particular issue with the "constant intrusion of Communist propaganda" into the research process, noting that all research is conducted from the perspective of the philosophies of Marx and Lenin (p. 354). This is the crux of the matter. While the large, centralized Communist government was able to create institutes and positions for applied psychologists, the regime imposed a particular ideology that eventually dictated not only how psychology could be conducted but what results were politically acceptable. This became an acute problem under Joseph Stalin, who gained power following the death of Lenin in

1924. Stalin's reign had deleterious effects on a number of scientific fields, including psychotechnics (Sirotkina & Smith, 2012).

Psychotechnics was accused of the perceived methodological error of *eclecticism*: the large-scale borrowing of theory and data from non-Soviet sources. As Shpil'rein explained, the purpose of science is to serve the workers in the struggle of building a socialist state. Soviet industrial psychologists criticized bourgeois industrial psychology at the Seventh International Conference on Psychotechnics, held in Moscow in 1931. This dismayed their international colleagues at the conference, who had no prior warning of the attack. Many of the participants dismissed the criticism of industrial psychology as propaganda alien to true science. However, there were real differences between the Soviet and Western workers. Much of Western industrial psychology assumed the existence of a literate and relatively skilled workforce, something that was lacking in the USSR. It is possible that this difference could have contributed to the change in orientation by the Russian psychologists. This new perspective did not save industrial psychology in the USSR. McLeish (1975) wrote that psychotechnics was eliminated in 1931; Joravsky (1989) noted that the psychotechnics journal ceased publication in 1934 and that by 1936 psychotechnic laboratories and research centers were closed.[15]

## Spain

After defeat in 1898 in a war against the United States, Spain entered into a period of modernization, and with it came the importation of modern psychology, primarily from Germany and France. In contrast to countries such as Germany and the United States where scientific psychology preceded the applied component, in Spain it was applied psychology that led to a scientific psychology. There was a particular interest in psychotechnology, in part due to its perceived successes in World War I.[16] Two separate centers for applied psychology were established, one in Barcelona and the other in Madrid, that differed in certain aspects but maintained close contact. The center for psychotechnology established at

---

[15] Morris Viteles (1974) reported that his friend Isaak Shpil'rein was murdered in a Stalin purge in 1935. Joravsky (1989) does not corroborate that year; he wrote that Shpil'rein's disappearance in the late 1930s was attributed to the leadership role he played in an outlawed discipline and to suspicion of his close relationships with foreigners. The Communist Party was inconsistent in whom it arrested. Gastev was arrested in 1938; however, Chelpanov and O. A. Ermanskii (1866–1941), who both displayed a degree of independence from Party doctrine, were not.

[16] Spain was not a participant in that conflict.

the school of Barcelona was under the direction of the physician Emilio Mira (1896–1964), who developed a biology-based psychotechnology. This center was involved in personnel testing of police officers and bus drivers. Mira forged connections with others working in psychotechnics, including Claparède, Lahy, and Moede, and was involved in the creation of International Association for Psychotechnology in Geneva in 1920. Mira advocated for a holistic approach to assessment rather than one based on a single test. He was involved in the establishment of a series of psychotechnical centers based in several provinces. Mira supported the losing Republic side in the Spanish Civil War. After that conflict, he immigrated to Brazil, where he continued his work in psychotechnology (Carpintero, 2012). In addition to his psychotechnology work, Mira was the first Spanish-speaking psychologist to write about psychoanalysis and behaviorism and authored more than thirty books that covered virtually all areas of psychology (Zusne, 1984).

## Switzerland

Industrial psychology came to Switzerland at an early date. At the same time that Hugo Münsterberg received the invitation to Harvard University in 1892, he also received one to the University of Zürich (Heller, 1929–30). Münsterberg chose Harvard, but it is interesting to speculate if the history of I-O psychology would have turned out differently if he had made the other choice. In 1913, the Swiss shoe manufacturer Ivan Bally, who was interested in the work of Münsterberg, asked Jules Suter of the University of Zürich if he could apply Münsterberg's ideas to Bally's factory. After Suter's work for Bally, he returned to the University of Zürich to work on employee selection and vocational guidance. In 1924, Suter established the Institute of Industrial Psychology. Sponsored and partially supported by the city of Zürich, the Institute eventually became independent and self-supporting. In 1927, that Institute merged with others, including one in Geneva, into a corporation named the Swiss Foundation for Industrial Psychology, which combined the measurement of separate abilities with the study of the entire personality (Heller, 1929–30).

In 1912, Edouard Claparède (1873–1940) established the *Institut J. J. Rousseau* (Jean Jacques Rousseau Institute), initially for the study of educational problems, but it eventually branched out into vocational research. In 1916, the Institute developed a number of tests for telephone operators (Kitson, 1921b). Claparède was a generalist with multiple interests. He had a medical degree (1897) from the University of Geneva and practiced neurology and psychiatry with a particular interest in sleep (Murchison, 1929; Pillsbury, 1941). Today Claparède is probably best remembered for his work in child psychology, which directly influenced Jean Piaget (Zusne, 1984). On the applied side of psychology, Claparède was the first president of what became the International Association for Psychology and Psychotechnics, a position he held from the informal beginnings of the association in 1920 to his death.[17] With Pierre Bovet, he organized the first International Conference of Psychotechnics in 1920 (Holman, 1927; Pickren & Fowler, 2013).

Franziska Baumgarten-Tramer (1886–1970) was an important figure in the development of industrial psychology in Switzerland. Born in Lodz, Poland, Baumgarten-Tramer abandoned her goal to be a writer after hearing her first university psychology lecture (Baumgarten, 1975). Educated at the Universities of Cracow, Paris, Zürich, Bonn, and Berlin, she received her Ph.D. from the latter in 1917 (Murchison, 1929; Stevens & Gardner, 1982). Baumgarten-Tramer's interest in industrial psychology was the result of a lecture on that subject by Hugo Münsterberg at the University of Berlin. "After this hour I know immediately, 'I shall become an industrial psychologist'" (Baumgarten, 1975, p. 489). She further noted that she had had an affinity for factories since childhood and that she had a great deal of respect for factory workers. Deeply concerned about issues such as inadequate pay and overwork, Baumgarten-Tramer said that Münsterberg showed her an avenue to deal with these worker concerns as a psychologist rather than a political activist (Baumgarten, 1975).

Baumgarten-Tramer's initial publication in industrial psychology was a 1919 paper titled *Einige Bermerkungen zur Frage der Berufseignungsprüfung (Comments on the Questions of a Job Suitability Test)* (cited in Canziani, 1975). She came to believe that in addition to ability and interest, it is important to assess qualities of character in determining an individual's chances for job success. She investigated traits such as dishonesty, gratitude, and "empathetic intuition" and also evaluated the whole character. Baumgarten-Tramer developed a typology of workers, published a standard text in 1930 – *Die Psychologie der Menschenbehandlung (The Psychology of Human Treatment in Industry)* (cited in Stevens & Gardner, 1982) – and also published historical accounts of industrial psychology. Similar to many psychologists of her generation who had an

---

[17] The Association became the International Association of Psychotechnics and, after 1955, the International Association of Applied Psychology (IAAP) (Gundlach, 1998).

interest in industrial psychology, Baumgarten-Tramer was an applied psychologist in the broad sense. In addition to her industrial work, she published work in developmental psychology, psychic distress, educational psychology, and other areas. Baumgarten-Tramer had a strong interest in morality and justice. The German industrial psychologist Curt Piorkowski described her as the "Conscience of Psychology" (Canziani, 1975). The section on Germany in this chapter illustrates this with her blistering critique of the actions of some German psychologists during the period of National Socialism.

## The Americas

### United States

Despite the many accomplishments of industrial psychologists in the United States, there was a fair amount of concern in the 1920s by leading American psychologists that their European counterparts were eclipsing them. For example, in the early 1920s, Viteles (1923) wrote that the scope of the field was greater in Great Britain, France, and Germany compared to the United States, where industrial psychology was primarily involved with employee selection along with some application to advertising.[18] Viteles (1928b) continued that theme, noting that in European countries industrial psychologists studied topics such as the effects of illumination and ventilation that in the United States have been ceded to engineers. Bingham (1929) observed that the United States was "relatively backward in certain essential respects" compared to the European industrial nations (p. 399), and he did opine a year earlier (Bingham, 1928) that "the significant and constructive contributions of industrial psychology in America have been meagre" (p. 187). Bingham believed the reasons for this included psychology's relative youth as a science, competition from other subdisciplines, and the high demand for psychologists in colleges and universities. Even regarding America's strong suit of selection, Kornhauser (1929–30a) believed that Germany had outdistanced both England and the United States in occupational test development. Moore and Hartmann (1931) stated that European countries such as Great Britain and Germany were more advanced in industrial psychology than the United States in the 1920s. And James McKeen Cattell (1929/1947) in his presidential address to

---

[18] By the 1920s, *industrial psychology* was the preferred term in the United States for applying psychology to business (Arthur & Benjamin, 1999).

the 1929 Ninth International Congress of Psychology claimed that despite a great deal of development in personnel and industrial management, America is "apparently somewhat behind Germany in the applications of psychology to industry" (p. 448).

Was there any basis for this inferiority complex? Probably not, as American industrial psychology made some real strides following World War I. As we will see in this section, the 1920s saw both advances and setbacks for industrial psychology. The 1920s and early 1930s were a period of growth for industrial psychology and for psychology in general in the United States. By the end of the 1920s, the number of doctoral-level American psychologists listed in Murchison's (1929) *Psychological Register* far outnumbered those in any other country. The 1920s saw substantial economic growth and overall prosperity in America. Following a brief recession at the beginning of the decade, in the ten-year period from 1919 to 1929 the gross national product (GNP) rose 39 percent (Cashman, 1989). Psychology experienced dramatic growth in the early part of that decade. Driven in part by the perceived success of the Army testing program, business managers showed an increased interest in the use of testing. The general public was open to intelligence testing, and intelligence tests began to be used in educational settings. After the war, Robert Yerkes, who oversaw the development of the Army Alpha and Beta exams, was inundated with informational requests about those exams (Kevles, 1968).

Economic expansion opened up opportunities for psychologists in industry and in consulting firms. This was particularly important for women, who because of pervasive gender bias in colleges and universities often had difficulty obtaining academic jobs.[19] While only nutrition and zoology had more female scientists than psychology, there were virtually no women in leadership roles in the APA and no female journal editors, division chairs, or administrative officers.[20] There were

---

[19] While there are numerous examples of biased or condescending attitudes toward women by prominent male psychologists during this period, I will offer only one. In the second edition of his *History of Experimental Psychology*, Boring (1950) stated that while psychology has a higher percentage of women than other sciences, this is not true of the experimental side of the field. While admitting it is dangerous to generalize, he proceeded to do just that, speculating that the reason there are more women in applied psychology (i.e., outside of academia) is because experimental psychology is quite technical, experimentalists need to know something about electronics, and "[w]omen take to testing more readily than to electronics" (p. 578).

[20] Women were not the only group who faced discrimination in academic jobs. As discussed in Chapter 5, African Americans faced pervasive discrimination. There was also anti-Semitism, particularly in elite universities (see Winston, 1996, 1998). In research conducted during this time period, it was not unusual to compare Jews and Gentiles on attributes such as personality characteristics (e.g., Sward, 1935; Thurstone & Thurstone, 1930). Morris Viteles (1974) recalled

some prominent psychologists who were supportive of women. James McKeen Cattell, for example, in 1893 nominated Mary Whiton Caulkins and Christine Ladd-Franklin for APA membership, declaring that psychologists should not discriminate against women (Sokal, 1992). Mary Caulkins did become president of the APA in 1905, but she and Margaret Washburn, who was elected in 1921, were the only females elected president of APA until Anne Anastasi was elected in 1972. In the 1920s and 1930s, women became a majority in applied areas (Furumoto, 2003). Noteworthy female industrial psychologists active during this era include Marion Bills, Elsie Oschrin Bregman, Grace Manson, Millicent Pond, and Sadie Myers Shellow.

Marion A. Bills (1890–1970) received her doctorate from Bryn Mawr College in 1917. She was hired by Walter Van Dyke Bingham as a research assistant at the Bureau of Personnel Research at the CIT Division of Applied Psychology, where she rose to the associate director position. Bills worked for the Life Insurance Research Bureau in 1924 and 1925, where she conducted a number of studies on employee retention (Bills, 1923, 1925, 1926–27a, 1926–27b, 1928). In 1926, she began a long association with the Aetna Life Insurance Association, where she consulted with management and developed job evaluation, wage incentive, and job classification systems (Austin & Waung, 1994, cited in Koppes & Bauer, 2006). Ferguson (1952) considered Bills's long-term research on retention and selection to be one of the first substantive collaborations between psychology and business. In 1951–52, Bills was the first woman elected president of Division 14, the industrial psychology division of the APA (Koppes, 1997).[21]

Prior to receiving a 1922 Columbia University Ph.D., Elsie Oschrin Bregman (1896–1969) worked for the R. H. Macy Company of New York City from 1919 to 1921. While at Macy's, Bregman conducted research and implemented procedures in selection and training for clerical and sales positions (Bregman, 1921; Oschrin, 1918). Bregman also worked as a research assistant and instructor at Columbia University. She was a longtime associate (1923–34) at one of the first applied psychology consulting firms, the Psychological Corporation. While there, she revised

---

his mixed emotions following his promotion to assistant professor at the University of Pennsylvania in 1925. He was informed by the administration through his chairperson that he "should not anticipate promotion beyond this level because there was already one Jew . . . in the department and two more in other departments of the university" (p. 467). In spite of this, Viteles was eventually promoted to full professor and eventually received an honorary LL.D. degree from Penn.

[21] A second female president was not elected for another twenty-eight years: Mary Tenopyr in 1979–80.

the Army Alpha General Intelligence Examinations for use by business, receiving a royalty of 10 percent on every sale for her lifetime. She may have been the only person to profit from that organization in its early, financially troubled years (Sokal, 1981). In addition to her work on the Army Alpha, Bregman published the Bregman Language Completion Scale (Bregman, 1935). Bregman coauthored three books with E. L. Thorndike and others between 1925 and 1934: *The Measurement of Intelligence* (1925), *Adult Learning* (1928), and *The Prediction of Vocational Success* (1934) (cited in Bregman Biography, 1970).

Grace Manson (1893–1967) was Head of the Psychology Department at Salem College from 1919 to 1921. In 1923, she became one of only four students to receive a doctorate from the pioneering applied psychology program at the Carnegie Institute of Technology (CIT). Manson was an instructor and investigator at CIT from 1923 to 1924. She was employed at the University of Michigan, where from 1924 to 1926 she was an investigator for the National Research Council on Human Migrations, and from 1926 to 1931, she was a research associate for the Bureau of Business Research in the School of Business Administration. While there Manson conducted research on selection techniques such as application blanks, rating scales, and personal history data in department stores and insurance companies (Cook & Manson, 1925–26; Manson, 1925a, 1925b, 1925–26a). With Margaret Elliott, Manson published a comprehensive survey of salaries for a sample of 14,000 business and professional women (Elliott & Manson, 1930). Manson (1931) developed an occupational interest inventory and assessed the occupational interests of 13,752 women. She also published an often-cited bibliography of psychological tests and measures in use by industry (Manson, 1925–26b).

Millicent Pond (b.1889) received her Ph.D. from Yale University in 1925. She worked as an employment interviewer at the Winchester Repeating Arms Company and then as director of employment test research and supervisor of employment research at the Scovill Manufacturing Company in Connecticut. At Scovill, Pond was responsible for selection, placement, and training and conducted a number of studies evaluating selection procedures that included intelligence tests, other employment tests, and application blanks to predict supervisor ratings, pay and pay progress, and job tenure (Pond, 1926–27; Scovill, 1928–29).

Sadie Myers Shellow (1895–1991) earned her doctorate from Columbia University in 1923. She was subsequently employed as a psychologist at the Milwaukee Electric Railway and Light Company, where she collaborated with Morris Viteles. Shellow developed a number of psychological tests and conducted research on their effectiveness (Shellow, 1925–26, 1926–27a, 1926–27b). Beginning in 1935, she worked as a personnel consultant for the Milwaukee Police Department, where she conducted research on and developed procedures for the selection of recruits, patrol officers, detectives, sergeants, lieutenants, captains, clerks, and laboratory assistants. In addition to selection, Shellow advised the department on placement and training.

By the end of the 1920s, there were approximately fifty psychologists working full time in industry (Katzell & Austin, 1992). One prominent practitioner was Henry Charles Link (1889–1952), whose work at the Winchester Repeating Arms Company was discussed in Chapter 4 and whose views on the construct of intelligence appeared in Chapter 5. Link received both his undergraduate and graduate degrees from Yale University, the Ph.D. in 1916. His book *Employment Psychology* (1919) was a seminal work on criterion-related test validation, praised by Arthur Kornhauser and Forrest Kingsbury (1924) for its sound scientific methods in test construction and standardization. In addition to his work at Winchester, Link also worked for US Rubber, Lord & Taylor, and the Gimbel Brothers Department Store. In 1931, he constructed one of the first market research surveys, the *Psychological Barometer* (von Mayrhauser, n.d., cited in Vinchur & Koppes, 2007).

Other psychologists employed in industry during the 1920s included Harry Hepner at Kaufmann's Department Store in Pittsburgh, H. G. Kenagy at Procter & Gamble, and Beardsley Ruml at Macy's Department Store. Ruml (1894–1960) was an instructor in the CIT applied psychology program, an officer in the Personnel Research Federation, a professor at the University of Chicago, director of the Laura Spelman Rockefeller Memorial Fund, chairman of both the R. H. Macy Company and the Federal Reserve Bank of New York, and architect of the federal pay-as-you-go income tax plan. He did his undergraduate work at Dartmouth College and received his Ph.D. from the University of Chicago in 1917 (*New York Times*, 1960). In addition to practitioners working full time in industry, academic psychologists continued to branch out into industry. Prominent among them were Morris Viteles, Harold Burtt, and Donald Paterson, whose careers are described in Chapter 8. Others included Douglas Fryer at New York University and Forrest Kingsbury at the University of Chicago.

*Industrial Psychology Consulting Firms and Organizations*
The immediate postwar period saw the emergence of nonacademic industrial psychology consulting firms. The first was the Scott Company,

founded in 1919 by Walter Dill Scott, along with Robert Clothier, Joseph W. Hayes, L. B. Hopkins, Stanley W. Mathewson, and Beardsley Ruml.[22] The firm was organized to provide industry with solutions to personnel problems; to share with industry research on social, economic, and psychological factors involved in employee adjustment; and "to offer to industry a consulting service which combines the industrial and the scientific points of view" (Scott Company announcement, n.d.). Consultants for the company included Mary Holmes Stevens Hayes (1884–1962), one of the first female consultant psychologists. In addition to her consulting work with the Scott Company, Hayes, whose 1910 doctorate was from the University of Chicago, coauthored *Science and Common Sense in Working with Men* with Walter Dill Scott (Scott & Hayes, 1921) and later was prominent in youth guidance and placement work (Koppes, 1997).

The Scott Company was founded to determine if the same type of personnel services the Committee on Classification of Personnel offered to the US Army in World War I could profitably be offered to private employers. The Scott Company thrived and expanded from its original office in Dayton, Ohio, to Chicago, Philadelphia, and Springfield, Massachusetts. Among its well-known client companies were Armour, Goodyear Tire and Rubber, Guardian Life Insurance, Hart, Schaffner, & Marx, National Cash Register, the Pennsylvania Railroad, and the US Civil Service Commission. Services offered included test development, training manuals, job classification and salary evaluation, staffing of personnel departments, labor relations and arbitration, and publication of technical manuals and books (Ferguson, n.d.). Notable achievements include early development work on the graphic rating scale (Freyd, 1923) and the point-system of job salary evaluation,[23] advice to the US Civil Service Commission about establishing a research section, and the publication of the influential text *Personnel Management* (1923) by Scott and

---

[22] While the Scott Company was the first industrial psychology consulting firm, it was not the first industrial consulting firm in America. Emerson Engineers, founded in 1907 by Harrington Emerson and based on Taylor's Scientific Management principles, preceded it (Muhs, 1986; Van De Water, 1997). And recall from Chapter 4 that the unsuccessful Economic Psychology Association, founded in 1915, was designed to provide psychological services to businesses along the lines of Bingham's academic-based program at the Carnegie Institute of Technology, a program that might also have a claim to being engaged in "consulting." It might be safest to describe the Scott Company as the first successful, nonacademic, industrial psychology consulting firm.

[23] Ferguson (n.d.) stated that this point-system of job evaluation was developed five years before the one developed by Merrill Lott, whose system usually gets credit as the first. Ferguson (1962) also mentioned the work done on job evaluation in the CIT program by Clary, Bills, and Benge.

Clothier. Three important concepts developed by the Scott Company were the idea of the "worker-in-his-work," a humane conception of labor in opposition to the commodity conception of labor, and a labor policy that was positive in nature. The Scott Company was ahead of its time in both its approach to labor relations and its philosophy of staffing personnel departments, attributed to Ruml, that the worker and the work were an integral unit. That is, both the work and the workers were plastic; either could change in response to the other. Employee selection, for example, was not simply a question of fitting the worker to the job (the "square peg in a square hole" approach). When a worker left, the worker-in-his-work unit was gone. Restoration was not simply a matter of replacing the worker; a completely new unit must be created taking into account the new worker's abilities, interests, and opportunities (Ferguson, 1961, 1962).

The Scott Company believed that workers had certain inalienable rights and it was up to firms to help them achieve their personal goals. The Scott Company did not work with companies perceived as not supporting workers, and it tried to foster a positive labor philosophy with the firms it did work with. For example, in a 1920 proposal to the Chicago Foundrymen's Association, Scott wrote that the Association had three options when dealing with potential unionization. It could ignore unions, an unrealistic choice. It could attempt to remain nonunion by fighting unionization. Or it could create an organization that would cooperate with the unions, which ideally would result in labor peace. Scott noted that the Association could choose option two, but it would have to proceed without help from the Scott Company. Scott would only assist with the cooperative option, and he offered a detailed plan of how his company could help the Association achieve labor harmony (Ferguson, 1962). While the Scott Company was successful, it had a short life span of only a few years. Possible contributing factors to its demise include the economic recession of 1921–22 and the company principals leaving for other opportunities (Ferguson, n.d., 1961).

The Psychological Corporation, founded by James McKeen Cattell in 1921, is still a viable operation today. Cattell (1923) envisioned this organization as a holding company for psychologists. The Corporation's purpose was to advance psychology through research and practice.[24] The Corporation had twenty prominent psychologists as directors – including the industrial

---

[24] Cattell (1922) wrote that of the 161 replies he received from an earlier mass mailing to psychologists proposing the corporation, all were supportive "with the exception of two letters from psychiatrists" (p. 213).

psychologists Walter Van Dyke Bingham, Harry L. Hollingworth, and Walter Dill Scott – and an additional 170 psychologists as stockholders. Branch offices were established in a number of states to provide services such as test preparation and employee selection. Cattell (1923) was explicit in his view that in addition to providing services to industrial leaders, obtaining the cooperation of organized labor was just as important. His goals for the Psychological Corporation were very ambitious. As Sokal (1984) noted, in addition to providing psychological services to the public and promoting research, Cattell hoped to drive unqualified non-psychologists out of the field. He wanted to improve the popularity, social standing, and finances of psychologists, although the pay structure for the psychologist stockholders was quite byzantine. In the early years of the corporation, Cattell's ambitions were not realized as the Corporation floundered financially under his leadership. He was not an industrial psychologist, and his ideas about selection, for example, were not as sophisticated as those proposed by the Scott Company (Sokal, 1981). The Psychological Corporation was reorganized in 1926 with the industrial psychologists Walter Van Dyke Bingham as President, Walter Dill Scott as First Vice President, Paul S. Achilles as Secretary-Treasurer, and Elsie O. Bregman as Assistant Secretary. Cattell was given the title of Chairman of the Board (Achilles, 1957; Notes and News, 1927). Under the new leadership the Psychological Corporation did achieve financial success.

The Personnel Research Federation (PRF) was founded in 1921 as a conduit for exchanging research information, to provide consultants for industry, and to conduct personnel research. Walter Van Dyke Bingham, in his capacity of chairman of the National Research Council's Division of Anthropology and Psychology, was instrumental in its founding. The PRF, through the initiation of the National Research Council, the American Federation of Labor (AFL), and the Engineering Foundation, fostered cooperation among universities, government, and independent research organizations (Bingham, 1928; Ferguson, 1962). The founding members were the National Research Council, the Engineering Foundation, the American Federation of Labor, the Bureau of Industrial Research, the National Committee for Mental Hygiene, Carnegie Institute of Technology's Bureau of Personnel Research, and divisions from the University of Pennsylvania and Bryn Mawr College. Beardsley Ruml was appointed acting director but left before the first meeting and was replaced by Leonard Outhwaite. By the first annual meeting, other government agencies and universities had become members. New members included the Civil Service Commission, the Bureau of Labor Statistics, Harvard University's

Graduate School of Business, and the University of Chicago's School of Commerce and Administration (Flinn, 1922–23).

The constitution of the PRF stated the goal of the group was cooperation among industry, commerce, education, and government on personnel research. To do so, the PRF would act as a clearinghouse for personnel research information and coordinate personnel research information. The first chairman was Robert Yerkes, and the vice chairman was Samuel Gompers of the American Federation of Labor (Flinn, 1922–23). In 1922, the PRF founded the *Journal of Personnel Research*. This journal, later renamed *The Personnel Journal*, was an important outlet for industrial psychology research.[25]

The Bureau of Personnel Administration was established in 1922. A private organization concerned with the public sector, the Bureau was administered by the Institute for Government Research along with an advisory board consisting of representatives from the Assembly of Civil Service Commissions, the United States Civil Service Commission, the National Civil Service Reform League, and the National Research Council (Thurstone, 1923). L. L. Thurstone, who previously was head of the Department of Education and Psychology at the Carnegie Institute of Technology, was the first Director of Research at the Bureau. Among the activities in the Bureau's charge were the study of the selection, transfer, and promotion of public sector employees; public service position classification; the training of federal employees; developing tests for postal carriers and clerks; and other personnel concerns of federal, state, and local government employees (News and Comment, 1922b).

*Progress and Then Decline in Psychological Testing*
In the 1920s, American psychologists made significant progress in selection methods, training, and other substantive areas of research and practice. In addition, there was substantial progress in establishing a unique professional reputation. Applied professional organizations were established, new journals were founded, and industrial psychologists made a concerted effort to distinguish themselves from unscientific purveyors of the same services provided by applied psychologists. Finally, the 1920s saw an

---

[25] In a 1957 letter to Leonard Ferguson, Paul Achilles wrote that Bingham gave him the title of "Field Representative" and that he functioned as a "handy man" for the organization: visiting member organizations and coordinating their activities, inviting articles for the journal, and advising Bingham, among other activities. Achilles recalled that Max Freyd worked for the PRF and Bruce V. Moore was employed there at various times. Ferguson (1962) wrote that Moore was "on loan" from Penn State University to the PRF in 1927–28.

increased emphasis on organizational topics, such as motivation, leadership, and job satisfaction, as exemplified by the iconic Hawthorne Studies. All of these topics are discussed in later chapters.

The enthusiasm for psychological testing and industrial psychology evident in the early years of the 1920s did not survive the decade. There were warnings of potential problems early on. Link (1919) warned of the overuse and misuse of the word *psychology* by the general public and of the perception that psychology can be "regarded as the panacea for all ills" (p. 6). Viteles (1921, 1974) used the same word *panacea* in describing "the rush to use intelligence tests – frequently inappropriately and without validation for the specific industrial situation in question – as a panacea for achieving economic goals in industry" (Viteles, 1974, p. 452). By the middle of the 1920s, both the public's and industry's interest in industrial psychology was fading. There were most likely multiple reasons for this disenchantment. The economy was booming, reducing turnover and perhaps also reducing the need for the expertise of psychologists (Hale, 1992). The effectiveness of psychological tests was oversold, resulting in an understandable backlash when they failed to deliver as promised. Commenting on these unreasonable expectations, Wembridge (1925) wrote: "The tests failed only in they could not do what no one had a right to expect they could do" (p. 163). Non-psychologists without adequate knowledge of test construction or validation offered their services, and practitioners of pseudoscientific procedures peddled their systems to the public.[26] Kingsbury (1923) noted that "[m]ost of the blame, probably, is to be placed on the promulgators of the innumerable varieties of fake psychology which are being foisted today upon and uncritical public" (p. 3). Reputable applied psychologists – Link (1919), Viteles (1921), and Kornhauser and Kingsbury (1924), for example – urged caution and an adherence to professional standards, but then, as now, it was difficult for users of psychological services to distinguish a qualified consultant from an unqualified one or a valid test or procedure from an invalid one. In the end, caution probably would not have made much difference. The business community were looking for quick and easy solutions to complex problems. Sokal (1984) noted that this was something a conscientious industrial psychologist simply could not provide.

*Performance Appraisal and Training*
There was industrial psychology work conducted in areas other than testing in the 1920s and early 1930s, for example, in performance appraisal

---

[26] We take a closer look at pseudo-psychology and industrial psychology in Chapter 9.

and employee training. In performance appraisal, Harry Hepner (1893–1984) discussed the potential advantage of using timely feedback from performance ratings to improve employee performance (Hepner, 1930), one of the first psychologists to do so (Farr & Levy, 2007). Farr and Levy (2007) also cited H. L. Humke's (1938–39) use of ratings to identify individuals for training, promotion, or termination and Herbert Moore's (1939) discussion of promotion ratings to create the perception of just decisions based on more than subjective supervisor opinions as notable 1930s developments. Among the rating scales available in the 1920s were the Specific Instance Scale and the Descriptive Term Scale. The Specific Instance Scale used scale anchors that were not developed by the raters, as in Scott's Man-to-Man Scale, but instead used examples of performance that were generated by the scale's authors. In this, the Specific Instance Scale was a forerunner of the well-known Behaviorally Anchored Rating Scale (BARS) developed in by Patricia Cain Smith and Lorne Kendall (1963). Another very popular scale in the 1920s, the Descriptive Term Scale, used descriptive adjectives for scale anchors (Farr & Levy, 2007).

By the 1920s, industrial psychologists were aware that raters could make systematic errors in evaluating performance. Frank L. Wells first mentioned what became known as the *halo* error in 1907 (cited in Guilford, 1936). Link (1919) wrote of "prejudices" by raters due to concentrating on only one particular quality of the worker. E. L. Thorndike (1920) discussed a "halo belonging to the individual as a whole," which he described as an inability of the rater to evaluate individual aspects of performance (p. 25). He noted: "Their ratings were apparently affected by a marked tendency to think of the person in general as rather good or rather inferior and to color the judgments of the qualities by this general feeling" (p. 25). Thorndike examined instances of this constant error, this "halo" as he termed it, in both industry and the military in World War I. Knight and Franzen (1922) discussed an additional error, "leniency," which is the tendency for raters to be overly lenient in their ratings.

Despite progress in training made during World War I, training was a rare professional activity for industrial psychologists in the 1920s, with contemporary texts allocating little space to training. After 1930, there was a shift in training from the supervisor to an expert in training; however, that expert trainer was generally not a psychologist (Kraiger & Ford, 2007). While training focused on skill acquisition, Henry Link (1923a) noted that this was insufficient, that training should arouse interest in the work and create what he termed "institutional goodwill" among the workers.

*The Early 1930s*

The severe 1930s economic depression triggered by the stock market crash of 1929 further diminished opportunities for industrial psychologists, with many firms retrenching and struggling to survive. In the early 1930s, test use in industry diminished; a 1932 Bureau of Labor Statistics study found test use in only 14 of 224 surveyed firms (Hale, 1992). Academia was not a viable employment option, as available academic jobs were scarce as the Great Depression continued. Even in the early years of the Depression, supply was outpacing demand for academic positions. For the academic years 1929–30, 1930–31, and 1931–32, there were 84, 92, and 100 new Ph.D. degrees and 271, 307, and 405 new M.A. degrees granted, yet for those same years only 30, 43, and 33 Ph.D. and 47, 54, and 40 M.A. academic positions were created, based on a survey of 350 American colleges and universities (Poffenberger, 1933). Despite the economic difficulty industry was experiencing, any growth in psychology in the United States during the Depression was in applied psychology (Capshew, 1999).

Notable industrial psychology work did occur in the early 1930s. There were important advances in measurement, such as L. L Thurstone's (1931) pioneering work on multiple factor analysis, and there was the emergence of the test validation strategy called curricular validity, later termed content validity (Rogers, 1995). In 1931, the Minnesota Employment Research Institute was established and subsequently produced a number of occupational tests. The National Occupational Conference founded a program to examine attitude measurement and its relation to job success; it also commissioned Walter Van Dyke Bingham's book *Aptitudes and Aptitude Testing* (1937), published later that decade. Morris Viteles published his landmark survey text *Industrial Psychology* (1932), documenting the scope and depth of the field.

# Oceania

## *Australia*

As was true in Great Britain and in the United States, the original impetus for industrial psychology was to improve the efficiency of work organizations. Intellectuals such as University of Sydney economics professor Robert F. Irvine (1861–1941) and Clarence H. Northcott (1880–1968), who later worked for Rowntree and was director of the Institute of Personnel Management in Great Britain, advocated during World War I for a scientific management approach to efficiency and for the use of psychological tests in employee selection (Blackburn, 1998). Australia's leading proponent of improving efficiency through the use of industrial psychology was Bernard Muscio.

*Bernard Muscio*
Bernard Muscio (1887–1926) received his B.A. in 1910 and his M.A. in 1912 in philosophy from the University of Sydney. He won a scholarship to the University of Cambridge, where he studied philosophy and, with C. S. Myers, psychology, receiving a B.A. in 1913 and an M.A. in 1919. Muscio worked as a demonstrator in experimental psychology at Cambridge from 1914 to 1916 and then returned to the University of Sydney as a lecturer from 1916 to 1919. In 1916, he delivered a series of talks on industrial psychology in Sydney, which later appeared in print as *Lectures in Industrial Psychology* (1917) (O'Neil, 1986). Muscio returned to Great Britain to work as one of the first investigators of the Industrial Fatigue Research Board in 1919 and then moved to the National Institute of Industrial Psychology in 1921. He was appointed Challis Chair of Philosophy at the University of Sydney in 1922, where he died prematurely of pneumonia and pleurisy four years later (Landauer & Cross, 1971).

Landauer and Cross (1971) note that those years at the Industrial Fatigue Research Board and the National Institute of Industrial Psychology were very important for Muscio, permitting him to subject theories he discussed in the *Lectures* to empirical investigation. Muscio's research focused on fatigue and vocational guidance. He recognized that fatigue can be physical or mental, and he accorded great importance to the role of attention in mental fatigue, particularly attention overload. Early in his career, Muscio (1920) was an advocate of scientific management. He, however, rejected the worker as machine analogy and took a holistic approach to the worker, believing that knowledge of the whole individual is necessary, in contrast to the more atomistic approach of scientific management (Landauer & Cross, 1971). This view was similar to that of his former professor C. S. Myers. The overarching goal of Muscio's approach, however, was to increase efficiency and therefore production (Blackburn, 1998).

With his return to the University of Sydney in 1922, Muscio and others expanded industrial psychology and developed links with interested employers. In 1923, Muscio and University of Sydney colleagues founded the *Australasian Journal of Psychology and Philosophy* with the express goal of fostering the application of psychology to increasing industrial efficiency. Topics included in the journal included vocational guidance, research on employee fatigue, and scientific management. After Muscio's death in 1926, Alfred Horatio Martin, along with his University of Sydney department head Henry Tasman Lovell, took up the cause of industrial psychology.[27] Martin, whose doctorate was from Columbia University, became the first director of the Australian Institute of Industrial Psychology. The Institute was founded in 1927 through the efforts of Frank Lincoln Edwards, who was Secretary of Chamber of Manufactures of New South Wales (Blackburn, 1998). This Institute was affiliated with the NIIP in Great Britain (Buchanan, 2012). Engaged primarily in psychological testing, it received funding from employers and had employers as committee members (Blackburn, 1998; Warr, 2007). The early 1920s also saw the first vocational guidance bureau in Australia, a joint effort between the New South Wales Education Department and local employers. Other, similar centers followed (Warr, 2007). Elton Mayo, a professor of philosophy at the University of Queensland, had an interest in the effects of industrialization and of trade unions (Griffin, Landy, & Mayocchi, 2002). Believing that discontent due to class consciousness could be alleviated by creating a more humane workplace, he saw industrial psychology as the vehicle for accomplishing this. Finding little support for his ideas at his university or in the business community, Mayo left to pursue them in the United States (Blackburn, 1998). There he became well known for his part in the Hawthorne Studies.[28]

### New Zealand

Industrial psychology emerged in New Zealand in the early 1920s at Canterbury College of the University of New Zealand. James Shelley (1884–1961), the first chair of education at Canterbury College, most likely gave the first lectures in industrial psychology there and also administered mental tests (Carter, 2012; Jamieson & Paterson, 1993). He and Clarence E. Beeby (1902–98) established a psychological clinic that included a vocational psychology component in 1927 (Jamieson & Paterson, 1993). Beeby was an educational psychologist who received his doctorate at Victoria College where his research was supervised by Charles Spearman. In 1927, Beeby was appointed lecturer in experimental education and experimental psychology at Canterbury, and he later became director of the educational and

---

[27] Lovell was appointed the first professor of psychology in Australia in 1921, as the McCaughey Associate Professor of Psychology at the University of Sydney. The psychology department there was the first in Australia, and Lovell became its first department head and first full professor in 1929 (Blackburn, 1998).

[28] The Hawthorne Studies are discussed in Chapter 10.

psychological laboratories, a post formerly held by Shelley. In 1929–30, Beeby visited psychological laboratories in Canada and the United States (Renwick, 2013). He also spent time in England, where he had some contact with a regional branch of the National Institute of Industrial Psychology. Beeby, along with Shelley, worked on industrial psychology topics, although Beeby candidly admitted that although in the early years they were enthusiastic, they lacked expertise (Beeby, 1979, cited in Jamieson & Paterson, 1993).

## Chapter Summary

Industrial psychology saw considerable expansion following its perceived successes in World War I. That expansion, along with the individuals who made it possible, was described in this chapter on a country-by-country basis. In China, interest in modern psychology, particularly American functionalism, began in the 1920s, with industrial psychology appearing in the early 1930s through the efforts of Chen Li. In Japan, initial interest in scientific management and the study of fatigue in the early twentieth century expanded to other topics such as selection following World War I. The Japanese military, advised by Matataro Matsumoto, was interested in aptitude testing and applying psychology to aviation. In Europe, Germany was prominent in psychotechnics through the efforts of both psychologists and engineers. A number of institutes were established to investigate industrial psychology concerns; prominent psychologists interested in industrial applications included Lipmann and Moede. While there was industrial psychology activity in the private sector, particularly railways, there was considerable industrial psychology work done in the German military. While some industrial psychologists benefited from the opportunities offered by this buildup, the intolerance of the Nazi regime had negative consequences for industrial psychology and tragic consequences for some industrial psychologists.

Other European countries embraced industrial psychology to greater or lesser degrees. In Czechoslovakia and Poland, psychotechnic work was similar to that done in the United States and in Germany. Much of the industrial psychology activity in Great Britain was conducted by the Industrial Fatigue Research Board and the Charles Myers' National Institute of Industrial Psychology. The two entities cooperated with each other and generally rejected mechanistic approaches such as scientific management in favor of more employee-centered ones. While applied psychology work in Italy, especially work in personnel selection and vocational guidance, was evident in the early years of the twentieth century, it was eventually co-opted by the

Fascist movement. There was also early interest in industrial psychology in Switzerland, where Franziska Baumgarten-Tramer was prominent. In Russia, the revolution that resulted in the USSR had an enormous impact on industrial psychology. While the revolutionary regime initially showed an interest, eventually industrial psychology was determined to be out of line with communist ideology and was therefore effectively eliminated in the early 1930s.

Economic prosperity along with the perceived success of the Army testing program in World War I contributed to a great deal of interest in industrial psychology in the United States in the early 1920s. The major focus was on employee selection, especially on the use of psychological tests. Industrial psychology offered opportunities for female psychologists who did not have equal access to academic positions. Consulting firms such as the Scott Company and the Psychological Corporation were established that provided psychological expertise to industry, and the Personnel Research Federation was founded to foster cooperation among industry, government, and universities. Personnel tests had a boom then bust cycle in the 1920s: initial enthusiasm followed by a decline possibly brought about by a combination of overselling the benefits of testing and an inability to control unqualified individuals from developing and marketing them. The economic depression of the 1930s further reduced test use by industry.

Personnel selection was the most prominent industrial psychology activity in America during the 1920s and 1930s. Chapter 7 examines personnel tests and the strategies used to evaluate them.

# Employee Selection in the 1920s

Applying psychology to the selection of employees was the most popular activity for industrial psychologists in the 1920s, certainly in America and to a large extent outside of it as well. Koppes and Pickren (2007) categorized topics from a sample of industrial psychology articles in four leading American psychology journals published between 1887 and 1927 and all articles in the *Journal of Applied Psychology* from its inception in 1917 through 1930. Of the 102 articles sampled, thirty-nine (38 percent) involved selection and/or placement, far outdistancing advertising (19 percent), vocational guidance (11 percent), performance evaluation (5 percent), and training (2 percent).[1] They also examined the frequency of topics in the *Journal of Personnel Research* between 1922 and 1930. Once again, selection/placement was the clear winner. Fifty-two (27 percent) involved selection and placement. The next highest total was seventeen (9 percent) for training. In addition, a number of the other topics listed, such as vocational tests, vocational interests, and job analysis, are related to employee selection. It is true that the amount of research published in journals is an imperfect proxy for overall activity in the profession, as noted by Marion Bills (1953). She discussed reasons for the paucity of published research by practitioners and gave examples of practice that never appeared in journals. While publications may not reflect all activity in industrial psychology, at least based on published research, it is clear that selection was the primary activity of industrial psychologists in America. This assessment is reinforced by contemporary observers such as Morris Viteles (1923).

---

[1] There were fifteen topics listed. The four journals sampled were *Psychological Review, Pedagogical Seminary, Psychological Bulletin,* and *Journal of Educational Psychology.* These journals were sampled every fifth year.

## The Validation Process

By the early 1920s, there was a generally agreed-upon methodology and a more or less standard set of predictors and criteria used for selection. In addition, the terminology used today for the validation process was becoming standard. *Reliability* was used to designate consistency, while *validity* was reserved for the determination of what the test was measuring. By the mid-1920s, the *prognostic value* and *diagnostic value* of a test were now termed *predictive validity* and *concurrent validity,* respectively (T. B. Rogers, 1995). A test was correlated with a behavioral measure, usually job performance, to determine predictive or concurrent validity.[2] This behavioral measure was now termed a *criterion.* The criterion was defined both as a measure of success or failure on the job (Bingham, 1926) and as a job proficiency index used to determine the validity of the test (Burtt, 1926; see Austin & Villanova, 1992). A persistent theme throughout the history of I-O psychology is the difficulty of obtaining and measuring relevant criteria, sometimes termed the *criterion problem.* In addition to reliable and valid tests, by the 1920s industrial psychologists were emphasizing the importance of reliable and valid criteria for test validation. Bingham (1924, 1926), Viteles (1925–26b, 1932) and others were concerned with the unreliability and inadequacy of criteria. They noted that much effort in test construction was wasted by attempting to validate using poor criteria. Viteles (1925–26b) wrote that in the majority of published selection studies, the criteria used were unreliable ratings and rankings, even when more objective criteria such as production data could have been obtained. Although the multidimensional nature of job performance was recognized, most selection studies did not use multiple criteria (Austin & Villanova, 1992).

In the 1920s, the main methods of conducting validation research were to correlate the predictor with the criterion, use some type of comparison method, or use both of these methods together. Comparison methods, described in Chapter 3, involved categorizing employees at different levels on the criterion and matching those levels to a test score or range of scores. The percentage comparison method, for example, gave the percentage of employees at a particular score level who were successful (or unsuccessful) on a criterion such as job performance. If high average test scores were

---

[2] Obtaining test scores from job applicants and later obtaining criterion information once the hired applicants had some time on the job, and then correlating the tests scores with criterion scores is a predictive validation strategy. Testing job incumbents and using available criterion data and correlating those scores is a concurrent validation strategy.

associated with successful job performance and low test scores with poor performance, that provided evidence that the test was doing what it was designed to do, that is, it was valid. I examined a sample of 163 validation studies conducted from 1906 through 1930. Sixty-eight percent (111) were published in American journals, and the remainder were from non-US journals, primarily from Germany, Great Britain, and France. Eighty-four (51 percent) of those studies assessed predictor validity through the use of a correlation, that is, a validity coefficient. Sixty-five studies (40 percent) used some type of comparison method, and fourteen (9 percent) used both correlational and comparison methods.[3] Based on this sample, it appears that while correlational methods were preferred, comparison methods were quite popular.

The postwar correlational predictor-criterion validation process was similar to the basic criterion-related validation strategy used today. Kornhauser and Kingsbury (1924) described the process in the following steps: Based on a job analysis of the job in question, a test or tests were either constructed or selected from existing tests to assess the knowledge or skills necessary for successful performance. The test was administered and test scores were obtained from job applicants or, if that was not possible, from job incumbents. Criterion data, such as production records or supervisor ratings, were obtained. The quantitative relationship between the test scores and the criterion was computed, generally by examining the size of the correlation between the two. That correlation coefficient, the validity coefficient, was compared to the validity of the current method in use. If the new test was superior, critical scores or standards for accepting, rejecting, or classifying applicants were then determined for that test. The procedure outlined by Freyd (1923–24) was similar, although he framed the process in more consciously scientific terms, referring to it as an experiment and to the applicants as subjects. He recommended as a first step engaging a cost consultant to identify the department that could best benefit from improved selection. Freyd also recommended that the experimenter ensure that the tests were properly administered and that the procedures should be checked periodically for accuracy and adjusted if needed. In addition to determining the test's validity, checking the

---

[3] The majority of the studies (151) were taken from Dorcus and Jones (1950), who summarized validity studies from 1906 through the late 1940s. This was not a comprehensive sample nor was it a random sample of validation studies. Dorcus and Jones selected the studies based on criteria that included identification of a specific job, reporting of sample size, explicit identification of the test and job proficiency criterion used, and reporting of either correlational or comparison results. I supplemented these studies with a dozen additional studies from that time period.

reliability of the test was also considered to be important (e.g., Bingham & Freyd, 1926). Burtt (1926) discussed the problem of redundancy or overlap when using multiple tests and described a partial correlation method to deal with this problem.[4] To allay the anxiety that applicants may experience before they take tests, Link (1919) recommended the use of "shock absorbers." This involved administering an initial easy and interesting test, which is not scored, to build confidence and put the applicant at ease.

Bingham and Freyd (1926) recommended that before embarking on a new selection program, psychologists should determine whether there was an actual problem with the current selection system and if there were more applicants than jobs. Selecting better employees was only possible if there was a sufficiently large pool of applicants. Also, there needed to be enough individuals employed in a specific job to make conducting a validation study feasible. Reliable and valid criteria should be available. And it is crucial to determine whether the organization was willing to cooperate with the psychologists implementing the program. Freyd (1923–24) described various methods to combine test scores when multiple tests are used. He recommended the use of multiple regression over other methods such as simply adding raw scores, weighting scores based on reliability, adding percentile standings, and the profile method, which relies on individual judgment rather than statistics.

The concept of selection *utility* had its roots in a 1928 book by Clark Hull that described his Index of Forecasting Efficiency (Taylor & Russell, 1939). Utility involves an assessment of the overall value of a test or tests to the organization, recognizing that factors other than the size of the correlation between the test and criterion can affect that value. Hull made a distinction between predicting average performance for a group and trying to predict performance for a single individual.[5] In the former case, given a large number of job applicants for a single job, even tests with moderate validity coefficients can be of considerable value to the

---

[4] Today the problem of high inter-correlations or redundancy among predictors is termed *multicollinearity*.

[5] It is very difficult to predict individual performance. Predictors used in selection are generally evaluated by how accurately they predict for the group, not for an individual. One may not be able to say which individual applicant will be successful and which will not, but with a valid predictor, you can say that the overall group of hires will be better performers than if the predictor was not used. Validity coefficients are generally quite modest, correlations in the 0.3 to 0.4 range are not uncommon. Therefore, perfect prediction is impossible. There will always be inaccurate predictions: *false positives* who are predicted to succeed but fail and *false negatives* who are predicted to fail but would have succeeded. Since false positives are more damaging to the organization than false negatives, cutoff scores on tests can be set to reduce the occurrence of these false positives, although this increases the proportion of the less worrisome false negatives.

organization.[6] Hull's work anticipated later conceptualizations of selection utility by Taylor and Russell (1939) and Brogden (1946, 1949).

While the statistical approach to employee selection was firmly established in American industrial psychology, not all industrial psychologists were completely comfortable with that orientation. Max Freyd and Morris Viteles debated the issue in the pages of the *Journal of Applied Psychology*, with Freyd defending the statistical approach and Viteles advocating for a more clinical perspective.[7] Viteles (1925) noted that reliance on a single test score is not adequate for diagnosis and that the idea that an individual without extensive psychological training, a "psycho-technician," can adequately interpret test scores is false. He argued for what he considered the more humane European approach. This approach focused on the interests and well-being of the individual employee, unlike the statistical approach which evaluated group performance. Viteles was not saying the statistical approach was unnecessary; in fact, he was a lifelong advocate for valid tests. He believed, however, that the use of valid tests should be combined with a more clinical, employee-centered approach.

Echoing E. L. Thorndike (1918), Freyd (1925) countered each of Viteles' arguments. He noted that the statistical approach provides verifiable evidence that the procedure is valid. Freyd assumed that there was a careful analysis of the job requirements and appropriate criterion selection, that the test had been properly constructed, and that there was a relatively strong correlation between the test and the criterion. The psychologist can then provide empirical evidence for using the predictor, placing selection on a firm scientific basis. Freyd saw difficulties with using judgmental methods, claiming there was no reason to assume the judgment of a psychologist was superior to that of a manager. He questioned the reliability of judgments and believed that bias in the clinical method was unavoidable. Freyd concluded that the task for the psychologist in industry is experimental research. In fact, at the 1925 APA annual conference, Freyd (1926) recommended that applied psychologists drop the "applied" in their name and call themselves experimental psychologists or simply "psychologists" to better reflect the approach they should apply to industrial problems. Disagreement among

---

[6] Today we would term that situation as having a *selection ratio* favorable to the organization. The selection ratio is the number of hires over the number of applicants. Low selection ratios are favorable to the organization because the organization can be more selective in choosing members. High selection ratios are not favorable for the organization, although they do favor applicants because they have less competition for the position.

[7] It is understandable that Viteles would favor a more clinical approach. His Ph.D. advisor at the University of Pennsylvania was Lightner Witmer (1867–1956), who established the first psychological clinic and who was arguably the first clinical psychologist (McReynolds, 1997).

psychologists about the relative accuracy of statistical versus clinical prediction has proved to be a durable topic in psychology, surfacing periodically over the past 100 or so years (see, for example, Meehl, 1954).

Validation studies appeared in many outlets through the 1920s including dissertations, theses, technical reports, and journals. Examination of the 163 validation studies used earlier in this chapter for comparing correlational and comparison validation strategies found 118 of these studies were published in journals. The seventy-nine studies published in American journals appeared in twenty-seven different journals, demonstrating that there was a wide range of journals willing to publish this type of work. Not surprisingly, industrial psychology journals published the most studies. The *Journal of Personnel Research* (later renamed *Personnel Journal*), with twenty-seven studies, published more than twice as many as any other journal, followed by the *Journal of Applied Psychology* with eleven and *Industrial Psychology* with five. While most of the other journals published only one or two studies, the following journals published three each: *Education Administration and Supervision, Electric Railway Journal, Forbes,* and *Journal of Educational Psychology.* The Australian journal *Australasian Journal of Psychology and Philosophy* also published three studies. The nine studies conducted in France were spread out pretty evenly among the journals *Archives de Psychologie (Archives of Psychology), Génie Civil (Civil Engineering), Journal de Psychologie (Journal of Psychology), L'année Psychologique (The Psychological Year),* and *Revue de la Science du Travail (Review of Labor Science).* Six studies were published in British journals, four in the *Journal of the National Institute of Industrial Psychology,* and two in the *British Journal of Psychology.* Twenty-one studies appeared in German journals, ten in *Industrielle Psychotechnik (Industrial Psychotechnics),* seven in *Psychotechnische Zeitschrift (Psychotechnical Journal),* three in *Zeitschrift für angewandte Psychologie (Journal of Applied Psychology),* and one in the engineering journal *Maschinenbau (Mechanical Engineering).* While this sample was neither random nor comprehensive, it does demonstrate the wide range of journals willing to publish validation research.

## Analysis of Predictors and Criteria

Table 7.1, taken from Vinchur (2007), provides a breakdown of the types of tests and criteria used in validation studies from 1906 to 1930.[8] The majority

---

[8] A list of studies used in the analysis is available from the author. The source of all but four of the studies used was Dorcus and Jones (1950).

Table 7.1 *Summary Information from Validity Studies: 1906–1930*

Functional Classification
of Tests

| | Frequency | Percent |
|---|---|---|
| *I. Tests of Proficiencies* | *46* | *6.6* |
| a. Educational Tests | 2 | .3 |
| b. Trade Tests | 44 | 6.3 |
| *II. Tests of Aptitudes* | *635* | *90.3* |
| a. General Aptitude Tests | 75 | 10.6 |
| 1. General Intelligence Tests | 65 | 9.2 |
| 2. Mechanical Aptitude Tests | 10 | 1.4 |
| b. Special Aptitude Tests | 560 | 79.7 |
| 1. Physical Tests | 44 | 6.3 |
| 2. Motor Tests | 117 | 16.6 |
| 3. Sensory Tests | 96 | 13.7 |
| 4. Special Mental Functions | 303 | 43.1 |
| *III. Tests of Character & Temperament* | *22* | *3.2* |
| Total | 703 | 100.0 |

Criteria

| | Frequency | Percent |
|---|---|---|
| *Objective* | *59* | *31.9* |
| Production | 19 | 9.9 |
| Sales | 14 | 7.3 |
| Accidents | 5 | 2.6 |
| Salary | 4 | 2.1 |
| Job Level | 3 | 1.6 |
| *Subjective* | *126* | *68.1* |
| Ratings | 94 | 49.0 |
| Ranking | 32 | 16.7 |

Type of Job

| | Frequency | Percent |
|---|---|---|
| Clerical & Office | 80 | 29.5 |
| Manufacturing | 69 | 25.5 |
| Sales | 34 | 12.5 |
| Teaching | 23 | 8.5 |
| Transportation | 23 | 8.5 |
| Service | 14 | 5.2 |
| Construction | 10 | 3.7 |
| Managerial | 8 | 3.0 |

Note: Some percentages may not add up to 100 percent due to unclassified entries.
Table information from Vinchur (2007).

of the studies analyzed, 147 of 170, were conducted between 1921 and 1930 (two studies were undated but from this period). Two-thirds of the studies were published in the United States; most of the others were from Germany, the United Kingdom, and France, in that order. The 170 studies contained 284 independent samples, with a median sample size of thirty-five (range = 4–5,002). Clerical and office workers comprised the largest sample group (29.5 percent), followed by workers in manufacturing plants (25.5 percent). To organize the predictor and criteria data in a time-period appropriate manner, Kornhauser and Kingsbury's (1924) functional classification approach was used. They categorized tests based on whether they measured proficiencies, aptitudes, or character and temperament. Tests of proficiencies were either educational or trade tests. Tests of aptitudes included general intelligence and mechanical aptitude along with special aptitude tests. Character and temperament tests were what today we would term *personality tests*. Vocational interest tests are included in this category. Not all the tests used as predictors were commercially available tests; a number were "homemade" and were difficult to cleanly classify into Kornhauser and Kingsbury's categories. For this reason, the classification results should be considered a rough estimate only, not a precise categorization of tests.[9]

Of the tests used as predictors, more than 90 percent are classified as aptitude tests. The use of trade tests was much lower, a little over 6 percent of the total. This may be because unlike aptitude tests, trade tests are keyed to specific jobs, making them less generalizable and more time-consuming to construct. Tests of character and temperament, today commonly termed *personality tests*, were used only a little over 3 percent of the time. Personality test use in employee selection did not become popular until the 1930s and later. Of the aptitude tests, tests of general aptitude, mostly general intelligence tests, comprised 10.6 percent of the sample. More popular (79.7 percent) were the special aptitude tests. Tests of specific mental functions were the most used of those, representing more than half of the special aptitude tests. Subjective criteria were twice as popular as objective criteria. As for type of subjective criteria, ratings were used approximately 70 percent of the time, rankings about 30 percent. Production was the most popular objective criterion, followed, in order, by sales, accidents, salary, and job level.

[9] Another difficulty in classifying was that some tests could be classified in more than one category depending on their use. For example, an arithmetic test could be considered an educational test in that setting or a special aptitude test if used in a vocational setting.

The preceding list of tests does not exhaust the types of predictors or criteria in use during the 1920s. In addition to the above, Burtt (1926) added academic records, success in same occupation, personal history or application blanks, letters of application, graphology, letters of recommendation, and interviews. Graphology was viewed with suspicion by industrial psychologists, as were other pseudo-scientific predictors such as phrenology and physiognomy.[10] Techniques used for selection in other countries varied from those used in America. In Germany, for example, while pencil-and-paper tests were used, there was a preference for tests of manual dexterity and the use of elaborate apparatus. This may have been due partially to the belief that such tests are more objective than written tests and more in line with the scientific methodology of the academic laboratory. It was not until the late 1940s and 1950s that written tests came to be preferred over the use of apparatus-type tests in Germany (van Drunen, 1997).[11]

Burtt (1926) categorized criteria into two groups: *Estimates by supervisors* with grouping, ranking, and linear scales (ratings) as examples; and *Production figures*. He also recognized that other criteria, such as quality of work, amount of preliminary training, and length of service, were available. Viteles (1932) discussed twelve types of objective criteria: those concerned with production (quantity and quality of output), reduction of production (amount of spoiled work, number of breakages, number of operating mistakes), number and cost of accidents, length of service or job stability, earnings (commission and bonus), rate of advancement, and Standard Trade Examinations. He also described eight variations of rating scales, including the popular graphic rating scale and the man-to-man comparison scale. The general consensus was that objective criteria were preferable to subjective (e.g., Burtt, 1926; Kornhauser & Kingsbury, 1924). Although there was a recognition that job performance is multidimensional, the majority of studies used only one or two criteria. One exception was Kornhauser (1923–24), whose research on billing clerks used the objective criteria of speed and accuracy in addition to speed and accuracy ratings (Austin & Villanova, 1992).

The following section examines predictors and criteria used in validation studies. For tests, categorization into tests of proficiencies, aptitudes, and character and temperament (which includes interest inventories), following Kornhauser and Kingsbury (1924), is used.[12] Interviews and

---

[10] These and other so-called "pseudo-psychological" techniques are reviewed in Chapter 9.

[11] Cf. the "Science and Scientific Psychology" section of Chapter 2.

[12] Another method to categorize tests was by occupation, for example, tests for clerical workers, tests for engineers, or tests for executives, or a combination of occupation and the type of psychological or physical attribute the test assessed (e.g., Manson, 1925–26b).

personal history data are also discussed. For some of the categories, examples of validation studies are presented. The studies presented are meant not to be representative but just to illustrate the kind of research conducted during this time period.

## Tests of Proficiencies

### Educational Tests

Proficiencies refer to knowledge, skills, and abilities that are acquired through learning and experience. Educational tests are a classic example of tests of proficiencies that have been used since teachers have been examining pupils, although it was not until the early twentieth century that these tests began to be standardized. For industrial psychology, educational tests provided a template for trade tests, tests that assess knowledge and skill in trades such a typist, bricklayer, lathe operator, and other standard trades (Chapman, 1923; Kornhauser & Kingsbury, 1924).

### Trade Tests

The major impetus behind the development of occupational trade tests was the US Army's need to fill a large number of skilled positions in World War I. As discussed in Chapter 5, the Committee on Classification of Personnel in the US Army was created in 1917 to give psychologists the opportunity to assist in this and other personnel needs. The Army needed a procedure to measure trade proficiency that would be applicable to all trades, could be administered by an examiner who has no particular knowledge of that trade, and could reliably differentiate among different levels of trade skill and knowledge. The Army recognized four levels of expertise in order from least to most proficient: novice, apprentice, journeyman, and expert. In addition, the test must be able to be administered quickly and scored in an objective manner independent of the judgment of the examiner. Three types of trade tests were created: oral, picture, and performance trade tests (Chapman, 1923).

The procedure for constructing an oral trade test was described by Chapman (1923). After reviewing the trade literature for a particular trade and consulting with supervisors and tradespeople, fifty or sixty initial questions were written. These questions were then administered to approximately a dozen tradespeople who represented apprentice, journeyman, and expert levels of experience. Based on their response to the test questions and to a series of follow-up questions, poor questions were eliminated. The total number of questions was reduced to approximately thirty to forty, taking care to ensure that each level of experience was represented in these items. This smaller subset of questions was then administered to a larger group, roughly twenty individuals at each of the four levels of expertise. Based on this administration, questions that were ambiguous, were questionably related to performance, or did not differentiate among expertise levels were eliminated. The final test, generally fifteen to twenty questions, was calibrated to determine the critical scores separating novice, apprentice, journeyman, and expert levels.[13]

Oral trade tests are useful when one can reasonably infer a strong relationship between knowledge of a trade and skill in carrying out that trade. Picture trade tests, whose construction is similar to that of an oral trade test, used pictures of tools, machinery, or work operations to approximate the actual work situation. Although more difficult to construct than oral trade tests, they have the advantage of appearing more relevant to the trade by the person taking the test. Performance trade tests were standardized samples of the actual job, using tools and materials characteristic of that occupation. A standardized test of typing is an example. Performance trade tests are useful when the connection between job knowledge and performance is weak (e.g., knowing about the operation of the typewriter does not necessary predict typing speed). They could also be used with candidates who lack English-language skills. A major difficulty in constructing these types of tests was procuring a sample of job behaviors that are representative of the whole job (Chapman, 1923). An example of a performance test is the driving test that was used to select train engineers for the Royal Saxon Railroads in Germany. Adapted by Walther Moede, Curt Piorkowski, and Max Brahn from a similar test developed by Piorkowski and Moede to select motorcar drivers in World War I, the railway test was first used in Dresden in 1917. The applicant sat in front of a stimulus canvas surrounded by various levers, handles, and indicators used on the job. After an explanation of the controls and an opportunity to practice, the candidate simulated driving a steam locomotive. Speed and precision of reaction were evaluated using standard psychology laboratory equipment such as the Hipp chronoscope (Gundlach, 1997).

---

[13] This procedure is recognizable as the current-day *content-oriented validation* strategy aka *content-oriented test development.*

Examples of trade test validation studies in the 1920s include the following: Filer and O'Rourke (1922) tested ninety general clerks using a civil service clerical examination. They found a correlation between test scores and efficiency ratings of 0.70. Paterson (1922–23) used the Scott Company file clerk test as the predictor and a criterion of supervisor ratings of trade status for a sample of forty-three clerks. The validity coefficient between the test scores and ratings was 0.82. As part of a larger study, Weber and Leslie (1926) correlated scores from the Thurstone Test for Clerical Work with supervisor ratings for a group of twenty-eight stenographers. They calculated a correlation between test scores and ratings of 0.69.[14]

## Tests of Aptitudes

### General Aptitude Tests

While proficiency tests measure an individual's current level of knowledge or current skill level, aptitude tests are designed to measure potential: individuals who have the intellectual, mechanical, or other aptitude to be successful on the job. Unlike proficiency tests, aptitude tests should not be dependent on specific prior knowledge, although as illustrated by the previous discussion of the US Army Alpha and Beta tests, this can be true more in theory than actuality.

### General Intelligence Tests

Also known as mental alertness tests, general ability tests, and learning ability tests, by the early 1920s general intelligence tests were such a prominent part of the culture that they were used as a synonym for a psychological test (Kornhauser & Kingsbury, 1924). In previous chapters, the history of these tests, from the early efforts of Binet through the group

---

[14] Originally I had intended to conduct a meta-analysis of validity studies for each of the predictor categories, reasoning the large amount of variability among validity coefficients was likely due to statistical artifacts such as sampling error. However, lack of useful studies in some categories and other complications such as lack of needed statistical information recorded, a tendency to average across disparate tests and only report the multiple correlation, and difficulty equating predictors within each category made the meta-analysis unworkable. To give the reader a rough idea of average validity for at least two categories, for trade tests, across 24 samples with a median sample size of 32.5, the average weighted correlation was 0.46. For general intelligence tests, across 21 samples with a median sample size of 43, the average weighted correlation was 0.24. Caution should be used in interpreting these values, as for both types of tests there were some correlations that were unusually high (in the 0.8 to 0.9 range), and the range of validity coefficients was often extreme.

intelligence tests used in World War I, was examined. Also discussed were some of the controversial issues that surrounded the use of these tests. The focus here is on the validity of the tests used by industrial psychologists. Examples of the tests used include revisions of the Army Alpha and Beta tests, the Scott Company Mental Alertness Test, the Otis Self-Administering Test of Mental Ability, the Morgan Mental Test, the CIT Bureau of Personnel Research Test VI, and the Terman Group Test of Mental Ability.

Examples of studies from the 1920s that examined the validity of intelligence tests include the following. Bingham and Davis (1924) evaluated the predictive validity of the Bureau of Personnel Research Test VI, which was based on the Army Alpha, for a sample of seventy-three businessmen. The criterion was business success as determined by a personal history inventory. They found a correlation between test scores and success ratings of −0.10, essentially no relationship between the test and success. A more positive result was found by Paterson (1922–23), who correlated scores on the Scott Company Mental Alertness Test with trade status for a group of forty-three file clerks. Paterson found a correlation of 0.63 between the test and criterion. Other studies that evaluated intelligence tests in the 1920s include Bills (1923), Cowdery (1922), Otis (1920), Scudder (1929), and Snow (1923).

*Mechanical Aptitude Tests*
These tests can require the applicant to perform a task, such as assembling a series of objects, or they can be pencil-and-paper-type tests that present pictures of machinery or tools. Mechanical aptitude tests differ from trade tests in that, although they are more or less tests of acquired ability, that ability is of a type useful across occupations and is not tied to a specific trade (Kornhauser & Kingsbury, 1924). Link (1919) provides an example of a validation study using a mechanical aptitude test from his text *Employment Psychology.* Link tested a small sample of twelve apprentice machinists using the Stenquist Mechanical Assembly test. Using instructor and foreman rankings as the criterion, he found a very high correlation of 0.84; however, because of the small sample size, it is difficult to evaluate this result. Crockett (1926–27), however, found a correlation of only 0.09 between the Stenquist and mechanical ability ratings for a group of twenty-seven tool and die maker apprentices.

*Special Aptitude Tests*

This varied group of tests assesses a narrower set of aptitudes than the general intelligence or mechanical aptitude tests and can be considered components of those larger tests.

*Physical Tests*

While they were designed to test physical or physiological aspects of individuals, physical tests were also viewed as having a psychological component. For example, success of a test of hand-grip strength depends not only on physical strength but also on a person's "will" (Kornhauser & Kingsbury, 1924). The physical attributes measured covered a wide range. Some examples were height, weight, muscular strength, resistance to fatigue using an ergograph, grip strength using a hand dynamometer, and amount of tremor using a tremometer. Kitson (1922–23) examined height and weight as predictors, with supervisor rankings of commissions earned as the criterion, for a group of ninety shoe salesmen. He found a correlation between height and the criterion of 0.11 and between weight and the criterion of 0.05.

*Motor Tests and Sensory Tests*

Motor aptitude tests assess characteristics such as speed and accuracy of movement and muscular control. Examples of these tests include finger dexterity tests, pegboards, tracing and line drawing tests, and tapping tests. Sensory tests measure the functioning of the sensory organs. Examples include visual acuity tests, tests of color blindness and color naming, hearing tests, and tests for balance or equilibrium. These tests were popular in Europe during the 1920s.

*Tests of Other Special Mental Functions*

This category involves tests of the various components, such as attention, perception, memory, and judgment, which together comprise overall mental functioning. A large variety of tests were included in this category. Examples include simple memory tests, spelling tests, cancellation tests, arithmetic tests, synonyms, antonyms, tests of directions, sentence completion tests, sorting tests, and tests of other functions, many of which are components of the omnibus general intelligence tests.

## Tests of Character and Temperament Traits

### *Personality Tests*

This category includes not only tests that today we would call personality tests but also tests of "moral judgment" and tests of interests. Woodworth's prototypical personality test, the *Woodworth Personal Data Sheet (WPDS)*, was revised by him after the war for civilian use. Like most American personality tests of the 1920s and early 1930s, Woodworth's test was designed to measure maladjustment. Identifying and eliminating potential or actual workers who displayed emotional instability was believed to be the solution to low productivity, labor organization, and other industrial concerns. This was consistent with the view that work difficulties were not primarily a function of external conditions such as low pay but were rather due to the personal maladjustment of workers. This belief was reinforced by psychologists such as Elton Mayo and by psychiatrists and other individuals who founded the *mental hygiene* movement (Gibby & Zickar, 2008).[15]

Most of the personality tests developed in the 1920s measured one or two dimensions and focused on maladjustment. Initially these tests borrowed items from Woodworth's inventory; eventually they borrowed from each other.[16] Donald A. Laird (1925a) of Colgate University developed the Colgate Mental Hygiene Test. It was based on Woodworth's WPDS and designed to identify persons "in need of mental hygiene" and to quantify "the degree and kind of deviation" (p. 128). In addition to the items measuring psychoneurotic traits, items assessing introversion and extroversion were later included (Hoitsma, 1925). Elwood (1927) compared female nursing students with female liberal arts college students on Colgate Mental Hygiene Test scores. He found the nursing students to be more emotionally stable and more extroverted than the college students. L. L. Thurstone and Thelma Gwinn Thurstone (1930) published the Personality Schedule, a neurotic inventory compiled to a large extent from existing tests including the WPDS, Laird's Colgate inventory, questions about ascendance-submission taken from Allport, and questions about introversion and extroversion taken from Freyd. Viteles (1932)

---

[15] Worker maladjustment and Elton Mayo are part of the discussion of organizational psychology in Chapter 10.

[16] An exception was the "cross-out" or cancellation tests developed by Pressey and Pressey (1919) (Gibby & Zickar, 2008). Pintner (1923) claimed the first use of a cancellation test was by the French psychologist Benjamin B. Bourdon in 1895.

identified this test, the Colgate Personality Inventory, and the Woodworth-Wells Psychoneurotic Inventory as tests used in industrial settings (Gibby & Zickar, 2008). An early example of a study evaluating a temperament test for predicting job performance was conducted by Ream (1922). He gave 122 insurance salesmen the Carnegie Bureau of Personnel Research Will-Temperament Test. Based on how much insurance they sold in an eleven-week training course, Ream divided them into Successful, Doubtful, and Unsuccessful groups. While he did not compute validity coefficients, he found that in the Successful group, sixty-one individuals passed the test while only eight failed. In the Unsuccessful group, twenty-seven failed the test and only three passed.

The early 1930s saw the advent of more multidimensional inventories, led by Robert Bernreuter's (1931) Bernreuter Personality Inventory (BPI). This test was followed a few years later by the Humm-Wadsworth Temperament Scale (HWTS), developed by Doncaster G. Humm and Guy W. Wadsworth Jr. (1933–34).[17] Bernreuter (1931) noted that existing personality tests assume that individual behavior in a given situation is associated with a single trait. His goal in constructing his inventory was to simultaneously assess several traits, assuming that behavior is the result of multiple traits operating to varying degrees. Bernreuter's test was designed to measure four traits: neurotic tendency, introversion-extroversion, ascendance-submission, and self-sufficiency.[18] He reported that split-half reliabilities for the individual scales were all above 0.80. Despite acceptable reliability, the validity of the test for predicting worker performance was disappointing (Gibby & Zickar, 2008).

### Interest Inventories

DuBois (1970) noted that interest tests applied to education appeared as early as 1912 by Edward L. Thorndike and in 1914 by Thorndike's doctoral student Truman Lee Kelley. For more industrial applications, pioneering work of the use of interests was conducted at the Carnegie Institute of Technology (CIT) in Pittsburgh, Pennsylvania, especially during the early 1920s. The applied psychology program at CIT was the first doctoral program in industrial psychology. Despite the program's short existence from 1915 to 1924, a great

---

[17] Application of and research on the HWTS occurred outside the time period covered in this history. The HWTS was heavily marketed to industry and quite popular. See Gibby and Zickar (2008) for a description of the test and its use.

[18] By 1935, two additional traits were added: self-consciousness and solitariness (Gibby & Zickar, 2008).

deal of important work was done there on employee selection, including the use of interests. Among the individuals who conducted research on interests were staff members James B. Miner (1922) and Clarence S. Yoakum. Yoakum supervised the doctoral program, whose four graduates, Bruce V. Moore, Merrill Ream, Max Freyd, and Grace Manson, all worked on interest research (Ferguson, 1962–65).[19] In 1919–20, Yoakum conducted a seminar on interests that resulted in a pool of approximately 1,000 items that were used in later studies (DuBois, 1970).

Bruce Moore (1921), building on an idea from James Miner, conducted his doctoral research on the use of interests to successfully differentiate new employees that were best suited for sales engineering careers from those best suited for design engineering careers at the Westinghouse Electric and Manufacturing Company. Merrill Ream (1924) extended this idea in an attempt to distinguish successful from unsuccessful salespersons. While he was unable to do so, Ream did offer a valuable insight: that items could be objectively scored based on how well they distinguished between the two groups, an early example of the contrasting criterion group method. Max Freyd (1922–23) applied this method to assessing personality differences between mechanically versus socially inclined students. While Freyd interpreted these differences in terms of the extroversion-introversion personality dimension, Edward K. Strong Jr., one of Freyd's advisors at CIT, thought it best to interpret these criterion score differences directly as job compatibility predictors rather than as personality indicators. Strong took this idea with him when he moved in 1923 to Stanford University, where with his student Karl Cowdery he developed his well-known Strong Vocational Interest Blank (Ferguson, n.d.).

At Stanford, Strong and Truman Kelley supervised Karl Cowdery's doctoral dissertation. Cowdery (1926–27) used a sample of medical doctors, lawyers, and engineers to improve on the interest inventory developed at CIT by constructing a weighting process that approximated multiple regression and by cross-validating the results on a new group of professionals. Using Cowdery's inventory as a template, Strong increased the number of occupations covered, increased the sample sizes, and simplified the item weight calculations. Strong published his Strong Vocational Interest Blank in 1927 and spent the remainder of his career refining it (DuBois, 1970). Grace Manson (1931) developed her own occupational interest test and used it to assess close to 14,000 women.

---

[19] These individuals and the CIT program are discussed in Chapter 8.

## Other Predictors

### *Interviews*

The interview was the most popular selection technique used by personnel departments in the 1920s and for the majority of organizations the sole procedure used (Viteles, 1932). Viteles noted a number of problems with interviews. Brevity is one. Viteles cited research discussed in Bingham and Moore (1931) that for two large organizations, the Kearny Works of the Western Electric Company and R. H. Macy and Company, initial interviews lasted only about one minute and second interviews averaged five or six minutes. Errors common in interviews included "conditioned reactions" (basing judgment on non-job-related characteristics such as gait, posture, or dress), unintentional bias due to the interviewer's attitude or "mental set," and failure to define the traits or terms used in the interview. Viteles wrote that interviews generally exhibit poor reliability, as assessed by level of agreement among interviewers, along with poor predictive validity.

The reliability of interviews had been questioned as far back as 1915 by Walter Dill Scott. While empirical research on the reliability and validity of the interview was relatively rare in the 1920s and early 1930s, there were a few studies conducted (Eder, Kacmar, & Ferris, 1989). Hollingworth (1922) had twelve experienced sales managers interview and rank-order fifty-seven job applicants. The rankings showed a great deal of variability, calling into question their reliability. Kenagy and Yoakum (1925) looked at the validity of the interview for salespersons using sales performance two months after hire as the criterion. Based on a half-hour interview, an executive rated thirty-four salespersons, while two other executives rated these individuals based on their performance in a two-week training program. The validity coefficient between the interview and sales performance was 0.27. The correlation between the interview and training ratings was 0.16, and between the interview and performance it was 0.21. Moss (1931) had interviewers rate medical school applicants' scholastic ability. If the interview ratings had been used, they would have identified 33 percent of the applicants who would have failed; however, they also would have eliminated 23 percent of students who earned an average of 85 percent or greater.

Recognizing the unreliability of interviews, Burtt (1926) had four suggestions for improvement. First was the use of multiple interviewers whose results could be pooled. Burtt emphasized the importance of establishing good rapport with the candidate. He advocated for the use of "crucial questions" that are relevant for the job and based on a job analysis and job specifications. Finally, Burtt said interviewers should keep in mind those traits that are most important to evaluate during the interview. To facilitate the last two suggestions, Burtt recommended using a rating scale to assess traits in a systematic manner.[20] Viteles (1932) also offered suggestions to improve the interview. He advocated careful selection and proper training of interviewers, clear definitions of the traits assessed and the methods used to measure them, repeated interviews and observation by independent individuals, and standardization of interview procedures.

## Application Forms and Personal History Data

Personal history data were used as predictors in the 1920s, although they predate that period. Personal history inventories and standardized application blanks date back at least to Thomas Peters in 1894. Peters developed an inventory while working for the Washington Life Insurance Company in Atlanta. In 1915, businessman Edward A. Woods of Pittsburgh attempted to differentiate successful employees from unsuccessful ones through the use of personal history items (Ferguson, n.d.).[21] Personal history inventories assessed a variety of information. Examples included age, marital status, number of dependents, education, work experience, membership in organizations, number of investments, and home ownership.

Among the studies that evaluated the validity of personal history inventories were the following. Holcombe (1922) had a sample of 148 life insurance salespersons complete a personal history inventory. Using production as the criterion, he found that 67 percent of successful salespersons had high scores on the inventory while only 27 percent of the failures had high scores. Goldsmith (1922) used a sample of 502 salespersons to evaluate personal history data with amount of insurance paid for as the criterion. Only 4 percent were successful in the low scoring group, while 53 percent were successful in the high scoring group. Using a large sample size of 4,178 insurance agents from eighteen companies, Manson (1925–26a) evaluated the validity of personal history items using the criterion of amount of insurance paid. She reported low correlations between the predictor and criterion.

---

[20] This suggestion anticipated the *structured interview*, where questions are standardized and based on knowledge and abilities shown to be important for job success. Structured interviews have generally been found to be more reliable and valid than unstructured ones (e.g., Schmidt & Hunter, 1998; Wiesner & Cronshaw, 1988).

[21] In Chapter 8, Woods's role in establishing the Bureau of Salesmanship Research at the Carnegie Institute of Technology is discussed.

## Chapter Summary

Using psychology to improve the employee selection process was a very popular activity for industrial psychologists in the 1920s. By that time, a standard set of predictors and criteria were coming into use. Predictors included various types of proficiency and aptitude tests, personality tests, interest inventories, interviews, and personal history data. Criteria were primarily job performance measures, either objective measures or subjective measures such as supervisor ratings. Predictors were validated for the most part either by comparing various test score levels with corresponding levels of performance or by correlating predictor scores with criterion scores. A typical procedure for the correlational method would have been to construct or select a test based on a job analysis, administer that test to either a group of applicants or a group of current employees, obtain criterion scores for that group, and then correlate the two sets of scores. If the relationship between those two variables was strong, the test was considered to be valid. In the 1920s, there was the beginning of a recognition that a strong correlation was not enough. Other factors, such as the percentage of applicants that must be selected and the percentage of employees who are already successful on the job, contributed to the usefulness, value, or utility of the test for the organization.

The analysis of a fairly large number of validation studies conducted from 1906 through 1930s found that more than 50 percent of the employees assessed worked in clerical, office, or manufacturing positions. The vast majority of tests used were classified as aptitude tests; the use of trade tests, personality tests, and interest inventories was much lower. Subjective criteria, such as ratings, were more than twice as popular as objective criteria that assessed actual production. The validity of these tests and other predictors such as interviews and personal history data was quite variable, probably a reflection of factors such as small sample sizes.

## CHAPTER 8

# The Education of Industrial Psychologists

## Education in Psychology Prior to 1900

While a formal scientific psychology is less than 150 years old, psychology was taught in colleges and universities well before that. Fay (1939) suggested that in the United States, psychology instruction began with Henry Dunster's presidency of Harvard College in 1640. While it is true that psychology was not yet distinct from philosophy and instruction on psychological topics did not take place in courses named *psychology*, the subject matter was recognizably psychological in nature. Fay divided pre-1890 American psychology into three periods: The *Theology and Moral Philosophy* period (1640–1776) relied on English scholastic education and the American Enlightenment; next, the *Intellectual Philosophy* period (1776–1861) focused first on Scottish philosophy and then, after the 1820s, on the use of American textbooks. From 1861 to 1890, the *British and German Influence* was most prominent.[1] It was during that latter period that the first graduate programs in psychology emerged.

In the beginning years of industrial psychology, there were no graduate programs specifically in that discipline.[2] The early industrial psychologists were for the most part generalists who, in addition to their applied work, had other often quite diverse interests. Contributions to industrial psychology also came from individuals trained in fields other than psychology, such as business, engineering, and medicine. Therefore, training for industrial psychology work was varied and nonstandard. Some of the pioneers in industrial psychology had medical degrees, such as Emilio Mira (Universidad Central de España, 1923), or both M.D. and doctoral degrees, such as Hugo Münsterberg (Ph.D., University of Leipzig, 1885; M.D., University of Heidelberg, 1887), Willy Hellpach (Ph.D., University of

---

[1] These dates are approximate, and there was some overlap among the divisions (Fay, 1939).
[2] The focus in this chapter is on doctoral education in the United States in psychology departments. For a history of undergraduate education in psychology, see McGovern and Brewer (2013).

Leipzig, 1900; M.D., University of Leipzig, 1903), Agostino Gemelli (Ph. D. in philosophy, University of Louvain, 1911; M.D., University of Pavia, 1902), Charles S. Myers (Sc.D., University of Cambridge, 1909; M.D., University of Cambridge, 1901), and Walther Poppelreuter (Ph.D., University of Königsberg, 1909; M.D., University of Munich, 1915) (Zusne, 1984).

In the late 1800s, the German university model was world-renowned. For individuals interested in obtaining a doctorate in psychology, Germany was the preferred destination. Wilhelm Wundt and his psychological laboratory at Leipzig produced some notable figures in early industrial psychology. Münsterberg and Hellpach received their doctorates at Leipzig with Wundt, as did the Americans James McKeen Cattell in 1886 and Walter Dill Scott in 1900, the British psychologist Charles Spearman in 1905, and the German psychologists Wilhelm Peters and Otto Klemm in 1904 and 1906, respectively (Tinker, 1932). Early contributors to what became industrial psychology who studied in universities other than the University of Leipzig include William Stern (Ph.D., University of Berlin, 1893) and Otto Lipmann (Ph.D., University of Breslau, 1904). Around 1900 and shortly thereafter, Americans important to the history of industrial psychology began completing their doctorates in the new psychology graduate programs in the United States. Those programs, with one exception, did not offer a doctorate in industrial psychology per se; it was, however, possible to get training in industrial psychology from faculty interested in the field. The exception was the program at the Carnegie Institute of Technology (CIT), where it was possible to obtain a doctorate in industrial psychology. Although short-lived, the program at CIT had an outsize influence on industrial psychology's development.

## Carnegie Institute of Technology Division of Applied Psychology

The first graduate program to focus specifically on training industrial psychologists began in 1915 at CIT, now named Carnegie Mellon University, in Pittsburgh, Pennsylvania. Because of the influence this program had on the development of I-O psychology in the United States and the many prominent industrial psychologists associated with it, it merits coverage in some detail. The industrialist Andrew Carnegie founded CIT in 1900 as Carnegie Technical Schools, a vocational training school for the children of blue-collar workers. In 1912, the name was changed to the Carnegie Institute of Technology, at which time the school began offering four-year degrees. Initially, CIT consisted of four schools: the

School of Applied Design, the School of Applied Industries, the School of Applied Science, and a school for women: the Margaret Morrison Carnegie School. Industrial psychology was a perfect fit for the practical, vocational orientation of CIT. At the 1914 annual meeting of the APA, the president of CIT, Arthur A. Hamerschlag, asked Dartmouth College professor Walter Van Dyke Bingham if he would be interested in evaluating the role psychology could play at CIT. Bingham agreed, and Hamerschlag was impressed enough with the report produced that he offered Bingham an appointment. Bingham accepted and arrived at CIT in January 1915 (Ferguson, 1962–65).

### *Walter Van Dyke Bingham*

Walter Van Dyke Bingham (1880–1952) was an inspired choice to lead the applied psychology program at CIT, based on his background, interests, and abilities. Born in Swan Lake City, Iowa, in 1880, Bingham (Figure 8.1) spent a year at the University of Kansas before transferring and obtaining his A.B. degree at Beloit College in 1901. Unlike the first generation of industrial psychologists such as Münsterberg and Scott who obtained their doctorates in Germany, Bingham did his graduate work at the University of Chicago, one of the epicenters of the functionalist orientation in American psychology. While at Chicago, Bingham worked with James Rowland Angell, functionalism's leading theorist, and was a student assistant for John B. Watson, the early proponent of the behavioral approach to psychology.[3] While a student, Bingham traveled to Europe. In Berlin, he met with Wolfgang Köhler and Kurt Koffka, two of the founders of the Gestalt approach to psychology. He also met with future industrial psychologist Hans Rupp. In England, Bingham met with leading psychometricians Charles Spearman and Cyril Burt along with Charles S. Myers, who would go on to become Great Britain's leading industrial psychologist (Bingham, 1952).

Prior to completing his doctorate in 1908, Bingham studied philosophy at Harvard University in 1907, where he worked with William James and other Harvard psychologists, including Hugo Münsterberg. Bingham

---

[3] John B. Watson's 1913 article *Psychology as a Behaviorist Views It* is credited with initiating the new behaviorist school of psychology in opposition to both structuralism and functionalism (Zusne, 1984). While Watson was primarily an animal researcher during his academic career at the University of Chicago and Johns Hopkins University, following his resignation from Johns Hopkins, he began a long and successful second career in advertising with the J. Walter Thompson agency in New York City in 1921 (Goodwin, 1999; Schultz & Schultz, 2004).

Figure 8.1  Walter Van Dyke Bingham. Courtesy of Beloit College Archives

began his academic career at Columbia University, where he became well acquainted with differential psychology and mental test development while working with Edward L. Thorndike. In 1910, Bingham accepted an appointment at Dartmouth College, where he remained until leaving for the CIT position in 1915 (Ferguson, 1962–65).

### The Division of Applied Psychology at CIT

Bingham's initial charges at CIT were to head a Department for Training of Teachers and to start a Bureau of Mental Tests; however, by the academic year 1916–17, he was named director of a Division of Applied Psychology (DAP),[4] with a wide range of responsibilities across all four CIT schools.[5] In addition to the Bureau of Mental

---

[4] The Division of Applied Psychology (1915–21) was renamed the Division of Cooperative Research from 1921 to 1924 (Ferguson, 1962).

[5] Bingham was not the first psychologist to teach at CIT. The first was George Alexander Hutchison, who taught from 1910 to 1913 (Ferguson, 1962–65).

Tests and the Department for Training of Teachers, the DAP consisted of the Department of Psychology and Education along with additional Departments of Psychology and Education in the School of Applied Industries and in the Margaret Morrison Carnegie School (Ferguson, 1962–65). The 1915–16 appointees in DAP were Bingham, whose initial title was Professor of Psychology and Education and Head of the Department for Training of Teachers; James B. Miner, Assistant Professor of Psychology; Margaret Louise Free and Louis L. Thurstone, Assistants in the Department of Psychology; Katherine Murdoch, Instructor in Psychology and Education; Jonathan Zerbe, Instructor in Psychology and Pedagogy; and Edwin H. Smith, Instructor in Manual Training. In 1916–17, Kate Gordon was added as Assistant Professor of Psychology and Education, Guy Montrose Whipple as a consultant and Lecturer in Applied Psychology, and Walter Dill Scott as Professor of Applied Psychology and Director of the Bureau of Salesmanship Research (Division of Applied Psychology 1915–1924, n.d.).

The DAP also included a number of cooperative enterprises with local businesses. These innovative ventures were some of the first examples of how business and academia can work together for their mutual benefit. The Bureau of Salesmanship Research, begun in 1916, was proposed to Bingham by the insurance executive Edward A. Woods. Woods conceived of the Bureau as a laboratory for developing and testing methods for the recruitment, selection, and training of sales personnel. Business partners would contribute capital and in return make use of the findings of the Bureau to improve sales. Among the eighteen original members were the Aluminum Company of America, Carnegie Steel, Ford Motor, B. F. Goodrich, H. J. Heinz, Westinghouse, and a number of insurance companies including John Hancock, Metropolitan Life, and Prudential. To direct the Bureau, Bingham brought in Walter Dill Scott, who took a leave from Northwestern University. At CIT, Scott was given the title of Professor of Applied Psychology, the first such designation in the United States. Shortly after the establishment of the Bureau, Scott and Bingham traveled to the first Salesmanship Congress in Detroit, Michigan, where with Guy Montrose Whipple they provided possibly the first empirical demonstration of the unreliability of the employment interview (Ferguson, 1962–65; n.d.; Scott, Bingham, & Whipple, 1916).

The initial student-staff associates were Charles H. Brundage, Kurt T. Friedlaender, Russell L. Gould, Dwight L. Hoopingarner, Mary La

Dame, Edward S. Robinson, and Charles Booth Tuttle.[6] Ferguson (1962–65) noted that these seven individuals were the first group of students educated specifically for a career in industrial psychology. Of that group, Brundage, Friedlaender, Gould, and Tuttle went on to business careers (Ferguson, 1962). Edward S. Robinson (1893–1937) earned a Ph.D. under James Angell at the University of Chicago and remained in academia at Yale University and at the University of Chicago. He did noteworthy work in the functionalist vein on learning, problem solving, social psychology, and law until his early accidental death (Zusne, 1984). Dwight Hoopingarner (1893–1955) became one of the early non-doctoral industrial psychologists to be employed in industry when, following his year at CIT in 1916–17, he was hired as director of employment and education at the National Bank of Commerce in New York City. Hoopingarner spent his career in labor relations in academia, law firms, and organizations such as New York Building Congress and the American Construction Council. He wrote *Labor Relations in Industry* in 1925. Like Hoopingarner, Mary La Dame's career was also in labor relations. Following her time at CIT, La Dame (1884–1972) investigated employment agency administration at state and federal levels for the Russell Sage Foundation. She then became executive secretary to the New York State Committee on Employment Problems, chaired by Frances Perkins, Commissioner of Labor for the State of New York. When Perkins became US Secretary of Labor in the Roosevelt administration, she asked La Dame to join her in Washington as Special Assistant to the Secretary of Labor. In that capacity, La Dame was instrumental in determining the policies and overall structure of the United States Employment Service (Ferguson, 1962).

Other cooperative ventures followed the creation of the Bureau of Salesmanship Research. At the urging of Edgar J. Kaufmann of the Pittsburgh-based Kaufmann Department stores, in 1918 the Bureau of Retail Training began first under the direction of James B. Miner and then later was directed by Werrett W. Charters.[7] Among the activities of

---

[6] Only Friedlaender, Gould, Hoopingarner, La Dame, and Robinson are listed as Fellows and Research Assistants in 1916–17 in the Cleeton Papers (Division of Applied Psychology 1915–1924, n.d.).

[7] In an undated memoir of the Bureau of Retail Training (possibly from the 1950s), Elizabeth Dyer, who worked at the Bureau from 1918 to 1922, remembers Kaufmann's "enthusiasm, drive, and initiative" and viewed him as the "power behind the throne" (p. 5). Dyer also wrote admiringly of the leadership of both Miner and Charters, discussed how "primitive" retailing in Pittsburgh was at the time, and discussed her impressions of staff and visitors to the program, noting that Whiting Williams was a particular favorite (Ferguson Collection, n.d.).

this bureau was pioneering work on the nature of applied research, job analysis procedures, and research on employer and employee attitudes regarding training.[8] In 1919, the School of Life Insurance Salesmanship was begun. The driving force behind this enterprise was Winslow Russell of the Phoenix Mutual Life Insurance Company. The first director was John A. Stevenson, at the time an assistant professor at the University of Illinois. Ferguson (n.d.) stated that this program "completely revolutionized the field of life insurance selling" by focusing on the needs of the consumer rather than the features of the insurance policies (p. 78). This philosophy was embodied in the Life Insurance Series of books produced by the School.

While Scott was involved in wartime activities, Guy Whipple served as acting director of the Bureau of Salesmanship Research. When it became clear that Scott would not be returning to CIT after the war's conclusion, Clarence Stone Yoakum was appointed director. In 1919, the Bureau of Salesmanship research was renamed the Bureau of Personnel Research, with an expanded scope of activities and staff. Three new staff members were hired: Marion A. Bills, Herbert G. Kenagy, and C. F. Hanson. Yoakum supervised the doctoral program; four students received their doctorates from the program. Ferguson (n.d.) stated that one of those students, Bruce V. Moore, earned the first doctorate from an industrial psychology program in the United States in 1921. The records of the Carnegie Mellon registrar, however, have Moore and Merrill Ream both earning their Ph.D. degrees on June 6, 1921. The other two doctorates were awarded to Max Freyd in 1922 and Grace Manson in 1923 (J. Papinchak, Carnegie Mellon University Registrar, personal communication, February 12, 2018).[9] Twenty master's degrees were awarded to eleven women and nine men, the first to Edward S. Robinson in 1917 (Division of Applied Psychology 1915–1924, n.d.).

While Bingham did return to the CIT program after the war, the DAP's days were numbered. Despite its success, the program closed in 1924. There appear to be a number of factors that contributed to the program's demise.

---

[8]  In addition to Whiting Williams, who was one the earliest researchers on employee attitudes, Frank and Lillian Gilbreth gave lectures at CIT (Ferguson, n.d.; Moore, 1962).

[9]  Commencement programs from CIT show Moore and Ream both receiving their doctorates in 1921 from the Division of Applied Psychology, while Freyd received his degree in 1922 and Manson in 1923 under the Division for Cooperative Research, the new name for the Division of Applied Psychology (J. Corrin, Carnegie Mellon University Archivist, personal communication, February 5, 2018). Freyd (1951) noted his degree was in psychology and personnel administration, although the Carnegie Mellon University Registrar does not have a record of a degree that included the phrase *personnel administration* (J. Papinchak, personal communication, February 12, 2018).

Richard S. Uhrbrock, a program graduate, cited three reasons: Bingham's increasing interest in a new venture, the Personnel Research Federation; the difficulty the new director, Clarence Yoakum, had in retaining corporate sponsorship; and an unsupportive CIT president (cited in Hilgard, 1987). It would appear that lack of support from the new CIT president, Thomas Baker, was a major factor. In his 1922–23 annual report, he stated that while financial considerations were important, the very popularity of the program was a factor in its demise. Baker noted that DAP housed virtually all of the graduate students at CIT. His belief was that the emphasis on applied research was misplaced and that "pure" research should be the priority. Baker also stated that psychology, while of use in training undergraduates, should not be a major department in a school of technology (Division of Applied Psychology 1915–1924, n.d.).[10]

The DAP program at CIT was an important one for the development of industrial psychology. It awarded the first graduate degrees in industrial psychology and presented a model for successful cooperation between academia and industry, and much innovative work was conducted there on employee selection and other areas of industrial psychology. Those accomplishments influenced industrial psychology applications in World War I and in the postwar years. Furthermore, the staff and students of the CIT program established themselves in academia and industry.

### CIT Program Aftermath: Staff and Students

A surprisingly large percentage of individuals associated with the CIT program went on to make major contributions to industrial psychology. Thumbnail sketches of some of these individuals appear in this chapter; other are discussed elsewhere in the book. As befits a history of industrial psychology, the focus is on psychologists; however, it is important to recognize that business leaders who were partners in the CIT program also played a significant role.[11] The careers of two psychologists associated with the CIT program, Marion A. Bills and Grace Manson, were previously described in Chapter 6. Arthur Kornhauser, who received his M.A.

[10] The Bureau of Retail Training moved to the University of Pittsburgh in 1923 (Ferguson, n.d.). Glen Cleeton was the only faculty member retained after the demise of DAP. The graduate program in industrial psychology at CIT was not revived until 1945 under the direction of B. von Haller Gilmer (Prien, 1991). Cleeton eventually became Dean of the Division of Humanistic and Social Studies at CIT (Cleeton, 1962).

[11] Space considerations preclude a comprehensive inventory of all of the contributors; see Ferguson 1962–65 for additional staff and students.

degree from CIT, is discussed in various places in this book; a short biography appears in Chapter 9 in the section on organized labor, a career-long interest of his. Walter Dill Scott's life and career have already been discussed in Chapter 4. His service in World War I was covered in Chapter 5, and his work in cofounding the first industrial psychology consulting firm, the Scott Company, was discussed in Chapter 6. Scott's career as an industrial psychologist pretty much ended in 1920 when he was appointed president of his alma mater, Northwestern University (Jacobson, 1951).

Walter Van Dyke Bingham served with Scott in World War I and then returned to CIT. Following the dismantling of the DAP program, Bingham moved to New York City to direct the Personnel Research Federation.[12] In World War II, Bingham again offered his services to the US military and served as chief psychologist for the Adjutant General. Bingham had a long and very productive career in industrial psychology. He published more than 200 books and articles (Zusne, 1984), including *Procedures in Employment Psychology* (1926) with Max Freyd, *How to Interview* (1931) with Bruce V. Moore, and *Aptitudes and Aptitude Testing* (1937).

Bruce V. Moore's (1891–1977) experience with applied psychology in World War I influenced his decision to enroll in the DAP program in 1919. Originally headed for study with E. L. Thorndike at Columbia University, he was invited to work on psychological tests in the war effort (Farr & Tesluk, 1997). Moore received his A.B. degree in 1914 and his M.S. in 1917, both from Indiana University. After receiving his industrial psychology doctorate from CIT in 1921, Moore joined the faculty at the Pennsylvania State College (now University) in 1920 and remained until he retired in 1952. Upon arrival, Moore taught one of the first courses to be called "Industrial Psychology" (Moore, 1962). He later established the graduate program in industrial psychology, in addition to serving for many years as psychology department head. Moore was the first president of the APA's Industrial and Business Psychology division, Division 14, which evolved into the present-day Society for Industrial and Organizational Psychology (SIOP).

Moore's fellow doctoral student Merrill Jay Ream (1893–1973) received his undergraduate degree from Washburn College and his master's degree from the State University of Iowa. In addition to conducting early research on personality testing (Ream, 1922), intelligence testing, and merit ratings,

---

[12] The Personnel Research Federation was discussed in Chapter 6.

Ream published *Ability to Sell* in 1924. Following his graduation from CIT, Ream went to work in the insurance industry (Murchison, 1929).

Max Freyd (1896–1951) earned a B.A. in psychology in 1918 and a M.S. in psychology and education in 1920, both from the University of Washington. After receiving his doctorate, he taught for a year at the University of Pennsylvania before joining John B. Watson at the J. Walter Thompson advertising agency. Freyd conducted research in advertising, marketing, and merchandizing. From 1925 to 1928, he was at the Personnel Research Federation, where in addition to conducting research he was managing editor of *Personnel Journal*. In 1928, Freyd went to the Retail Research Association as head of its Merchandizing Research Division. In 1936, he moved to Washington, DC, and took a position as head of the Personnel Division of the Social Security Board and later supervised development of personnel manuals for the Civil Service Commission (Freyd, 1951).[13]

Freyd (1922–23) published research on employee interests, was instrumental in the development of the graphic rating scale (Freyd, 1923), coauthored with Bingham *Procedures in Employment Psychology* (Bingham & Freyd, 1926), and championed a quantitative approach to employee selection (Freyd, 1923–24, 1925). A prolific researcher, he was an active participant in a number of important industrial psychology organizations, including the CIT program and the Personnel Research Federation. Poor health forced Freyd to retire in the summer of 1946. In a 1951 response to a request for information from Leonard Ferguson about the CIT program, Freyd modestly stated that "I have always considered myself one of the lesser lights of the C.I.T. group" and then praised Walter Van Dyke Bingham as the key to the success of the program. Freyd was a strong advocate for a scientific approach to industrial psychology who made substantial contributions to industrial psychology.

Best known for his pioneering work in measuring vocational interests (Strong, 1927), Edward K. Strong Jr. (1884–1963) received his Ph.D. from Columbia University in 1911. While he completed his dissertation under the supervision of James McKeen Cattell, the topic on the relative merits of various advertisements was suggested to him by Harry Hollingworth (Hansen, 1987). This work is the earliest example of an American psychology dissertation on a business-related topic that I have been able to

---

[13] A March 8, 1936, *New York Times* announcement stated that Max Freyd had been appointed instructor in the Department of Psychology at the Stevens Institute of Technology in Hoboken, NJ, but apparently he did not start and/or remain there.

locate.[14] Following graduation from Columbia University, Strong worked in advertising and marketing for three years and later worked on Scott and Bingham's Committee on Classification of Personnel during World War I (Darley, 1964). He joined the faculty at CIT in 1919 and then moved to Stanford University in 1923, developed his eponymous interest inventory, and remained there until his 1949 retirement.

Another CIT staff member who went on to make important contributions to psychology was Louis Leon Thurstone (1887–1955). While still a graduate student at the University of Chicago, L. L. Thurstone was selected by Bingham to be an assistant in the Department of Psychology in the Division of Applied Psychology at CIT. Thurstone rose to full professor and chair of that department. Prior to his time at CIT, he earned a master's of engineering degree from Cornell University, had a brief stint working as an assistant to Thomas Edison at his Menlo Park laboratory, and was an instructor at the University of Minnesota. Thurstone completed his doctorate at the University of Chicago in 1917 under James Angell. He worked on trade tests for the US Army during World War I and in 1923 worked for a year on civil service personnel methods for the Institute of Government Research in Washington, DC. From 1924 to 1952, Thurstone was a professor at his alma mater, the University of Chicago. He then moved to the University of North Carolina (Adkins, 1964; Ferguson, 1962–65; Jones, 1998; Thurstone, 1952). While Thurstone's early work was primarily in test construction, employee selection, and vocational guidance (e.g., Thurstone, 1919a, 1919b), he later concentrated on psychometrics and statistics. In particular, his work on psychological scale construction (e.g., Thurstone, 1927, 1929) and factor analysis (e.g., Thurstone, 1931, 1935, 1947) had a major impact not only on I-O psychology but on psychology as a whole.[15]

Clarence Stone Yoakum, Guy Montrose Whipple, and James B. Miner were also involved in the program. Like Bingham, Kornhauser, and Thurstone, Yoakum (1879–1945) received his 1908 Ph.D. from the University of Chicago. Initially interested in studying animal learning and fatigue in humans, Yoakum became chair of the psychology department at the University of Texas (Pillsbury, 1946). Commissioned as a first lieutenant in World War I, he obtained the rank of major and field supervisor of mental testing for the US Army. Yoakum and his team

---

[14] Lillian Gilbreth, whose work in scientific management was discussed in Chapter 2, also had an early dissertation from Brown University in 1914 that focused on an industrial psychology topic: the application of scientific management to teaching (Koppes, Landy, & Perkins, 1993).

[15] Adkins (1964) provides a complete bibliography of Thurstone's published works.

revised an early cognitive ability group test into the *Army Alpha* test in an intensive three-month period (Bingham, 1946). As noted in the summary of the Army testing program he published with Robert Yerkes, that test was administered to more than 1.5 million soldiers in World War I (Yoakum & Yerkes, 1920). Following his military service, in 1919 Yoakum replaced Scott as professor of applied psychology and director of the Bureau of Personnel Research at CIT. While he did adapt the *Alpha* for civilian use, Yoakum was also interested in supplementing cognitive ability tests with other selection predictors such as personality factors, past accomplishments, and interests. He supervised the four students who received their doctorates from the CIT program, and these dissertations influenced the work of Strong when developing his own vocational interest inventory. In 1925, Yoakum coauthored with H. G. Kenagy *Selection and Training of Salesmen*. After his time at CIT, Yoakum embarked on a career as a professor of personnel management at the University of Michigan, followed by an administrative career as director of the Bureau of Research at Michigan (where he worked with his former student Grace Manson), a short time (1929–30) as dean of the college of liberal arts at Northwestern University, and then a return to the University of Michigan as dean of the graduate school and vice president (Bingham, 1946; Pillsbury, 1946).

Guy M. Whipple (1876–1941) received his doctorate at Cornell University in 1900 under the tutelage of E. B. Titchener, the leading American advocate for the structuralist orientation in psychology.[16] Along with Raymond Dodge and F. L. Wells, Whipple was a member of the CIT Division of Applied Psychology's original advisory committee, was acting director of the Bureau of Salesmanship Research after Scott, and held the rank of professor of applied psychology (Ferguson, 1962–65). He was also a member of Yerkes and Yoakum's team that developed the *Army Alpha* test in World War I (Bingham, 1946). James B. Miner (1873–1943) was a graduate student of Cattell's at Columbia University. Miner received his doctorate in 1903. After teaching at the Universities of Illinois, Iowa, and Minnesota, he joined the CIT program as an assistant professor of psychology and education in the Department of Training for Teachers and then served as executive secretary and acting director of the Bureau of Retail Training and as a Bureau of Salesmanship Research consultant. His

---

[16] Titchener (1867–1927) was a staunch foe of functionalism and applied psychology who promoted psychology as strictly a laboratory science, with introspection as the only appropriate research method. Kept alive to a large extent through the force of Titchener's influence and personality, his structuralist orientation pretty much ended as a viable system when he died (Bjork, 1983).

interest in assessing vocational interests had an influence on Strong (Ferguson, n.d.; Strong, 1927). Miner's contributions to quantitative analysis in psychology included authorship of an annual review of correlation in the journal *Psychological Bulletin*. In 1921, he moved to the University of Kentucky, where he spent the remainder of his career (White, 1943).

## The Education of Industrial Psychologists in the 1920s

While the CIT program was unique in its emphasis on graduate education in industrial psychology, there were other programs where it was possible to learn about the field in a more informal manner. With the exception of the short-lived CIT program, doctoral degrees specifically in industrial psychology were not granted in the United States until after the Second World War (Katzell, 1992). There were, however, a number of colleges and universities where an interested student could work with faculty who had industrial psychology expertise. Already mentioned was Cattell's graduate program at Columbia University and some of the early graduates who contributed to industrial psychology. Beginning in the 1920s, there was a major in vocational guidance at Columbia, a direct precursor to the more formal program begun in the 1950s. The program was developed by Harry D. Kitson (1886–1959), who like many applied psychologists at the time was interested in both vocational guidance and industrial psychology (Thompson, 1992). Kitson received his doctorate from the University of Chicago in 1915 and, after teaching there and at Indiana University, began a long career at Columbia University's Teachers College from 1925 to 1951. While Kitson's primary interest was in vocational guidance, he did write *The Mind of the Buyer: The Psychology of Selling*, an early book on the psychology of sales (Kitson, 1921a).

In addition to the previously discussed James B. Miner, Harry Hollingworth, and Edward K. Strong Jr., two Columbia University graduates who were important to the history of industrial psychology are Albert Poffenberger and Edward L. Thorndike. Albert T. Poffenberger (1885–1977) received his undergraduate degree from Bucknell University in 1909 and his doctorate from Columbia in 1912. He spent his entire academic career at Columbia University, beginning as a lecturer in 1912 and retiring in 1950, a span that included time as executive department head from 1927 to 1941. Poffenberger served as a captain in the US Army in World War I and was responsible for psychological testing at Camp Wheeler, Georgia. He coauthored the 1917 text *Applied Psychology* with Harry Hollingworth and also wrote *Psychology in Advertising* (1925) and *Applied Psychology: Its Principles and Methods* (1927). Poffenberger was president of APA in 1934 and of the American Association of Applied Psychology in 1943–44 (Wenzel, 1979).

Edward L. Thorndike (1874–1949) made wide-ranging contributions to psychology both as an educator and as a researcher. He had undergraduate degrees from Wesleyan and Harvard, and he earned his Ph.D. at Columbia University under Cattell in 1898. The following year he began teaching at Columbia and remained on the faculty until 1940. Familiar to undergraduate psychology students today for his work in animal and human learning and his "law of effect" and "law of exercise," Thorndike did some of the earliest work in psychological measurement (e.g., Thorndike, 1904) and became a leader in educational psychology. His industrial psychology work included selection research in World War I, psychological test development, and work in vocational guidance (Ferguson, 1962–65; Thorndike, 1991). The author or coauthor of more than 450 articles and books (Zusne, 1984), Thorndike was described as a "dynamo" by his former assistant Walter Van Dyke Bingham (Bingham, 1952). Thorndike was elected president of the APA in 1912 and the American Association for the Advancement of Science (AAAP) in 1934.

The 1920s cohort of Columbia University graduates included psychologists who made significant contributions to industrial psychology. Herbert Anderson Toops (1895–1972) completed his B.A. and M.A. degrees at the Ohio State University and received his Columbia doctorate in 1921 under E. L. Thorndike. During World War I, Toops worked on trade tests, or work sample tests (Ferguson, 1962–65), and he took this as his dissertation topic. Hired back at Ohio State in 1923, he developed with Harold Burtt an industrial psychology program there (Austin, 1992). Herbert W. Rogers (1890–1964), who also received his doctorate in 1921, published one of the early papers on the validation of employee selection procedures (Rogers, 1917). He chaired the psychology department at Lafayette College from 1929 until he retired in 1957.[17] Based on biographical information in the Lafayette College archives, Rogers (1946) may have been the first master's-level psychologist to be employed full time in a business setting, the Charles Williams Stores in New York City in 1916 (Vinchur & Koppes, 2007).[18] Two other

---

[17]  Rogers was married to Margaret V. Cobb, also a Columbia University Ph.D. Cobb was a member of the group of psychologists who developed the Army Alpha and Beta tests in World War I (Ferguson, 1962–65).

[18]  Henry C. Link, who began at the Winchester Repeating Arms Company in 1917, may have been the first Ph.D.-level psychologist to work full time in industry (Ferguson, 1962–65). The first psychologist to work full time in government was L. J. O'Rourke, who became director of Personnel Research for the Civil Service Commission in 1922 (Hilgard, 1987).

graduates who received their doctorates from Columbia University in the 1920s were Elsie Oschrin Bregman and Sadie Myers Shellow, whose careers were discussed in Chapter 6.

Bingham (1928) noted that by the late 1920s there existed a number of universities that offered some advanced training in industrial and "commercial" psychology. He listed as "hospitable" to industrial psychology research the universities of Chicago, Iowa, Michigan, Ohio, Pennsylvania, and Pittsburgh as well as Columbia University, Northwestern University, and Stanford University. On the business side, he saw promising developments at the Harvard School of Business Administration and Yale University. In their history of I-O psychology education in the United States, Lowman, Kantor, and Perloff (2007) discuss a handful of other programs in addition to those mentioned by Bingham where a student could receive an education in industrial psychology prior to 1930. The additions are Ohio State University, Pennsylvania State University, George Washington University, New York University, and the University of Minnesota.

Ohio State's program was founded by Harold Burtt, who joined the faculty in 1919, and Herbert Toops, who arrived in 1923 (Austin, 1992). Burtt (1890–1991) received his undergraduate degree from Dartmouth College in 1911, where he was influenced by Walter Van Dyke Bingham, who suggested Burtt contact Hugo Münsterberg at Harvard to discuss a career in psychology. Although Burtt was assigned an advisor other than Münsterberg, he did get to work with him on an applied project evaluating streetlight illumination and safety (Burtt, 1953).[19] After receiving his doctorate from Harvard in 1915, Burtt taught at Harvard and Simmons College before his World War I service as chair of the Committee on Psychological Problems in Aviation (Ferguson, 1962–65). He then taught at Ohio State University for forty-one years until 1960, with twenty-two of those years as department chair. Burtt published a number of influential textbooks on industrial psychology (Burtt, 1926, 1929, 1948) and on advertising (Burtt, 1938) (Austin, 1992; Thayer & Austin, 1992). Like his almost as long-lived contemporary Morris Viteles, Burtt's career spanned almost the entire history of I-O psychology in the twentieth century. Burtt (1953) recalled working with Hugo Münsterberg prior to World War I and

---

[19] Burtt's dissertation advisor was Herbert Sidney Langfeld, a sensation and perception researcher who captured Burtt on his first day at Harvard and assigned him a dissertation topic on imagery (Burtt, 1953). In an interview with Frank Landy (1991) when Burtt was 100 years old, Burtt, who had no interest in studying imagery, retained some bitterness at the memory more than seventy-five years later.

how Münsterberg's support of Germany cost him friendships. Burtt noted that he was the graduate assistant who accompanied Münsterberg to his last, fatal lecture at Radcliffe College.

The program at what was then Pennsylvania State College was developed by Bruce V. Moore, who received his doctorate in industrial psychology from the CIT program. Instruction at New York University began with the 1924 hiring of Douglas H. Fryer. George Washington University offered instruction in industrial psychology in the 1920s, as did the University of Minnesota with the hiring of Donald Gildersleeve Paterson in 1921 (Lowman, Kantor, & Perloff, 2007). Paterson (1892–1961) was an influential figure in the education of industrial psychologists. Despite not having a Ph.D. himself (he held A.B. and M.A. degrees from Ohio State University), Paterson supervised nearly 300 master's students and eighty-eight doctoral students in his thirty-nine years at the University of Minnesota. He served as the US Army's chief psychological examiner at Camp Wadsworth in World War I and then worked for two years for the Scott Company industrial psychology consulting firm. Paterson authored or coauthored more than 300 publications, was editor of the *Journal of Applied Psychology* for twelve years, and was involved in the founding of the Minnesota Mechanical Abilities Project, the Minnesota Employment Stabilization Research Institute, the University of Minnesota Industrial Relations Center, and the Minnesota Studies of Vocational Adjustment and Rehabilitation ("Donald G. Paterson 1892–1961," 1961; Dunnette, 1993).

### Morris S. Viteles

The University of Pennsylvania's Department of Psychology was founded in 1887. James McKeen Cattell was its first professor of psychology, and the department's first chair was Lightner Witmer, another Wundt Ph.D. who founded the first psychological clinic in 1896. Morris Simon Viteles (1898–1996), who received his doctorate under Witmer and Edwin B. Twitmyer in 1921,[20] in essence became the industrial psychology program at Penn from that date until his retirement from the faculty in 1968. Viteles

---

[20] Twitmyer (1873–1943) received his A.B. from Lafayette College in 1896 and his Ph.D. from the University of Pennsylvania in 1902. Along with much better known Ivan Pavlov, Twitmyer has a legitimate claim as a co-discoverer of the classical conditioning paradigm. In his 1902 dissertation (posthumously published in 1974), Twitmyer used the human knee jerk rather than Pavlov's well-known dogs. Unlike Pavlov; however, after presenting his results at the 1904 APA conference, Twitmyer never followed up on his findings (see Coon, 1982).

Figure 8.2  Morris Viteles. The Drs. Nicholas and Dorothy Cummings Center
for the History of Psychology, The University of Akron.

(Figure 8.2) mentored those Penn students interested in industrial psychology throughout his long career (Thompson, 1992). Born in Zvanetz, Russia, he moved to England and then at age six to the United States. In addition to his doctorate, Viteles received his undergraduate and master's degrees from the University of Pennsylvania; he also spent his entire academic career there as a faculty member and administrator. Along with Witmer and Twitmyer, Viteles cited the British industrial psychologist Charles Myers and Walter Van Dyke Bingham as major influences on his career, Myers for his intellectual outlook and Bingham for his encouragement and the professional opportunities he provided. Viteles noted that when he was considering a career in industrial psychology, he was familiar with the books by Münsterberg (1913), Hollingworth (1916), and Link (1919), but he is sure that he was not aware of neither Scott's (1911) book nor the work being done by Bingham and his staff and students at CIT (Viteles, 1967).

Viteles was an early advocate of what today is termed the "scientist-practitioner" model. He practiced what he preached, spending his long career juggling responsibilities in academia and industry. Viteles advocated a close association between experimental and applied psychology and the need for industrial psychologists to be broadly trained in psychology. He was a lifelong critic of "looseness" in research and of theory unsupported by research (Viteles, 1967, 1974). On the practitioner side, Viteles had long-term consulting arrangements with companies such as Bell Telephone, the Philadelphia Electric Company,[21] and the Yellow Cab Company of Philadelphia. In 1926, Viteles founded the first university-based vocational guidance program (Thompson, 1998), and his job psychograph method was a very early job analysis technique (Viteles, 1974). His landmark textbook, *Industrial Psychology* (1932), defined the field and was used by generations of students. Viteles served as an officer in World War I and as chairman of the National Research Council Committee on Aviation Psychology in World War II. After the Second World War, he began a revision of *Industrial Psychology*; however, Viteles found when working on the "Motives in Industry" chapter that so much additional research had been conducted on work motivation that he dropped the revision and instead wrote *Motivation and Morale in Industry* (1953). He noted that "fifteen pages in *Industrial Psychology* became a book of approximately five hundred pages" (Viteles, 1974, p. 482).

Of particular note was Viteles's lifelong effort to internationalize industrial psychology. In 1922–23, he toured Europe and met with psychologists involved in industrial applications. In France, Viteles met with Jean Marie Lahy; in Germany, he was impressed with the work of Otto Lipmann, William Stern, and Fritz W. O. Giese. Viteles was less impressed with the more mechanical *psychotechnics* approach advocated by Walter Moede and Curt Piorkowski, among others. Viteles found a kindred spirit in Charles S. Myers of London, whose view of how basic and applied psychology could complement each other matched his own. Viteles traveled in the Soviet Union on a fellowship in 1934–35 and reviewed the work of applied psychologists there. While he admired the efforts of individual industrial psychologists, he was critical of the oppressive ideology of the Soviet system. In recognition of his long interest in cooperation among psychologists across the globe, he was the first psychologist from the United States elected to a term, from 1958 to 1968, as president of the International

---

[21] Viteles's professional relationship with the Philadelphia Electric Company lasted from 1927 to 1984: fifty-seven years (Russell, 1991).

Association of Applied Psychology. After fifty years of service at the University of Pennsylvania, Viteles retired in 1968 at the age of seventy (Viteles, 1967, 1974). He remained active in the profession of industrial psychology for more than twenty-five additional years.

## Early Industrial Psychology Textbooks

Examining early books on industrial psychology in chronological order can provide a window on the development of the discipline. Over the years, topics were added and excised, were emphasized and deemphasized, and expanded and contracted. While there were a fair number of books published on specific topics relevant to industrial psychology, such as advertising, in this section the focus is on books that take a broader perspective or that emphasize employee selection, the most popular activity of industrial psychologists during that time. Already discussed in a previous chapter were two of the earliest books about industrial psychology: Scott's (1911) *Increasing Human Efficiency in Business* and Münsterberg's (1913) *Psychology and Industrial Efficiency.* Münsterberg followed up his 1913 book with *Psychology: General and Applied* (1914) and *Business Psychology* (1918). Other notable books published before 1920 include Hollingworth's *Vocational Psychology* (1916), Hollingworth and Poffenberger's *Applied Psychology* (1917), Muscio's *Lectures on Industrial Psychology* (1917), and Link's *Employment Psychology* (1919).

In addition to covering industrial psychology, Hollingworth and Poffenberger's *Applied Psychology* (1917) surveyed the broader field of applied psychology. There are chapters covering psychology and the law, medicine, social work, and education. The authors also examined efficiency and its relation to heredity, learning, sex, age, environmental conditions, drugs, work, sleep, fatigue, and rest periods. Three chapters focus directly on industrial psychology. "Chapter XI: Psychology and the Executive" covers the three primary ways psychology can be put to practical use: improved employee selection, motivation and training programs, and improved environmental conditions. The chapter includes a rudimentary validation procedure, a list of tests and an examination of what today would be labeled validity coefficients for those tests across a number of occupations, a summary of the Taylor system of management, and a discussion of environmental factors such as lighting and ventilation and their effects on fatigue and accidents. "Chapter XII: Psychology in the Workshop" focuses on the worker. Among the topics discussed are the effect of "mental set," how effort should be distributed with an emphasis on rest periods, the use of time and motion study, and the psychological reaction of the worker. This chapter relies heavily on scientific management for its orientation but also raises interesting questions about the effects of routinized work on spontaneity and individuality. "Chapter XIII: Psychology and the Market" looks at psychology applied to advertising. Hollingworth and Poffenberger discussed subjects such as trademark infringement and confusion, but little space is devoted to what makes advertisements effective. There is a section on salesmanship, with the conclusion that salesmanship was more complex than advertising and research into it was less developed than advertising research.

Henry C. Link (1919) took a self-consciously scientific perspective in *Employment Psychology*. Viteles (1974) called Link's book the first comprehensive text in industrial psychology in the United States. Link divided his text into four parts (see Table 8.1). Part I describes a series of "experiments" Link conducted, using psychological tests to select assemblers, clerks, machine operators, and applicants for other jobs. He also discussed test administration and the value and scope of tests, and he included a chapter on the nature of intelligence. In Part II, Link covered trade tests (which he states are also psychological tests) and other applications of psychology to industry, including job analysis and training. Part III, labeled "Selection and Retention," is for the most part a discussion of performance appraisal. In the concluding section, Part IV, Link discussed industrial psychology's difficulties with organized labor, the problem of nonqualified individuals ("quacks") offering quick fixes, and the importance of maintaining a strong link between laboratory psychology and application. Interestingly, Link included a chapter on "The Applicant's Point of View," an attempt to see things from the perspective of the employee under evaluation.

After 1920, as a consensus was building as to what constituted industrial psychology, there was an increase in books devoted to the discipline. Among the books published in the 1920s and the early 1930s are *Fundamentals of Vocational Psychology* (Griffitts, 1924), *Industrial Psychology* (Myers, 1925), *The Psychology of Selecting Men* (Laird, 1925b), *Principles of Employment Psychology* (Burtt, 1926), *Industrial Psychology in Great Britain* (Myers, 1926), *Applied Psychology: Its Principles and Methods* (Poffenberger, 1927), *Methoden der Wirtschaftspsychologie (Methods of Economic Psychology)* (Giese, 1927, cited in Geuter, 1992), *Psychology and Industrial Efficiency* (Burtt, 1929), *Lehrbuch der Psychotechnik (Textbook of Psychotechnics)* (Moede, 1930, cited in Zusne, 1984), *Psychology in Modern Business* (Hepner, 1930), *Readings in Industrial Psychology* edited by Moore and Hartmann (1931), and the magisterial *Industrial Psychology* (Viteles,

Table 8.1 Employment Psychology: The Application of Scientific Methods to the Selection, Training and Grading of Employees *(Link, 1919)*

| | Table of Contents |
|---|---|
| Foreword | Part I – Psychological Tests |
| I. | Employment Psychology |
| II. | A First Experiment |
| III. | Applying the Results |
| IV. | Selecting Girls as Assemblers |
| V. | The Portable Laboratory |
| VI. | Testing Men Assemblers |
| VII. | Clerks |
| VIII. | Stenographers, Typists, and Comptometrists |
| IX. | Testing to Specification |
| X. | Machine Operators |
| XI. | Apprentice Toolmakers |
| XII. | General Intelligence: A Dialogue |
| XIII. | Language and Literacy Tests |
| XIV. | The Technique of Giving Tests |
| XV. | The Vocational Value of Tests |
| XVI. | The Scope of Psychological Tests |
| | With Special Reference to the Selection of Higher Executives |
| XVII. | The Scope of Psychological Tests (cont'd) |
| Foreword | Part II – Trade Tests and Other Applications of Employment Psychology |
| XVII. | How to Ask Questions, the Question of Trade Tests |
| XIX. | The Observational Method |
| XX. | Job Analysis |
| XXI. | Selection and Training, the Vestibule School |
| Foreword | Part III – Selection and Retention |
| XXII. | The Measure of Comparative Productiveness |
| XXIII. | Measuring by Limited Impressions |
| Foreword | Part IV – Conclusions |
| XXIV. | A Practical Combination of Employment Methods |
| XXV. | The Applicant's Point of View |
| XXVI. | Employment Psychology, Labor and Industry |

1932). A sample of these books are described and contrasted to illustrate their evolution, cumulating with Viteles's 1932 book.

*Fundamentals of Vocational Psychology* (1924) by Charles H. Griffitts was designed for use as a textbook. He emphasized general principles and methods, reasoning that good practice is based on sound theory. The opening two chapters of the book's seventeen chapters cover individual differences (variability) and correlation. Next are two chapters on the use of physiognomy, which include a discussion of the reasons for its popularity.[22] The following two chapters on the interview also cover recruitment, letters of application, application blanks, and the qualifications of a good interviewer. Next is a chapter on rating scales, and then nine chapters about various types of tests, which include trade tests, tests of strength and motor control, sensory and perceptual tests, tests of imagery and imagination, intelligence tests, and tests of instincts and character. The final chapter of Griffitts's text is a discussion of how an individual can choose an occupation.

Charles S. Myers's (1925) *Industrial Psychology* is based on five lectures he gave at Columbia University in the summer of 1924. The book describes industrial psychology in the United Kingdom. After stating that the discipline first developed in the United States, Myers pointed out two major differences between industrial psychology in the United States and in Great Britain. First was the greater strength of trade unions in the UK and their higher level of cooperation with industrial psychologists. Myers attributed this cooperation to industrial psychologists in Great Britain using motion study "primarily to secure greater *ease* of work" rather than just to increase efficiency (p. 7, italics in original). Second, Myers pointed out that in contrast to the decentralized development of the field in America, in the United Kingdom industrial psychology had been confined for the most part to two centralized bodies: the Industrial Fatigue Research Board and the National Institute of Industrial Psychology.[23]

Myers defined industrial psychology as an applied science that encompasses the study of management–labor relations, work incentives, workers' tools, materials, posture and movements, the timing of rest and work, physical work environment, employee selection and training, and psychological factors in product sales. He did not draw a distinction between psychology and physiology and noted that industrial psychologists must have an understanding of both mental and bodily processes. The first book chapter covers the history and activities of the Industrial Fatigue Research Board and the National Institute of Industrial Psychology followed by a chapter that examines industrial fatigue. Myers discussed improving the quantity and quality of output through movement study (e.g., Taylorism).

[22] Physiognomy is the determination of traits and abilities by evaluating physical characteristics. See Chapter 9.
[23] The history of the Industrial Fatigue Research Board and the National Institute of Industrial Psychology appeared in Chapter 6.

The final two chapters focus on vocational guidance and selection and include the use of tests for assessing vocational abilities.

In the introductory chapter to his *Principles of Employment Psychology* (Table 8.2), Harold E. Burtt (1926) stated what for him is the fundamental principle of employment psychology: "We must first *test the test*" (p. 5, italics in original). That is, tests used in selection for a given occupation must be given to workers in that occupation, and the "efficiency" of the tests must be compared to the "efficiency of workers" in that job. There must be a relationship between test scores and job performance. In the next chapter, Burtt took on the "intellectual underworld" of astrology, spiritualism, phrenology, and physiognomy along with its practitioners, who sometimes purport to be psychologists. The next two chapters describe types of mental tests and their use, stressing standardization in administration and scoring. It is notable that Burtt devoted an entire chapter to the criterion, illustrating his view of its increasing importance for industrial psychologists. Subsequent chapters describe the process of validation, examine intelligence and interests as predictors, and evaluate rating scales.

Table 8.2  Principles of Employment Psychology *(Burtt, 1926)*

|  |  |
|---|---|
|  | Contents |
| I. | Introduction |
| II. | Psychology Gold Bricks |
| III. | History of Scientific Vocational Psychology |
| IV. | Types of Mental Tests |
| V. | Mental Test Technique |
| VI. | The Criterion |
| VII. | The Subjects Used in Evaluating Tests |
| VIII. | Special Capacity Tests: Total Mental Situation |
| IX. | Special Capacity Tests: The Mental Components of the Job |
| X. | Intelligence and Vocational Aptitude |
| XI. | Interests in Employment Psychology |
| XII. | Rating Scales |
| XIII. | Miscellaneous Determinants of Vocational Aptitude |
| XIV. | Trade Tests |
| XV. | Job Analysis |
| XVI. | The Outlook for Employment Psychology |
| Appendix |  |
| I. | Illustrating the Technique of Correlation |
| II. | Combining Rankings with Incomplete Data |
| III. | Illustrating the Derivation of a Regression Equation |
| Bibliography |  |
| Index |  |

Table 8.3  Readings in Industrial Psychology *(edited by Moore and Hartmann, 1931)*

|  | Contents |
|---|---|
| Preface | |
| Author Biographies | |
| Introduction | |
|  | Chapter I |
|  | Introduction |
| A. | The Field of Industrial Psychology |
| B. | Backgrounds of Industrial Psychology |
| C. | Basic Psychological Concepts |
| D. | Why Men Work |
| E. | Plan of the Book |
|  | Chapter II |
|  | Basic Principles |
| A. | The Field of Applied Psychology |
| B. | Psychological Problems in Industry |
| C. | The Problem of Selection and Placement |
|  | Chapter III |
|  | Popular versus Scientific Procedures in Appraising Men |
| A. | Physiognomy |
| B. | Stereotypes |
| C. | Graphology |
| D. | Phrenology |
| E. | Lower Depths of the Psychological Underworld |
| F. | Scientific Interpretation |
|  | Chapter IV |
|  | Technique of Personnel Selection |
| A. | Basic Principles for Selection and Placement |
| B. | Job Analysis and Job Specification |
| C. | Applications and Records as Aids in Selection |
| D. | The Employment Interview |
|  | Chapter V |
|  | Rating Scales |
| A. | Kinds of Scales |
| B. | Factors Influencing Judgment |
|  | Chapter VI |
|  | Mental Tests and Individual Placement |
| A. | Measures of General Intelligence |
| B. | Special Aptitude and Trade Tests |
| C. | Limitations of a Testing Program |
|  | Chapter VII |
|  | Analysis of Occupational Interests |
| A. | Discriminating Engineering Interests |
|  | Chapter VIII |
|  | Vocational Guidance |
| A. | Nature of the Problem |
| B. | Predicting Careers |
|  | Chapter IX |
|  | Training the Worker |

Table 8.3  (cont.)

| | |
|---|---|
| A. | Organization of Training Education |
| B. | Economical Methods of Instruction |
| C. | Results of Training |
| | Chapter X |
| | Efficiency and Scientific Management |
| A. | Time and Motion Study: the Traditional Engineering Approach |
| B. | Enhancing Productivity: the Psychotechnologist's Approach |
| | Chapter XI |
| | Fatigue and Rest Pauses |
| A. | The Facts of Industrial Fatigue |
| B. | Influences of Rest Pauses on Production |
| | Chapter XII |
| | The Working Environment |
| A. | Illumination and Vision |
| B. | Ventilation |
| | Chapter XIII |
| | Accidents |
| A. | External Factors in Accidents |
| B. | Individual Differences in Susceptibility to Accidents |
| C. | Methods of Prevention |
| | Chapter XIV |
| | Monotony |
| A. | Causes of Monotony |
| B. | Effects of Monotony |
| C. | Suggested Remedies |
| | Chapter XV |
| | Morale: Motivation and Satisfaction in Work |
| A. | Drives and Urges in Making a Living |
| B. | Sources of Dissatisfaction |
| C. | The Control of Morale |
| | Chapter XVI |
| | Labor Unrest and Strikes |
| A. | Explanation of Strikes |
| B. | The Workers' Attitude |
| C. | Conflict and Solution |
| | Chapter XVII |
| | Leadership and Social Adjustment |
| A. | Qualities of Leaders |
| B. | Inadequacies of Management |
| C. | Constructive Industrial Guidance |
| | Chapter XVIII |
| | Distributing the Product |
| A. | Principles Fundamental to Salesmanship and Advertising |
| B. | Determining the Effective Advertisement by Experiment |
| C. | Abuses in Advertising |
| D. | Goodwill |
| Index | |

There is a chapter on "miscellaneous determinants" of occupational aptitude such as academic record, personal history information, letters of
recommendation, and the interview and also separate chapters on trade
tests and job analysis. Formulas for statistical computation appear in
a series of appendices.

Bruce Moore's and George Hartmann's (1931) edited work *Readings in
Industrial Psychology* was an attempt to offer a comprehensive view of
industrial psychology, something they viewed as unavailable in book
form up to that point. Because Moore and Hartmann had to rely on
mimeographed materials in their own courses, they decided to develop
this book (Moore, 1962).[24] The eighteen chapters of the book are composed of 223 mostly brief excerpts from books and articles. The authors
were a diverse group of psychologists and non-psychologists from a variety
of countries. The chapters, along with chapter subheadings, are listed in
Table 8.3. While this makes for a lengthy list, it is instructive to consider
what topics were considered a part of industrial psychology circa 1930.
Perennial subjects such as personnel selection, pseudo-psychology, scientific management, vocational guidance, fatigue, accidents, and advertising
are represented. Training and occupational interests have their own chapters, the latter possibly due to Moore's own pioneering work on that
subject. There is also a chapter on labor relations that examines the reasons
why workers strike and considers methods for resolving labor conflicts.
Of particular note is the increasing emphasis on "organizational" topics:
motivation, job satisfaction, and leadership. Moore (1962) recalled that it
was L. L. Thurstone who suggested that Moore not limit his industrial
psychology course to selection and placement, and therefore Moore and
Hartmann included the material on motivation, morale, and satisfaction in
the *Readings* book. The scope of industrial psychology was coming into
focus; what was now needed was an authoritative text to pull it all together:
Morris Viteles's *Industrial Psychology*.

### The Industrial Psychology "Bible"

The publication of Morris Viteles's 1932 text *Industrial Psychology* indicated
that industrial psychology was now a mature field with well-defined
methods and content. Bruce Moore (1962) characterized Viteles's book

---

[24] Moore and Hartmann's timing for their book was not optimal. Moore (1962) noted that Viteles's
(1932) comprehensive *Industrial Psychology* appeared the year after Hartmann and his *Readings* was
published and that Viteles's book to some extent overshadowed their own edited book.

Table 8.4 Industrial Psychology *(Viteles, 1932)*

|  | Contents |
|---|---|
|  | Section One |
|  | The Foundations of Industrial Psychology |
| I. | Introduction to the Study of Industrial Psychology |
| II. | The Economic Foundations of Industrial Psychology |
| III. | Social Foundations of Industrial Psychology |
| IV. | The Psychological Foundations of Industrial Psychology |
| V. | The Rise and Scope of Industrial Psychology |
| VI. | The Nature and Distribution of Individual Differences |
| VII. | The Origin of Individual Differences |
|  | Section Two |
|  | Fitting the Worker to the Job |
| VIII. | Basic Factors in Vocational Selection |
| IX. | Job Analysis |
| X. | The Interview and Allied Techniques |
| XI. | Standardization and Administration of Psychological Tests |
| XII. | Standardization and Administration of Psychological Tests (continued) |
| XIII. | Tests for Skilled and Semi-Skilled Workers |
| XIV. | Tests in the Transportation Industry |
| XV. | Tests for Office Occupations, Technical and Supervisory Employees |
|  | Section Three |
|  | Maintaining Fitness at Work |
| XVI. | Safety at Work |
| XVII. | Psychological Techniques in Accident Prevention |
| XVIII. | Accidents in the Transportation Industry |
| XIX. | The Acquisition of Skill |
| XX. | Training Methods |
| XXI. | Industrial Fatigue |
| XXII. | The Elimination of Unnecessary Fatigue |
| XXIII. | Machines and Monotony |
| XXIV. | Specific Influences in Monotonous Work |
| XXV. | Motives in Industry |
| XXVI. | The Maladjusted Worker |
| XXVII. | Problems of Supervision and Management |

as "monumental" and wrote that with the publication of this text "the new profession of industrial psychology was on its way" (p. 5). Called the "bible" both inside and outside the United States, it was the standard text for generations of industrial psychology students (Thompson, 1998). Viteles (1974) recalled that because of a series of reviews of industrial psychology that he published in the *Psychological Bulletin* beginning in 1925, he was able to complete the text in only nine months while maintaining both his university and consulting jobs. Weighing in at more than 650 pages, *Industrial Psychology* was a comprehensive compendium of the state of the field in the early 1930s. In keeping with Viteles's interest in international cooperation among psychologists, the text was global in scope.

As seen in Table 8.4, the book was divided into three sections. Section One covers industrial psychology's economic, social, and psychological foundations. A description and critical assessment of scientific management are included in the economic foundations chapter, and the organization of personnel departments is discussed in the social foundations chapter. In keeping with Viteles's emphasis on the importance of careful research, the psychological foundations chapter describes the experimental basis of psychology. Also included in Section One are a short history of industrial psychology both in the United States and in Europe and two chapters on individual differences. One chapter describes these differences, and the other examines their possible hereditary and environmental origins.

Section Two is concerned with employee selection and psychological testing: "Fitting the Worker to the Job." This section includes chapters on job analysis, selection techniques such as the interview and application blank, and test construction, standardization, and administration. There are three chapters that examine tests for occupational groups: skilled and semiskilled workers, transportation workers such as train motormen and automobile operators, and white-collar workers such as office employees and supervisors. The final section, "Maintaining Fitness at Work," covers a wide range of topics related to worker productivity and satisfaction. There are chapters on safety and on accident prevention and a separate chapter on transportation accidents. Two chapters are devoted to training along with two that examine the nature of industrial fatigue and how to reduce or eliminate it in the workplace. There are also two chapters on mental fatigue or monotony devoted to the nature of repetitive work and to the various individual difference characteristics and environmental conditions that affect monotony. The chapter on "The Maladjusted Worker" is concerned with emotional maladjustment and its effects. Finally, the book has two chapters on "organizational" topics; one on financial and nonfinancial motivations that includes criticism of the instinct explanation for motivated behavior and one on leadership that covers morale, group processes, and conflict.

Moore and Hartmann (1931) and Viteles (1932) both included chapters on motivation and leadership. While interest in these topics was not unknown in industrial psychology (e.g., Scott's coverage of motivation in his 1911 text), these topics were not typical in industrial psychology or employment psychology books in the 1920s. Their inclusion signals an expansion of the scope in the field, a topic explored in Chapter 10. It is also interesting that Viteles chose not to cover advertising in his text. The psychology of advertising and sales was a salient topic for industrial psychologists in the United States from the very genesis of the profession, yet Viteles decided it did not fit within his conception of industrial psychology topics. This decision foreshadowed subsequent practice. Similar to vocational psychology and human factors, psychology applied to advertising eventually established an identity separate from I-O psychology.

## Chapter Summary

The first generation of individuals who applied psychology to industry were trained as experimental psychologists, physicians, or sometimes both. For the most part, they were generalists whose interest in industrial psychology constituted only part of their bodies of work. Many of these psychologists received their doctorates in the German university system. Some, such as Münsterberg and Scott, worked with Wundt at the University of Leipzig. In the United States, after 1900 it became more common to complete the Ph.D. at an American university. While with the exception of the Carnegie Institute of Technology program these doctorates were not specifically in industrial psychology, sympathetic faculty at various colleges and universities offered training in industrial psychology. Examples are Columbia University with Cattell, Thorndike, and Poffenberger; Ohio State University with Burtt and Toops; and the University of Pennsylvania with Viteles.

The short-lived (1915–24) Carnegie Tech Division of Applied Psychology did offer doctoral-level training in industrial psychology; however, the program graduated only four Ph.D. recipients. The Division, under the direction of Walter Van Dyke Bingham, had a substantial impact on the development of industrial psychology. It produced innovative research, particularly in employee selection, and provided a model of how academia and business could cooperate to the mutual benefit of both parties. Staff and students associated with the Division constitute a virtual "who's who" of American industrial psychology. In addition to Bingham, a partial list includes Marion Bills, Max Freyd, Grace Manson, Bruce V. Moore, Walter Dill Scott, Edward K. Strong Jr., L. L. Thurstone, and Clarence Yoakum.

Texts used by students and others interested in industrial psychology increased in scope and sophistication from the 1910s to the early 1930s. Notable among those books was Morris Viteles's *Industrial Psychology* (1932), a comprehensive compendium of the state of the field at that time. The texts progressed from a focus on testing and selection to an inclusion of "organizational" topics such as leadership and motivation. One result of increased educational opportunities in industrial psychology was increased professionalization and professional identity. In Chapter 9, factors that contributed to the professionalization of industrial psychology are explored.

# Establishing a Profession

## Establishing a Professional Identity

Much of this book thus far has been concerned with how industrial psychology established itself as a separate profession. The educational, research, and practice activities described up to this point have contributed to that goal, some more explicitly than others. This chapter sums up those efforts and examines the more self-conscious aspects of establishing a professional identity, such as forming professional societies, hosting conferences, creating journals, and separating industrial psychologists from other, unwelcome competitors.

Defining a "profession" is not straightforward, as the definition of a profession has evolved over the past 100 years. Today it is often used simply as a synonym for a job or a career, but our interest is with the more traditional use of the term: an occupation requiring advanced training in the arts or in science. Professionals possess a high degree of systematic knowledge and are oriented toward and loyal to their professional community. This community defines and administers professional rewards and regulates members' activities. Critically, a profession is different from craftwork in that craftwork can be assessed directly by a client, for example, the consumer can determine directly whether a mechanic successfully repairs an automobile. Professions, because of the complexity of subject matter they deal with, often need results to be interpreted for the client (Brown, 1992). The outcomes realized after engaging a professional are not always a reliable indicator of the quality of the service. A physician may not be successful in curing a disease or an attorney may not be successful in obtaining an acquittal, but that does not necessarily mean they were incompetent or they did not give good value for their services. Interpretation is needed. It is not that results are unimportant but that success or failure alone do not give sufficient information to pass judgment on the competency of the professional.

JoAnne Brown (1992) noted that the first task for members of a new profession is to persuade their clientele of the value of that profession's services. At the same time, however, professionals must keep their knowledge and skills secret or incomprehensible enough to maintain a monopoly on those services. Older, established professions such as medicine and law concentrate on the latter goal; their value is well established. The new profession of industrial psychology needed to focus both on the popularity aspect and on the development of a level of expertise that is not available to the general public. Industrial psychologists needed to differentiate themselves from other types of professionals and from nonprofessionals. There was an inevitable tension between these two goals, particularly for a scientific profession such as industrial psychology that placed a high value on public dissemination of knowledge.

In addition to creating value and establishing a monopoly, prestige or status is a key component of a profession. Napoli (1981) defined a profession as an occupational group that maintains high prestige with a number of constituencies, such as clients, employers, the public, and other professions. In his analysis of the professionalization of psychology in the United States, Napoli found that applied psychology's quest for professional status differed from other professions in three important ways. First, the professionalization of applied psychology was influenced not only by general cultural trends such as industrialization but also by specific events, for example, World War I and the Great Depression. Next, between 1920 and 1945, applied psychologists kept internal disagreements to a minimum and were therefore able to present a united front. And finally, psychology was the first profession to arise directly from the university. This resulted in tension between academics and practitioners, but practitioners came already equipped with the prestige conferred by an advanced degree.[1]

The early industrial psychologists employed a number of strategies to establish a professional niche. This is a process that continues to the present day. I-O psychologists are still trying to differentiate themselves from a wide variety of management consultants who provide similar services and address similar problems. Then and now, prominent psychologists used the popular press to educate the public about their science.

---

[1] Napoli (1981) was discussing applied psychology in general, which includes industrial psychology. He did note that the three main branches of applied psychology – clinical, educational, and industrial psychology – have their own unique professional history. In some respects, industrial psychology had an easier time than the other two disciplines. For example, it did not have to deal with opposition from the medical profession to the extent that clinical psychology did.

Between 1890 and 1930, hundreds of articles by psychologists were published in popular magazines. Hugo Münsterberg was one of the most prolific, putting himself forth as an expert in all matters psychological, including industrial psychology (Benjamin, 2006). Establishing the perception that the industrial psychologist is an expert, someone capable of understanding human behavior and using that knowledge to solve organizational problems, was critical to establishing a professional identity.

The process of establishing a professional identity for industrial psychology was an outgrowth of the process of establishing a professional identity for the parent discipline of scientific psychology. This process had two steps. First, beginning in the late 1800s, the new science of psychology carved out a place for itself among the more established sciences by founding laboratories and, eventually, academic departments separate from philosophy; by forming professional societies to promote its interests; and by establishing journals to propagate theory and research. Next, the various branches of applied psychology, including industrial psychology, began to establish their own identities under the umbrella of psychology as a whole. The strategy used by industrial psychologists was similar to that used by the larger profession: teaching courses and offering degrees in industrial psychology,[2] creating industrial psychology professional organizations and journals, and establishing an identity separate from others who offered comparable services. In addition, industrial psychologists had to deal with the approbation of their non-applied colleagues on one hand and with indifference from professional managers, the very clientele they were trying to serve.

Earlier in the text we saw examples of the tension between the academic and applied sides of psychology, for example, Boring's (1929, 1950) exorcism of applied psychology in his *History of Experimental Psychology* and Walter Dill Scott's reluctance to give a talk on advertising to a group of businesspersons for fear it would hurt his academic career. This interdisciplinary conflict was set aside during World War I, when experimental psychologists joined their applied colleagues in supporting the war effort. This foray into applied work was viewed by many experimentalists as an interlude from their laboratories, not as a viable direction for scientific psychology. Bruce V. Moore (1962) provided an illustration. While attending graduate school in the Division of Applied Psychology at CIT, Moore attended the APA convention and was introduced to an unnamed "eminent psychologist," who upon learning where Moore was studying remarked: "Well, now that the war is

---

[2] As noted in previous chapters, with the exception of the CIT program, specialized degrees in industrial psychology in the United States began after World War II.

over, psychologists ought to be getting back to the real science of psychology" (p. 3). Moore realized that, despite applied psychology's successes in the war, it was still far from accepted in academia. Another CIT alumnus, Glen U. Cleeton (1962), noted that at the time Walter Dill Scott was publishing his early texts on applied psychology in the early 1900s, "the very thought of a technology of psychology ... came close to heresy" (p. 32). The early institutional history of the APA, discussed later in the chapter, provides an illustration of the hostility of academic psychologists against their applied colleagues

In addition to disagreement between academic and applied psychologists, there were industrial psychologists who were critical of their colleagues' superficial knowledge of their client industries. Henry Link, one of the first full-time industrial psychology consultants, was direct in his criticism of these colleagues who worked in industry but failed to try to understand those industries. He noted that there have been many applications "of psychology *to* industry, but not so many *in* industry" (Link, 1920, p. 336, emphasis in the original). Eliott Frost (1920b) made essentially the same point, concerned that psychological applications to industry will not progress unless psychologists develop an interest in both psychology and industry. Frost believed industrialists are inclined to be overly concerned with quick results to the bottom line, while psychologists tend to miss important factors such as management history, production control, and types of products that vary from industry to industry.

## Early Professional Organizations

The early industrial psychologists joined existing professional organizations and created their own. This section is concerned not with previously discussed private and public practice and research organizations, such as the Scott Company in the United States and the National Institute for Industrial Psychology in Great Britain, but with those organizations whose purpose is furthering professionalism through activities such as developing professional standards, policing members' behavior, disseminating knowledge, and presenting a public face for the field.

### The American Psychological Association and Other Professional Organizations

National psychological societies began to appear in the late 1800s. The American Psychological Association (APA) was first, founded in 1892 and adopting its first constitution in 1894. This was followed by the

British Psychological Society and the French Psychological Society in 1901, the German Society for Experimental Psychology in 1904, the Italian Psychological Society in 1910, the Chinese Psychological Society in 1921, the Indian Psychological Association in 1925, the Japanese Psychological Association in 1927, the Hungarian Psychological Association in 1928, and the Norwegian Psychological Association in 1934 (Benjamin & Baker, 2012).

The constitution adopted in 1894 at the third annual meeting of the APA stated in Article I: "The object of the Association is the advancement of Psychology as a science. Those are eligible for membership who are engaged in this work" (Cattell, 1895, p. 150). This scientific goal was viewed by many members as incompatible with applied efforts. By 1917, Cattell (1946) estimated that only seventeen of the APA's more than 300 members were involved in applying psychology. This is not surprising given that starting in 1906, the APA made membership standards more restrictive by requiring published research for those not in full-time academic psychology positions. Copies of publications were required in 1911, and by 1915 those in academia who did not hold the professorial rank were banned (Napoli, 1981). Attempts by applied psychologists to organize within the APA were frustrated, so they formed their own, primarily state-based, applied organizations. The New York State Association of Consulting Organizations, established in 1921, was the largest of these organizations. Under the direction of New York University psychologist Douglas Fryer (1891–1960), this organization was renamed the Association of Consulting Psychologists (ACP) in 1930. ACP's goal was to transcend state boundaries and establish a national presence (Benjamin, 1997a).

During the 1930s, the APA continued to be unresponsive to the needs of applied psychologists. Fryer once again led the attempt to establish a new national professional organization. The American Association of Applied Psychology (AAAP), proposed in 1937, was divided into clinical, consulting, educational, and industrial sections. The latter section was called Section D, Industrial and Business Psychology. Having become superfluous, the ACP voted to end its existence (Benjamin, 1997a). Following a merger between the APA and AAAP in 1941, in 1945 Division 14, Industrial and Business Psychology, was created (Benjamin, 1997b).

It is interesting that despite the APA's attempts to exclude applied psychologists, a number of APA presidents were involved in industrial psychology applications in industry or in the military during the first third of the twentieth century. Of the forty-two individuals (William James and G. Stanley Hall served twice) who were president of APA between 1892 and

1935, at least fifteen have some link to industrial psychology. While only a few, Hugo Münsterberg (APA president in 1898), Walter Dill Scott (1919), and Harry Hollingworth (1927) would be considered primarily industrial psychologists, another dozen are discussed in this book for their industrial work. James McKeen Cattell (1895) started the Psychological Corporation and was instrumental in early testing work. His Columbia University colleagues E. L. Thorndike (1912), Robert Woodworth (1914), and Albert Poffenberger (1935) all contributed to industrial psychology. John Watson (1915) was part of the World War I effort and spent much of his career in advertising. John W. Baird (1918) was a cofounder of the *Journal of Applied Psychology*, and L. L. Thurstone (1933), in addition to his work in the applied psychology program at CIT, conducted selection research before concentrating on psychological measurement. George M. Stratton (1908), Robert M. Yerkes (1917), Knight Dunlap (1922), Lewis M. Terman (1923), and Edwin G. Boring (1928) were part of the military's psychology efforts in World War I. It is true that many of these psychologists identified as experimental psychologists and spent the bulk of their careers in academia. Nevertheless, it would appear that for some of the most prominent psychologists of the first third of the twentieth century, the line between basic and applied psychology could be porous depending on the circumstances.

In early 1920s Germany, applied psychology and academic psychology were perceived for the most part as separate entities. Applied psychologists founded their own organizations. The most significant early one was *Verband der prakischen Psychologen (Association of Practical Psychologists)*. The roots of the association were in the 1921 congress of Society for Experimental Psychology, which organized a subcommittee, consisting of William Stern and Otto Lipmann, to consider an applied psychology congress in Berlin. Outside of the society, the Association of Practical Psychologists was established, with Karl Marbe as chair, Walther Moede as vice chair, and Otto Lipmann as secretary. The new association met with the Society subcommittee in 1922. Despite sentiment by Fritz Giese that the association should be an organization of full-time practitioners, throughout the 1920s university faculty members with applied interests were most prominent. Marbe remained chair until 1927, and professors Walther Moede, Walther Poppelreuter, Johann Rieffert, Narziss Ach, Gustaf Deuchler, and Giese himself all served at various times on the executive committee in the 1920s and early 1930s. The word *German* was added to the name of the association in the mid-1920s, and in 1926, the membership criteria of academic training with dissertation along with proof of applied work were established. After 1933, the association became relatively inactive and did not become reestablished until the 1940s (Geuter, 1992).

## Regulation of Practice

In addition to creating professional organizations, another strategy for creating a niche for industrial psychology was the use of credentials to keep unqualified individuals from practicing the profession. This has been a very successful strategy for medical and legal professions, especially when backed by the force of law. Psychologists had less success with this strategy, at least in the early years. It is true that membership in APA was strictly regulated, although this, at least initially, was of little use to nonacademic psychologists since the intent of those strict membership guidelines was to keep them out. Even when those requirements were relaxed to admit applied psychologists, the problem remained of how to deal with the others outside the organization calling themselves psychologists or practicing psychology without proper training. There are a limited number of strategies available in this situation. Professional licensing along the lines of the medical profession is one. Industrial psychology did not pursue this strategy in its formative years.

Whether or not a professional is licensed, it is still important to maintain standards of practice for those within that profession. While professional standards have no direct effect on competitors outside the profession, they do offer clients some assurance that those within the profession are behaving ethically and competently. By maintaining standards, professionals can hope to differentiate themselves from competitors who cannot or will not maintain those standards. By the second decade of twentieth century, for example, psychologists were discussing developing standards for the use of psychological tests. In 1915, the APA passed a resolution declaring that only individuals with the proper training in psychology should use these tests. Unfortunately, the APA had little influence over applied psychologists, who had been systematically excluded from membership, or with the general public. The resolution had little or no effect (Napoli, 1981).

## International Conferences and the International Association of Psychotechnics

The International Association of Applied Psychology (IAAP), formerly known as the International Association of Psychotechnics, was the first international organization of individual psychologists (Pickren & Fowler,

2013). There is some question as to when it was founded.[3] Holman (1927) gives the year as 1920, with the Swiss psychologist Edouard Claparède as its first president. While there appeared to be an informal society formed then, there was no official society until 1927, when Claparède's group merged with the International Association of Psychology and Psychotechnics to become the International Association of Psychotechnical Conferences, at some point informally shortened to the International Association of Psychotechnics (Gundlach, 1998).[4] Claparède and Pierre Bovet organized the first International Congress of Psychotechnics Applied to Vocational Guidance in Geneva in 1920. Given the devastation in Europe brought about by World War I, there was hope that applied psychology could contribute to the reconstruction and that neutral Switzerland would be an ideal choice to begin reconciliation among former enemies (Gundlach, 1998). The first conference was a small affair, about fifty participants from continental Europe. There were no participants from Germany, Russia, the United Kingdom, or the United States. Claparède was the congress president. Despite its small size, the conference was well received, and the second congress was planned for the following year in Barcelona, Spain, again with Claparède as president (Benjamin & Baker, 2012).

The 1921 congress, the Second International Conference of Psychotechnics Applied to Vocational Guidance and Scientific Management, was organized into three sections: I. Vocational selection, II. Vocational guidance in general, and III. Psychotechnics applied to vocational guidance. Among the participants who presented papers at the conference were J. H. Lahy from France; Franziska Baumgarten, Walther Moede, Otto Lipmann, and Kurt Piorkowski from Germany;[5] Cyril Burt, Eric Farmer, George H. Miles, and Max Tagg from Great Britain; Guilio Cesare Ferrari from Italy; Emilio Mira from Spain; and Edouard Claparède from Switzerland. The United States was represented by the scientific management experts Frank and Lillian Gilbreth (Kitson, 1922b). Three more congresses were held in the 1920s. The third congress was held in 1922 in Milan, Italy, with G. C. Ferrari presiding. The fourth in 1927 was in Paris; Edouard Toulouse was the conference president. It was at this conference that the membership decided on the merger of organizations that resulted in the International Association of Psychotechnics (Holman,

---

[3] Unfortunately, the archives of the association were destroyed in World War II; therefore, substantial information about the founding and early years has been lost (Pickren & Fowler, 2013).

[4] The shortened name was not official until Franziska Baumgarten, the general secretary, changed it shortly after World War II ended (Gundlach, 1998).

[5] Although Baumgarten, later Baumgarten-Tramer, was Swiss, she was at that time living in Berlin.

1927). In 1928, the fifth congress was held in Utrecht, the Netherlands, with Franciscus M. Roels presiding. There were three conferences in the 1930s: the sixth conference in Barcelona Spain in 1930 with Mira as president; the seventh in 1931 in Moscow, Russia, with Isaak N. Shpil'rein presiding; and in 1934, the eighth congress in Prague, Czechoslovakia, with František Šeracky as president (Benjamin & Baker, 2012).

## Journals

In previous chapters, a number of journals devoted to applied psychology generally or industrial psychology specifically were mentioned. For example, one of the earliest journals for applied psychology was the German journal *Zeitschrift für angewandte Psychologie (Journal for Applied Psychology)*, founded in 1907 by William Stern and Otto Lipmann. Journals were important to the professionalization of industrial psychology for a number of reasons. In addition to disseminating the results of research studies and building a knowledge base for the field, they contributed to the scientific prestige of the field and fostered a sense of community among the participants.

The first journal in America devoted in large part to psychological applications in industry and business, the *Journal of Applied Psychology* was first published in March 1917. The founders were G. Stanley Hall and two of his Clark University colleagues John Wallace Baird and L. R. Geissler (Ross, 1972). Hall, Baird, and Geissler served as the initial editors. The list of cooperating editors included prominent industrial psychologists Walter Van Dyke Bingham, Harry Hollingworth, Walter Dill Scott, Daniel Starch, and Edward K. Strong Jr.

Granville Stanley Hall (1844–1924) is best known for his pioneering work in developmental psychology. Hall's 1878 doctorate under William James at Harvard University was the first Ph.D. awarded in psychology in the United States. Hall founded the APA and served as its first president. In addition to cofounding the *Journal of Applied Psychology*, in 1887 he established the *American Journal of Psychology*, the first American psychology journal. While serving as president of Clark University, Hall brought the psychoanalyst Sigmund Freud for his only visit to the United States in 1909 (Ross, 1972).[6] John Wallace Baird (1869–1919) earned his Ph.D. at Cornell University with E. B. Titchener. Although trained in Titchener's brand of "pure" experimental psychology, Baird later became interested in

---

[6] See Ross (1972) for a book-length biography of Hall.

applied psychology. He served as president of APA in 1918. Ludwig Reinhold Geissler (1879–1932) was born in Leipzig, Germany, and attended classes at that city's university before completing his undergraduate degree at the University of Texas. Like Baird, Geissler received his doctorate under Titchener at Cornell. Geissler's applied work included time as a research psychologist at the National Electric Lamp Association in Cleveland, Ohio, and work on the effectiveness of advertising in Athens, Georgia, while on the faculty at the University of Georgia (Kozlowski, Chen, & Salas, 2017).

The scope of the journal delineated in the first volume was quite broad. While the application of psychology to vocational activities was listed first, also included were the study of individual differences; the influence of environmental conditions such as climate, nutrition, and fatigue; and the psychology of everyday activities such as reading and playing games. Excluded were tests used for educational or clinical purposes ("Introduction," 1917). In the foreword to the first volume, Hall, Baird, and Geissler (1917) explained why they saw a need for the new journal. They noted a striking growth in the application of psychology to business and industry, first in advertising, then salesmanship, and then personnel selection. The editors discussed the need for a psychology that could contribute to human happiness along with a journal that could pull together research from various applied fields from both within the United States and abroad. They also noted the need for a journal to coordinate applied psychology with "pure psychology." Hall, Baird, and Geissler continued to edit the journal until midway through 1919, when Baird passed away. In 1920, James P. Porter and William F. Book became editors. Book was editor until 1927, and Porter was then the sole editor until 1942. The *Journal of Applied Psychology* was an important outlet for industrial psychology research and, as the longest continuously published scholarly journal in I-O psychology, remains so today (Kozlowski, Chen, & Salas, 2017).[7]

The German monthly journal *Praktische Psychologie (Practical Psychology)* began in October 1919. Edited by Walther Moede and Curt Piorkowski, it covered the entire field of applied psychology with a special

---

[7] Kozlowski, Chen, and Salas (2017) did a decade-by-decade analysis of the journal and noted some interesting differences between the early and recent volumes. Book reviews comprised a substantial 40 percent of journal content during the 1917–26 period; they disappeared in the mid-1950s. Average article length in 2007–16 (12.89 pages) was more than double that of 1917–26 (6.10 pages). In the first forty years of publication, sole authors were by far the most common. By 2007–16, sole authorship had all but disappeared.

emphasis on industrial psychology and experimental pedagogy. The journal emphasized two components of industrial psychology. First were vocational aptitudes and vocational guidance; the second was the reorganization along rational lines of the apprentice system and of working methods in general (Link, 1921). Two later German journals that focused on psychotechnics were *Industrielle Psychotechnik (Industrial Psychotechnics)*, founded in 1924, and *Psychotechnische Zeitschrift (Psychotechnical Journal)*, founded the following year (Geuter, 1992).[8] In Great Britain, the *Journal of the National Institute of Industrial Psychology* began publication in January 1922. The official publication of the National Institute of Industrial Psychology (NIIP), the journal was edited by the NIIP director Charles S. Myers, who was a founder and editor of the *British Journal of Psychology*. Reflecting the goals of the Institute, the journal's focus was research on the mental and physical health of the workers, whether such research originated in the Institute or outside it (News and Comment, 1922a). The stated purpose of the journal was to publish, in nontechnical language, the methods and results of the application of science to industry and commerce (News Notes, 1922–23).

Also in 1922, the *Journal of Personnel Research*, the official publication of the Personnel Research Federation (PRF), began publication with Leonard Outhwaite of PRF as editor-in-chief and Clarence Yoakum of the Carnegie Institute of Technology as managing editor. One of the editorial board members was Matthew Noll, vice president of the American Federation of Labor. With an expanded second volume in 1923–24, Walter V. Bingham took over as editor, L. L. Thurstone was added as associate editor, and Yoakum remained as managing editor. In 1926–27, Max Freyd became managing editor, with Yoakum replacing Thurstone as associate editor. The name of the journal was changed to *Personnel Journal* in 1927.

The first popular magazine devoted to industrial psychology in the United States was founded in January 1926 by Donald A. Laird (1897–1969), a Colgate University professor and author of textbooks on applied psychology. Laird was the chief psychological editor, and Percy S. Brown, president of the Taylor Society, was chief industrial editor (Notes and News, 1925). *Industrial Psychology* took a more scholarly approach than other popular psychology journals. There were articles from both psychologists and businesspersons along with summaries of research findings, book reviews, and news and notes of interest to those

---

[8] Viteles (1932) gave the start date for *Industrielle Psychotechnik*, which replaced *Praktische Psychologie*, as 1923 and the start date of *Psychotechnische Zeitschrift*, edited by Rupp, as 1926.

in psychology and industry. There were special issues, including one on women in industry. The magazine was short-lived, however, folding after only three years of publication at the end of 1928 (Benjamin & Bryant, 1997).

## Separating from Pseudo-Science

### Phrenology, Physiognomy, and Other Competitors

Of particular concern to the early industrial psychologists were practitioners of what psychologists considered pseudo-science or, more specifically, pseudo-psychology. Pseudo-psychology, the use of unscientific methods applied to such activities as measuring personality traits and vocational abilities, took a number of different forms. Examples are palmistry, physiognomy, phrenology, and graphology (Yates, 1946). Kingsbury (1923) added telepathy, spiritism, clairvoyance, occultism, and, interestingly, hypnotism and dream interpretation. Paterson (Patterson [sic.], 1923) included astrology and fortune telling. Burtt (1926) devoted the second chapter of his text to "Psychology Gold Bricks," a discussion and debunking of astrology, spiritualism, phrenology, and physiognomy. Moore and Hartmann (1931) discuss palmistry and mind reading in a section titled "Lower Depths of the Psychological Underworld." Not all pseudo-psychology practices are relevant to the history of early industrial psychology. Some were deemed not worthy of serious attention. Others, however, provided direct competition for the scientific interventions championed by industrial psychology. Chief among those were graphology, phrenology, and physiognomy – especially the character analysis system of the physician Katherine Blackford.

Graphology is a system of determining personality characteristics from handwriting analysis. This information can then be used to make predictions about future performance. Note that two inferences are necessary if graphology is a valid procedure: first, that handwriting analysis can accurately assess traits; and second, that these traits are predictive of performance. While it is possible to trace graphology as far back as Camillo Baldo of Italy in the mid-1600s, a more direct ancestor of present-day graphology is the "sign" method of graphology that was developed around 1860 by Abbé Michon of France. The sign method analyzes details of script, such as how a particular letter is formed. Later methods emphasized the script as a whole rather than just the details (Yates, 1946).

Phrenologists determine traits and abilities by analyzing the shape of the skull. Its origins date to the late 1700s and the physician and anatomist Franz Joseph Gall (1758–1828) of Vienna. Gall, who called his system "cranioscopy," believed in the localization of faculties in the brain and postulated that the ridges and indentations in the skull's surface reflect the strength of those faculties. As developed by Gall and his one-time collaborator Johann K. Spurzheim (1776–1832), who coined the term *phrenology*, phrenology's basic principles can be summarized as follows: The brain is the correlate of the mind; humans have a finite number of independent mental faculties that occur on a specific region of the surface of the brain; the size of those regions correlates with the amount of the corresponding faculty; and finally, the amount of each faculty can be determined by examination of the surface of the skull. There are thirty-six faculties in total (Goodwin, 2005; Yates, 1946). By determining an individual's strengths and weaknesses, the phrenologist can advise that person on personal decisions, including occupational ones. Phrenology was an early example of an attempt to objectively measure individual differences.

While Gall should be given credit as one of the first to appreciate the brain's role in emotion and intellect and for recognizing that there is localization of function in the brain, his specific system of determining faculties from skull topography was refuted by subsequent neurological research. By the mid-nineteenth century, his system was viewed as nonscientific by the scientific community. In the United States, however, phrenology proved to be very popular with the general public. Spurzheim gave an American lecture tour in 1832. Unlike Gall, who believed faculties were innate, Spurzheim believed faculties could be strengthened through education. This notion appealed to many Americans and was popularized by the New York firm of Fowler and Wells. Founded by Orson Fowler and Samuel Wells in 1844, with branches in Philadelphia and Boston, the firm was the premier popularizer of phrenology until the early twentieth century. As an example of their services, the *Choice of Pursuits*, a book advertised in the October 1881 issue of the *Phrenological Journal*, described seventy-five occupations and the temperaments and abilities necessary for each. The *Phrenological Journal* was published until 1911 (Goodwin, 1999).

Phrenology was also popular in the United Kingdom, although it was never particularly popular elsewhere in Europe. Spurzheim, who lectured in Edinburgh, influenced George Combe (1788–1858), who wrote a widely read book on phrenology, *The Constitution of Man, Considered in Relation to External Objects* (1828, cited in Evans, 2016). At one time, more than 200 lecturers spread the phrenological gospel across the United Kingdom. Phrenology, however, was formally rejected by the British Association for the Advancement of Science, and after 1850, its reputation was declining (Evans, 2016).

Physiognomy is the evaluation of physical characteristics to determine abilities and psychological traits. Body type, facial features, and even hair color have all been used as predictors of temperament and traits. Physiognomy has a long pedigree. The Greek physician Hippocrates (c. 460–c.370) described two basic body types and ascribed different temperaments to each. Cesare Lombroso (1836–1909), an Italian physician and criminologist, believed that criminals could be distinguished from non-criminals through "stigmata" or "atavistic signs," which are physical abnormalities in the shape of the head, eyes, ears, jaw, or other areas that indicate degeneracy (Dazzi & Mecacci, 1997; Yates, 1946). German psychiatrist Ernst Kretschmer's (1888–1964) constitutional theory of personality postulated three basic body types: thin or *asthenic*, associated with schizophrenia; stout or *pyknic*, associated with what today is termed bipolar disorder; and *athletic*, like the asthenic type also associated with schizophrenia.[9] Normal individuals exhibited similar characteristics to abnormal ones, just not to the same degree (Yates, 1946; Zusne, 1984). The best-known American empirical studies linking physique and temperament were those conducted by the psychologist and physician William H. Sheldon (1898–1977). Although the bulk of his research was published toward the end of the time period covered in this book, the outline of his system was evident in the 1920s and available to the industrial psychology community (e.g., Sheldon, 1927–28). Sheldon's system is worth describing as an example of an empirical approach to physiognomy.

It is not quite fair to locate our discussion of Sheldon, or Kretschmer for that matter, in a section on pseudo-psychology. Sheldon was a psychologist who took an empirical approach, and it was empirical studies that eventually called his system into question. Nevertheless, the story is interesting as an example of a physiognomic approach that, unlike Blackford's system, developed inside psychology. Based on measurements taken from thousands of photographs of individuals, Sheldon determined that there were three basic body types, or somatotypes: the thin, lightly muscled *ectomorph*; the athletic, muscular *mesomorph*; and the rounded *endomorph*. In practice, these were not discrete categorizations, but they represented somatotypes on a continuum. Each body type was associated with a particular

---

[9] Extremely abnormal physiques constituted a fourth category: *dysplastic* (Zusne, 1984).

temperament. For example, ectomorphs are introverted, mesomorphs love physical activity, and endomorphs are jovial and sociable (Zusne, 1984). Sheldon claimed high correlations between his somatotypes and associated temperaments. His claims have not been supported however. The evidence against them is summarized by Strelau (1998). Factor analytic studies have shown that his three somatotypes can easily be reduced to two. The impressive correlations Sheldon found did not hold up. Subsequent research found the correlations between the somatotypes and objective measures of personality to be much lower and often statistically insignificant. And there is serious concern with some of the foundations of Sheldon's approach, chiefly that it is the innately determined body type that determines the innately determined temperament. If individuals with different somatotypes are treated differently by others, it could be the stereotypical treatment that results in particular behaviors and personality traits. This approach also assumes that because they are innate, somatotypes and personalities are relatively resistant to environmental factors, a questionable assertion at best.

In his seminal text *Psychology and Industrial Efficiency* (1913), Münsterberg wrote that it is possible to assess individual difference characteristics indirectly through group membership, such as ethnic group. But then he proceeded to undermine his own assertion by noting that individual group members may differ dramatically from the group norm and by giving examples of factory employees who individually varied considerably from an assessment of the capabilities of their particular ethnic groups. Münsterberg further stated that "average characteristics are found out with scientific exactitude by statistical and experimental methods, and not that they are simply deduced from superficial impressions" (p. 130). While his chapter on groups may not read as particularly enlightened from a present-day perspective, Münsterberg emphasized that any assertion must withstand empirical scientific scrutiny, even the stereotypes prevalent at the time. Examples of early studies that empirically demonstrated how stereotypes can lead to judgment errors include Anderson (1921) and Rice (1926–27).[10]

---

[10] Eliott Frost (1920a) of the Rochester, New York, Chamber of Commerce gave an address to American Psychological Association, "What Industry Does and Does Not Want from the Psychologist," that provides a window into how at least one person viewed industrial psychology and the topic of "race" psychology. Along with reasonable requests for psychology's help in reducing turnover, educating workers, and training supervisors, Frost cites the "Americanization of the Alien" as an important need. He notes that certain "races" are easily assimilated, while "[o]thers are distinctly clannish" (p. 21). Frost then proceeds to give examples of ethnic group stereotypes, such as the "emotional Italian," the "placid Swede," and the "keen-witted Jew" (p. 22) and how that knowledge can help in job placement.

## Industrial Psychology versus Pseudo-Psychology

For industrial psychology to establish itself as a legitimate applied science, it was critical for the early industrial psychologists to separate themselves from the "various charlatans who invade our cities, advertise extensively in the newspapers and on the bill boards, give free lectures in the best hotels or theatres and then conduct large classes for four to six weeks at so much per head" (Patterson [sic.], 1923, p. 101). Psychologists noted that anyone can call him or herself a psychologist and that even well-meaning lay practitioners often have insufficient knowledge of psychological tests and other methods to use them appropriately (Kingsbury, 1923). Even some psychologists at times oversold the benefit of testing despite warnings to proceed with caution from reputable colleagues such as Kornhauser and Kingsbury (1924). Using the scientific method can be a slow process; people grow impatient and seek out shortcuts, which the character analysts were only too happy to supply (Dunlap, 1923). To establish their own reputation, it was important that industrial psychologists discredit their unscientific competitors.

Character analysis is a blanket term that included those systems, such as physiognomy and phrenology, that purported to read personality from anatomical characteristics. One particularly influential system of character analysis was the Blackford system.[11] *The Job, the Man, the Boss* (1914), authored by Katherine Blackford and Arthur Newcomb, describes the Blackford Plan of Employment. Many of their suggestions would be judged as perfectly reasonable to their industrial psychologist contemporaries or to a present-day reader. Blackford and Newcomb even quote Walter Dill Scott to the affect that business failure or success is more dependent on mental attitude than mental capacity. Their definition of successful selection, "selection for each job in our organization of the one man out of all others who, by natural aptitudes, training, and experience, is best fitted to fill all the requirements of that job, and suited to its environment and conditions" (pp. 12–13; italics omitted), would not be out of place in an industrial psychology textbook. In addition, Blackford and Newcomb stated that workers should be able to see and enjoy the results of their work, that reduced work hours and rest periods actually result in greater

---

[11]  Bruce V. Moore (1962), for example, recalled that when in graduate school at CIT in the early 1920s, he was assigned to work on employee selection for the Westinghouse Electric and Manufacturing Company. The first obstacle he had to overcome was the current use of Blackford's system for selecting and training engineers.

productivity, that employees should have expectations of promotion, and that supervision should be tailored to the individual employee. The Blackford Plan calls for uniformity of policy and methods, elimination of waste, the establishment of an "employment department" to handle all phases of personnel activities, and scientific employment by experts. Where Blackford differed from psychologists was in how she selected individuals for employment. For Blackford and Newcomb, character analysis provided the method for their "scientific" selection.

The Blackford selection system analyzed character based on nine physical variables: color, form, size, structure, texture, consistency, proportion, expression, and condition. Regarding hair color, for example, blond individuals were described as active, hopeful, positive, quick, variety-loving, dynamic, aggressive, impatient, speculative, changing, driving, and domineering. Brunettes were mirror opposites: thoughtful, serious, painstaking, cautious, specializing, conservative, deliberate, patient, imitative, static, plodding, submissive, slow, and negative (Blackford & Newcomb, 1914). Paterson and Ludgate (1922–23) put "Dr. Blackford's generalizations to the acid test" (p. 123). They had ninety-four judges pick two blondes and two brunettes they knew and rate them on these traits. There were no differences found between brunettes and blondes on the traits rated; the correlation between trait ratings for blondes and brunettes was a very high 0.96.

Other pseudo-psychological systems were evaluated and found wanting. Phrenology was evaluated by Cleeton and Knight (1924). They made a number of careful phrenological measurements of the head that purported to measure the following character traits: sound judgment, intellectual capacity, frankness, will power, ability to make friends, leadership, originality, and impulsiveness. Two groups of raters were used: close associates of the assessed individuals and a group of casual observers. Cleeton and Knight found little or no agreement between phrenological measures and the trait ratings for either group. Graphology fared no better than physiognomy and phrenology (e.g., Hull & Montgomery, 1919), although at least one psychologist (Dunlap, 1923) saw the technique as more promising than systems based on anatomy. Reviews of research studies provided additional evidence for the questionable validity of character analysis (Brandenburg, 1926; Dunlap, 1923; Moore and Hartmann, 1931). Brandenburg (1926) concluded that character analysis "is wholly devoid of any scientific basis" (p. 588).

Discrediting pseudo-psychology was not limited to the United States. For example, in Switzerland, Franziska Baumgarten-Tramer (1926, cited in

Canziani, 1975) demonstrated the falsity of the electro-diagnostic method of determining psychological characteristics. This procedure was propagated by Zachar Bissky of the Ukraine, who claimed to be able to evaluate an individual's capacity for a job by stimulation of the forehead and the skull. In addition, Baumgarten-Tramer debunked the widely known Polish hypnotist Radwan, who was working as a psychotechnician (Canziani, 1975).

It is hard to gauge how effective these types of disconfirming studies were in persuading employers to abstain from using pseudo-psychological methods and to instead adopt the psychologists' services.[12] Industrial psychology had neither the size nor the standing to make much of an impression on the bulk of business managers. How widespread was the belief in pseudo-psychology in the general public? In an admittedly limited attempt to answer that question, Donald Paterson quizzed his University of Minnesota summer school Applied Psychology students regarding their beliefs in various systems. Of his twenty students, sixteen (80 percent) had a "Positive Belief" in psychology's usefulness in vocational guidance; however, twelve (60 percent) also had a positive belief in mental telepathy and eleven (55 percent) had a positive belief in physiognomy. Astrology, fortune telling, graphology, spiritualism, palmistry, and phrenology had considerably less support, ranging from two to five students expressing a positive belief (Patterson [sic.], 1923). While based on a very limited sample, the result that more than half the class viewed physiognomy positively is intriguing.[13]

In an autobiography written in the 1940s but not published until 2013, Harry Hollingworth (2013) shared an anecdote illustrating both the inaccuracy and tenacity of pseudoscientific methods. Prior to World War I, Hollingworth accepted an offer by the practicing phrenologist daughter of Orson Fowler to devise a test of the accuracy of phrenology. Recall that Orson Fowler was the cofounder of the popular phrenology firm of Fowler

---

[12] It is also hard to gauge how popular these methods were with employers at the time, given a paucity of employer surveys on the topic. In one study, Kornhauser and Jackson (1922) questioned 100 employment managers of industrial plants and 100 insurance agency managers about their use of character analysis. Of the sixty-five responses returned, six reported using character analysis, in five cases Blackford's system or that system in combination with another system.

[13] Longstaff (1947) replicated Paterson's study in 1946 using two University of Minnesota classes, Occupational and Vocational Psychology and Psychology in Personnel Work, with a total sample size of 177. Belief in physiognomy dropped dramatically, from 55 percent in Paterson's sample to 3 percent in Longstaff's sample. Interestingly, belief in the vocational guidance statement: "Psychology can determine what specific job a man is best fitted for" dropped from 80 percent in the 1923 sample to 48 percent in the 1946 sample.

and Wells. Hollingworth "jumped at this opportunity to convey an impressive lesson" to his students at Barnard College (p. 102). Having just tested these students on intelligence and on musical ability, Hollingworth rank-ordered the students on these two traits and then challenged Ms. Fowler to assess the same students on these traits using phrenology. The correlation between the two rank-orders was zero, at which point Fowler declared the standardized tests as worthless. Next, Hollingworth brought in a masked man and asked Fowler to give a complete reading of his traits and aptitude using phrenology. The following picture emerged. Among other things, the man was a dreamer, financially irresponsible, a poor bargainer, and of artistic temperament. The anonymous victim turned out to be Walter Dill Scott, whose professional record would seem to emphatically contradict all of these results. Fowler simply noted that Scott had missed his true calling. None of this seemed to make a lasting impression on many of Hollingworth's students, who later paid for readings at the phrenologist's studio.

## Relations with Other Groups

In developing a professional identity of their own, psychologists looked to and maintained relationships with other, more established professions, especially engineering and medicine. As illustrated by the complicated relationship between American psychologists and the engineers who developed and practiced scientific management as well as the sometimes fractious relationship between German psychologists and engineers in their early efforts in psychotechnics, interactions between engineers and psychologists were marked by both cooperation and criticism. Scientific management had an influence on industrial psychology, and industrial psychologists adopted its ethos of efficiency and productivity. Yet they also needed to identify scientific management's shortcomings in dealing with the human element to create a niche that psychology could fill. Bingham (1928) noted that industrial psychologists seemed content to cede a number of psychological topics in industry to engineers and practitioners of scientific management. Examples are studies of illumination, fatigue, accidents, and work simplification. He went on to note that while industrial psychologists and engineers, particularly advocates of scientific management, have the same ultimate goal of increasing organizational productivity and efficiency, they differ in emphasis. For Bingham, the psychologist's first priority is the worker: Improving selection, training, and working conditions all is in the service of improving workers' adjustment and satisfaction. This in turn should also lead to greater productivity.

While psychologists were active in teaching and research on industrial psychology topics in 1920s Germany, in industry, psychotechnics was the domain of engineers. The new occupation of production engineer had responsibility for labor force deployment, and as such engineers often took responsibility for applying psychological methods. Geuter (1992) stated that of sixty-three firms identified in the 1926 volume of *Industrielle Psychotechnik* as having a psychotechnical test station, forty-one were headed by engineers and not one by a psychologist. The psychologist Walther Moede directed the Institute for Industrial Psychotechnics at the Technical College of Berlin-Charlottenburg; however, the courses were mostly taken by engineers. In a 1920 volume of *Zeitschrift für angewandte Psychologie*, the psychologist Hans Paul Roloff criticized the brief training engineers received in assessing intelligence, while the engineer Georg Schlesinger defended the competence of engineers. Psychologists continued to argue that applying psychology should be left to trained psychologists, while engineers such as K. A. Tramm opposed the idea that engineers are not qualified to perform activities such as administering aptitude tests (Geuter, 1992). It was not until the 1930s that psychologists began to gain parity with engineers in psychotechnics in industry (McCollom, 1968).

Psychology, including industrial psychology, has had a complicated relationship with the medical profession. Recall that a number of the psychologists important to the development of industrial psychology, such as Hugo Münsterberg and Charles S. Myers, held medical degrees in addition to their doctorates. There were also a fair number, among them James McKeen Cattell, Elton Mayo, and Robert Yerkes, who either expressed an interest in a medical career or began one but did not complete it. Unlike their colleagues the clinical psychologists, the early industrial psychologists generally did not compete directly with physicians and were therefore spared the difficulty of competing with the older, more established professionals. World War I was an exception; medical officers and psychologists involved in testing needed to find a way to coexist. Walter Dill Scott was wary of psychologists becoming subservient to physicians in the medical corps; he believed the best way for psychologists to contribute to the war effort was as civilian consultants, not as commissioned officers. Robert Yerkes disagreed, reasoning that an association with physicians would lead to a boost in prestige for psychologists. He successfully lobbied for a commission as a major in the Sanitary Corps. Yerkes's psychological testing program had mixed success, however, and he believed that it never received the resources and respect it deserved.

One strategy that psychologists used to enhance their professional standing was to appropriate the metaphors used in engineering and medicine. Industrial psychologists spoke of efficiency and productivity and used engineering analogies in discussing their services. The role of the psychologist was conceptualized in medical terms. Tests could be used to objectively diagnose a problem in the same way that a medical test is used for diagnosis. Psychologists not only adopted the language of engineering and medicine, they also adopted the professional demeanor, the "cool, impersonal, technical style as their own" (Brown, 1992, p. 126). This neutral tone had its basis in the scientific laboratory. JoAnne Brown (1992) discussed these metaphors as they related to the history of intelligence testing between 1890 and 1930, roughly the same time period covered in this book. Since testing was such an integral part of industrial psychology, it is not surprising that the engineering and medical metaphors were incorporated into industrial psychology as well.

There was a third group with a long, complicated relationship with industrial psychology. Interactions between industrial psychology and organized labor have been discussed at various points in this text, for example, Loren Baritz's (1960) *Servants of Power* and his characterization of industrial social scientists, including psychologists, as biased against labor. As discussed in the next section, during the early years of I-O psychology, organized labor and industrial psychology had a complex relationship. Industrial psychologists were sometimes supportive, sometimes oppositional, and often simply indifferent to unions and their concerns.

### Organized Labor

In the United States, the earliest recorded union was the shoemakers union in Philadelphia, the Federal Society of Journeymen Cordwainers, founded in 1794 (Freeman, 1991).[14] Early local craft unions, which limited themselves to a single skilled job, focused on improving pay and working conditions for their members. By the 1830s, the first national unions began to appear. By the end of that century, there were thirty national unions with a total membership of approximately 300,000 workers. The Knights of Labor, formed in 1869, was the first union to admit workers across crafts. Unusually for its time, workers were admitted regardless of religion or race. By 1886, membership had grown to about 700,000. By the

[14] A cordwainer is a shoemaker who makes shoes from new leather.

end of the century, however, the Knights had all but disappeared due to internal conflict and the aftermath of the Haymarket Square Riots, a violent confrontation between protesters and the authorities in Chicago. In 1886, Samuel Gompers founded the American Federation of Labor (AFL), an umbrella organization whose membership comprised various craft unions rather than direct membership like the Knights of Labor. Also unlike the Knights, the AFL focused exclusively on improving labor contracts and working conditions rather than a broader agenda of legislative and political activities. Seen as a mainstream alternative to more radical and violent unions like Eugene V. Debs's American Railway Union and the Industrial Workers of the World (the "Wobblies"), by the end of World War I, the AFL had more than 5 million members. In 1938, an alternative to the AFL, the Congress of Industrial Organizations (CIO), was formally established by John L. Lewis of the United Mine Workers.[15] Unlike the AFL, the CIO admitted both skilled and unskilled workers (DeNisi & Griffin, 2001).

The labor movement of the late 1800s and early 1900s, particularly the more radical elements, was characterized by antagonism and strife between the workers and management. Management held the bulk of the power, aided at times by enforcement assistance from the government and by favorable judicial decisions. For example, the US Supreme Court twice, in 1908 and in 1915, upheld so-called "yellow dog" contracts, which permitted companies to fire workers who joined unions (Zickar, 2001). Employees resorted to work slowdowns and strikes. Employers often responded aggressively with the use of replacement workers called "scabs." Violent confrontations between strikers and company police or state militia some-times occurred as a result. In addition, in the 1920s, companies portrayed union leaders as communists to give cover for government intervention and reduce public sympathy (DeNisi & Griffin, 2001).

Strikes have been a part of American industry since even before the United States was an independent country; the first recorded strike, tailors protesting a wage reduction, occurred in New York in 1768. During the time period covered in this history of I-O psychology (roughly the 1880s to the early 1930s), European and American workers struck with about the same frequency; however, strikes in the United States tended to be both longer and more violent. In America, the first nationwide railroad strike in

---

[15] Lewis broke away from the AFL in 1935 because the craft unions were unsupportive of his organizing efforts. He formed the Committee for Industrial Organization, which in 1938 became the Congress of Industrial Organizations (Freeman, 1991).

1877 involved approximately 100,000 workers and led to more than 100 deaths. By the mid-1880s, the number of strikes averaged more than a thousand a year. In 1886 alone, there were about 1,500 strikes that idled more than half a million workers. Examples include the 1892 Carnegie steel strike in Homestead, Pennsylvania; the 1894 Pullman railway workers strike; and a number of strikes by miners in the western United States. State and federal troops were sometimes used against the strikers. Workers won concessions in approximately half of the strikes that took place in the 1880s and 1890s. Even though unions did begin to turn to both private and government mediation, the years immediately prior to World War I saw an increased volume of strikes. Despite a pledge by the AFL to avoid strikes during the conflict, they continued to rise in number, peaking right after the war. The year 1919 saw the highest proportion of workers on strike in America's history, with a fifth of the workforce, 4 million workers, idled. After 1922, the volume of strikes began to drop due an economic turndown in 1921, a propaganda campaign equating unionism with foreign radical-ism, and repression by the government. The labor movement did not quickly recover, and the number of strikes did not increase until the 1930s, helped by the formation of the CIO and the 1935 passage of the National Labor Relations Act (NLRA) (Freeman, 1991).

Rather than the use of force, another management strategy for dealing with the threat of unionization was to give workers a voice in management and to improve compensation and working conditions to the point where a union was no longer needed. The Western Electric plant in Hawthorne, Illinois, the site of the iconic Hawthorne Studies discussed in the next chapter, provides an illustration. In 1906, the Hawthorne Works introduced a pension plan that awarded benefits at the discretion of management. "Welfare capitalism" continued with the opening of a medical department in 1908, an athletic complex in 1921, and a gymnasium in 1927. Besides sponsoring athletic teams and events, the company offered evening courses, a club store, and a savings and loan association (Gillespie, 1991). Eliminating the need for a union was not the only motivation behind these amenities; it was also hoped that these improvements would lead to increased company loyalty and improved productivity. Reducing collective worker action, how-ever, was a major rationale for this employer interest in worker welfare.

## Organized Labor and Industrial Psychology

The relationship between organized labor and industrial psychology for much of the twentieth century was generally one of mutual indifference, with some notable exceptions described in this chapter. Unionists viewed industrial psychologists with suspicion because of the company the psychologists kept. Industrial psychologists were identified with management. Psychologists were dependent on managers for applied work and for access to organizations to conduct research. The perception, often accurate, was that industrial psychology was biased toward management. In addition, Gordon and Burt (1981) noted that industrial psychologists were seen by unionists as representative of an intellectual and academic community that was perceived as using unions as a means to advance their own political agendas. They also stated that industrial psychologists were conflated with their contemporaries, the practitioners of scientific management, a movement that engendered a great deal of animosity from workers. Organized labor therefore saw no reason to reach out to industrial psychology, and industrial psychologists, preoccupied with establishing their own field and often aligned with management, saw no reason to try to bridge that gap.

There was no general philosophical aversion by industrial psychology to the needs of workers in industrial psychology's early years. From the earliest days of industrial psychology, there was a belief that the interventions of industrial psychologists would benefit both manager and worker alike. And while some of the early pioneers such as Münsterberg (1913) argued for a neutral stance regarding the results of their work, a more general consensus evolved that the industrial psychologist has an obligation to be concerned about the welfare of workers (e.g., Viteles, 1932). Individuals important to the development of industrial psychology in the United States, such as Walter Dill Scott, James McKeen Cattell, Walter Van Dyke Bingham, and even Hugo Münsterberg, were not anti-labor. They saw labor as well as management as important constituencies. In the 1920s, Bingham and Cattell corresponded with Samuel Gompers on matters of mutual interest. Bingham was part of a group that worked with Gompers when establishing the Personnel Research Federation (Flinn, 1922–23; Zickar, 2004). Cattell (1923) and Gompers exchanged letters about how psychology, and specifically the Psychological Corporation, could help unions reach their goals. And as early as 1913, Münsterberg collaborated with Gompers in administering job satisfaction questionnaires to blue-collar workers (Hale, 1980). As discussed in Chapter 6, Walter Dill Scott's Scott Company refused to work for companies that were anti-labor. For example, when asked by the Chicago Foundrymen's Association for help in anti-union activity, the Scott Company refused unless the Association changed its stance to one of cooperation. Dwight Hoopingarner, who worked for a year with Walter Dill Scott in the Carnegie Institute of Technology program, had an interest in labor relations and cooperative management, authoring a book on the subject, *Labor Relations in Industry*, in 1925 (Ferguson, 1962–65).

Arthur W. Kornhauser (1896–1990) was an industrial psychologist who not only was sympathetic to unions but was actively interested in working with them. After earning a B.S. degree from the University of Pittsburgh, Kornhauser received his M.A. from the CIT program in 1919 and then a Ph.D. from the University of Chicago in 1926. He worked on the Army trade tests with Scott in World War I. He then joined Scott for a year in 1919 in the first industrial psychology consulting firm, the Scott Company. Kornhauser worked part time for the Psychological Corporation from 1935 to 1943 and also consulted with the Life Insurance Sales Research Bureau (LISRB) from 1932 to 1939. On the academic side, he was at the University of Chicago from 1921 to 1943 and at Wayne State University from 1947 to 1962.[16] He made significant contributions to at least four areas of industrial psychology: psychological testing and selection (e.g., Kornhauser & Kingsbury, 1924), employee attitude surveys (e.g., Kornhauser & Sharp, 1931–32), labor relations and unions, and employee mental health (e.g., Kornhauser, 1965). As early as the late 1920s, Kornhauser was criticizing industrial psychology for its pro-management orientation, a critique he maintained throughout his career (Kornhauser, 1929–30b, 1947). He also criticized pollsters for anti-union bias (Kornhauser, 1946–47) and testified before the US Congress about these views. Kornhauser facilitated forums where various constituencies such as management, labor, and psychologists could discuss issues. He was one of the few psychologists who conducted research on labor unions and worked to make them more effective (Zickar, 2003).

During the Great Depression in 1935, the US Congress passed the National Labor Relations Act (NLRA) to try to reduce the conflict between labor and management. Commonly known as the Wagner Act, its purpose was to level the playing field between management and labor. The National Labor Relations Board (NLRB) was created to administer the Act. The Act gave workers the legal right to organize, to bargain

---

[16] Ross Stagner (1909–97) was a colleague of Kornhauser's at Wayne State University. Like Kornhauser, Stagner was pro-labor and wrote a number of books on union–management relations. Stagner received his doctorate from the University of Wisconsin in 1932 (Lachman, 1998). Although his contributions to industrial psychology occurred after the time period covered in this text, he was an example of the relatively rare industrial psychologist who, like Kornhauser, could never be accused of being pro-management in outlook.

collectively, and to strike to attain their goals. It also prohibited unfair labor practices such as discrimination in hiring, promotion, or termination due to union membership (DeNisi & Griffin, 2001). In the past, companies could simply fire workers who were members of unions or who had union sympathies. This was no longer legal. Similar to the Hawthorne Works example earlier, firms could try to improve working conditions and compensation to reduce or eliminate the need for unions. Another strategy was to form internal unions to represent the workers that could be controlled by management. A third, much rarer strategy was more subtle: to use personality tests to try to identify workers who were sympathetic to unionization and eliminate those individuals.

As described by Zickar (2001), this practice was probably not pervasive, but it did occur. Postwar personality tests, such as the X-O Tests for Investigating the Emotions (Pressey & Pressey, 1919), Personal Inventory (Laird, 1925a), Thurstone Personality Schedule (Thurstone & Thurstone, 1930), and Bernreuter Personality Inventory (Bernreuter, 1933), were designed to measure emotional stability. The belief at the time was that workers engaged in union activity not just because of dissatisfaction with external factors such as pay but because they were psychologically maladjusted.[17] The rationale for the use of these tests was that they could identify individuals with psychological problems, who could be terminated before they could act on their pro-union inclinations. Of course, because of the NLRA, the reasons for this weeding out could not be directly stated; instead, code words for union sympathizers such as *agitators, troublemakers,* and *hotheads* were used. Despite the use of this strategy, there is no evidence that these personality inventories were valid predictors of potential union activity.

## Chapter Summary

The early industrial psychologists engaged in a number of strategies to try to establish their field as a profession. Similar to the efforts of psychology in general, industrial psychologists taught courses in industrial psychology; founded specialty journals; created regional, national, and international organizations; engaged in public relations to educate the public; and took steps to separate themselves from and discredit perceived unscientific competitors. The first national psychological association, the American Psychological Association, was initially hostile to applied psychologists,

---

[17] This belief is explored in the discussion of the Hawthorne Studies in Chapter 10.

motivating them to establish their own practice-oriented organizations. The largest of these, the American Association of Applied Psychology, eventually merged with the APA. On the international level, the International Association of Psychotechnics was informally begun in 1920 and became an official society in 1927. The first international conference on psychotechnics took place in Geneva in 1920. Other international conferences occurred in Spain, Italy, France, the Netherlands, Russia, and Czechoslovakia throughout the 1920s and early 1930s. Industrial psychology journals were established in the 1910s and 1920s. Among them were the *Journal of Applied Psychology* and the *Journal of Personnel Research* in the United States, *Industrielle Psychotechnik* in Germany, and the *Journal of the National Institute of Industrial Psychology* in Great Britain.

Psychologists conducted research to discredit practitioners of what they considered pseudo-psychology. They subjected the claims of graphologists, phrenologists, and proponents of physiognomy to empirical study and found no basis for the efficacy of these practices. The character analysis system of Katherine Blackford was a particular target for American psychologists. Industrial psychologists also appropriated metaphors and the professional demeanor of other professions such as engineering and medicine. Despite criticism that industrial psychology was biased toward management (e.g., Baritz, 1960), the discipline's relationship with organized labor in the early years was variable. While largely indifferent, there were examples of pro-labor industrial psychologists and of cooperation between unions and industrial psychologists.

By the early 1930s, industrial psychology had made significant progress toward establishing itself as a profession. It had its own professional organizations, conferences, and journals. It had established itself in university and college curricula. And through texts such as Viteles (1932), the content and methods of the discipline were coming into focus. While, in America at least, industrial psychologists for the most part concentrated on personnel-related issues such as selection, there was increasing interest in broader organizational topics such as leadership, motivation, employee attitudes, and group processes. The history of these and other topics that comprise the "organizational" side of I-O psychology is the subject of Chapter 10.

# The Beginnings of Organizational Psychology

Ten years after the end of World War I, Walter Van Dyke Bingham (1928) described the scope of industrial psychology as encompassing a series of six psychological questions or problems about human nature. First is the *worker in relation to his work*. This phrase, which described a guiding principle of the Scott Company, refers to assisting the employee discover the natural way of performing his or her job, of increasing productivity, reducing fatigue, eliminating injuries and accidents, and increasing satisfaction and a sense of accomplishment. The next set of questions comes from the *relations between a worker and his fellow workers*: how to reduce conflict, develop solidarity, avoid restriction of output, and ensure that experienced employees will be helpful to new employees. The third group of questions centered on the *relations of the worker and his immediate supervisor*. To avoid difficulty, the supervisor should be reasonable, fair, and clear in assigning work. The next group of questions involved the *worker's relations to management*. These questions revolved around financial and nonfinancial compensation and recognition, adequacy of machinery, attention to grievances and concerns, and expectation of stable employment. *Group relations* between workers and management defined a fifth set of potential problems, in particular, difficulty with interactions between management and organized labor. Finally, there are those problems that arise from the worker's relationship *to the entire circle of contacts* inside and outside the organization. This is a recognition that an employee's behavior is affected not only by what goes on in the organization but also by her or his family relations, money worries, and other nonwork concerns. Bingham recognized the balancing act for management between helping the employee with nonwork concerns while at the same time avoiding paternalism and respecting the worker's independence and self-respect.

Much of this book to this point has focused on Bingham's (1928) first set of questions: How can we make organizations more productive and efficient? Industrial psychology in the first third of the last century, particularly in America, to a large extent was concerned with individual differences and their application, especially in employee selection. While there has always been interest in the other questions Bingham raised, toward the end of the 1920s, that interest was on the rise. These questions about employee attitudes, motivation, group processes, supervision and leadership, and other topics are today grouped under the "O" umbrella in I-O psychology. While some early work relevant to these areas has already been covered, this chapter focuses specifically on the history of those topics.

Histories of organizational psychology and its more interdisciplinary sibling organizational behavior (OB) tend to reference a number of different landmarks than the ones we have described for industrial psychology. Much of that history occurred after the 1930s. Industrial psychology and its focus on human resource management topics such as selection dominated the field in the early years. One way to conceptualize the history of I-O psychology is as the development of three separate threads, one that evolved into present-day industrial or personnel psychology, another into organizational psychology and OB, and a third into engineering psychology or human factors. Industrial psychology developed from an interest in and measurement of individual differences, with influences that included scientific management. Industrial psychology topics, such as employee selection, performance appraisal, and training, are now associated with personnel or human resource management. There was interest in and investigation of organizational psychology topics, such as work motivation, leadership, and employee attitudes, by early industrial psychologists. But at least in America, these areas were not the primary focus.

Organizational psychology, known previously as social-industrial psychology, has its intellectual roots in the work of individuals such as Max Weber, Henri Fayol, and Mary Parker Follett. It was influenced by industrial psychology, by landmark research such as the Hawthorne Studies, and by later work of psychologists associated with the human relations movement. The third thread was concerned with adapting machinery and the work environment to the capabilities of the worker. That approach evolved into engineering psychology or human factors. The three threads of industrial, organizational, and engineering psychology evolved relatively independently, with the industrial and organizational approaches merging into present-day I-O psychology and engineering psychology or human factors breaking away to form its own subdiscipline (Landy, 1989).[1] While there is some heuristic merit to this conceptualization, it downplays the interdependence among the three areas. Early industrial psychologists participated in all three areas, and all three areas share some common influences and precursors.

How the history of I-O psychology is told depends on the perspective and orientation of the person telling the story. History told from the "I" perspective will differ somewhat from one told from the "O" perspective. In addition, although organizational psychology and OB are very similar, historians may emphasize different landmarks when describing the history of one or the other. Organizational psychology has been characterized as more parochial or insular, focusing on individual and small group behavior and relying on research from inside psychology. OB, on the other hand, is viewed as taking a broader approach that includes not only individual and group behavior but also the functioning of the organization as a whole. OB is viewed as more multidisciplinary than organizational psychology, drawing not only on psychology but also on fields such as sociology, anthropology, economics, management, political science, and history. A historian from an organizational psychology perspective might emphasize the role of psychology and psychologists such as Kurt Lewin in that history. A history written from an OB perspective might take a more interdisciplinary approach, discussing, for example, the work of sociologists such as Peter Blau, Alvin Gouldner, Robert K. Merton, and Philip Selznick.

Why is this a concern? Since this is a book about the early history of I-O psychology, the logical approach would be to emphasize developments inside the field of psychology. Further, since there is a consensus (e.g., Miner, 2006) that OB as a field did not develop until the 1950s, well after the period covered in this book, the history of OB would appear to be beyond the scope of this history of early I-O psychology. It is not quite that simple, however. While the distinctions between organizational psychology and OB detailed in the previous paragraph are fine in theory, in reality there is so much overlap between the two that drawing a bright-line separation is impossible. Examination of current textbooks in organizational psychology and OB shows that they cover the same topics, including the more "macro" topics such as organizational theory, culture, and change in the psychology texts, and draw on the much of the same research, quite

---

[1] Landy (1989) argued that given engineering psychology's subject matter and approach, it still remains a natural fit within I-O psychology.

a bit of it interdisciplinary. Therefore, it is reasonable that organizational psychology and OB share a common set of precursors, such as scientific management and industrial psychology itself.[2]

## Theoretical Foundations of Organizational Psychology

Max Weber, Henri Fayol, and Mary Parker Follett are theorists whose work had a lasting influence on organizational psychology. The German scholar Max Weber (1864–1920) attended the universities of Heidelberg, Berlin, and Göttengen. Trained as a lawyer, Weber made significant contributions to legal history, economics, religion, and political science. While he did teach intermittently at Berlin, Freiburg, and Heidelberg, Weber had substantial means and spent much of his career as an independent scholar. Adopted by sociologists as one of the founders of that discipline, Weber did not consider himself a sociologist until late in life. In 1918, he accepted the chair in sociology at the University of Vienna, and in 1919, the year before his death, he moved to the chair in sociology at the University of Munich (Magnusson, 1990). Weber became well known for his theory that capitalism is the result of the rise of Protestantism over Catholicism in Europe and for his discussion of the "Protestant work ethic" (Miner, 2006). For our purposes, it is his work on bureaucracy in organizations that is most relevant.

Weber (1922/1946), writing in the early years of the twentieth century, peppered his description of the characteristics of modern bureaucracy with historical examples of political, religious, and military organizations. For Weber, bureaucracies were rule-based entities with a defined hierarchy of authority. Weber stressed the importance of the maintenance of written documents in managing the organization. According to Weber, officials in an ideal bureaucracy are appointed, not elected, and authority resides in the position, not the individual official. Entry is based on ability to perform the job, and advancement is based on performance at work. Organizational members are protected against the arbitrary use of authority. Weber viewed the ideal bureaucracy as the quintessential modern organizational form. Rationality is inherent in this structure. Reliance on rules and records, a hierarchy of authority with unity of command, clear lines of communication and control, division of labor and function, and rewards based on

---

[2] Many of the landmark influences on organizational psychology and OB occurred after the time period covered in this chapter. Examples include the work of human relations theorists such as Abraham Maslow, Douglas McGregor, Rensis Likert, and Chris Argyris and the later work of Kurt Lewin. See the Appendix for a discussion of this work.

an impersonal evaluation of competence provide a measure of predictability for employees and guard against favoritism and nepotism.

Weber did not invent bureaucracy; he described and analyzed it. As organizations grew larger and more complex, bureaucracy became the only viable way to structure them. Bureaucracy has had its share of critics. As a closed system, bureaucracies have been criticized as slow to change. Excessive rules and regulations can lead to lack of innovation and "red tape." Workers may feel stifled by the rigid structure, and job satisfaction may suffer. Nevertheless, for large organizations, bureaucracy's many strengths make it the dominant type of structure for large organizations.

Henri Fayol (1841–1925) was a mining engineer who wrote about management at roughly the same time as Max Weber, although they did not seem to influence one another. His final work, *General and Industrial Management*, first published in in 1916, appeared at a time when there was a great need for management training and when theory in management was sorely lacking (Miner, 2006). Fayol (1916/1949) described fourteen general principles of management, cautioned against their inflexible use, and noted that they should be adapted as circumstances dictate. He also emphasized that his list is not exhaustive. His principles are summarized in Table 10.1 (Fayol, 1949/1960). These common-sense principles have much in common with Max Weber's characteristics of bureaucracy in advocating, for example, division of labor, scalar chain of authority, and unity of command. Particularly interesting is Fayol's recognition that the degree of centralization is contingent on factors such as the size of the organization and his distinction between rule-based justice and equity. The latter combines justice and kindness. Fayol thought equity should permeate the organization, as it is essential for establishing worker loyalty. In addition to his principles of management, Fayol (1916/1949) discussed the essential functions of industrial organizations, namely, technical, commercial, financial, security, accounting, and managerial functions. He is probably best remembered today for summarizing the five elements of management: planning, organizing, commanding, coordinating, and controlling (Miner, 2006).

Mary Parker Follett (1868–1933) had a varied career as a social worker and social activist. She worked for women's suffrage, played a major role in the development of neighborhood community centers, advocated for vocational guidance and placement, and wrote books on political power, the nature of democracy, and group studies. Follett accomplished this despite having to deal with a chronic, debilitating illness for much of her adult life. Follett developed her ideas about organizations from her years of

Table 10.1  Summary of Henri Fayol's (*1916/1949*) General Principles of Management

1.  *Division of Work*: Fayol saw specialization as a part of the natural order, with the result that more and better work can be produced with the same amount of effort. He believed this principle could be applied to all work, not just technical tasks, but noted that there are limits to dividing up the work that should not be exceeded.

2.  *Authority and Responsibility*: Although a distinction can be made between official and personal power, they complement each other and both should be used. The power to reward or punish is a natural consequence of authority. Fayol believed that the judgment needed for effective use of sanctions should be based on high moral character, impartiality, and firmness, and that the best defense against abuse of power is character and integrity.

3.  *Discipline*: Discipline is essential for the proper functioning of a business. The best way to establish discipline is to place good superiors throughout the organization. Also be certain that agreements between management and employees are as clear and fair as possible and use sanctions judiciously.

4.  *Unity of Command*: An employee should receive orders from one superior, and one superior only. Fayol provided examples of how this principle can be violated, and noted that these kinds of violations are a recipe for havoc.

5.  *Unity of Direction*: One plan and one head is needed for any group of activities with the same objective. This is distinct from Unity of Command, although Fayol noted Unity of Command cannot exist without Unity of Direction.

6.  *Subordination of Individual Interest to General Interest*: Individual interests should not prevail over that of the business concern. How to reconcile competing interests is one of the great difficulties that managers face.

7.  *Renumeration of Personnel*: Payment for services rendered has a major influence on the success of the business. In general, compensation should be fair, it should reward well-directed effort, and it should not result in overpayment. Fayol discussed the advantages and disadvantages of three modes of payment: *Time rates* where employees are paid a set rate for a predetermined time period; *Job rates* where employees are paid at the completion of a job, regardless of the time needed for completion; and *Piece rates* where workers are paid for each discrete piece of work they produce. He also discussed the use of bonuses, profit-sharing, and non-financial compensation.

8.  *Centralization*: The degree of centralization or decentralization is dependent on a number of factors such as the size of the firm. This is an early recognition of the importance of what today are termed contingency factors.

9.  *Scalar Chain*: The scalar chain illustrates the hierarchy of authority from top to bottom. While these lines of communication should generally be followed, Fayol did concede that this can be time-consuming and at times should be bypassed for the good of the firm.

10. *Order*: This is the application of the aphorism "A place for everything and everything in its place." Order is important not only for materials, but also for workers, the "social order." There should be an appointed place for each employee, and that employee should be in that appointed place.

11. *Equity*: Fayol distinguished justice, defined as executing established conventions, from equity, which he defined as the result of combining justice and kindness. Equity is necessary to instill loyalty in workers, and should permeate the entire scalar chain.

Table 10.1 (cont.)

| | |
|---|---|
| 12. | *Stability of Tenure of Personnel*: Employees should be given sufficient time to become proficient in their jobs. While successful firms exhibit stability, change is inevitable due to factors such as age, illness, and retirement. Balance between stability and change is the key. |
| 13. | *Initiative*: Conceptualizing and executing a plan requires the power of initiative. Superior managers foster initiative in their subordinates. |
| 14. | *Esprit de Corps*: Managers should foster harmony in the organization. They should avoid sowing dissention among their subordinates and also avoid an overreliance on written communication, which can be misinterpreted and can lead to conflict. |

observation and experience as an activist. She wrote and lectured about organizational conflict, power, authority, leadership, and group processes in ways that anticipated much current thinking on these topics. Follett's work has been rediscovered on a number of occasions since her death in 1933, and it continues to be the subject of scholarly inquiry in multiple fields (Tonn, 2003).

The approaches of Weber and Fayol with their emphasis on structure and process constitute part of what is now termed classic organization theory. These mechanistic approaches, caricatured tongue in cheek by Perrow (1986) as the "forces of darkness," were sometimes used as a foil for the human relations theorists (who advocate for what Perrow termed the "forces of light"). Unlike Fayol and Weber, the work of Follett is viewed as more in the spirit of the human relations movement. Despite the historical antagonism between the classical and human relations approaches to organizations, they each have their respective strengths and weaknesses.

## Early Concern for Worker Welfare

The large-scale industrial organizations that developed as part of the Industrial Revolution could be grim places to work, with employees barely earning enough to survive. As Wren and Bedeian (2009) noted, however, misery was not unique to the factory system; most people lived at subsistence levels before then. "The Industrial Revolution did not create poverty; it inherited it" (Wren & Bedeian, 2009, p. 56). While the majority of factory owners were more concerned with profits and production than worker welfare, there were exceptions. Notable among them is Robert Owen (1771–1858), a Welsh social reformer who owned cotton mills in New Lanark, Scotland. Owen improved working and housing conditions for his employees and established a school and store for them. The school was perhaps the first to include a day nursery and playground and also offered evening classes (Magnusson, 1990). Owen was a cofounder of the consumer cooperative movement, and in 1824 in the United States, he led an unsuccessful commune experiment in New Harmony, Indiana (Merrill, 1960). In his efforts to convince other factory owners to pay as much attention to their "vital machines" as they did to the actual machinery of their plants, Owen (1825/1960) appealed not just to their altruism but also to their concern for profitability. He claimed returns exceeding 50 percent, soon to approach 100 percent, from his investment in his workers' welfare at the New Lanark mills.

From a present-day perspective, Owen's methods can be criticized as paternalistic; however, for his time, his approach was revolutionary in showing genuine concern for his employees. At roughly the same time as Owen's reforms were taking place, a management method that came to be known as the Lowell system was evolving in the textile mills of Massachusetts. In 1823, the Boston Manufacturing Company built a complex of fully mechanized mills in East Chelmsford and named them in honor of the company's founder, Francis Lowell. To recruit young women from the surrounding area and to reassure their families that they were safe and treated well, the mill owners paid unusually high wages, constructed boardinghouses, and supervised the women closely both in those boardinghouses and on the job. The women responded positively, maintaining excellent work records and engaging in off-the-job self-improvement programs. The Lowell system was used as a national example of the benefits of the humane treatment of workers. Wage cuts due to recession in the 1830s, the speeding up of the machinery without a wage increase, overexpansion, and the influx off immigrant labor in the 1840s effectively ended the system by the 1850s (Foner & Garraty, 1991).

## Industrial Psychology and Employee Welfare

The distinction between the quantitative, efficiency-oriented approach of the early industrial psychologists and the more worker-oriented approach that is associated with organizational psychology is not clear-cut. Historical treatments in introductory I-O psychology textbooks can give the impression that, at least in the United States, industrial psychologists took mechanistic approaches to increasing productivity until the Hawthorne Studies opened their eyes to the importance of employee attitudes and well-being. A case can be made that interest in topics such as motivation, job satisfaction, and group processes was underdeveloped in the early days of industrial psychology. But industrial psychologists have been interested in employee welfare from the very beginning of the field. Early industrial psychologists in a number of countries criticized the mechanistic scientific management approach for its perceived lack of concern for the worker. The British psychologist C. S. Myers's (1920) longstanding interest in employee discontent was reflected in the activities of the National Institute of Industrial Psychology that he cofounded with Welch in 1921. A major principle of that Institute was to not focus solely on increasing output by relying on financial incentives but to "ease the effort required by the worker" (Farmer, 1958, p. 265). In Germany, Otto Lipmann believed that optimal selection procedures were not enough, that more attention should be paid to worker satisfaction and motivation (Hausmann, 1930–31).

What was true for Europe was true for the United States. On the scientific management front, as early as 1903, in a paper presented to the American Society for Mechanical Engineering, the engineer and scientific management consultant Henry Gantt advocated for obtaining the cooperation of the worker and for leading, rather than driving, employees (cited in Merrill, 1960). In industrial psychology, Hollingworth and Poffenberger (1917) wrote how modern management was "discarding . . . traditional incentives of fear, punishment, and compulsion" and emphasizing "initiative, mental attitude, coöperation, loyalty, professional pride, etc." (p. 212). They discussed "industrial democracy," where employees have a decisive say in policies such as hours worked, pay, and supervisor selection. Link (1919) included a chapter in his text describing the employment process from the applicant's point of view, claiming no book on employment psychology would be complete without one. Link noted that it is easy to view the applicant "as though he were a mere bit of mechanism, an inanimate pawn in the game of industry" (p. 361). He claimed that all applicants want to be treated fairly, to maintain their self-esteem, and to be able to look after their self-interests. In an article describing the mechanics of employee selection, L. L. Thurstone (1924–25) stated that the most serious personnel problem is when individuals see the realm of work and nonwork ("living") as necessarily antagonistic. He noted: "The goal of personnel research is to harmonize these two realms as far as possible by providing situations of productive work which are not hated as a necessary evil, which include opportunities for self-expression, the enjoyment of power, mastery, freedom, control, social approval, and self-advancement" (p. 56).

## The Hawthorne Studies

The Hawthorne Studies were conducted at the Western Electric plant in Hawthorne, Illinois. These studies are viewed as a watershed event in the history of American I-O psychology and as the impetus for moving away from the mechanistic approach of industrial psychology toward a more expansive, worker-oriented organizational approach. While there is some truth to this generalization, as with most generalizations things are not quite so simple or straightforward. As discussed previously, the topics researched at the Hawthorne, Illinois, Western Electric Plant were not new to industrial psychology. In fact, many of the "discoveries" of the Hawthorne researchers were not really new at all. An emphasis on employee welfare was not new to large organizations either. By the early 1920s, Western Electric's parent company, American Telephone and Telegraph (AT&T), was discussing how to increase employees' commitment to the organization and foster cooperation and integration among executives, managers, and workers (Gillespie, 1991). There is also a tendency to gloss over the fact that these more worker-oriented approaches that focused on motivation, group processes, job satisfaction, and other organizational topics had as their primary goal increasing the efficiency and productivity of the employee; that is, a happy worker is a productive worker. Any incidental benefit to the employee was welcome but not the main point.

As with any study or group of studies that achieve iconic status, the Hawthorne Studies have received their fair share of criticism and revisionist history. Whether or not the research findings hold up to scrutiny, the overall message taken from these studies was that the field clearly needed to focus more on the attitudes and well-being of the worker and less on mechanistic approaches to productivity and efficiency. When the Hawthorne researchers obtained results that seemed counterintuitive or puzzling, instead of discarding the research as corrupted, they delved deeper into the possible reasons for these results. Those reasons, disseminated in books such as those by Fritz Roethlisberger and William Dickson (1939) and Elton Mayo (1933), generated what many believe to be a paradigm shift from mechanistic approaches to a human relations approach in dealing with organizational concerns. As Roethlisberger (1941) put it, human problems in employee relations require human solutions; the research conducted at the Hawthorne plant represented "the road back to sanity" (p. 8).

*Initial Studies*

By the mid-1920s, the Hawthorne Works of the Western Electric Plant was considered to be a model large manufacturing plant, employing nearly 22,000 workers. Western Electric was a subsidiary of and produced telephone equipment for AT&T (Gillespie, 1991). The initial group of studies that became known as the Hawthorne Studies, conducted between the fall of 1924 and the spring of 1927, were supervised by the Committee on Industrial Lighting, an independent group from the gas and electric lighting industry. Taking the type of mechanistic approach to improving productivity common at the time, the Committee set out to demonstrate that improved lighting would result in improved employee satisfaction and productivity. The Committee was influenced by the writings of industrial psychologists such as Walter Dill Scott and Hugo Münsterberg (Highhouse, 2007). C. E. Snow, the head of the electrical engineering department at the Massachusetts Institute of Technology (MIT), supervised the initial research (Hilgard, 1987). The study appeared to be well designed and conducted, and in addition to illumination, the researchers examined supervision and compensation (Miner, 2006). Contrary to expectations, the researchers found that any variation in illumination, whether brighter or dimmer, resulted in improved productivity. Only when the illumination level was too dim for the workers to see did productivity drop.

Research continued with a small sample of six women whose job it was to assemble telephone relays. The relay assembly test room experiments, which were conducted from 1927 to 1933, examined the effects on fatigue and monotony of varying rest periods and workday and workweek length. Similar to the earlier study, no matter how the researchers varied these interventions, productivity increased (Hilgard, 1987). Intrigued by these results, Hawthorne management invited a group of researchers from the Harvard Graduate School of Administration and from MIT to examine these findings further. Elton Mayo (1923), one of the Harvard researchers, had earlier attributed increased output under these conditions to be due to improved group dynamics and the increased attention given to the workers. This type of effect later became termed the *Hawthorne effect*. Additional studies were conducted using armature straighteners, mica splitters, additional relay assemblers, and typists as participants to examine the effect of payment systems on productivity (Miner, 2006).

## Elton Mayo and "Revery"

Elton Mayo (1933) and Fritz Roethlisberger and William Dickson (1939) were three of the principal investigators who published accounts of the research. (George) Elton Mayo (1880–1949) emerged as an early spokesperson and the chief publicist for the Hawthorne Studies (Hilgard, 1987). Mayo (Figure 10.1), who spent the first forty-two years of his life in Australia, started but failed to complete an M.D. degree. He did complete an undergraduate degree in philosophy and psychology. Immigrating to the United States in 1922, Mayo obtained a research position at the University of Pennsylvania funded by the Rockefeller family and conducted research in Philadelphia textile mills. At age forty-six, he moved to the Harvard Business School in 1926, became involved in the Hawthorne Studies in 1928, and remained at Harvard until his retirement in 1947. Mayo had little in the way of scientific research training (Miner, 2006).[3]

Figure 10.1 Elton Mayo. State Library of South Australia, B 13694

[3] See Trahair (1984) for a biography of Mayo.

Well before his involvement in the Hawthorne Studies, Mayo was advocating a broad approach to the management of organizational employees. He was highly critical of simply grafting the experimental methods of the psychological laboratory to industry. Mayo (1924) believed that studies that were intensely focused on only one or at best a few environmental variables missed the importance of the "total situation." For Mayo, focusing only on working conditions ignored the reality that poor adjustment to the workplace can be due to the personal history of the worker or some combination of working conditions and personal history. In underlining the importance of considering the personal concerns of the employees, many that originate from nonwork problems such as family issues, Mayo anticipated today's work–nonwork balance discussion. His particular focus was on *revery*, or daydreaming, which along with concentration, hypnoid states, and sleep he believed to be the four types of mental states. Drawing on the findings of medical psychology rather than experimental psychology, Mayo gave numerous examples of how negative reveries due to unresolved personal problems can negatively affect work performance. Financial worries, marital problems, traumatic war experiences, and other problems generate negative reveries at work, with subsequent detriment of performance.

What can the organization do about the revery problem? Mayo was not opposed to all revery, just "pessimistic reflection." He noted that the routine, habitual nature of operating machines fosters a low-grade pessimistic revery. One possible solution was to make the work itself interesting: "If the conditions of work are good or the work interesting, then his job acts as a corrective of any tendency to pessimism or as an antidote to any actual difficulties of problems" (Mayo, 1924, p. 258). For Mayo, another solution was to introduce frequent rest breaks and instruct the workers on the proper method of relaxation during those breaks, thereby reducing negative revery. He illustrated the application of this method, with a successful result of a 15 percent productivity increase, in the spinning department of a textile mill (Mayo, 1924–25). On a more global scale, Mayo (1924a) advocated for a paternalistic approach by personnel departments toward workers to deal with their pessimistic reflections. Information about physical condition, medical history, personal history, reveries, the worker's "domestic situation" and about his or her adaptation to work should all be collected. Mayo understood that collecting this information takes sensitivity on the part of management. But he was confident that once employees understand that management has their happiness and well-being as their concern and that the information will be kept in confidence, data collection was feasible.

Fritz Jules Roethlisberger (1898–1974) became part of the Hawthorne research team in 1930. Mayo, who obtained funding for Roethlisberger at Hawthorne, was a mentor to Roethlisberger. Roethlisberger had a long career focusing on communications, counseling, and training and eventually became a full professor at Harvard Business School. In 1929, William Dickson worked a summer job at Hawthorne to help finance his Ph.D. degree in economics. Instead of completing his degree, he remained at Hawthorne in personnel research until 1969, taking a break at Harvard Business School from 1932 to 1936 to coauthor *Management and the Worker* with Roethlisberger. One of many personnel managers at Hawthorne who were involved in the research, Dickson was the main communicator from the company to the public (Miner, 2006).[4]

### Later Studies

Mayo (1933) saw the Hawthorne effect and subsequent increased production not as the result of an environmental manipulation such as an illumination change but as due to social variables such as group processes, group norms, and communication processes (Hilgard, 1987). Between 1928 and 1931, Western Electric Management began a plant-wide program of individual, confidential conferences between trained interviewers and employees to permit employees to express their opinions. Analysis of these interviews showed money was not the only incentive workers cared about. Work interest, good sanitation, and available social contact were examples of factors other than money that motivated workers. The relationship between the worker and her or his immediate supervisor was found to be the critical factor for employee satisfaction, morale, and productivity (Viteles, 1932). Mayo (1933) saw a direct link between worker satisfaction and productivity.

The Bank Wiring Room Study, conducted in 1931 and 1932, was the final formal study at the Hawthorne plant. This research was heavily influenced by the anthropologist W. Lloyd Warner (1898–1970). The group dynamics of fourteen men who wired telephone banks were observed. The major finding of the observer was that the men adhered to a group norm in

---

[4] In addition to Mayo, Roethlisberger, and Dickson, Clair Turner, a professor of biology and public health at MIT, was involved in the relay assembly studies independent of Mayo. Miner (2006) stated that Turner did not participate in the study's interpretation and had minimal overall input to the research.

restricting their output below what could be theoretically produced.[5] The probable reason for this restriction of output was a concern that management would exploit the workers if they performed to full capacity. Because the workers were paid on an incentive system, this restriction did reduce their compensation. Nevertheless, the group enforced adherence to the level of output that it considered a fair day's work for a fair day's pay, and employees took a graduated series of steps against offenders who produced below or above that norm. Steps ranged from minor verbal harassment through physical harassment through the most severe step of socially isolating the recalcitrant offender (Vecchio, 1995). The results of the bank wiring room observation suggested that management had only limited control over employee output (Miner, 2006).

A personal counseling program was begun in 1936 with the goals of increasing productivity and reducing worker dissatisfaction by generating a type of "positive Hawthorne effect" using counselor, rather than experimenter, attention and concern (Highhouse, 2007, p. 335). From 1942 to 1948, the counseling program expanded to other Western Electric plants. By 1948, at the Hawthorne plant alone, fifty-five counselors were employed. After 1948, the program was increasingly evaluated negatively by the Hawthorne plant management, and by 1956, no counselors were active. On paper, however, the program lasted until 1961 (Miner, 2006). Reasons for the termination of the program included the high cost; lack of a clear goal; changes that lessened the need for counseling, such as smaller, more decentralized plants that decreased the gap between worker and management; the growth of unions to represent worker interests; and better human relations training for supervisors (Gillespie, 1991). As Highhouse (2007) described the counseling program: "The major practical outcome of the Hawthorne research, therefore, has resulted in a failed exercise in managerial paternalism" (p. 336).

## Influence, Interpretation, and Criticism

There is no question that the Hawthorne Studies had a profound effect, not only on I-O psychology but also on organizational behavior, sociology, anthropology, and management. The genesis of the human relations movement in organizations can be found in these studies. Today in organizational psychology and organizational behavior it is widely accepted that a knowledge of worker attitudes and social processes is

---

[5] Restriction of output was not a new concept. Frederick Taylor (1903/1972, 1911), for example, who referred to restriction of output as "soldiering," had discussed it decades earlier.

critical for understanding organizations and ensuring their proper functioning. In the ninety or so years since the beginning of the Hawthorne Studies, an enormous body of research on job satisfaction and other employee attitudes, formal and informal group processes, supervision, and other Hawthorne-related topics has been conducted. While the impact of the results of the Hawthorne Studies is indisputable, it is an open question as to whether those results and interpretations were actually supported by the research data.

Because of their influence, the Hawthorne Studies have been minutely analyzed, interpreted, and reinterpreted. Alternative explanations other than social factors for the findings of the Hawthorne researchers included financial incentives, fear of layoffs, and managerial discipline. The Hawthorne researchers were aware that other explanations were possible; Roethlisberger and Dickson (1939), for example, were quite circumspect in their interpretations. In general, Mayo, Roethlisberger, and Dickson saw the Hawthorne results as a vindication of the importance of social factors in organizations, a topic that they believed had not been given the attention it merited.

Mayo saw the Hawthorne Studies in broad, societal terms. He did not view industrial work as inherently boring or fatiguing. Mayo believed that maintenance of a balanced inner equilibrium made workers resistant to aversive work conditions. Therefore, complaints about external working conditions, especially supervision, were irrational in that they reflected an internal disequilibrium, not a response to those actual conditions. The ultimate cause of this disequilibrium, reflected in the work situation, was the general breakdown of societal norms and values fostered by an industrial society. Mayo's solution, as illustrated by the relay assembly room study, was to encourage teamwork and cooperation, which in turn will result in the security of group membership. Employees should be able to confide in supervisors, and supervisors should be trained to deal with workers' concerns. Mayo was a critic of then-current scientific approaches; he viewed them as inadequate to understand workers (Miner, 2006). Consistent with his earlier writings (e.g., Mayo, 1923), Mayo believed that the root of many of the problems in organizations was maladjusted individual workers. In order to remedy these problems, the focus should be on the improving the psychological adjustment of these employees.[6]

---

[6] This view was similar to that of industrial psychiatrists, who in the early part of the twentieth century played a part in developing the new field of *mental hygiene*, whose practitioners were interested in ameliorating the stress brought about by the industrial revolution. Mental hygienists were also interested in prison reform, in preventing and curing mental illness, and in preventing alcohol abuse (Gibby & Zickar, 2008).

Roethlisberger and Dickson were also skeptical that employee complaints were indicative of poor company policies. They viewed social organization as necessary for maintaining employees' internal equilibrium and a precondition for successful collaboration. All parts of the organization are interconnected; changes in one part can disturb equilibrium in another part. Increases in output, as in the relay assembly room, were not due to less fatigue from more frequent breaks. The breaks created the opportunity for more social interaction, which fostered increased output. Economic incentives are not a primary motivator but must be used in conjunction with social factors (Miner, 2006).

Whether the conclusions drawn by the Hawthorne researchers are supported by the data they collected remains an open question. There is evidence that they went beyond what the data supported in their interpretations. Reanalysis of the data by later researchers has not proven particularly useful. For John Miner (2006), the reason for this ambiguity is straightforward: The Hawthorne researchers were not trained experimenters, and therefore the research was poorly designed and conducted. None of the social factors touted by the Hawthorne researchers were even measured experimentally. There were numerous confounds, or alternative explanations, other than social factors that could have resulted in increased productivity. For example, in the relay assembly test room experiments, financial incentives were given and unproductive workers were dismissed, which provided two alternative explanations for the results. In addition, conclusions were drawn based on a tiny sample size. In the bank wiring room study, no experimental manipulations were even attempted; the results were based on observation only. Given these limitations, it is not surprising that it is possible to draw multiple, conflicting conclusions from the studies. As Viteles (1959) put it: "All that can be truly said about the Hawthorne studies is that no valid conclusions can be drawn from them" (p. 101).[7]

Despite the Hawthorne researchers' limitations in scientific methodology, there is no question that the message sent by their work has resonated with generations of organizational researchers. While possibly most influential in organizational sociology, the Hawthorne Studies have had an impact on multiple fields, including I-O psychology (Miner, 2006).

---

[7] In light of the influence that the Hawthorne Studies had on I-O psychology, it is interesting that none of the Hawthorne researchers had doctorates in psychology. C. E. Snow of MIT was an electrical engineer. Fritz Roethlisberger had an undergraduate degree in engineering and a master's degree in philosophy. William Dickson was enrolled in a Ph.D. program in economics but never completed it. Elton Mayo did have some training in psychology but never obtained a doctorate.

It would be difficult to find an introductory I-O psychology textbook that does not include a description of them.

## Leadership

Writing in 1927, Walter Van Dyke Bingham stated that "[l]eadership is the organization of activities of a group for the achievement of a common purpose" (Bingham, 1927/1980, p. 245). What makes a good leader? Is successful leadership a trait or constellation of traits that an individual possesses, perhaps innately to some degree? If a person is lucky enough to have these traits, he or she will emerge as a successful leader. Or is successful leadership a skill that can be learned like any other skill? Can an individual be taught to be a successful leader, in the same manner that one can be taught to be a successful accountant, carpenter, or physician?

While discussion of these questions was not unknown in early industrial psychology, examination of industrial psychology texts through the 1920s shows that leadership was not considered a topic worthy of chapter-length treatment. Books on industrial psychology, vocational psychology, and applied psychology published before 1920, such as Scott (1911), Münsterberg (1913), Hollingworth (1916), Hollingworth and Poffenberger (1917), Muscio (1917), and Link (1919), did not include a chapter on leadership. Nor did texts published in the 1920s, for example, Griffitts (1924), Myers (1925, 1926), Laird (1925b), and Burtt (1929). Discussion of leadership was included in some social psychology textbooks, and articles in the popular press about business leaders appeared periodically, although few of these were empirical in nature. By the early 1930s, chapters on leadership began to appear in industrial psychology books. In their edited book, Moore and Hartmann (1931) include a selection of short readings on leadership in a chapter titled "Leadership and Social Adjustment." Viteles (1932) did write a chapter on leadership in his text *Industrial Psychology*, the first industrial psychology text to contain one (Day & Zaccaro, 2007). There were only a few books published in the 1920s that focused on business leaders (e.g., Craig & Charters, 1925).

Traditionally, the dominant view was that leadership is a talent or trait. One of the earlier expressions of this "Great Man" perspective of leadership was put forth by the Scottish historian and essayist Thomas Carlyle (1795–1881), who in a series of lectures published in the 1840s advocated a strong hero figure as the best solution for societal problems (Magnusson, 1990). The idea that leadership is an innate or mostly innate characteristic of an individual was typical in the beginning years of industrial psychology, and although there were exceptions, this conception had an influence into the 1930s (Day & Zaccaro, 2007). Craig and Charters (1925), in what Day and Zaccaro (2007) called the first empirically based book to focus on industrial leadership, listed a number of oft-cited personal qualities or abilities that they believed were characteristic of successful leaders. This inventory included both traits and behaviors. Listed were characteristics such as forcefulness, ability to command respect, and self-confidence that are clearly traits; others (e.g., ability to train, ability to give clear and detailed instructions, ability to get and use suggestions from subordinates) were more behavioral. While at the time traits were generally considered to be innate and therefore difficult to modify, the characteristics of successful leaders were assumed to be something that could be developed (Day & Zaccaro, 2007).

Early social psychology textbooks discussed leadership in general terms, although some of the discussion dovetails with the coverage in the industrial psychology literature. C. A. Ellwood (1917), a professor of sociology, discussed social leadership. Consistent with the "Great Man" perspective, Ellwood wrote that although everyone possesses leadership ability to some degree, the outstanding leader is that exceptional individual whose "biological" constitution is superior to that of the average of the social group. He did recognize that followers also have power. Ellwood noted that, for good or bad, the leader is always selected by the social group and that the leader's power is to an extent limited by the group. Floyd H. Allport (1924) focused on leadership as an agent of social change. He wrote that the most important factor in leader emergence is "personal prestige," which he perceived as something that exists not within the person but rather within the attitudes of others toward the leader. This personal prestige can be reinforced by symbolic devices such as titles and ranks. In assessing the personality of the leader, Allport thought the trait of ascendance to be of the greatest importance; a leader must be domineering. Ascendance is generally combined with physical power, although Allport conceded that smaller, frailer individuals can compensate by displaying great endurance and energy. Ascendance must be moderated by tact and concern for social welfare. Among the other traits that Allport saw as useful for a leader to possess were high intelligence, tenacity, and drive.

In his *Introduction to Social Psychology*, Bernard (1926) wrote that the chief determinant of successful leadership is the ability to focus the attention of the group on a common object of interest. To be successful, the leader must be able to respond to each follower individually, a task that requires a high level of intelligence and "gamesmanship." As to the innate nature of leadership ability, however, Bernard is blunt: "Such leaders are not born, as some poetic temperaments have maintained, but must be trained, either formally or in the hard school of experience" (pp. 530–531). Nevertheless, Bernard claimed that some inherited characteristics may be of value, as the best training for leadership success is the actual practice of leadership, with the support of theoretical training and natural ability. For face-to-face leadership, the characteristics he believed most important are an imposing physical presence and an attitude of sympathy and under-standing. Also of major importance are a strong justice sense, courage, persistence, and "insight"; one must know human nature generally and be a good judge of the character of each individual follower. To that list, Bernard added other desirable abilities such as originality, initiative, men-tal flexibility, moral vision, cheerfulness, even temper, and self-confidence.

In the industrial psychology literature, Viteles's (1932) leadership chap-ter also covered group processes, power, and conflict, topics that would merit their own chapters in a present-day organizational psychology text-book. He discussed the use of rewards and punishment by leaders. After elaborating on the pitfalls of using punishment, Viteles noted that even the use of rewards can be a problem because they, like punishment, are externally applied. Citing the work of F. C. Bartlett and O. Tead, Viteles made a distinction between *discipline*, which is enforced obedience to an outside authority, and the preferred *morale*, defined as "*obedience to exter-nal circumstances which has its source of authority within the man or group*" (p. 616, italics in original). Discipline is most often enforced through rewards and punishments, while development of morale requires the reed-ucation of both management and workers to substitute individual and group standards for external commands. To create an environment where employees take personal responsibility to achieve organizational goals, the "boss" must become a leader who understands influences on group beha-vior and who can effectively manage conflict (Bartlett, 1927; Tead, 1929; both cited in Viteles, 1932).

Viteles (1932) included a discussion of group processes and conflict. Drawing on the writings of Mary Follett, he noted that conflict in orga-nizations is not necessarily detrimental. According to Viteles, competition between organizations, groups, and individuals can result in improved work processes. Unsatisfactory means of dealing with conflict are to allow one party to dominate another and, following Follett, to engage in compromise. Compromise involves sacrifice on the part of both parties, increasing the probability that the conflict will arise again in the future. *Integration* is the preferred method of ameliorating conflict. To achieve this, the whole situation must be analyzed taking both workers' and management's views into account to find a solution that adequately meets the needs of both groups in a manner that benefits the entire organization. Viteles called for a change in the quality of leadership in industry, one that substitutes morale for discipline and uses integration when dealing with conflict. Following Bartlett, he described three types of leaders: those who depend on the *prestige* of their position, those who *dominate* their employees, and those who have the ability to *persuade* the workers.[8] It was Viteles' belief that a new kind of leader was needed, one who does not depend on "prestige, dominance, or persuasion, but on the capacity to integrate the abilities and desires of individual members of a group to a common purpose" (p. 627).

Walter Van Dyke Bingham (1927/1980) contributed a chapter on leadership to Henry Metcalf's *The Foundations of Psychological Management* that in many ways was ahead of its time in its conception of leadership. He stressed that leadership can occur at many levels in the organization and that the designated leader may not be the actual leader of the group. Planning and foresight are key for a successful leader, as are a technical knowledge of the industrial process and the ability to clearly communicate goals to employees. Bingham cautioned that speed in decision making is not the most important factor. Decisions need to be based on factual information, which can take time to collect. He was adamant that individuals are not born with an innate set of skills that predispose them to be successful leaders; rather, leadership ability can be learned like any other ability or skill: "Leadership ability is complex, but it is entirely capable of analysis; when you break it into its elements and note the specific sorts of behavior which differentiate the successful leader from the unsuccessful, you discover that these components of leadership are capable of development through training" (Bingham, 1927/1980, p. 255). At the time, Bingham's statement was more an article of faith than the reflection of a systematic research program. It would take another twenty or so years for industrial psychology research to disavow the trait approach and transition to a behavioral approach to leadership.[9]

---

[8] It is interesting to compare Bartlett's classification of leaders with French and Raven's (1959) well-known classification of types or sources of power. Prestige based on office would correspond to position power or legitimate authority; domination would be akin to reward and punishment power; and ability to persuade is similar to referent power, or power based on personal charisma.

[9] Day and Zaccaro (2007) noted that given the paucity of coverage in textbooks in the 1920s, Bingham's ideas about leadership had little influence on his contemporaries. It was not until the Ohio State and University of Michigan studies in the 1950s that the behavioral orientation and subsequent interactional approaches began in earnest.

## Work Motivation and Job Satisfaction

Work motivation and job satisfaction were often discussed in tandem in the early years of industrial psychology. "Man is 'driven' to work by the imperiousness of his wants. If these wants can function freely and have a reasonable opportunity of being fulfilled, then satisfaction normally ensues" (Moore and Hartmann, 1931, p. 415). In this conceptualization, motivation and satisfaction are viewed as two sides of the same coin.[10] With an increasing recognition of the importance of the human factor in work, there was a corresponding increased interest in behaviors and attitudes that promoted efficiency and satisfaction and, with those factors that underlie those attitudes and behaviors, what Viteles (1932) called *motives-in-work.*

Prior to the mid-1800s, very little attention was paid to work motivation because capital investment was minimal and production was limited to small groups of workers. This changed with the advent of the Industrial Revolution. Capital investment increased dramatically, and efficiency and productivity became of paramount concern, including the efficiency and productivity of the individual workers. Efforts at motivation focused almost exclusively on monetary incentives (Dunnette & Kirchner, 1965). It was not that incentives other than money were not recognized. Even Frederick Taylor's scientific management approach recognized incentives other than money; nevertheless, in practice, the focus was on tying performance to financial incentives, generally with some variation of a piece-rate system. As illustrated by the Hawthorne Studies; however, by the 1920s, it was evident that increasing financial incentives did not necessarily result in maximum performance; workers would voluntarily restrict their output. While some of this restriction can be attributed to union rules, voluntary restriction of output was widespread. Possible reasons for this were resistance to speeding-up machinery, fear of layoffs if production increased, and a lack of trust between the workers and management (Viteles, 1932).

Walter Dill Scott agreed with Taylor that workers were underperforming, that a "first-class man" can perform at a level two to four times that of the average worker. Scott's *Increasing Human Efficiency in Business* (1911) is essentially a book about motivation. The book discussed various strategies for increasing worker efficiency. For the most part, that translated to increasing motivation through means such as imitating desirable role

---

[10] Research on job satisfaction for its own sake was fairly rare until the 1950s; since then, it has been a popular area of study. As an illustration, in the *Journal of Applied Psychology* between 1917 and 1946, only two articles appeared with work satisfaction or job satisfaction in the title (Wright, 2006).

models, creating loyalty to management, increasing workers' ability to concentrate, manipulating wages, developing proper habits, and fostering a "love of the game." Scott wrote that three conditions are necessary for developing a love of the game in business. First, the worker must be able to take personal responsibility for his or her work. The job must provide opportunity for personal initiative, for creativity, and for personal expression. Second, the work should provide social prestige or social approval for the worker. And finally, the worker must view the work as important and useful. In today's terms, love of the game is akin to intrinsic motivation, where the work itself is motivating. One of Scott's strategies, "pleasure as a means of increasing human efficiency," concerns the use of job satisfaction to improve performance. In *Psychology and Industrial Efficiency* (1913), Hugo Münsterberg also discussed factors other than money that can influence individual worker performance. Examples include fatigue, working hours, alcohol, weather and other atmospheric conditions, and what he termed "mental monotony." Münsterberg did recognize that social factors are important in the workplace. Some of his suggestions for fostering social interaction seem almost whimsical, for example, giving the workers a pet cat.

Scott relied heavily on the use of instincts to explain motivation. Instincts, an innate propensity to respond to stimuli in a particular way, were popular as an all-purpose theory of behavior, including economic behavior, in the early part of the twentieth century. Postulated instincts ranged from the pervasive, such as Freud's libido, to the highly specific, such as the economist C. H. Parker's sixteen instincts that included the housing instinct, hunting instinct, and leadership instinct (Viteles, 1932). By the mid-1920s, even those who were favorably inclined to instinctual explanations recognized that most human behavior is partially the result of experience (Griffitts, 1924). At least in the United States, the increasing popularity of Watsonian behaviorism led psychologists to deemphasize innate tendencies, ignore them, or deny their existence altogether. Viteles (1932) viewed instincts as "nothing more than logical abstractions" and found no structural or neurological evidence for their existence in humans (p. 567). Research on Viteles's motives-in-work led to systematic investigations of attitudes through the use of interviews, rating scales, and observations to determine the effect of various conditions on the workers and to examine how these conditions affect worker productivity.

As an illustration, Viteles (1932) described Otto Lipmann's research in the mining industry when Lipmann was director of the Efficiency Committee of the German Industrial Inquiry Board. Technology had dramatically changed the German anthracite coal mining industry.

In 1913, 95 percent of the coal was hand-mined; by 1926, the use of machinery had reduced that amount to 33 percent. Lipmann found that workers, particularly older workers, strenuously objected to the introduction of the new machinery. Given the choice, however, they preferred to use it rather than return to their pickaxes. Rather than dismiss this seeming contradiction as just talk on the part of the workers, Lipmann delved deeper into the reasons for the resistance. He found that workers tended toward conservatism; that is, they did not like change. In addition, they did not like to be deprived of the social aspects of hand mining, the companionship of the other miners. They were also fearful that increased mechanization could cost the miners their jobs. Lipmann (1928–29) was concerned that technical innovations were severing the link between the worker and his or her work, with the result of decreased job satisfaction.[11]

In the United States, the Hawthorne Studies generated a long list of variables associated with motivation and job satisfaction. Examples ranged from proper ventilation, lighting, temperature, and noise levels to opportunity for social contact, interesting work, and an opportunity for advancement. The single factor found to be most critical for morale, happiness, positive attitude, and efficiency was the relationship between the worker and his or her immediate supervisor (Putnam, 1929–30), a finding reinforced by the results of a study conducted by Arthur Kornhauser and Agnes Sharp (1931–32). Kornhauser and Sharp used interviews and questionnaires to assess the attitudes of women performing routine operations in a paper manufacturing plant. This study is interesting in that, unlike much previous work, Kornhauser and Sharp did not find the expected relationship between worker efficiency and worker attitudes. That is, productivity and satisfaction were not strongly related. One other finding was that the women did not seem particularly invested in this type of factory work. It was simply what one did after completing school; it provided a needed paycheck, and paid work was marginally better at this point in their lives than the only realistic alternative of housework.

In the early 1930s, Robert Hoppock conducted one of the earliest large-scale studies on job satisfaction for his doctoral dissertation. In the town of New Hope, Pennsylvania, Hoppock (1935) approached the measurement of job satisfaction from a number of perspectives. He reviewed previous job satisfaction studies and found that in twenty-one of thirty-two studies, less than a third of participants reported being dissatisfied with their jobs. He

---

[11] This study anticipated the better-known Tavistock Institute coal-mining studies conducted by Trist and Bamforth (1951). This research is described in the Appendix.

conducted in-depth interviews with forty employed workers who held twenty-eight different occupations and with forty unemployed individuals who last engaged in thirty-one different occupations. Hoppock assessed the level of job satisfaction of 500 teachers and then compared the 100 most satisfied with the 100 least satisfied. With these groups, he found a relation between job satisfaction and a number of variables, including emotional adjustment, religion, superiors, associates, vocational choice, community size where one worked, feelings of success, praise, family influence, interest in work, and social status. Dissatisfied workers reported more fatigue and monotony than satisfied ones, and the satisfied group was seven and a half years older on average than those who were unsatisfied.

Hoppock also had an assistant attempt to contact every adult resident of New Hope and complete a satisfaction questionnaire.[12] The response rate was 88 percent (309 of 351 residents). Only 15 percent of the residents did not like their jobs, and another 15 percent disliked their jobs about half the time. Sixteen percent said that they disliked their jobs more than they believed other workers disliked their jobs. Asked if they could have any job in the world, 48 percent reported they would remain in the job they had. Finally, 66 percent said that they received more satisfaction from their jobs than from any leisure activity. These results should be interpreted with caution, as the country was dealing with the Great Depression and, given the rising unemployment rate, perhaps workers were happy to have any job.

## Chapter Summary

The 1920s and early 1930s saw an increased interest in topics that today would be considered part of organizational psychology and organizational behavior. While psychological testing, employee selection, and other human resource topics remained the dominant interest of industrial psychologists in many parts of the world, including the United States, more attention was directed at understanding organizational leadership, motivation, group processes, and employee attitudes such as job satisfaction. It is true that much of the formal history of organizational psychology and organizational behavior occurred via the human relations movement after the time period covered in this book. That history, however, is best viewed as a natural outgrowth of the interests of the early industrial psychologists. Other than industrial psychology and scientific management, other

---

[12] The research assistant was Hoppock's recently retired father-in-law (Landy, 1989).

influences on this history include Max Weber and his bureaucratic theory, Henri Fayol's theory of management, and the ideas on conflict, power, and leadership of Mary Follett.

The Hawthorne Studies, conducted at the Western Electric Plant in Hawthorne, Illinois, are widely considered to have generated interest in America in leadership, group processes, conflict, employee attitudes, and other organizational topics. These studies, begun in the 1920s and popularized by researchers Elton Mayo (1933) and Fritz Roethlisberger and William Dickson (1939), were wide-ranging. The researchers examined the effects of levels of illumination on production and found attention paid to the workers to be the critical factor in productivity. They observed group processes among workers wiring banks of equipment to study restriction of output and set up counseling programs for employees. The Hawthorne Studies were certainly the genesis for a great deal of theorizing and research on the human aspects of organizations. It does not, however, appear that the conclusions drawn by the researchers were particularly well supported by the data they generated.

Leadership theories evolved in the 1920s and early 1930s from traditional approaches that emphasized innate traits and instincts to more of a hybrid of traits and behaviors to even in some cases (e.g., Walter Van Dyke Bingham [1927/1980]) a truly behavioral approach. That is, effective leadership was becoming viewed as a set of behaviors that could be taught rather than strictly a talent or trait. Ideas about employee motivation were undergoing a similar reevaluation, from theories based on instincts to a consideration of environmental variables, such as working conditions and quality of supervision. Job satisfaction was one of those variables that was assumed to influence motivation and therefore productivity. Notable among studies that examined job satisfaction was a large-scale study by Hoppock (1935) that assessed satisfaction levels of workers in New Hope, Pennsylvania.

This chapter on organizational psychology brings to a close our narrative of the early years of I-O psychology, from the late 1800s to the early 1930s. In Chapter 11, I will reflect on that history and offer concluding remarks. For the reader interested the story of I-O psychology after the early 1930s, there is a capsule history of important historical developments in the Appendix.

# Reflections on the Early Years of Industrial Psychology

## Concluding Remarks

In the foreword of the first volume of the *Journal of Applied Psychology*, the editors G. Stanley Hall, John W. Baird, and L. R. Geissler (1917) stated their vision for applied psychology:

> Yet the problem which is here concerned is one that must appeal to the interest of every psychologist who besides being a "pure scientist" also cherishes the hope that in addition to throwing light upon the theoretical problems of his science, his findings may also contribute their quota to the sum total of human happiness; and it must appeal to every human being who is interested in increasing human efficiency and human happiness by the more direct method of decreasing the number of cases where a square peg is condemned to a life of fruitless endeavor to fit itself comfortably in a round hole. (p. 6)

A little later in the essay, they continued: "The psychologist finds that the old distinction between pure and applied science is already obscured in his domain; and he is beginning to realize that applied psychology can no longer be relegated to a distinctly inferior plane" (p. 6).

These two short passages highlight a number of themes that characterized the early years of industrial psychology. They include industrial psychology's dual goals of increasing the efficiency of organizations while at the same time increasing the well-being of organizational members. The editors allude to the use of selection as a means to achieve these goals, of matching up the square pegs with square holes and round pegs with round holes. The dichotomy between "pure" or basic science and applied work was mentioned, along with the inference that applied psychology had less status than basic science, that applied psychology has been "relegated to a distinctly inferior plane." Yet there is optimism here too, a belief that the rift between basic and applied science was already fading and that applied psychologists could not only increase productivity and efficiency but that in doing so they could also "contribute their quota to the sum total of human happiness."

In reviewing the beginning years of what evolved into I-O psychology, what, if any, conclusions can be drawn about industrial psychology during that time? Did the first few generations of industrial psychologists reach their goals of increasing productivity and efficiency? Did they contribute to the well-being of workers? Were they able to establish industrial psychology as a viable scientific and professional enterprise? These questions present us with a classic criterion problem: How exactly do we define success? Relevant criteria might include the growth in numbers of industrial psychologists and of the topics they study, the degree of global expansion of the field, the reliability and validity of procedures used, and the level of acceptance of I-O psychology by managers in organizations. The remainder of this chapter is a reflection on these questions and a consideration of some of the trends, themes, and conflicts in the historical narrative. While for the most part the focus is on industrial psychology's development to the early 1930s, there is also some discussion of the overall history of I-O psychology and of how those early efforts influenced current practice. When contrasting the past with the present, an effort was made to be sensitive to the contextual factors that influenced the lives and work of the early industrial psychologists. Their world was not the same as ours.

## The Importance of Context

I-O psychology was the result of the interaction between individuals interested in applying psychology to industry and an environment that was supportive of that goal. One is inseparable from the other. Psychology's adaptation of the scientific method provided the first generation of industrial psychologists with a set of tools for solving organizational problems that was different from those used by nonscientific competitors. This scientific approach was also in harmony with industry's increasing faith in science. Advances in the physical sciences and engineering seemed to promise innovative solutions to longstanding problems in organizations. Perhaps the new science of psychology had something to contribute to this effort. As organizations became larger and more complex, they became increasingly difficult to manage. Industrial psychologists were there to offer their expertise to help manage them. Convincing managers that this expertise was needed was not easy, nor was differentiating industrial psychology from competitors who had beliefs and practices antithetical to empirical verification.

Earlier chapters discussed a number of local and more widespread events that had a major influence on the early development of industrial psychology. Industrialization, Progressivism, World War I, and the Bolshevik revolution in Russia are examples. Scientific psychology and the increased popularity and respect given to that field transferred a measure of legitimacy to the fledgling field of industrial psychology. The expansion of the higher education system provided increased opportunities for relevant graduate-level training. The emergence of professional managers who, at least to a degree, were willing to seek experts from outside their organizations gave industrial psychologists an opportunity to apply their theories and practice in real-world settings. Advances in psychological measurement and statistics were of critical importance to the early industrial psychologists. In turn, industrial psychologists began to contribute psychometric and quantitative innovations of their own.

## *General Trends and Themes*

A number of general trends can be identified in the history of I-O psychology from its origins to the present day. One is growth. The field became larger: more I-O psychologists, more graduate schools, more countries involved in I-O psychology, increased specialization, more journals, and more books. While the fundamental themes of increasing productivity and improving worker well-being endured, theories explaining organizational behavior grew more complex, and practice became more sophisticated. Finding a balance between the needs of managers and the needs of the workers continues to challenge I-O psychologists. As they did in the early years, I-O psychologists still struggle with establishing a professional identity both within psychology and in the organizations they work in.

Reviewing the entire history of I-O psychology in the United States, Zickar and Gibby (2007) identified four enduring themes. These themes were also characteristic of the early years of the field. First was an emphasis on productivity and efficiency. The Progressive Era's obsession with efficiency and productivity was taken up by practitioners of scientific management and then later by their industrial psychology successors. Improving economic performance through increased productivity by individual workers was the goal of scientific management. It also became the goal of industrial psychologists. Next was an emphasis on quantification. Quantification was critical to the scientific orientation of the early industrial psychologists. Psychological tests provided a means to assess individual differences, and by quantifying the predictive accuracy of their tests, industrial psychologists could empirically demonstrate the usefulness of their interventions. In addition, the use of empirical verification gave industrial psychologists a way to separate themselves from their pseudo-psychology competitors.

Third was a focus on individual differences and on employee selection. Employee selection was the major activity of early industrial psychology before 1930, particularly in Germany and the United States. Research on employee selection and psychological testing dominated journal space, and selection and testing were the topics given most coverage in textbooks of the era. Finally, there was the tension and interdependence between practice and science. While acrimony between the academic and applied sides of psychology was not a universal event and the size of the rift varied from country to country, in the United States, the approbation of academic psychologists was one of the hurdles their applied colleagues had to contend with.

The following sections expand on these and other themes that characterized the beginning years of industrial psychology. The importance to the field of the measurement of individual differences and employee selection is examined as well as the science versus practice debate. Industrial psychology's perceived bias toward management is reviewed. The chapter closes with a discussion of the expansion of the field and an examination of the influence of the early years on present-day science and practice.

### *The Importance of Individual Differences, Quantification, and Employee Selection*

I-O psychology was built on the existence and measurement of individual differences. The ability to quantify those differences provided a foundation for psychological applications to business and industry, including to employee selection. Selection, along with advertising, provided psychologists with an entrée into business. As organizations grew in size and complexity, managers needed a way to systematically select those individuals with the best chance of succeeding. Scientific management, while recognizing the importance of selection, was not up to the task. Industrial psychology was. The key advantage for industrial psychologists was their ability to empirically verify the effectiveness of their tests. By demonstrating the ability to measure individual difference characteristics in a reliable manner and by further providing, through the validation process, empirical evidence that these measures could be used to predict job performance, the early industrial psychologists were able to rely on the authority of science to separate themselves from other practitioners. In the United States, the perceived success of psychological testing in World War I convinced the public that applied psychology could be useful. While that initial postwar boost was short-lived, industrial psychologists took advantage of the opportunity it afforded them to demonstrate the viability of their profession.

The acceptance of this empirically based, quantitative approach to selection varied both across and within countries. For example, in the 1920s, the American psychologists Max Freyd and Morris Viteles debated the use of strictly statistical selection procedures versus a more clinically oriented approach. Freyd (1925) emphasized the advantages of objective, bias-resistant statistical techniques. Viteles (1925) was concerned that strict reliance on such an approach would remove psychological judgment from the process. He believed a wholly statistical approach would result in a mere technology with no need for the psychologist's expertise. In the United States, the advocates of statistical validation carried the day. Other countries relied on the use of tests to varying degrees, with some, such as Germany, preferring more laboratory-influenced apparatus approaches to selection and more subjective, global assessments of applicants (van Drunen, 1997).

From a present-day perspective, there is much to criticize about the tests and procedures used. It is quite remarkable, however, how resilient the basic criterion-related validation model developed by the early industrial psychologists has been. It is still in use today. The predictors that the early industrial psychologists used are still the mainstays of present-day selection programs. Interviews, cognitive ability tests, job knowledge tests, personal data forms, and interest and personality inventories are all used in modern selection research and practice. It is true that some tests were used and interpreted in the early years in ways that would cause concern today. As illustrated by the application of the US Army Alpha and Beta test results, the hereditarian views of many of the early testers led them to a belief in the innate, immutable nature of intelligence. Hereditarian views, overconfidence in the accuracy of their tests, and acceptance of the stereo-types prevalent at the time led some psychologists to draw conclusions about racial and ethnic differences in intelligence not supported by the evidence. Industrial psychologists, however, such as Henry Link (1923b) and Morris Viteles (1928a) spoke out vigorously against these conclusions. They pointed out how the tests were biased against individuals who lacked exposure to American culture and educational opportunity. Eventually some of those psychologists most committed to a hereditarian viewpoint recanted (e.g., Brigham, 1930). While this reconsideration of their views could have been due in part to changes in professional mores, it is also plausible that they were convinced by the scientific evidence that demonstrated that their earlier claims of group differences were flawed.

In addition to the disagreement between psychologists who supported innate differences and those who were open to environmental influences, two other conflicts stand out. One is the science–practice divide, also framed as an academic–practitioner dichotomy. The other involves determining where the industrial psychologist's primary responsibility lies. Is it to the manager who employs the psychologist and controls access to the organization? Or is it to the worker, whose well-being has been put forth as a major concern of the field? Is it possible for industrial psychologists to satisfy both the worker and the manager? Can they increase productivity and improve organizational functioning and at the same time increase the satisfaction and well-being of the employees?

### *Science versus Practice*

Whether framed as a tension between science and practice or between academics and practitioners, this conflict is as old as industrial psychology itself. It did not occur everywhere to the same degree, and in some places, such as Germany, it did not seem to be a major concern. In Great Britain, the opposing viewpoints of Charles Myers, who was convinced of the importance of applied psychology, and his former student Frederic Bartlett, who was just as convinced of the primacy of the experimental lab, provide an illustration of the conflict (Bartlett, 1948; Bunn, 2001). In the United States, disapproval by laboratory psychologists tended to decrease as industrial psychology grew in size and influence. This was especially true when applied psychology demonstrated its value during times of national crisis such as World War I. Individual psychologists did change their views about applied psychology. Early in his career, even as iconic a figure in industrial psychology as Hugo Münsterberg was quite hostile to practical applications of psychology outside the laboratory (Benjamin, 2006). Psychologists considering the leap from the laboratory to the factory did have cause for concern. Because of the stigma associated with applied psychology, industrial psychologists such as Walter Dill Scott and Harry Hollingworth were initially reluctant to take on applied work. Hollingworth would eventually disavow the important work he did in industrial psychology, claiming he had preferred experimental psychology all along (Hollingworth, 2013). Psychologists who did practice often held on to their academic positions for prestige and security. For others, however, academic opportunities were limited or nonexistent. For them, practice was the only viable option.

I can find little evidence for a reciprocal hostility by industrial psychologists toward experimental psychology. I suspect there was some resentment toward those academics who stigmatized practice, although applied work was defended by some academics (e.g., Thorndike, 1919). The early industrial psychologists believed in the importance of basic research and theory. However, at least in the United States, industrial psychologists did not rely on their basic science colleagues for guidance. They developed their own methods and practice and did not find basic research methods such as introspection useful (Danziger, 1990). Many of the early industrial psychologists who straddled both industry and academia viewed themselves as scientist-practitioners. Morris Viteles is a representative example. In their autobiographies, the German psychologists Otto Klemm (1936) and Karl Marbe (1936) both emphasized the critical importance of both theory and practice, as did leading American industrial psychologists such as Walter Van Dyke Bingham (1928). The whole approach of the early psychologists, illustrated most starkly perhaps by their employee selection work, was self-consciously empirical and quantitative. This identification with the prestige of science was critical to establishing their own professional identity separate from the multitude of other competitors. The all-out mobilization to win World War I brought about a temporary truce between academic and applied psychologists. Many academic psychologists, including those hostile toward applied psychology, engaged in applied work during the war. For some, such as Charles S. Myers (1936), that exposure to applied work resulted in a career change toward industrial psychology. For others, such as Edwin Boring, George Stratton, Robert Yerkes, and Knight Dunlap, the war was an interruption whose end signaled a return to the "real" science of the laboratory.

### Manager versus Worker

As exemplified by Baritz's book *The Servants of Power* (1960), industrial psychology has been criticized for its perceived managerial bias in practice and in research. In the United States, industrial psychologists were viewed as serving the upper echelons of the organization while ignoring the needs of nonmanagement employees and exhibiting, at best, indifference toward organized labor. While this generalization may contain a grain of truth, many counterexamples occurred. Psychologists such as James McKeen Cattell (1923) at the Psychological Corporation and Walter V. Bingham (1928) at the Personnel Research Federation cooperated with organized labor. Walter Dill Scott refused to allow his consulting firm to be used by client organizations against labor (Ferguson, 1962). Textbook authors such as Morris Viteles made explicit the industrial psychologist's obligation to protect the well-being of the workers. Psychologists such as Arthur Kornhauser (1929–30b) warned colleagues of the managerial bias problem, noting that industrial psychologists are content "to be judged by the standards of the accountant," showing little concern "over intangible and unmeasurable attitudes or satisfactions" (p. 348). Similar to advocates of scientific management, industrial psychologists for the most part believed that their interventions would benefit both labor and management. If the proper person is selected for a job, the organization benefits by having a productive worker and the worker benefits from having a job he or she is interested in and good at performing. Proper training makes workers more productive and makes their jobs more manageable. Increasing worker motivation or job satisfaction results in happier workers who will be productive, remain on the job, and not be tempted to join a union. Beliefs such as these allowed industrial psychologists to perceive their efforts as helping both manager and worker alike.

It is not as if the early industrial psychologists did not listen to the concerns of workers. They interviewed them, surveyed them, and occasionally even counseled them. But this concern was generally in service of management's aims of increasing productivity, reducing resistance to change, and quelling worker unrest. The assumption was that the psychological "expert" had knowledge and skills not available to either workers or managers. The power differential may not have been as stark as it was in scientific management, but it was there. This is not to imply that workers never benefited from the efforts of industrial psychologists or that psychologists did not have the welfare of the workers in mind. Nor is it to suggest that increasing the effectiveness of the workforce and the productivity of organizations are not legitimate goals. It is simply to point out that power resided with management and that it was management that employed industrial psychologists. It is therefore not surprising that workers would perceive industrial psychologists as part of the management power structure. Nor is it surprising that industrial psychologists would identify with managers and take managerial aspirations as their own. While some industrial psychologists conceded that this was cause for concern, they believed that it was possible to help the organization achieve its goals while still benefiting the employees. In addition, there were industrial psychologists who believed that the welfare of the worker was a higher priority than increasing efficiency and productivity.

## The Expansion of Industrial Psychology

The field saw considerable growth in the first third of the twentieth century. From an initial handful of interested individuals with backgrounds in experimental psychology, engineering, medicine, and business, by the 1930s, industrial psychologists had proliferated. Industrial psychology expanded across Europe and into Asia and Oceania. Countries did vary considerably in their acceptance of industrial psychology, depending on their economic, political, and social circumstances. And there were setbacks, for example, Stalin's ban on industrial psychology altogether in the USSR in the 1930s (Joravsky, 1989). There was also an increase in the number of topics industrial psychologists were interested in. The field expanded from the early topics of fatigue, advertising, and selection to areas such as training, performance appraisal, work motivation, leadership and supervision, group processes, and job satisfaction. While industrial psychology also shed interest areas, this occurred primarily after the 1930s. Even by the 1930s, however, it was clear that areas such as human factors and advertising would establish themselves as entities independent of industrial psychology or, in the case of vocational psychology, find a home outside industrial psychology.

Industrial psychology provided opportunities for women that were not available in academia. Because university faculty positions were difficult for women to obtain, applied psychology provided a career path for doctoral- and non-doctoral-level female psychologists. It is difficult to accurately gauge the number of women who were involved in industrial psychology, particularly in the early part of the twentieth century when someone working in industry might have been known simply as an applied psychologist. We have, however, seen many examples throughout the text of women industrial psychologists and women who, although they may not have identified as industrial psychologists, contributed to the field nonetheless. While a few women held academic positions, most spent most or all of their careers outside academia. Before 1920, Lillian Gilbreth was a leading figure in scientific management, and Tsuruko Haraguchi in Japan was conducting research on fatigue. The National Institute of Industrial Psychology in Great Britain employed women researchers, including the psychologists Winifred Spielman and May Smith.

The Swiss industrial psychologist Franziska Baumgarten-Tramer was an academic who conducted research on industrial topics. Mary Holmes Stevens Hayes worked for the Scott Company consulting firm, and Elsie Oschrin Bregman was employed as a psychologist at Cattell's Psychological Corporation and Macy's. Marion Bills was associate director of the Carnegie Institute of Technology (CIT) program before her long association with the insurance industry. She was also the first woman elected president of the APA Division for Industrial Psychology. Grace Manson, one of only four Ph.D. graduates from the CIT program, conducted applied research at the University of Michigan. Other women, such as Millicent Pond at Scovill Manufacturing Company and Sadie Myers Shellow at the Milwaukee Police Department, worked in industry. These individuals were true scientist-practitioners who, in addition to their applied work, conducted and published research.

## *From the Early Years to the Present Day*

Before discussing the influence of early industrial psychology on present-day science and practice, it is interesting to examine how industrial psychologists at the time viewed their field during those developmental years. Writing toward the end of the 1920s, Walter Van Dyke Bingham (1928) reflected on how psychology influenced industry in the United States. He saw three major types of influence: psychology as a science, psychology as a point of view, and psychology as a method. To illustrate psychology's influence as a science, Bingham gave examples that included how psychology influenced personnel procedures through the measurement of sensory, motor, cognitive, and personality individual difference characteristics. He believed that research in basic learning affected training in organizations and basic science in such areas as sensory processes influenced engineering. For example, Bingham discussed how the work of C. E. Ferree on visual efficiency under varying conditions of illumination changed how engineers illuminated workplaces. Less tangible but no less influential was psychology's view that human behavior is a natural phenomenon. Therefore, like all natural phenomena, it can be understood through empirical research. Superficial explanations (e.g., that an employee is accident-prone) gave way to a search for underlying causes, such as adequacy of training, visual acuity, length of working hours, and timing of breaks. Discovering and acting on these underlying causes can be beneficial for the worker and organization alike. While conceding that some psychologists have focused primarily on management's needs,

Bingham stated that the industrial psychologist's first concern is the worker. As a methodology, psychology has introduced the experimental method and use of statistics to explaining behavior and attitudes in organizations. These methods have proven useful for improving industrial productivity and efficiency.

Comparisons between the early years of industrial psychology and present-day I-O psychology science and practice show dramatic differences in scale. The field has grown dramatically in numbers of psychologists and in the scope of their interests. The number of topic areas has greatly expanded, resulting in a field that is increasingly specialized. Today, as was true in the early years, the field continues to contend for that unique niche as *the* scientific experts on behavior in organizations. The strategies are familiar: professional organizations to advance the field's goals, credentialing based on advanced degrees and training, and separation from the seemingly unending parade of purveyors of unscientific, unsupported, or otherwise questionable approaches to solving organizational problems. While some of those approaches, such as Katherine Blackford's character analysis, are no longer salient, others such as graphology that were questioned in the 1920s are still being questioned today. The quest to educate the business community and the public in general about just what it is that an I-O psychologist does (and does not do) continues. In a little over 100 years, I-O psychology is now a global enterprise employing thousands of psychologists in industry, consulting, government, and academia. Yet for all of the undeniable progress, the topic areas, methodology, and concerns of the early industrial psychologists are still with us today.

Employee selection provides an example of the durability of early practice and research. While it is true that recent innovations such as meta-analysis have expanded understanding of predictors and criteria, I-O psychologists are still using essentially the same predictors and criteria that were used in those early years. They have improved those cognitive ability tests, personality tests, interest inventories, interviews, job samples, and other predictors but have not generated much in the way of new ones. And while considerable progress has been made in understanding job performance, I-O psychologists still use rating forms and formats that would be recognizable to an industrial psychologist in the early 1920s. The predictor-criterion validation model described by Freyd (1923–24) and Kornhauser and Kingsbury (1924) has proven remarkably resilient; it is essentially the same procedure used to validate a predictor today. There is still the same emphasis on using psychology to make the organization more productive and efficient. What has changed in roughly 100 years is that today there is much more emphasis on theory and on understanding the underlying determinants on job performance and hopefully more empathy for the applicant.

In considering well over a century of history, it is interesting to note the cyclic nature of many of the interests of and procedures used by industrial psychologists. A new, popular procedure or approach eventually wanes, lies dormant, and then is rediscovered and revived. Employee selection provides a number of examples. Following World War I, cognitive ability tests showed a great deal of popularity and then fell out of favor due to over-selling and attacks on their fairness. They remained, however, an important tool for industrial psychologists until the 1960s when concerns about their fairness for minority groups caused organizations to reconsider them and I-O psychologists to look for alternatives. Their validity was reestablished in the 1980s and 1990s via meta-analysis, and once again they are widely viewed in the profession as valid predictors across jobs. Personality tests, popular in the 1930s and 1940s, came under increasing attack from outside the profession primarily for privacy concerns and inside the profession in the 1960s for their lack of validity. After a period of decreased use, advances in personality theory, test construction, and statistics led to a more positive reappraisal of their validity and utility.

Internationalization is another example. The field started with a great deal of international contact and cooperation followed by a long period of insular work. More recently, there has been a resurgence of interest in internationalization and cross-cultural issues. Similar cycles can be demonstrated for the use of interviews, for the importance of moderator variables,[1] and for the viability of job satisfaction as a predictor of performance. The point is not that I-O psychologists are going in circles, continually reinventing the wheel, although that may sometimes occur. The point is that like any good scientists, I-O psychologists are continually conducting research and reevaluating their practices. If those practices are found wanting, they are improved or discarded for a more valid procedure.

This is the essence of the scientist-practitioner model. This is how progress is made in any scientific endeavor. The early industrial psychologists knew this. They had faith in the scientific method. They believed that the new science of psychology could have a positive effect on business

---

[1] A moderator variable moderates or changes the relationship between two other variables. For example, if age moderates the relationship between a selection test and job performance, it would mean that the test is a better predictor for one age group than for others.

and industry despite skepticism from their academic colleagues and limited interest from the managers they set out to assist. By any fair, objective assessment, the early industrial psychologists faith was not misplaced. I-O psychology has made considerable progress as a science and a profession. There may be workers who have never heard of I-O psychology, but there are very few who have escaped its influence.

# I-O Psychology from the 1930s to the Twenty-First Century

## From Then to Now: A Whirlwind Tour

Because this book's coverage of the history of I-O psychology ends in the mid-1930s, more than eighty years of history is left unexamined. In the interest of providing some measure of closure, a capsule history of events subsequent to these early years is presented in this Appendix. The past eighty years saw a dramatic increase in the number of research publications, practice opportunities, and I-O psychologists. Because of the steady expansion of content, the decade-by-decade descriptions presented in this Appendix invariably lose detail and can appear somewhat telegraphic. Space limitations preclude any attempt at comprehensive coverage of all relevant global developments. Inevitably, not all important landmarks can be included.

### 1930s

A number of notable events occurred in the mid- to late 1930s. On the legislative front in the United States, the Fair Labor Standards Act of 1938 was passed. This law set a minimum wage and maximum hour limit for workers engaged in interstate commerce and prohibited children under the age of sixteen from working in mining or manufacturing jobs (Yellowitz, 1991). As the 1930s progressed, the worldwide economic depression deepened, and countries moved toward a second worldwide military conflict. In the United States, although test use in industry was down compared to the 1920s, employee selection continued to be the primary activity for industrial psychologists. By the mid-1930s, selection research was declining in Europe, and the United States was becoming the center of that activity (Salgado, Anderson, & Hülsheger, 2010). There were refinements made in the statistics used in testing and selection. In 1937, Kuder and Richardson developed an improvement of split-half estimates of test reliability they named KR-20. Taylor and Russell (1939) published a series of tables that considered the selection ratio, the base rate, and the validity coefficient when determining the utility of a selection test.[1] The US Employment Service published the initial volume of the *Dictionary of Occupational Titles* (DOT) in 1939, the first comprehensive listing of occupations in the United States. Also in 1939, work began on the Army General Classification Test (AGCT), a replacement for the Army Alpha and Beta tests of World War I vintage (Harrell, 1992). Walter Van Dyke Bingham, who played a pivotal role in the personnel testing program in World War I, was appointed chair of the Committee on Classification of Military Personnel.

By 1936, applied psychology research and practice was prohibited in those countries controlled by the USSR. A particular point of contention was the practice of distinguishing among individuals based on psychological differences, which conflicted with communist ideology. This began a long period of isolation from Western psychologists for Soviet psychologists that lasted until the end of the 1950s (Warr, 2007). The first industrial psychology text in China was published in 1935. Industrial psychology work there concentrated on working conditions and employee selection and guidance (Wang, 1994).

After immigrating to the United States from Germany in 1933, Kurt Lewin (1890–1947) conducted groundbreaking work in social psychology, particularly in the study of group dynamics. While at the University of Iowa, Lewin and his colleagues conducted a classic study contrasting authoritarian, democratic, and laissez-faire leadership styles (Lewin, Lippitt, & White, 1939). The same year that study was published, Lewin was invited to the Harwood Manufacturing Company by Alfred J. Marrow, a company vice president who also held a doctorate in psychology (Highhouse, 2007).[2] The Harwood Company was experiencing a turnover problem. Lewin and his students Alex Bavelas and John R. P. French Jr. conducted a series of studies to attempt to alleviate this problem. For a time, what became known as the Harwood Studies rivaled the Hawthorne Studies in notoriety, and similar to those studies, they were subjected to criticism and reinterpretation (Highhouse, 2007; Hilgard,

[1] The selection ratio is the ratio of applicants hired over the total number of applicants. Low selection ratios are more favorable for organizations because they can be more selective in hiring. The base rate refers to the percentage of current employees who are successful. The higher the base rate, the more difficult it is for a new selection procedure to have an impact.
[2] Marrow (1969) also wrote a book-length biography of Lewin.

1987). Lewin's work at Harwood was the genesis of his action research model, an approach that proved influential in organizational development (OD) practice (French, 1982).

In 1938, New Jersey Bell executive Chester Barnard published *The Functions of the Executive.* In this influential book, Barnard described organizations as cooperative systems, with leaders who valued cohesion and power that originated from the bottom instead of the top of the organizational hierarchy. He also discussed upward communication and the formation of natural groups in the organization (Perrow, 1986). Perrow believed Barnard's book was the first effective counterargument to the scientific management system.[3] Lawrence (1987) viewed *The Functions of the Executive* as a plausible starting point for the organizational behavior perspective, along with two other works from the 1930s that described the Hawthorne Studies, Elton Mayo's *Human Problems of Industrial Civilization* (1933) and Fritz Roethlisberger's and William Dickson's *Management and the Worker* (1939). By the early 1930s, the psychology of advertising and selling, one of the seminal applications of psychology to business, had grown so specialized and distinctive that Viteles (1932) chose to omit that topic from his landmark text *Industrial Psychology.* In 1938, of the 2,318 members and associates of the APA, 1,923 reported employment in psychological work (the remainder were students or retirees or did not list a position). Of those employed, sixty-one identified as industrial psychologists. This did not include individuals who identified as "guidance and personnel workers" or as consultants (Finch & Odoroff, 1939).

### 1940s

World War II took place from 1939 to 1945. Like World War I, the Second World War gave psychologists an opportunity to apply their expertise to large numbers of individuals. In particular, there was an enormous need for an expansion of the military's selection and classification systems. To illustrate, the United States had a failure rate for aviators of 40 to 60 percent before the war; however, this was not a significant problem because so few pilots were needed. For example, only twelve pilot applicants were accepted in 1937, but by 1942, that total had increased to more than 293,000 (Napoli, 1981). By 1940, the Army General Classification Test (AGCT) was ready for use (Harrell, 1992). Two years later, the US Navy

---

[3] As discussed earlier in the book, industrial psychologists also provided much criticism of scientific management, and research such as the Hawthorne Studies provided an alternative to that approach.

established its Applied Psychology Panel, which developed more than 250 tests on topics such as reading, arithmetic reasoning, mechanical knowledge, and aptitude. The Navy's aviation psychology program was directed by John G. Jenkins (Napoli, 1981). In the Army Air Force, John C. Flanagan (1948) supervised the construction of the Aviation Cadet Qualifying Exam. The military created research centers that evolved after the war's end into the Army Research Institute (ARI), the Navy Personnel Research and Development Center (NPRDC), and the Air Force Human Resources Laboratory (AFHRL) (Katzell & Austin, 1992).

By the beginning of World War II, the German military employed approximately 200 psychologists. These psychologists conducted job analyses and developed selection tests for aviators, sound detectors, tank drivers, marksmen, and others. Psychologists were also involved in training, morale-building, and propaganda. One of the main activities of military psychologists was the selection of officer candidates. The candidates went through a two-day selection process that assessed characteristics such as leadership ability, willpower, and practical intelligence. Among the procedures used were interviews, life history items, a leaderless group discussion procedure, handwriting analysis, and analysis of speech and facial expressions. Assessment of the candidate's entire personality was the objective (Ansbacher, 1941). The whole process laid the foundation for what after the war became known as an assessment center. This combination of pencil-and-paper tests and situational tests was pioneered by the German military following World War I (Ansbacher, 1951) and by the Hungarian Army in the 1930s (Salgado, Anderson, & Hülsheger, 2010). The assessment center concept made the leap from the German to the British military and then to the American military. Among the Americans involved was Henry Murray of Harvard University, who was instrumental in constructing situational tests for applicants of the Office of Strategic Services, a forerunner of the Central Intelligence Agency (CIA).

From a present-day perspective, the German military system was a mix of potentially valid procedures (e.g., aptitude tests, leaderless group discussion) and ones whose validity was questionable at best (e.g., analysis of handwriting, speech, and facial expressions). Davis (1947) reported that the emphasis was on the clinical assessment of character, not on more psychometrically sound approaches. No serious attempts at conventional validation of the selection procedures were made. There was a great deal of conflict between the psychology program and the German High Command, which decided to terminate the Army and Air Force programs in December 1941, early in the war. The Navy's psychology program limped along in a much reduced state after that time. About 1943, industrial psychology in Germany ground to a halt (Warr, 2007). The German ally Japan began using tests for military officers in 1942 (McCollom, 1968).

The largest military selection program in Europe during World War II took place in Great Britain (Salgado, Anderson, & Hülsheger, 2010). Many of the tests used were adapted from those developed in the United States, although British psychologists took a less quantitative approach to scoring than the Americans and preferred interviews and biographical data to standardized tests. A nonverbal cognitive ability test, the Progressive Matrices Test, was administered to approximately 3 million British Army and Royal Navy recruits. At least 2 million women and men took a battery of five or more tests (Vernon, 1947).

In the United States after the war, Hubert E. Brogden (1946, 1949; Brogden & Taylor, 1950) extended previous work on selection utility by demonstrating that the size of a validity coefficient is directly proportional to the percentage of gain one would expect to see if selection was based on the criterion itself; that is, the maximally effective method.[4] Salgado (2001) noted that all subsequent utility analysis work is based on Brogden's insights. Wagner (1949) reviewed the employment interview literature and noted that structured interviews showed promise for improving the traditionally low reliability and validity of unstructured ones. The journal *Personnel Psychology* began publication in 1947, and toward the end of the decade, Edwin Ghiselli and Clarence Brown (1948) and Robert L. Thorndike (1949) published influential books on employee selection.

In performance appraisal, Wiener's (1948) cybernetic theory about how systems adapt as a result of prior performance information likely influenced the use of performance feedback in I-O psychology (Farr & Levy, 2007). Robert L. Thorndike's (1949) text included his popular classification of criteria into immediate, intermediate, and ultimate levels, with the ultimate criterion representing the final goal of selection or training (Austin & Villanova, 1992).

By the 1940s, the shortcomings of the trait approach to leadership were becoming evident. A shift from these trait approaches to a behavioral approached occurred, most notably at Ohio State University and the

---

[4] For example, if the validity coefficient of a test used for selection is 0.40, using the test would provide 40 percent of the value of selecting without error by using the criterion itself for selection, which is generally not practical. Brogden also demonstrated how the selection ratio and the standard deviation of job performance affect economic utility (Schmidt, Hunter, McKenzie, & Muldrow, 1979).

University of Michigan. The Ohio State Leadership Studies, begun in 1945, were a major program of the Personnel Research Board, an interdisciplinary research group that conducted organizational research for industry, the military, and the government (Meyer, 2007).[5] In motivational research, the humanist psychologist Abraham Maslow published his influential needs theory in 1943. Developed in the 1930s and based on Maslow's observations of individuals struggling in the Great Depression (Latham & Budworth, 2007), Maslow postulated a hierarchy of needs, starting with physiological needs; ranging through security, social, and esteem needs; and cumulating with self-actualization. Once a lower set of needs is more or less satisfied, the set above it motivates the individual. Although not particularly well supported empirically, Maslow's need theory was popular in organizations.

In 1944, Kurt Lewin founded the Research Center for Group Dynamics at the Massachusetts Institute of Technology (MIT) (Salas, Priest, Stagl, Sims, & Burke, 2007). In 1946, Lewin, Kenneth Benne, Leland Bradford, and Donald Lippitt attempted to reduce racial tension in New Britain, Connecticut. Their efforts to change attitudes there resulted in the T-group method, also known as laboratory training and sensitivity training (Benne, 1964; Highhouse, 2007). The following year, Lewin (1947) published his influential three-step process for changing group standards: unfreezing, moving, and freezing. In 1948, the Center for Group Dynamics joined Rensis Likert's Michigan Survey Research Center and the Center for Utilization of Scientific Knowledge to form the University of Michigan Institute for Social Research (ISR). Topics such as organizational conflict, power, and decision making were receiving increased attention in the 1940s (Perrow, 1986). An example was the work on goal conflict by the sociologist Philip Selznick (1949) in his study of the Tennessee Valley Authority.

In 1946, the Tavistock Institute of Human Relations was established in London through a grant from the Rockefeller Foundation. At the Institute, psychologists, psychiatrists, and anthropologists worked together using the socio-technical systems model to conduct research on topics such as group processes, worker health and well-being, and conflict (Trist, Emory, Murray, & Trist, 1997). One of the better-known studies conducted was the Tavistock coal-mining study (Trist & Bamforth, 1951). Management changed the mining process from the "short-wall" method, where miners worked in small, autonomous groups, to the highly specialized "long-wall" method. While the latter was more efficient from an engineering perspective, use of the long-wall method disbanded the autonomous work teams

---

[5] The major findings of the Ohio State Studies are described in the 1950s section.

that provided social support to the miners. The long-wall method was not initially a success, emphasizing the importance of taking social factors into account when making technological changes; that is, adopting a socio-technical approach. Erich Trist, a leading spokesperson for the Institute, was influenced by psychoanalysis, Kurt Lewin, open systems theory, and the humanist approach to research (John B. Miner, 2002). Because traditional academic publications could be unsympathetic to psychiatrically based social science, the Tavistock Institute began publishing its own journal *Human Relations* in 1947 to provide an outlet for this type of research (Warr, 2007).

In 1947, a year prior to the founding of the state of Israel, Louis Guttmann established a behavioral unit in the Israeli military. This unit later became the Israel Institute for Applied Social Research. Also in 1947, an English translation of Max Weber's *The Theory of Social and Economic Organization* was published, initiating interest in bureaucratic organizational structure. Germany divided into East and West Germany in 1949. From that point, psychology in East Germany came under the influence of the USSR, while the United States was the main influence on psychology in West Germany (Warr, 2007).

### 1950s

In contrast to the early years of industrial psychology, in the 1950s, selection research was concentrated in the United States, and there was very little collaborative activity between American academics and those in other countries. This situation would last until the mid-1970s (Salgado, Anderson, & Hülsheger, 2010). The assessment center technique made the transition from the military to private industry, most prominently in the mid-1950s at AT&T. Management studies on assessment centers at AT&T that demonstrated the usefulness of the technique were conducted by Douglas Bray, Richard Campbell, and Donald Grant (Bray & Campbell, 1968; Bray & Grant, 1966; Bray, Campbell, & Grant, 1974; see Howard, 2010, for an historical summary). Bernard Bass conducted notable work on a technique often used in assessment centers, the leaderless group discussion (Bellows, 1951; Heron, 1954). Another procedure used primarily for selecting managers, individual assessment, saw an increase in research and practice during the 1950s (Highhouse, 2002; Prien, Schippmann, & Prien, 2003).[6]

---

[6] *Assessment Centers* evaluate groups of applicants by groups of assessors using multiple techniques, including interviews, paper-and-pencil tests, and group situational tests, such as the *Leaderless Group*

Advances in measurement, test validation, and test construction relevant for I-O psychology included the introduction of Item Response Theory (IRT) in 1952 by Frederic Lord (Austin, Scherbaum, & Mahlman, 2002). IRT was an attempt to bring ratio-level measurement to psychological testing. Other noteworthy developments included the following: Lee Cronbach (1951) developed a reliability coefficient with more general application than KR-20, his coefficient *alpha*. Cronbach, along with Paul Meehl, published an influential article on the concept of construct validity (Cronbach & Meehl, 1955). A year earlier, Meehl (1954) published a controversial book that demonstrated the clear superiority of statistical prediction versus clinical prediction. The statistical approach to selection continued in the 1950s to be the most popular approach in the profession (Katzell, 1957). Cronbach and Gleser (1957) extended Brogden's 1940s work on utility analysis. The critical incident technique, a procedure that proved popular in both job analysis and performance appraisal, was introduced by John C. Flanagan in 1954. The importance of appropriate criteria in selection received attention, although as Wallace and Weitz (1955) noted, actual criterion research about concerns such as criterion relevance, deficiency, and contamination was lacking. Robert Wherry's work on the effect of psychological, situational, and procedural variables on the accuracy of ratings was an exception (Farr & Levy, 2007).[7] Important selection-related publications included the collaborative *Technical Recommendations for Psychological and Diagnostic Techniques* (APA, AERA, & NCMUE, 1954) in the United States and, on the international level, the first edition of the *International Classification of Occupations for Migration and Placement* in 1952 and the first edition of the *International Standard Classification of Occupations* in 1958 (both cited in Salgado, 2001).

Despite criticism from outside the profession (e.g., Whyte, 1954), research on and the use of personality tests increased during the 1950s (Brown & Ghiselli, 1952). A review of studies conducted on biographical data inventories found considerable predictive validity for them (Taylor & Nevis, 1961). Long criticized for its questionable reliability and validity, the employment interview continued to be the most popular selection technique used by employers (Kendall, 1956). Because employers were resistant to giving up the interview, Heron (1954) advised psychologists to stop simply

---

*Discussion*, where a group of applicants is given a task and evaluated both on the quality of their solutions and on group interaction. *Individual Assessment* uses multiple assessment techniques but with a single applicant and a single assessor.

[7] Wherry's theory of rating research was not published until the 1980s (Wherry, 1983; Wherry & Bartlett, 1982).

documenting its deficiencies and work on improving its reliability and validity.

George Homans's (1950) *The Human Group* analyzed groups in terms of systems and established the paradigm for analyzing group behavior in organizations (Lawrence, 1987). In other human relations–based theory and research, Douglas McGregor (1957, 1960) discussed managerial beliefs about subordinates. Two examples, Theory X managers (who believe that because of the aversive nature of work employees must be tightly controlled) and Theory Y managers (who believe that if employees find the work intrinsically motivating, they will be self-motivated and can be trusted) have shown considerable staying power in organizational theory. In a similar human relations vein, Chris Argyris (1957) introduced his developmental model of organizational behavior, demonstrating conflict between the policies of modern organizations and the personalities of mature adults. By the middle of the decade, the human relations or organizational behavior (OB) perspective focused on the fit between the individual employee and the organization, with the assumption that a good fit benefits both (Shafritz & Ott, 1996).

In Great Britain, Joan Woodward (1958) discovered that the type of structure most effective for an organization depended on the type of technology the organization employed. Large-batch or mass production organizations were most successful when they were bureaucratic in structure, whereas small-batch and continuous process organizations tended to have more humanistic or organic structures.

Progress was made in understanding power and decision making in organizations. Dorwin Cartwright, in a 1953 address, argued that organizational variables such as leadership and attitude change could only be understood if viewed through the prism of power (cited in Ott, 1989). At the end of the decade, Richard Cyert and James March discussed how power affects organizational goals (Shafritz & Ott, 1996), and John R. P. French, Jr. and Bertram Raven (1959) introduced their five bases of power: reward, coercive, legitimate, expert, and referent. In decision theory, Cyert, March, and Herbert Simon discussed human cognitive limits when making decisions. They noted that rather than always working toward the optimal outcome, people will employ a "satisficing" strategy to obtain a suboptimal but good enough solution (March & Simon, 1958; Simon, 1947).

By the mid-1950s, motivation had become a central issue in industrial psychology (Ryan & Smith, 1954). Motivation was explicitly discussed in the industrial psychology literature, and theories of motivation were being developed in what had previously been a largely atheoretical area (Latham & Budworth, 2007). Many of these theories combined motivation and job satisfaction. Some, influenced by Freud's conception of the unconscious and by Henry Murray's (1938) work on personality, focused on employee needs. Maslow's need theory, described in the previous section, is the most notable example. Frederick Herzberg and his colleagues developed a need theory specifically for work situations. In their *two-factor theory*, the two sets of needs are hygiene factors, such as pay, and motivator factors that have to do with the intrinsic nature of the work itself. Meeting only hygiene needs will result in a worker who is in a neutral state: neither satisfied nor dissatisfied, neither motivated nor unmotivated. Only meeting the intrinsic motivator needs through job enrichment results in a satisfied, motivated employee (Herzberg, Mausner, & Snyderman, 1959). Attuned to the increased emphasis on motivation in industrial psychology, Morris Viteles's attempted revision of his classic 1932 text resulted in a book focused on motivation and attitudes: *Motivation and Morale in Industry* in 1953 (Viteles, 1967). Peter Drucker (1954) introduced management by objectives, a performance appraisal technique based on the motivational concept of goal setting. The procedure involved the manager and employee setting mutually agreed-upon, explicit goals and receiving performance feedback regarding progress toward those goals.

The 1950s saw the following additional developments. In training, Donald Kirkpatrick (1959) introduced four levels of training program evaluation criteria: reactions, learning, behavior change, and performance change. A review by Brayfield and Crockett (1955) found little evidence for a significant relationship between employee attitudes and job performance, casting doubt on the "satisfied worker is a productive worker" axiom. In Great Britain, the professional category of Psychologist was established in the Civil Service in 1950 (Warr, 2007). Among notable publications from this decade were the *Handbook of Applied Psychology* by Fryer and Henry, which appeared in 1950, and the journal *Administrative Science Quarterly*, which was first published in 1955. Due in part to explosive growth in military applications, human factors or engineering psychology was now distinct from industrial psychology; its own APA division was created in 1956. In 1958, the journal *Human Factors* was first published, and the Human Factors Society was formed. Vocational counseling was now considered part of counseling psychology instead of industrial psychology, continuing a trend that began in the 1930s (Savickas & Baker, 2005). In the United States, at least 1,000 psychologists were employed full time in industry by the end of the decade (McCollom, 1959).

In the United States, the decade opened with a lament from Taylor and Nevis (1961) that with the expansion of industrial psychology topics, the venerable practice of personnel selection was losing it cachet. It would in fact be a decade of challenges for psychologists involved in selection research and practice. The US Congress passed legislation outlawing discrimination against employees. This required industrial psychologists to substantially reevaluate their modus operandi. The Equal Pay Act of 1963 banned compensation differences based solely on employee sex, the Age Discrimination in Employment Act of 1967 prohibited age discrimination, and Title VII of the Civil Rights Act of 1964 banned discrimination in employment decisions based on race, sex, religion, color, or national origin. Industrial psychologists increasingly had to consider not only professional standards and employer needs but also the legal ramifications of their practice.

The following notable activity occurred in employee selection research and practice. The problem of unqualified testers administering nonvalid tests, present since the beginning of industrial psychology, received renewed attention (Dunnette, 1962; Taylor & Nevis, 1961). The basic selection validity model that had been relatively unchanged for close to fifty years was now criticized for being overly mechanistic and simplistic (Dunnette, 1962; Guion, 1967; Porter, 1966). Efforts to expand those models included Edwin Ghiselli's (1963) use of moderator variables to improve selection for homogenous subgroups and Marvin Dunnette's (1963) examination of variables such as job behaviors, job situations, and subgroups of applicants that intervene between the predictor and the criterion. Wernimont and Campbell (1968) proposed an alternative to the traditional validity model. Their behavioral consistency model preferred measures of behavior, or "samples," over "signs," such as tests, as predictors. In the 1960s, there was an increased interest in a broader view of the selection process, of integrating selection into the larger personnel system (Sells, 1964), and of taking a systems approach to selection itself (Dudek, 1963). Predictors of job performance continued for the most part to be cognitive ability tests, biographical data inventories, interest inventories, and personality tests, although the latter continued to be criticized for lack of validity by industrial psychologists (Guion & Gottier, 1965) and for violation of privacy by individuals outside psychology (e.g., Gross, 1962). Guion and Gottier's (1965) critique led to the perception that personality test selection research was not a fruitful activity, although that was not their intent (Guion, 1967, 1991). In the 1960s, Edwin Fleishman began his longtime research program on a taxonomy of human motor performance (Fleishman, 1988).

Notable publications this decade include Robert Guion's (1965) text on personnel testing, the first edition of *Standards for Educational and Psychological Tests and Manuals* (APA, 1966), the second edition of *International Standard Classification of Occupations* (1968, cited in Salgado, 2001), and the third edition of the DOT (1968). The historian Loren Baritz wrote *The Servants of Power* (1960), a book-length critique of how social scientists were co-opted by management. Also in 1960, applied psychologists in the United States interested in advertising and other consumer behavior established their own APA division. Over the objections of the industrial psychology division, the APA Council approved the new Division of Consumer Psychology, establishing for consumer psychologists an identity separate from industrial psychology (Schumann & Davidson, 2007).

Performance appraisal research emphasized behavioral measurement in the 1960s. There was a move away from trait ratings to behavioral ratings and a focus on measurement issues, accuracy of ratings, and rating format development (Farr & Levy, 2007). The trend toward behavior ratings was exemplified by the Behaviorally Anchored Rating Scale (BARS) introduced by Smith and Kendall in 1963. Also evident by the early 1960s was an increased interest on performance appraisal feedback and on the effect these evaluations have on employees' careers and lives (Farr & Levy, 2007). Herbert Meyer's work at General Electric on performance appraisal feedback suggested that two separate sessions should be held with employees. One should focus on development, the other on administrative concerns such as salary and promotion (Meyer, Kay, & French, 1965). Despite cognitive approaches surfacing in other areas of industrial psychology, psychologists interested in training still favored a behavioral approach (Kraiger & Ford, 2007). McGehee and Thayer (1961) published their text *Training in Business and Industry*, which included a description of training needs analysis.

In the 1960s, there was the beginning of a shift from need-based theories to more cognitive approaches to motivation. Victor Vroom's (1964) *expectancy theory* of motivation had its roots in the work of Kurt Lewin and the purposive behaviorism of Edward Tolman along with earlier work in organizations in the 1950s by Basil Georgopoulos, Gerald Mahoney, and Nyle Jones (John B. Miner, 2002). Expectancy theory posits that effort is a function of an individual's expectations that her or his effort will lead to successful performance, the expectation that performance will lead to a successful outcome, and the value or valence of that outcome for the individual. Another cognitive theory to emerge in this decade was *equity theory*, which views both motivation and satisfaction as the result of a comparison that each individual makes between two ratios: his or her ratio of perceived outcomes over inputs compared to a referent or relevant other's ratio. If, for example, an employee believes that she or he is putting in twice the amount of effort as a coworker yet only receiving half the reward, that employee will be dissatisfied. The employee will be motivated to either increase the amount of reward received or reduce his or her amount of effort in an attempt to bring the ratios of the employee and coworker closer to equity. J. Stacey Adams (1965), a developer of this approach, was influenced both social justice theories and Leon Festinger's cognitive dissonance theory (John B. Miner, 2002). A third cognitive motivational theory that received a great deal of attention was *goal-setting theory*, developed into a modern theory of motivation by Edwin Locke (1968), who later collaborated with Gary Latham.

Leadership research made the transition from behavioral approaches to situational or contingency approaches in the 1960s (Day & Zaccaro, 2007). Rather than search for behaviors that characterize effective leaders across situations, contingency approaches recognize that leader behavior is moderated by the situation. What may be effective leader behavior in one situation may be ineffective in another. Fred Fiedler's (1967) contingency theory is a classic early example. Fiedler's theory had two components: leadership style, which can be relationship- or task-oriented; and situation favorableness, based on how strong leader–member relations are, how structured the task is, and how much position power or formal authority the leader holds. Task-oriented leaders are most effective when situation favorableness is either very high or very low; with moderate situation favorableness, relationship-oriented leaders do best. Paul Hersey and Kenneth Blanchard (1969) proposed their life cycle situational theory of leadership, positing that to be an effective leader, one should match leadership style to the maturity level of the subordinates, where maturity is defined as the ability to perform the job unaided.

Interest in job satisfaction continued, although little evidence was found for a strong relationship between satisfaction and performance. A review by Vroom (1964) found an average correlation of only 0.14 between those two variables. The Job Descriptive Index (JDI) for measuring job satisfaction was introduced by Smith, Kendall, and Hulin in 1969. In time, the JDI became the "gold standard" for measuring job satisfaction (Balzer, Locke,

& Zedeck, 2008). Lofquist and Dawis (1969) introduced their theory of worker adjustment, which resulted in the Minnesota Satisfaction Questionnaire.

Other notable 1960s publications on organizational psychology topics include Rensis Likert's (1961) *New Patterns of Management* that described his "linking pin" model for small group integration and his four systems of management ranging from the exploitive-authoritarian System 1 to the participative System 4 (Hilgard, 1987). That same year, Burns and Stalker (1961) contrasted mechanistic and organic systems of management; the following year formal and informal components of organizations were described by Blau and Scott (1962). In 1964, Robert Kahn and his colleagues discussed the effect of role conflict and role ambiguity on individuals in organizations (Kahn, Wolfe, Quinn, Snoek, & Rosenthal, 1964), and in 1966, Kahn and Daniel Katz introduced open-systems theory to organizations in *The Social Psychology of Organizations* (Katz & Kahn, 1966). One final development worth mentioning from the 1960s was the importation of quality circles (QC) from Japan to other countries. These small volunteer groups that analyze and solve organizational problems were thought to have originated in the United States in the 1950s; however, the modern form is most associated with Japanese professor Kaoru Ishikawa (Salas, Priest, Stagl, Sims, & Burke, 2007).

### *1970s*

Employee discrimination lower court cases triggered by the equal employment opportunity legislation of the 1960s eventually made their way to the US Supreme Court in the 1970s, resulting in landmark decisions that had an impact on personnel selection practices. In *Griggs v. Duke Power* (1971), for example, the justices ruled that when a selection procedure has differential impact on a protected minority group, that procedure must be job-related; that is, the employer must demonstrate that the procedure is valid. In line with the employer guidelines distributed by the Equal Employment Opportunity Commission (EEOC), the government agency charged with enforcing Title VII of the 1964 Civil Rights Act, job-relatedness came to imply that the employer needed a professional validation study. In *Griggs* and other Supreme Court decisions, in the basic Title VII paradigm, the initial burden of proof was on the plaintiff, the person or group suing for discrimination, who had to demonstrate that an employer procedure had a differential impact on a protected group (Arvey & Faley, 1988).[8] The burden of proof then shifted to the defendant, usually the employer, who had to show a sound business reason for using the procedure; that is, that the procedure is valid. In 1975, the APA Division for Industrial-Organizational Psychology issued guidelines for test validation in employee selection: *Principles for the Validation and Use of Personnel Selection Procedures*. In 1978, four agencies of the federal government – the EEOC, the Civil Service Commission, the Department of Justice, and the Department of Labor – issued their own guidelines – the *Uniform Guidelines on Employee Selection Procedures* – where selection is viewed broadly enough to include virtually any employer decision (e.g., you can be selected for a job, a raise, or a promotion or for termination).

Federal legislation and subsequent court decisions drove a fair amount of selection research in the 1970s on statistical models of test fairness and on topics such as differential validity, where tests demonstrate different validity coefficients for different groups (Bray & Moses, 1972). One related line of research had far-reaching ramifications for selection research. Validity coefficients were long held to be mostly situation specific; that is, specific to the time, the organization, and/or the group used when they were initially determined. Predictors therefore had to be validated for each new situation. Contrary to that belief, the validity generalization (VG) research of Frank Schmidt and John Hunter (1977) demonstrated that, at least for cognitive ability tests, much or in some cases virtually all of the variability in validity coefficients across groups and situations was not due to substantive factors but rather was due to statistical artifacts such as sampling error, unreliability of measures, and restriction of range.

Other notable developments in test validation and employee selection included the following. There was increased interest in job analysis (Ash & Kroeker, 1975), beginning with Prien and Ronan's (1971) review article and highlighted by the first comprehensive book on job analysis by McCormick (1979). Functional Job Analysis was developed (Fine & Wiley, 1971), as was the Position Analysis Questionnaire (PAQ)

---

[8] A key point in the court's decisions had to do with the interpretation of the language of Section 703 (h) of Title VII, which states that a procedure is illegal if it is designed, intended, or used to discriminate. In *Griggs*, for example, the lower courts focused on employers' intent, which is difficult to prove. The Supreme Court focused on "used"; that is, the result of the procedure. Plaintiffs could generally meet their initial burden of proof by demonstrating "adverse impact," that the selection rate for the minority group is less than 80 percent of the rate for the majority group. If adverse impact is present, then the employer had to demonstrate the challenged procedure is psychometrically valid. If unable to do so, as in *Griggs v. Duke Power*, the employer would most likely lose the case (Arvey & Faley, 1988).

(McCormick, Jeanneret, & Mecham, 1972), which was destined to be one of the most researched job analysis inventories (Wilson, 2007). Notable work on utility analysis included Schmidt, Hunter, McKenzie, and Muldrow's (1979) method for estimating the standard deviation of job performance in a dollar metric, which simplified the use of what was now known as the Brogden-Cronbach-Gleser utility models. The use of assessment centers increased dramatically during the 1970s (Ash & Kroeker, 1975). A theoretical foundation for biographical data was proposed by Owens (1976). And the traditional validity model continued to undergo modification, which was viewed by Tenopyr and Oeltjen (1982) as one of the most important developments in selection research in recent years. Robert Guion (1976) emphasized that validity is a unitary concept. The traditional trio of criterion-related, content, and construct validation represent three different strategies for determining the meaningfulness, usefulness, and appropriateness of test score inferences, not three different types of validity. While much of the work in selection over the previous decades had been centered in the United States, beginning in the mid-1970s, Europe underwent a resurgence in employee selection research and practice (Salgado, Anderson, & Hülsheger, 2010).

Campbell (1971) noted that theory and research in training was substandard at the beginning of the decade. By the mid-1970s, things had improved, as illustrated by Goldstein's (1974) instruction systems design (ISD) model, a systems approach to the training process. Performance appraisal formats continued to build on the behavioral rating approach of Smith and Kendall (1963) with variants such as the Mixed Standard Scale (Blanz & Ghiselli, 1972) which included a check for logical errors in rater judgment and the Behavior Observation Scale (Latham & Wexley, 1977), in which the rater assessed actual occurrences of behavior rather than comparing the ratee against a hypothetical anchor.

On the organizational side, additional contingency theories of leadership were proposed. Examples include Path-Goal Theory, in which the effectiveness of four leadership styles was viewed as dependent both on the situation and on subordinate maturity levels (House, 1971); and vertical dyad linkage theory, which postulated that leaders respond differently to subordinates depending on whether those employees are perceived as in-group or out-group members (Graen, 1976). Toward the end of the decade, *transformational leaders* who inspire their followers were contrasted with *transactional leaders* whose leadership is based on rules and social contracts (Burns, 1978). Hackman and Oldman (1975, 1976, 1980) introduced their job enrichment theory, postulating that increasing the interest level, autonomy, responsibility level, and overall significance of a job would increase both motivation and job satisfaction. Regarding group processes, Irving Janis (1972) described *groupthink*, the situation where concurrence-seeking becomes the dominant mode of thinking in the group and conformity becomes the norm, resulting in poor-quality group decisions. In motivation theory, Albert Bandura (1977) introduced social learning theory, later renamed social cognitive theory. Bandura viewed behavior as a continuous reciprocal interaction among behavioral, cognitive, and environmental variables (Latham & Budworth, 2007).

In other developments, the first edition of the *Handbook of Industrial and Organizational Psychology* (1976), edited by Marvin Dunnette, was published. By the 1970s, in the United States, the venerable term *industrial psychology* became *industrial-organizational psychology* (*I/O* or *I-O psychology*). In Great Britain, the National Institute of Industrial Psychology (NIIP), an important center for industrial psychology since its founding in 1921, closed due to financial difficulties in 1973. The NIIP's journal *Occupational Psychology* was taken over by the British Psychological Society, was renamed the *Journal of Occupational Psychology* in 1975, and became international in scope. In China, psychology endured years of neglect during Mao's Cultural Revolution from 1966 to 1976. Following Mao Zedong's death in 1976, China became more open to outside ideas, and in 1978, the Chinese Psychological Association created a national committee of industrial psychology consisting of engineering psychology and organizational psychology branches (Warr, 2007).

### 1980s

In the United States, John Hunter and Frank Schmidt extended their validity generalization work into an innovative and influential meta-analysis procedure (Hunter, Schmidt, & Jackson, 1982).[9] By eliminating the statistical "noise" across research studies, researchers could make sense of often contradictory research results among the studies. They could then estimate population effect sizes and draw strong conclusions if variability across study results could be substantially accounted for by statistical

---

[9] The Hunter and Schmidt (1990) meta-analysis procedure estimates how much of the variability across research studies is due to statistical artifacts, principally sampling error, and how much is left over to be accounted for by moderator variables. They have found (e.g., Hunter & Hunter, 1984) that much of the perceived variability can be accounted for by these artifacts, allowing one to avoid the fruitless search for nonexistent moderators and to therefore draw strong conclusions about the population effect size based on existing studies.

artifacts. Meta-analysis, particularly the Hunter-Schmidt version, rapidly became the standard procedure in I-O psychology for summarizing results across individual studies; that is, for conducting a quantitative literature review. For example, meta-analyses conducted in the 1980s found cognitive ability tests have substantial validity across occupations (e.g., Hunter & Hunter, 1984).

Biodata inventories, although underused, continued to show substantial validity (Schmidt, Ones, & Hunter, 1992). The use of personality tests, long maligned for their lack of validity, underwent a resurgence due to the increased acceptance of the Five-Factor Model of personality (Digman, 1990). It appeared that much of the low validity attributed to personality tests in the past was due to confusion over multiple trait names and inconsistency in defining these traits. There was an upswing of interest in the use of integrity tests for identifying dishonest applicants (Schmidt, Ones, & Hunter, 1992). On the criterion end of validation, the decades-long trend away from output measures and toward behavioral measures continued (Austin & Villanova, 1992; see Campbell, 1990a, for an example). A highlight of the 1980s was the seven-year Project A: Army Selection and Classification Project conducted by the US Army, one of the largest selection studies ever attempted. Project A researchers evaluated multiple predictors and job performance constructs and developed a multidimensional model of job performance (Campbell, 1990b; Campbell & Knapp, 2010; Borman, Klimoski, & Ilgen, 2003).

In Europe, despite little or no evidence for its validity, the use of graphology as a selection procedure continued to be popular (Guion & Gibson, 1988). In Canada, Wiesner and Cronshaw's (1988) meta-analysis demonstrated the superiority of structured over unstructured interviews. In performance appraisal, Landy and Farr (1980) called for a moratorium on research that focused on formats and a shift toward understanding the cognitive processes that underlie the appraisal process. In the 1980s, that shift began to occur, along with a recognition of the importance of the social context that surrounds the performance appraisal process. There was also interest in performance ratings from multiple sources, sometimes known as 360-degree feedback (Farr & Levy, 2007). In job analysis, Gael (1988) published the first handbook of job analysis (Wilson, 2007).

The concept of organizational culture became popular. Edgar Schein's (1985) *Organizational Culture and Leadership* provided an overview. In work motivation, Greenberg (1987) extended equity theory by addressing workplace fairness and trust with his organizational justice theory (Latham & Budworth, 2007). Work on group processes and work teams included examination of how teams form, evolve, and perform; work on the construction of team taxonomies and classifications; and research on the measurement of team performance (Salas, Priest, Stagl, Sims, & Burke, 2007).

## 1990s and Beyond

As we approach the present day, it becomes difficult to summarize major events in the field in a few paragraphs. The continuing expansion of I-O psychology, the increased specialization by I-O psychologists, and lack of sufficient time to gain historical perspective make trying to determine what contributions will stand the test of time more of an exercise in prediction than history. With that caveat in mind, I will mention a few developments that appear worthy of interest. The US Congress passed the Americans with Disabilities Act of 1990, which codified requirements to provide reasonable accommodations for individuals with physical or mental disabilities, including accommodations for selection of employees and in other job-related areas. Meta-analyses estimated the average size of validity coefficients for various predictors, and the procedure was also offered as a component of an alternative research model that avoids the perceived pitfalls of the traditional null hypothesis testing model (see Schmidt, 1992). Barrick and Mount's (1991) meta-analytic review of the Big Five personality traits found substantial evidence for the validity of the trait conscientiousness across occupations. In a review of meta-analysis research that spanned eighty-five years, Frank Schmidt and John Hunter (1998) found general cognitive ability, work samples, peer ratings, the personality trait *conscientiousness*, integrity tests, and interviews to have substantial validity for selection, with structured interviews outperforming unstructured interviews. Poor predictors included graphology, educational level, interest inventories, and age of the applicant. There was an increase in research that evaluated selection from the perspective of the applicant (Borman, Hanson, & Hedge, 1997). The US Army's Project A continued to have an influence; for example, Campbell, McCloy, Oppler, and Sager (1993) developed a construct-based theory of job performance based on that research.

The use of computers and the internet was beginning to affect practice in the 1990s. For example, the paper version of the US Department of Labor's Dictionary of Occupational Titles (DOT) was revised and expanded into an internet version, the occupational information network (O*Net) (Wilson, 2007). In training, technology-delivered instruction

(TDI) methods such as web-based instruction and distance learning increased in popularity (Kraiger & Ford, 2007). The international nature of organizations combined with new technology has generated interest in virtual teams, although evidence for their effectiveness was not yet in evidence (Salas, Priest, Stagl, Sims, & Burke, 2007).

In work motivation, Latham and Budworth (2007) noted the continued endurance of equity and of goal-setting theories of motivation, with the latter garnering considerable evidence for their validity and usefulness. In the 1990s, several trends in leadership research were noted, including interest in transformational leadership and neo-charismatic leadership. Of note is the Global Leadership and Organizational Behavior Effectiveness (GLOBE) study. This study attempted to identify culturally specific and universal leadership behaviors across sixty countries, determining that there were some attributes endorsed by middle managers across countries (Chhokar, Brodbeck, & House, 2007; Lowe & Gardner, 2000).

I-O psychology continued to grow more international in outlook. Many I-O consulting firms had become multinational, with offices spread throughout the globe. In the 1990s, new journals were established with an explicit international perspective, such as the *International Journal of Selection and Assessment*, founded in 1993, and the *International Journal of Training and Development*, founded in 1997 (Warr, 2007). The number of international members in the Society for Industrial and Organizational Psychology (SIOP) was increasing, and SIOP collaborated with both the International Association of Applied Psychology and the European Association of Work and Organizational Psychology to form the Alliance of Organizational Psychology, whose goals include advancing the science and practice of I-O psychology and improving the quality of working life (Peiró, 2009, cited in Koppes Bryan & Vinchur, 2012). When the second edition of the Dunnette's (1976) *Handbook of Industrial and Organizational Psychology* expanded to four volumes (Dunnette & Hough, 1990–92; Triandis, Dunnette, & Hough, 1994), the subject of the fourth volume was cross-cultural I-O psychology.

I-O psychology has entered both the twenty-first century and its second century of existence. It is currently a vital, expanding field with a future that appears bright. I-O psychologists hold academic positions in psychology departments and business schools, they maintain consulting firms, and they are directly employed in business and government. While it is impossible to predict what the future will bring for I-O psychology, it is a safe bet that the same combination of internal and external forces that shaped the field during the past century will continue to do so. Changes in the social, cultural, and economic environments that I-O psychology is embedded within will have an influence. Technological changes and changes in the nature of work – for example, the increasing sophistication of robotics and artificial intelligence – will force corresponding changes in research and practice. Advances in psychology and neuroscience in understanding behavior and the nervous system should lead to advances in our understanding of work behavior.

There will be no shortages of challenges. How will I-O psychologists meet them? The basic scientist-practitioner model has served the field well over the past century. It should do the same in the future. Reliance on empirical evidence, genuine concern for worker welfare as well as the bottom line, and adherence to high ethical and professional standards will ideally guide future efforts.

# References

Achilles, P. (1957, November 30). [Letter to Leonard W. Ferguson] Carnegie-Mellon University (Ferguson Collection, Box 2), Pittsburgh, PA.

Adams, J. S. (1965). Inequity in social exchange. In K. Berkowitz (ed.), *Advances in experimental social psychology* (Vol. 2, pp. 267–299). New York, NY: Academic Press.

Adkins, D. C. (1964). Louis Leon Thurstone: Creative thinker, dedicated teacher, eminent psychologist. In N. Frederiksen & H. Gulliksen (eds.), *Contributions to mathematical psychology* (pp. 1–39). New York, NY: Holt, Rinehart, & Winston.

Aitken, H. G. J. (1985). *Scientific management in action: Taylorism at Watertown arsenal, 1908–1915.* Princeton, NJ: Princeton University Press.

Alford, L. P. (1934). *Henry Laurence Gantt: Leader in industry.* New York, NY: The American Society of Mechanical Engineers.

Allport, F. H. (1924). *Social psychology.* Boston, MA: Houghton Mifflin Company.

Allport, G. W. (1938). William Stern: 1871–1938. *American Journal of Psychology, 51*, 770–773.

American Psychological Association (n.d.). Guidelines and principles for accreditation of programs in professional psychology. Quick reference guide to doctoral programs. Retrieved from www.apa.org/ed/accreditation/about/policies/doctoral/aspx.

American Psychological Association (1966). *Standards for educational and psychological tests and manuals.* Washington, DC: American Psychological Association.

American Psychological Association, American Educational Research Association, & National Council on Measurement Used in Education (Joint Committee) (1954). Technical recommendations for psychological tests and diagnostic techniques. *Psychological Bulletin, 51*, 201–238.

Anderson, L. D. (1921). Estimating intelligence by means of printed photographs. *Journal of Applied Psychology, 5*, 152–155.

Ansbacher, H. L. (1941). German military psychology. *Psychological Bulletin, 38*, 370–392.

Ansbacher, H. L. (1951). A history of the Leaderless Group Discussion technique. *Psychological Bulletin, 48*, 383–391.

Argyris, C. (1957). *Personality and organization.* New York, NY: Harper & Row.

Arthur, Jr., W., & Benjamin, Jr., L. T. (1999). Psychology applied to business. In A. M. Stec & D. A. Bernstein (eds.), *Psychology: Fields of application* (pp. 98–115). Boston, MA: Houghton Mifflin.

Arvey, R. D., & Faley, R. H. (1988). *Fairness in selecting employees* (2nd ed.), Reading, MA: Addison-Wesley.

Ash, P., & Kroeker, L. P. (1975). Personnel selection, classification, and placement. In M. R. Rosenzweig & L. W. Porter (eds.), *Annual review of psychology* (pp. 481–507). Palo Alto, CA: Annual Reviews, Inc.

Austin, J. T. (1992). History of industrial-organizational psychology at Ohio State. *The Industrial-Organizational Psychologist, 29*, 51–59.

Austin, J. T., & Villanova, P. (1992). The criterion problem: 1917–1992. *Journal of Applied Psychology, 77*, 836–874.

Austin, J. T., Scherbaum, C. A., & Mahlman, R. A. (2002). History of research methods in industrial and organizational psychology: Measurement, design, analysis. In S. G. Rogelberg (ed.), *Handbook of research methods in industrial and organizational psychology* (pp. 3–33). Hoboken, NJ: Blackwell Publishers.

Bagley, W. C. (1922). Educational determinism; or democracy and the I.Q. *School and Society, 15*, 373–384.

Balzer, W. K., Locke, E., & Zedeck, S. (2008). Patricia Cain Smith (1917–2007). *American Psychologist, 63*, 198.

Bandura, A. (1977). Self-efficacy: Toward a unifying theory of behavioral change. *Psychological Review, 84*, 191–215.

Baritz, L. (1960). *The servants of power: A history of the use of social science in American industry*. Middletown, CT: Wesleyan University Press.

Barnard, C. I. (1938). *The functions of the executive*. Cambridge, MA: Harvard University Press.

Bartol, C. R., & Bartol, A. M. (2013). History of forensic psychology. In I. B. Weiner & R. K. Otto (eds.), *Handbook of forensic psychology* (4th edn., pp. 3–34). Hoboken, NJ: John Wiley & Sons.

Barrick, M. R., & Mount, M. K. (1991). The Big Five personality dimensions and job performance. *Personnel Psychology, 44*, 1–26.

Bartle, P. M. (1997). Lillian M. Gilbreth. In W. G. Bringmann, H. E. Lück, R. Miller, & C. E. Early (eds.), *A pictorial history of psychology* (pp. 501–502). Chicago, IL: Quintessence Publishing.

Bartlett, F. C. (1946). Dr. Charles S. Myers, C.B.E., FR.S. *Nature, 158*, 657–658.

Bartlett, F. C. (1948). Charles Samuel Myers 1873–1946. *Obituary Notices of the Fellows of the Royal Society, 5*, 767–777.

Baumgarten, F. (1933–34). Otto Lipmann – Psychologist. *Personnel Journal, 12*, 324–327.

Baumgarten, F. (1975). II. Autobiographical notes: Prof. Dr. Franziska Baumgarten. *Perceptual and Motor Skills, 41*, 487–490.

Baumgarten-Tramer, F. (1948). German psychologists and recent events. *Journal of Abnormal and Social Psychology, 43*, 452–465.

Bäumler, G. (1997). Sports psychology. In W. G. Bringmann, H. E. Lück, R. Miller, & C. E. Early (eds.), *A pictorial history of psychology* (pp. 485–489). Chicago, IL: Quintessence Publishing.

Beckman, R. O., & Levine, M. (1929–30). Selecting executives. *Personnel Journal*, *8*, 415–420.

Bellows, R. M. (1951). Industrial psychology. In C. P. Stone & D. W. Taylor (eds.), *Annual review of psychology* (pp. 173–192). Stanford CA: Annual Reviews.

Benjamin, L. T., Jr. (1996). Harry Hollingworth: Portrait of the generalist. In G. A. Kimble, C. A. Boneau, & M. Wertheimer (eds.), *Portraits of pioneers in psychology* (Vol. 2, pp. 119–135). Washington, DC: American Psychological Association & Hillsdale, NJ: Lawrence Erlbaum Associates.

Benjamin, L. T., Jr. (1997a). Organized industrial psychology before Division 14: The ACP and the AAAP (1930–1945). *Journal of Applied Psychology*, *82*, 459–466.

Benjamin, L. T., Jr. (1997b). A history of Division 14 (Society for Industrial and Organizational Psychology). In D. A. Dewsbury (ed.), *Unification through division: Histories of the divisions of the American Psychological Association*: (Vol. 2, pp. 101–126). Washington, DC: American Psychological Association.

Benjamin, L. T., Jr. (2000). Hugo Münsterberg: Portrait of an applied psychologist. In G. A. Kimble & M. Wertheimer (eds.), *Portraits of pioneers in psychology* (Vol. 4, pp. 113–129). Washington, DC: American Psychological Association & Mahwah, NJ: Lawrence Erlbaum Associates.

Benjamin, L. T., Jr. (2004). Science for sale: Psychology's earliest adventures in American advertising. In J. D. Williams, W. Lee, & C. P. Haugtvedt (eds.), *Diversity in advertising: Broadening the scope of research directions* (pp. 21–39). New York, NY: Psychology Press.

Benjamin, L. T., Jr. (2006). Hugo Münsterberg's attack on the application of scientific psychology. *Journal of Applied Psychology*, *91*, 414–425.

Benjamin, L. T., Jr. (2013). Introduction. In L. T. Benjamin, Jr., & L. R. Barton, *From Coca-Cola to chewing gum: The applied psychology of Harry Hollingworth* (Vol. 2, pp. ix–xx). Akron, OH: University of Akron Press.

Benjamin, L. T., Jr., & Baker, D. B. (2009). Recapturing a context for psychology: The role of history. *Perspectives on Psychological Science*, *4*, 97–98.

Benjamin, L. T., Jr., & Baker, D. B. (2012). The internationalization of psychology: A history. In D. B. Baker (ed.), *The Oxford handbook of the history of psychology: Global perspectives* (pp. 1–17). New York, NY: Oxford University Press.

Benjamin, L. T., Jr., & Bryant, W. H. M. (1997). A history of popular psychology magazines in America. In W. G. Bringmann, H. E. Lück, R. Miller, & C. E. Early (eds.), *A pictorial history of psychology* (pp. 585–593). Chicago, IL: Quintessence Publishing.

Benjamin, L. T., Jr., Rogers, A., & Rosenbaum, A. (1991). Coca-Cola, caffeine, and mental deficiency: Harry Hollingworth and the Chattanooga trial of 1911. *Journal of the History of the Behavioral Sciences*, *27*, 42–55.

Benne, K. D. (1964). History of the t-group in the laboratory setting. In L. P. Bradford, J. R. Gibb, & K. D. Benne (eds.), *T-group theory and laboratory method* (pp. 80–135). New York, NY: John Wiley & Sons.

Bernard, L. L. (1926). *An introduction to social psychology*. New York, NY: Henry Holt and Company.

Bernreuter, R. B. (1931). *The personality inventory*. Stanford, CA: Stanford University Press.

Bernreuter, R. B. (1933). The theory and construction of the Personality Inventory. *Journal of Social Psychology, 4*, 387–405.

Bills, M. A. (1923). Relation of mental alertness score to positions and permanency in the company. *Journal of Applied Psychology, 7*, 154–156.

Bills, M. A. (1925). Social status of the clerical worker and his permanence on the job. *Journal of Applied Psychology, 9*, 424–427.

Bills, M. A. (1926–27a). Permanence of men and women office workers. *Journal of Personnel Research, 5*, 402–404.

Bills, M. A. (1926–27b). Stability of office workers and age at employment. *Journal of Personnel Research, 5*, 475–477.

Bills, M. A. (1928). Relative permanency of women office workers. *American Management Association, 5*, 207–208.

Bills, M. A. (1953). Our expanding responsibilities. *Journal of Applied Psychology, 37*, 142–145.

Bingham, W. V. (1919). Army personnel work. With some implications for education and industry. *Journal of Applied Psychology, 3*, 1–12.

Bingham, W. V. (1923). On the possibility of an applied psychology. *Psychological Review, 30*, 289–305.

Bingham, W. V. (1924). What industrial psychology asks of management: Patience, discrimination, research opportunities, reliable criteria. *Bulletin of the Taylor Society, 9*, 243–248.

Bingham, W. V. (1926). Measures of occupational success. *Harvard Business Review, 5*, 1–10.

Bingham, W V. (1927/1980). Leadership. In H. C. Metcalf (ed.), *The psychological foundations of management* (pp. 244–260). Easton, PA: Hive Publishing Company [reprint of the 1927 ed. published by A. W. Shaw Co., Chicago].

Bingham, W. V. (1927–28). The Paris Congress of Technopsychology: Fourth International Conference of Technopsychology Applied to Vocational Guidance and Scientific Management, October 10–14, 1927. *Personnel Journal, 6*, 295–301.

Bingham, W. V. (1928). Industrial psychology: Its progress in the United States – Psychology as science, as point of view and as method. *Bulletin of the Taylor Society, 13*, 187–198.

Bingham, W. V. (1929). Industrial psychology in the United States: An appraisal. *Annals of Business Economics and Science of Labor, 3*, 398–408.

Bingham, W. V. (1937). *Aptitudes and aptitude testing*. New York, NY: Harper.

Bingham, W. V. (1946). Clarence Stone Yoakum 1879–1945. *American Psychologist, 1*, 26–28.

Bingham, W. V. (1952). Walter Van Dyke Bingham. In E. G. Boring, H. S. Langfeld, H. Werner, & R. M. Yerkes (eds.), *A history of psychology in autobiography* (Vol. 4, pp. 1–26). New York, NY: Appleton-Century-Crofts.

Bingham, W. V., & Davis, W. T. (1924). Intelligence test scores and business success. *Journal of Applied Psychology, 8,* 1–22.

Bingham, W. V., & Freyd, M. (1926). *Procedures in employment psychology: A manual for developing scientific methods of vocational selection.* New York, NY: McGraw-Hill.

Bingham, W. V., & Moore, B. V. (1931). *How to interview.* Oxford, England: Harpers.

Bjork, D. W. (1983). *The compromised scientist: William James in the development of American psychology.* New York, NY: Columbia University Press.

Blackburn, K. (1998). The quest for efficiency and the rise of industrial psychology in Australia, 1917–1929. *Labour History, 74,* 122–136.

Blackford, K. M. H., & Newcomb, A. (1914). *The job, the man, the boss.* Garden City, NY: Doubleday, Page.

Blanz, F., & Ghiselli, E. E. (1972). The mixed standard scale: A new rating system. *Personnel Psychology, 25,* 185–200.

Blau, P. M., & Scott, W. R. (1962). *Formal Organizations.* San Francisco, CA: Chandler.

Blowers, G. H. (1998). Chen Li: China's elder psychologist. *History of Psychology, 1,* 315–330.

Blumenthal, A. L. (1975). A reappraisal of Wilhelm Wundt. *American Psychologist, 30,* 1081–1088.

Boring, E. G. (1923). Intelligence as the tests test it. *New Republic, 36,* 35–37.

Boring, E. G. (1929). *A history of experimental psychology.* New York, NY: Century.

Boring, E. G. (1950). *A history of experimental psychology* (2nd ed.). New York, NY: Century-Appleton-Crofts.

Boring, E. G. (1961). The beginning and growth of measurement in psychology. *Isis, 52,* 238–257.

Borman, W. C., Hanson, M. A., & Hedge, J. W. (1997). Personnel selection. In J. T. Spence, J. M. Darley, & D. J. Foss (eds.), *Annual review of psychology* (pp. 299–337). Palo Alto, CA: Annual Reviews, Inc.

Borman, W. C., Klimoski, R. J., & Ilgen, D. R. (2003). Stability and change in industrial and organizational psychology. In W. C. Borman, D. R. Ilgen, & R. J. Klimoski, (eds.), *Handbook of psychology: Volume 12: Industrial and organizational psychology* (pp. 1–17). Hoboken, NJ: John Wiley & Sons.

Bowman, M. L. (1989). Testing individual differences in ancient China. *American Psychologist, 44,* 576–578.

Brandenburg, G. C. (1926). Do physical traits portray character? *Industrial Psychology, 1,* 580–588.

Bray, D. W., & Campbell, R. J. (1968). Selection of salesmen by means of an assessment center. *Journal of Applied Psychology, 52,* 36–41.

Bray, D. W., & Grant, D. L. (1966). The assessment center in the measurement of potential for business management. *Psychological Monographs: General and Applied, 80.*

Bray, D. W., & Moses, J. L. (1972). Personnel selection. In P. H. Mussen & R. Rosenzweig (eds.), *Annual review of psychology* (pp. 545–576). Palo Alto, CA: Annual Reviews, Inc.

Bray, D. W., Campbell, R. J., & Grant, D. L. (1974). *Formative years in business: A long term AT&T study of managerial lives.* New York, NY: John Wiley & Sons.

Brayfield, A. H., & Crockett, W. H. (1955). Employee attitudes and employee performance. *Psychological Bulletin, 62,* 396–424.

Bregman Biography (1970, March 12). Finding guide. Bregman Papers. Archives of the History of American Psychology, The Drs. Nicholas and Dorothy Cummings Center for the History of Psychology, University of Akron.

Bregman, E. O. (1921). A study in industrial psychology – Tests for special abilities. *Journal of Applied Psychology, 5,* 127–151.

Bregman, E. O. (1935). *Bregman Language Completion Scales: Forms A and B.* New York, NY: The Psychological Corporation.

Brigham, C. C. (1923). *A study of American intelligence.* Princeton, NJ: Princeton University Press.

Brigham, C. C. (1930). Intelligence tests of immigrant groups. *Psychological Review, 37,* 158–165.

Brock, A. C. (2017). The new history of psychology: Some (different) answers to Lovett's five questions. *History of Psychology, 20,* 195–217.

Brogden, H. E. (1946). On the interpretation of the correlation coefficient as a measure of predictive efficiency. *Journal of Educational Psychology, 37,* 64–76.

Brogden, H. E. (1949). When testing pays. *Personnel Psychology, 2,* 171–183.

Brogden, H. E., & Taylor, E. K. (1950). The dollar criterion: Applying the cost accounting concept to criterion construction. *Personnel Psychology, 3,* 133–154.

Brown, C. W., & Ghiselli, E. E. (1952). Industrial Psychology. In C. P. Stone & D. W. Taylor (eds.), *Annual review of psychology* (pp. 205–232). Stanford CA: Annual Reviews, Inc.

Brown, J. (1992). *The definition of a profession: The authority of metaphor in the history of intelligence testing, 1890–1930.* Princeton, NJ: Princeton University Press.

Brown, P. S. (1925). The work and aims of the Taylor Society. *Bulletin of the Taylor Society, 10,* 164–168.

Buchanan, R. D. (2012). Australia. In D. B. Baker (ed.), *The Oxford handbook of the history of psychology: Global perspectives* (pp. 18–33). New York, NY: Oxford University Press.

Bunn, G. (2001). Charlie and the chocolate factory. *The Psychologist, 14,* 576–579.

Burns, J. M. (1978). *Leadership.* New York, NY: Harper & Row.

Burns, T., & Stalker, G. M. (1961). *The management of innovation.* London: Tavistock Publications.

Burt, C. (1947). Charles Samuel Myers. *Occupational Psychology, 21,* 1–6.

Burtt, H. (1926). *Principles of employment psychology.* New York, NY: Harper.

Burtt, H. (1929). *Psychology and industrial efficiency*. New York, NY: Appleton.

Burtt, H. (1938). *Psychology of advertising*. Oxford: Houghton Mifflin.

Burtt, H. (1948). *Applied psychology*. New York, NY: Prentice-Hall.

Burtt, H. (1953, January 14). [Letter to Leonard Ferguson]. Carnegie-Mellon University (Ferguson Collection, Box 2),] Pittsburgh, PA.

Butterfield, H. (1931/1965). *The Whig interpretation of history*. New York, NY: Norton.

Campbell, J. P. (1971). Personnel training and development. *Annual review of psychology, 22*, 565–602.

Campbell, J. P. (1990a). Modeling the performance prediction problem in industrial and organizational psychology. In M. D. Dunnette & L. M. Hough (eds.), *Handbook of industrial and organizational psychology* (2nd ed., Vol. 1, pp. 687–732). Palo Alto, CA: Consulting Psychologists Press.

Campbell, J. P. (1990b). An overview of the Army Selection and Classification Project (Project A). *Personnel Psychology, 43*, 231–239.

Campbell, J. P. (2007). Profiting from history. In L. L. Koppes (ed.), *Historical perspectives in industrial and organizational psychology* (pp. 441–457). Mahwah, NJ: Lawrence Erlbaum Associates.

Campbell, J. P., & Knapp, D. J. (2010). Project A: Twelve years in R & D. In J. L. Farr & N. T. Tippins (eds.), *Handbook of employee selection* (pp. 865–886). New York, NY: Routledge.

Campbell, J. P., McCloy, R. A., Oppler, S. H., & Sager, C. E. (1993). A theory of performance. In N. Schmitt & W. C. Borman (eds.), *Personnel selection in organizations* (pp. 35–70). San Francisco, CA: Jossey-Bass.

Canziani, W. (1975). Contributions to the history of psychology: XXIII. I. Franziska Baumgarten-Tramer. *Perceptual and Motor Skills, 41*, 479–486.

Capshew, J. H. (1999). *Psychologists on the march: Science, practice, and professional identity in America, 1929–1969*. Cambridge: Cambridge University Press.

Carpintero, H. (1992). International development of psychology as an academic discipline. In A. E. Puente, J. R. Matthews, & C. L. Brewer (eds.), *Teaching psychology in America: A history* (pp. 89–121). Washington, DC: American Psychological Association.

Carpintero, H. (2012). Spain. In D. B. Baker (ed.), *The Oxford handbook of the history of psychology: Global perspectives* (pp. 513–537). New York, NY: Oxford University Press.

Carter, I. (2012). Shelley, James. In *The dictionary of New Zealand biography. Te Ara – The encyclopedia of New Zealand* (updated October 30, 2012). Retrieved from www.TeAra.gov.nz/en/biographies/4s23/shelley-james.

Cashman, S. D. (1989). *America in the twenties and thirties*. New York, NY: New York University Press.

Cattell, J. M. (1890/1947). Mental tests and measurements. *Mind, 15*, 373–381. Reprinted in *James McKeen Cattell: Man of science, Vol. 1: Psychological Research* (pp. 132–141). Lancaster, PA: Science Press.

Cattell, J. M. (1895). IV. Proceedings of the third annual meeting of the American Psychological Association. Princeton, N.J., 1894: Report of the Secretary and Treasurer. *Psychological Review, 2*, 149–152.

Cattell, J. M. (1922). Notes and comments. *Journal of Applied Psychology, 6,* 213.

Cattell, J. M. (1923). The Psychological Corporation. *Annals of the Academy of Political and Social Science, 110,* 165–171.

Cattell, J. M. (1929/1947). Psychology in America. In *James McKeen Cattell: Man of science, Vol. 2: Address and formal papers* (pp. 441–484). Lancaster, PA: Science Press.

Cattell, J. M. (1946). Retrospect: Psychology as a profession. *Journal of Consulting Psychology, 10,* 289–291.

Cerullo, J. J. (1988). E. G. Boring: Reflections on a discipline builder. *American Journal of Psychology, 101,* 561–575.

Chandler, A. D., Jr., (1991). *Industrial revolution.* In E. Foner & J. A. Garraty (eds.), *The reader's companion to American history* (pp. 559–563). Boston, MA: Houghton Mifflin Company.

Chapman, J. C. (1923). Tests for trade proficiency. *Annals of the American Academy of Political and Social Science, 110,* 45–59.

Chhokar, J. S., Brodbeck, F. C., & House, R. J. (eds.) (2007). *Culture and leadership across the world: The GLOBE book of in-depth studies of 25 societies.* Mahwah, NJ: Erlbaum.

Cimino, G., Foschi, R. (2012). Italy. In D. B. Baker (ed.), *The Oxford handbook of the history of psychology: Global perspectives* (pp. 307–346). New York, NY: Oxford University Press.

Clark, W. (1922). *The Gantt chart: A working tool of management.* New York, NY: Ronald Press.

Cleeton, G. U. (1962). A tribute to pioneering leadership in industrial psychology. In B. V. Gilmer (ed.), *Walter Van Dyke Bingham: Memorial Program/March 23, 1961* (pp. 31–33). Pittsburgh, PA: Carnegie Institute of Technology.

Cleeton, G. U., & Knight, F. B. (1924). Validity of character judgment based on external criteria. *Journal of Applied Psychology, 8,* 215–231.

Colella, A., Hebl, M., & King, E. (2017). One hundred years of discrimination research in the *Journal of Applied Psychology*: A sobering synopsis. *Journal of Applied Psychology, 102,* 500–513.

Cook, H. E., & Manson, G. E. (1925–26). Abilities necessary in effective retail selling and a method for evaluating them. *Journal of Personnel Research, 4,* 74–82.

Coon, D. J. (1982). Eponymy, obscurity, Twitmyer, and Pavlov. *Journal of the History of the Behavioral Sciences, 18,* 255–262.

Coon, D. J., & Sprenger, H. A. (1998). Psychologists in service to science: The American Psychological Association and the American Association for the Advancement of Science. *American Psychologist, 53,* 1253–1269.

Cowdery, K. M. (1922). Measures of general intelligence as indices of success in trade learning. *Journal of Applied Psychology, 6,* 311–330.

Cowdery, K. M. (1926–27). Measurement of professional attitudes: Differences between lawyers, physicians, and engineers. *Journal of Personnel Research, 5,* 131–141.

Cowles, M. (2001). *Statistics in psychology: An historical perspective* (2nd ed.). Mahwah, NJ: Lawrence Erlbaum.

Craig, D. R., & Charters, W. W. (1925). *Personal leadership in industry.* New York, NY: McGraw-Hill.

Crockett, A. C. (1926–27). Testing apprentices for the Burroughs Adding Machine Company. *Journal of Personnel Research, 5,* 259–266.

Cronbach, L. J. (1951). Coefficient alpha and the internal structure of tests. *Psychometrika, 6,* 671–684.

Cronbach, L. J., & Gleser, G. C. (1957). *Psychological tests and personnel decisions.* Urbana, IL: University of Illinois Press.

Cronbach, L. J., & Meehl, P. E. (1955). Construct validity in psychological tests. *Psychological Bulletin, 52,* 281–302.

Crunden, R. M. (1991). Progressivism. In E. Foner & J. A. Garraty (eds.), *The reader's companion to American history* (pp. 868–871). Boston, MA: Houghton Mifflin Company.

Cumming, G., & Corkindale, K. (1969). Human factors in the United Kingdom. *Human Factors, 11,* 75–80.

Cunningham, J. L. (1997). Alfred Binet and the quest for testing higher mental functioning. In W. G. Bringmann, H. E. Lück, R. Miller, & C. E. Early (eds.), *A pictorial history of psychology* (pp. 309–314). Chicago, IL: Quintessence Publishing.

Danziger, K. (1980). The history of introspection reconsidered. *Journal of the History of the Behavioral Sciences, 16,* 241–262.

Danziger, K. (1990). The autonomy of applied psychology. In K. Danziger, *Problematic encounter: Talks on psychology and history.* E-book retrieved from www.kurtdanziger.com.

Darley, J. G. (1964). Edward Kellogg Strong, Jr. (1884–1963). *Journal of Applied Psychology, 48,* 73–74.

Darwin, C. (1859/1986). *The origin of the species: By means of natural selection or the preservation of favored races in the struggle for life.* New York, NY: New American Library.

Davis, D. R. (1947). Post-mortem on German applied psychology. *Occupational Psychology, 21,* 105–110.

Day, D., & Zaccaro, S. (2007). Leadership: A critical historical analysis of the influence of leader traits. In L. L. Koppes (ed.), *Historical perspectives in industrial and organizational psychology* (pp. 383–405). Mahwah, NJ: Lawrence Erlbaum Associates.

Dazzi, N., & Mecacci, L. (1997). Early Italian psychology. In W. G. Bringmann, H. E. Lück, R. Miller, & C. E. Early (eds.), *A pictorial history of psychology* (pp. 577–581). Chicago, IL: Quintessence Publishing.

Deary, I. J., Lawn, M., & Bartholomew, D. J. (2008). A conversation between Charles Spearman, Godfrey Thomson, and Edward L. Thorndike: The International Examinations Inquiry Meeting 1931–1938. *History of Psychology, 11,* 122–142.

DeNisi, A. S., & Griffin, R. W. (2001). *Human resource management*. Boston, MA: Houghton Mifflin Company.

Dewey, J. (1896). The reflex arc concept in psychology. *Psychological Review, 3,* 357–370.

deWolff, C. J., & Shimmin, S. (1976). The psychology of work in Europe: A review of a profession. *Personnel Psychology, 29,* 175–195.

Dewsbury, D. A. (2003). Archival adventures in the history of comparative psychology. In D. Baker (ed.), *Thick description and fine texture: Studies in the history of psychology* (pp. 143–161). Akron, OH: University of Akron Press.

Digman, J. M. (1990). Personality structure: Emergence of the five-factor model. In M. R. Rosenzweig & L. W. Porter (eds.), *Annual review of psychology* (pp. 417–440). Palo Alto, CA: Annual Reviews, Inc.

Division of Applied Psychology: Carnegie Institute of Technology 1915–1924 (n.d.). Cleeton Papers, Archives of the History of American Psychology, the Drs. Nicholas and Dorothy Cummings Center for the History of Psychology, University of Akron.

Division of Industrial-Organizational Psychology, American Psychological Association (1975). *Principles for the validation and use of personnel selection procedures*. Dayton, OH: Industrial-Organizational Psychologist.

Dobrzyński, M. (1981). Work psychology in Poland. In C. J. deWolff, S. Shimmin, & M. Montmollin (eds.), *Conflicts and contradictions: Work psychologists in Europe* (pp. 73–75). London: Academic Press.

Dockeray, F. C., & Issacs, S. (1921). Psychological research in aviation in Italy, France, England and the American expeditionary forces. *Journal of Comparative Psychology, 1,* 115–148.

Donahue, P., & Falbo, B. (2007). (The teaching of) reading and writing at Lafayette College. In P. Donahue & G. F. Moon (eds.), *Local histories: Reading the archives of composition* (pp. 38–57). Pittsburgh, PA: University of Pittsburgh Press.

Donald G. Paterson 1892–1961 (1961). *Journal of Applied Psychology, 45,* 352.

Dorcus, R. M., & Jones, M. H. (1950). *Handbook of employee selection*. New York, NY: McGraw-Hill.

Drever, J. (1955). Godfrey Hilton Thomson: 1881–1955. *American Journal of Psychology, 68,* 494–496.

Drucker, P. (1954). *The practice of management*. New York, NY: Harper & Row.

DuBois, P. H. (1970). *A history of psychological testing*. Boston, MA: Allyn & Bacon.

Dudek, E. E. (1963). Personnel selection. In P. R. Farnsworth, O. McNemar, & Q. McNemar (eds.), *Annual review of psychology* (pp. 261–284). Palo Alto, CA: Annual Reviews, Inc.

Dunlap, K. (1923). Fact and fable in character analysis. *Annals of the Academy of Political and Social Science, 110,* 74–80.

Dunlap, K. (1932). Knight Dunlap. In C. Murchison (ed.), *A history of psychology in autobiography* (Vol. 2, pp. 35–61). Worcester, MA: Clark University Press.

Dunnette, M. D. (1962). Personnel management. In P. R. Farnsworth, O. McNemar, & Q. McNemar (eds.), *Annual review of psychology* (pp. 285–314). Palo Alto, CA: Annual Reviews, Inc.

Dunnette, M. D. (1963). A modified model for test validation and selection research. *Journal of Applied Psychology, 47*, 317–323.

Dunnette, M. D. (ed.) (1976). *Handbook of industrial and organizational psychology*. Chicago, IL: Rand-McNally.

Dunnette, M. D. (1993). Applied psychology at Minnesota. *The Industrial-Organizational Psychologist, 31*, 67–76.

Dunnette, M. D., & Hough, L. M. (eds.) (1990–92). *Handbook of industrial and organizational psychology*, (2nd ed., Vol. 1–3). Palo Alto, CA: Consulting Psychologists Press.

Dunnette, M. D., & Kirchner, W. K. (1965). *Psychology applied to industry*. New York, NY: Appleton-Century-Crofts.

Dyer, E. (n.d.). [Reminiscence of the Research Bureau for Retail Training: Carnegie Institute of Technology 1918–1922.] Box 4, Ferguson Collection, Carnegie-Mellon University.

Early, C. E., & Bringmann, W. G. (1997). The history of psychology. In W. G. Bringmann, H. E. Lück, R. Miller, & C. E. Early (eds.), *A pictorial history of psychology* (pp. 518–526). Chicago, IL: Quintessence Publishing.

Eder, R. W., Kacmar, K. M., & Ferris, G. R. (1989). Employment interview research: History and synthesis. In R. W. Eder & G. R. Ferris (eds.), *The employment interview: Theory, research, and practice* (pp. 17–31). Newbury Park, CA: Sage.

Elliott, M., & Manson, G. E. (1930). Earnings of women in business and in the professions. *Michigan Business Studies, 3(1)*.

Elliott, R. M. (1952). Richard M. Elliott. In E. G. Boring, H. S. Langfeld, H. Werner, R. M. Yerkes (eds.), *A history of psychology in autobiography* (Vol. 4, pp. 75–95). New York, NY: Russell & Russell.

Ellwood, C. A. (1917). *An introduction to social psychology*. New York, NY: D. Appleton and Company.

Elwood, R. H. (1927). The role of personality traits in selecting a career. *Journal of Applied Psychology, 11*, 199–201.

Equal Employment Opportunity Commission, Civil Service Commission, Department of Labor, & Department of Justice (1978). Uniform guidelines on employee selection procedures. *Federal Register, 43*, 38290–38313.

Evans, R. J. (2016). *The pursuit of power: Europe 1815–1914*. New York, NY: Viking.

Fancher, R. E. (1997). Galton's hat and the invention of intelligence tests. In W. G. Bringmann, H. E. Lück, R. Miller, & C. E. Early (eds.), *A pictorial history of psychology* (pp. 53–55). Chicago, IL: Quintessence Publishing.

Farmer, E. (1958). Early days in industrial psychology: An autobiographical note. *Occupational Psychology, 32*, 264–267.

Farr, J. L., & Levy, P. E. (2007). Performance appraisal. In L. L. Koppes (ed.), *Historical perspectives in industrial and organizational psychology* (pp. 311–327). Mahwah, NJ: Lawrence Erlbaum Associates.

Farr, J. L., & Tesluk, P. E. (1997). Bruce V. Moore: First president of Division 14. *Journal of Applied Psychology, 82*, 478–485.

Fay, J. W. (1939). *American psychology before William James*. New Brunswick, NJ: Rutgers University Press.

Fayol, H. (1916/1949). *General and industrial management*. London: Pitman Publishing.

Fayol, H. (1949/1960). General principles of management. In H. F. Merrill (ed.), *Classics in management* (pp. 217–241). New York, NY: American Management Association.

Ferguson, L. W. (n.d.). *New light on the history of industrial psychology*. Unpublished manuscript, Ferguson Collection, Carnegie Mellon University.

Ferguson, L. W. (1952). A look across the years 1920–1950. In L. L. Thurstone (ed.), *Applications of psychology: Essays to honor Walter V. Bingham* (pp. 7–22). New York, NY: Harper.

Ferguson, L. W. (1961). The development of industrial psychology. In B. V. Gilmer (ed.), *Industrial psychology* (pp. 18–37). New York, NY: McGraw-Hill.

Ferguson, L. W. (1962). Industrial psychology and labor. In B. V. Gilmer (ed.), *Walter Van Dyke Bingham: Memorial Program/March 23, 1961* (pp. 7–22). Pittsburgh, PA: Carnegie Institute of Technology.

Ferguson, L. W. (1962–65). *The heritage of industrial psychology* [14 pamphlets]. Hartford, CT: Finlay Press.

Fernberger, S. W. (1936). *Elementary general psychology*. Baltimore, MD: Williams & Wilkins.

Fiedler, F. E. (1967). *A theory of leadership effectiveness*. New York, NY: McGraw-Hill.

Filer, H. A., & O'Rourke, L. J. (1922). Progress in Civil Service tests, part 2. *Journal of Personnel Research, 1*, 489–520.

Finch, F. H., & Odoroff, M. E. (1939). Employment trends in applied psychology. *Journal of Consulting Psychology, 3*, 118–122.

Fine, S. A., & Wiley, W. W. (1971). *An introduction to functional job analysis*. Washington, DC: The Upjohn Institute.

Fisher, R. A. (1925). *Statistical methods for research workers*. Edinburgh: Oliver & Boyd.

Fisher, R. A. (1935). *The design of experiments*. Edinburgh: Oliver & Boyd.

Fitts, P. M. (1946). German applied psychology during World War II. *American Psychologist, 1*, 151–161.

Flanagan, J. C. (1948). *The aviation psychology program in the Army Air Forces* (Rep. No. 1). Washington, DC: US Government Printing Office.

Flanagan, J. C. (1954). The critical incident technique. *Psychological Bulletin, 51*, 327–358.

Fleishman, E. A. (1988). Some new frontiers in personnel selection research. *Personnel Psychology, 41*, 679–701.

Flinn, A. D. (1922–23). Development of Personnel Research Federation. *Journal of Personnel Research, 1*, 7–17.

Foner, E., & Garraty, J. A. (eds.) (1991). *The reader's companion to American history.* Boston, MA: Houghton Mifflin Company.

Ford, J. K., Hollenbeck, J. R., & Ryan, A. M. (eds.) (2014). *The nature of work: Advances in psychological theory, methods, and practice.* Washington, DC: American Psychological Association.

Forster, V. (1928–29). A test for drivers. *The Personnel Journal, 7,* 161–171.

Foschi, R., Giannone, A., & Giuliani, A. (2013). Italian psychology under protection: Agostino Gemelli between Catholicism and Fascism. *History of Psychology, 16,* 130–144.

Foster, W. S. (1919). Psychology of morale (Proceedings of the twenty-seventh annual meeting of the American Psychological Association, Baltimore, December 27 and 28, 1918). *Psychological Bulletin, 16,* 46–48.

Freeman, J. B. (1991). Labor. In E. Foner & J. A. Garraty (eds.), *The reader's companion to American history* (pp. 627–634). Boston, MA: Houghton Mifflin Company.

French, J. R. P., Jr., & Raven, B. (1959). The bases of social power. In D. P. Cartwright (ed.), *Studies in social power* (pp. 150–167). Ann Arbor, MI: Institute for Social Research, University of Michigan.

French, W. L. (1982). The emergence and early history of organizational development: With reference to influence on and interaction among some of the key actors. *Group and Organization Studies, 7,* 261–278.

Freyd, M. (1922–23). The measurement of interests in vocational selection. *Journal of Personnel Research, 1,* 319–328.

Freyd, M. (1923). The graphic rating scale. *Journal of Educational Psychology, 14,* 83–102.

Freyd, M. (1923–24). Measurement in vocational selection. *Journal of Personnel Research, 1,* 215–249; 268–284; 377–385.

Freyd, M. (1925). The statistical viewpoint in vocational selection. *Journal of Applied Psychology, 9,* 349–356.

Freyd, M. (1926). What is applied psychology? *Psychological Review, 33,* 308–324.

Freyd, M. (1951, March 7). [Letter to Leonard. W. Ferguson]. Carnegie Mellon University (Ferguson Collection, Box 4), Pittsburgh, PA.

Frost, E. (1920a). What industry does and does not want from the psychologist. *Journal of Applied Psychology, 4,* 18–25.

Frost, E. (1920b). Should psychology bake bread? *Journal of Applied Psychology, 4,* 294–305.

Fryer, D. H. (1923–24). Psychology and industry in France and Great Britain. *Journal of Personnel Research, 2,* 396–402.

Fryer, D. H., & Henry E. R. (eds.) (1950). *Handbook of applied psychology* (2 vols.). New York, NY: Rinehart.

Furumoto, L. (1989). The new history of psychology. In I. S. Cohen (ed.), *The G. Stanley Hall lecture series* (Vol. 9, pp. 9–34). Washington, DC: American Psychological Association.

Furumoto, L. (2003). Beyond great men and great ideas: History of psychology in sociocultural context. In P. Bronstein & K. Quina (eds.), *Teaching gender and multicultural awareness: Resources for the psychology classroom* (pp. 113–124). Washington, DC: American Psychological Association.

Gael, S. (ed.) (1988). *The job analysis handbook for business, industry, and government.* New York, NY: John Wiley & Sons.

Gantt, H. L. (1901). A bonus system of rewarding labor. *Transactions of the American Society of Mechanical Engineers, 23,* 241–360.

Gemelli, A. (1952). Agostino Gemelli. In E. G. Boring, H. S. Langfeld, H. Werner, R. M. Yerkes (eds.), *A history of psychology in autobiography* (Vol. 4, pp. 97–121). New York, NY: Russell & Russell.

Geuter, U. (1992). *The professionalization of psychology in Nazi Germany* (R. J. Holmes, trans.). Cambridge, England: Cambridge University Press.

Ghiselli, E. E. (1963). Moderating effects and differential reliability and validity. *Journal of Applied Psychology, 47,* 81–86.

Ghiselli, E. E., & Brown, C. W. (1948). *Personnel and industrial psychology.* New York, NY: McGraw-Hill.

Gibby, R. E., & Zickar, M. J. (2008). A history of the early days of personality testing in American industry: An obsession with adjustment. *History of Psychology, 11,* 164–184.

Gilbreth, F. B. (1923/1960). Science in management for the one best way to do work. In H. F. Merrill (ed.), *Classics in management* (pp. 245–291). New York, NY: American Management Association.

Gilbreth, L. M. (1914). *The psychology of management.* New York, NY: Sturgis & Walton.

Gilbreth, L. M. (1925). The present state of industrial psychology. *Mechanical Engineering, 47,* 1039–1042.

Gilbreth, Jr., F. B., & Carey, E. G. (1948). *Cheaper by the dozen.* New York, NY: Thomas Y. Crowell Co.

Gillespie, R. (1991). *Manufacturing knowledge: A history of the Hawthorne experiments.* Cambridge, UK: Cambridge University Press.

Goldsmith, D. B. (1922). The use of the personal history blank as a salesmanship test. *Journal of Applied Psychology, 6,* 149–155.

Goldstein, I. L. (1974). *Training: Program development and evaluation.* Monterey, CA: Brooks/Cole.

Goodwin, C. J. (1999). *A history of modern psychology.* New York, NY: John Wiley & Sons.

Goodwin, C. J. (2005). *A history of modern psychology* (2nd. ed.). Hoboken, NJ: John Wiley & Sons.

Gosset, W. S. (1908). The probable error of a mean. *Biometrika, 6,* 1–24.

Gordon, M. E., & Burt, R. E. (1981). A history of industrial psychology's relationship with American unions: Lessons from the past and directions for the future. *International Review of Applied Psychology, 30,* 137–156.

Gould, S. J. (1981). *The mismeasure of man.* New York, NY: W.W. Norton & Company.

Graen, G. (1976). Role making processes within complex organizations. In M. D. Dunnette (ed.), *Handbook of industrial and organizational psychology* (pp. 1201–1245), Chicago, IL: Rand McNally.

Greenberg, J. (1987). A taxonomy of organizational justice theories. *Academy of Management Review, 12*, 9–22.

Grether, W. F. (1968). Engineering psychology in the United States. *American Psychologist, 23*, 743–751.

Griffin, M. A., Landy, F. J., & Mayocchi, L. (2002). Australian influences on Elton Mayo: The construct of revery in industrial society. *History of Psychology, 5*, 356–375.

Griffitts, C. H. (1924). *Fundamentals of vocational psychology.* New York, NY: Macmillan.

*Griggs v. Duke Power* (1971). 401 US 424.

Gross, M. L. (1962). *The brain watchers.* New York, NY: Random House.

Guilford, J. P. (1936). *Psychometric methods.* New York, NY: McGraw-Hill.

Guilford, J. P. (1939). *General psychology.* New York, NY: Van Nostrand.

Guion, R. M. (1965). *Personnel testing.* New York, NY: McGraw-Hill.

Guion, R. M. (1967). Personnel selection. In P. R. Farnsworth, O. McNemar, & Q. McNemar (eds.), *Annual review of psychology* (pp. 191–216). Palo Alto, CA: Annual Reviews.

Guion, R. M. (1976). Recruiting, selection, and job placement. In M. D. Dunnette (ed.), *Handbook of industrial and organizational psychology* (pp. 777–828). Chicago, IL: Rand McNally.

Guion, R. M. (1991). Personnel assessment, selection, and placement. In M. D. Dunnette & L. M. Hough (eds.), *Handbook of industrial and organizational psychology* (2nd. ed., Vol. 2, pp. 327–397). Palo Alto, CA: Consulting Psychologists Press.

Guion, R. M., & Gibson, W. M. (1988). Personnel selection and placement. In M. R. Rosenzweig & L. W. Porter (eds.), *Annual review of psychology* (pp. 349–374). Palo Alto, CA: Annual Reviews, Inc.

Guion, R. M., & Gottier, R. F. (1965). Validity of personality measures in personnel selection. *Personnel Psychology, 18*, 135–164.

Gundlach, H. U. K. (1997). The mobile psychologist: Psychology and the railroads. In W. G. Bringmann, H. E. Lück, R. Miller, & C. E. Early (eds.), *A pictorial history of psychology* (pp. 506–509). Chicago, IL: Quintessence Publishing.

Gundlach, H. U. K. (1998). The 1920 Geneva Congress. In H. Gundlach (ed.), *Applied psychology Volume 1: The First Congress Geneva, 1920* (pp. 25–41). London: Routledge.

Gundlach, H. U. K. (2012). Germany. In D. B. Baker (ed.). *The Oxford handbook of the history of psychology: Global perspectives* (pp. 255–288). New York, NY: Oxford University Press.

Guthrie, R. V. (1998). *Even the rat was white: A historical view of psychology* (2nd ed.). Boston, MA: Allyn and Bacon.

Hackman, J. R., & Oldman, G. R. (1975). Development of the job diagnostic survey. *Journal of Applied Psychology, 60*, 159–170.

Hackman, J. R., & Oldman, G. R. (1976). Motivation through the design of work: Test of a theory. *Organizational Behavior and Human Performance, 16*, 250–279.

Hackman, J. R., & Oldham, G. R. (1980). *Work redesign.* Reading, MA: Addison-Wesley.

Hale, M. (1992). History of employment testing. In A. Widgor & W. R. Garner (eds.), *Ability testing: Uses, consequences, and controversies* (pp. 3–38). Washington, DC: National Academy Press.

Hale, M., Jr. (1980). *Human science and the social order: Hugo Münsterberg and the origins of applied psychology.* Philadelphia, PA: Temple University Press.

Hall, G. S. (1917). Practical relations between psychology and the war. *Journal of Applied Psychology, 1,* 9–16.

Hall, G. S., Baird, J. W., & Geissler, L. R. (1917). Foreword. *Journal of Applied Psychology, 1,* 5–7.

Hansen, J. C. (1987). Edward Kellogg Strong, Jr.: First author of the Strong Interest Inventory. *Journal of Counseling and Development, 66,* 119–125.

Harari, Y. N. (2015). *Sapiens: A brief history of humankind.* New York, NY: Harper.

Harrell, T. W. (1992). Some history of the Army General Classification Test. *Journal of Applied Psychology, 77,* 875–878.

Hartmann, G. W. (1931–32). Industrial psychology today in Germany and Russia. *Personnel Journal, 10,* 352–354.

Hausmann, M. F. (1930–31). Otto Lipmann and industrial psychology in Germany [Review of *Grundriss der arbeitswissenschaft und ergebnisse der arbeitswissenschaftlichen statistik*]. *Personnel Journal, 9,* 417–420.

Hearnshaw, L. S. (1964). *A short history of British psychology 1840–1940.* Westport, CT: Greenwood Press.

Heidbreder, E. (1933). *Seven psychologies.* New York, NY: Century.

Heller, W. J. (1929–30). Industrial psychology and its development in Switzerland. *Personnel Journal, 8,* 435–441.

Henmon, V. A. C. (1919). Air service tests for aptitude in flying. *Journal of Applied Psychology, 3,* 103–109.

Hepner, H. W. (1930). *Psychology in modern business.* New York, NY: Prentice-Hall.

Heron, A. (1954). Industrial psychology. In C. P. Stone & Q. McNemar (eds.), *Annual review of psychology* (pp. 203–228). Stanford CA: Annual Reviews, Inc.

Hersey, P., & Blanchard, K. H. (1969). Life cycle theory of leadership. *Training and Development Journal, 23,* 26–34.

Herzberg, F., Mausner, B., & Snyderman, B. S. (1959). *The motivation to work.* New York, NY: John Wiley & Sons.

Highhouse, S. (2002). Assessing the candidate as a whole: A historical and critical analysis of individual psychological assessment. *Personnel Psychology, 55,* 363–396.

Highhouse, S. (2007). Applications of organizational psychology: Learning through failure or failure to learn. In L. L. Koppes (ed.), *Historical perspectives in industrial and organizational psychology* (pp. 331–352). Mahwah, NJ: Lawrence Erlbaum Associates.

Hilgard, E. R. (1987). *Psychology in America: A historical survey.* San Diego, CA: Harcourt, Brace, Jovanovich.

Hilgard, E. R., Leary, D. E., & McGuire, G. R. (1991). The history of psychology: A survey and critical assessment. *Annual review of psychology*, *42*, 79–107.

Hoitsma, R. K. (1925). The reliability and relationship of the Colgate Mental Hygiene Test. *Journal of Applied Psychology*, *9*, 293–303.

Holcombe, J. M., Jr. (1922). A case of sales research: Report on first steps in a study of the selection of life insurance salesmen. *Bulletin of the Taylor Society*, *7*, 112–121.

Hollingworth, H. L. (1911). The influence of caffeine on mental and motor efficiency. *Archives of Psychology*, *3*, 1–166.

Hollingworth, H. L. (1916). *Vocational psychology: Its problems and methods*. New York, NY: Appleton.

Hollingworth, H. L. (1922). *Judging human character*. New York, NY: Appleton-Century-Crofts.

Hollingworth, H. L. (2013). *From Coca-Cola to chewing gum: The applied psychology of Harry Hollingworth*, Volume II (L. T. Benjamin, Jr. & L. R. Barton [eds.]). Akron, OH: University of Akron Press.

Hollingworth, H. L., & Poffenberger, A. T. (1917). *Applied psychology*. New York, NY: Appleton.

Holman, P. (1927). The Fourth International Congress of Psychotechnique. *Journal of Applied Psychology*, *11*, 519–526.

Homans, G. C. (1950). *The human group*. New York, NY: Harcourt, Brace.

Hoopingarner, D. L. (1925). *Labor relations in industry*. Chicago, IL: A. W. Shaw.

Hoppock, R. (1935). *Job satisfaction*. New York and London: Harper and Brothers.

Hoskovec, J. (2012). Czech Republic. In D. B. Baker (ed.), *The Oxford handbook of the history of psychology: Global perspectives* (pp. 138–161). New York, NY: Oxford University Press.

House, R. J. (1971). A path-goal theory of leader effectiveness. *Administrative Science Quarterly*, *16*, 321–338.

Houser, J. D. (1927). *What the employee thinks*. Cambridge, MA: Harvard University Press.

Howard, A. (2010). The Management Progress Study and its legacy for selection. In J. L. Farr & N. T. Tippins (eds.), *Handbook of employee selection* (pp. 843–864). New York, NY: Routledge.

Hsueh, Y., & Guo, B. (2012). China. In D. B. Baker (ed.), *The Oxford handbook of the history of psychology: Global perspectives* (pp. 81–124). New York, NY: Oxford University Press.

Hulin, C. L. (2014). Work and being: The meanings of work in contemporary society. In J. K. Ford, J. R. Hollenbeck, & A. M. Ryan (eds.), *The nature of work: Advances in psychological theory, methods, and practice* (pp. 3–33). Washington, DC: American Psychological Association.

Hull, C. L. (1928). *Aptitude testing*. Yonkers-on-Hudson, NY: World Book.

Hull, C. L., & Montgomery, R. B. (1919). An experimental investigation of certain alleged relations between character and handwriting. In B. V. Moore &

G. W. Hartmann (eds.), *Readings in industrial psychology* (pp. 78–80). New York, NY: D. Appleton-Century Company.

Humke, H. L. (1938–39). Full use of employee ratings. *Personnel Journal, 17*, 292–295.

Humm, D. G., & Wadsworth, G. W. (1933–34). The Humm-Wadsworth Temperament Scale: Preliminary report. *Personnel Journal, 12*, 314.

Humphreys, L. (1983). Review of *The mismeasure of man. American Journal of Psychology, 96*, 407–416.

Hunter, J. E., & Hunter, R. F. (1984). Validity and utility of alternative predictors of job performance. *Psychological Bulletin, 96*, 72–98.

Hunter, J. E, & Schmidt, F. L. (1990). *Methods of meta-analysis: Correcting error and bias in research findings.* Newberry Park, CA: Sage.

Hunter, J. E., Schmidt, F. L., & Jackson, G. B. (1982). *Meta-analysis: Cumulating research findings across studies.* Beverly Hills, CA: Sage.

Introduction (1917). *Journal of Applied Psychology, 1*, 1–3.

Jacobson, J. Z. (1951). *Scott of Northwestern.* Chicago, IL: Louis Mariano.

Jamieson, B., & Paterson, J. (1993). Industrial/Organizational psychology in New Zealand. *New England Journal of Psychology, 22*, 1–8.

Janis, I. L. (1972). *Victims of groupthink: A psychological study of foreign policy decisions and fiascoes.* Boston, MA: Houghton Mifflin.

Jarausch, K. H. (2015). *Out of ashes: A new history of Europe in the twentieth century.* Princeton, NJ: Princeton University Press.

Jastrow, J. (1930). Joseph Jastrow. In C. Murchison (ed.), *A history of psychology in autobiography* (Vol. 1, pp. 135–162). Worcester, MA: Clark University Press.

Jastrow, J., Baldwin, J. M., & Cattell, J. M. (1898). Physical and mental tests. *Psychological Review, 5*, 172–179.

Jones, E. S. (1917). The Woolley-Test series applied to the detection of ability in telegraphy. *Journal of Educational Psychology, 8*, 27–34.

Jones, L. V. (1998). L. L. Thurstone's vision of psychology as a quantitative rational science. In G. A. Kimble & M. Wertheimer (eds.), *Portraits of pioneers in psychology* (Vol. 3, pp. 85–102). Washington, DC: American Psychological Association and Mahwah, NJ: Lawrence Erlbaum Associates.

Joravsky, D. (1989). *Russian psychology: A critical history.* Oxford, UK: Basil Blackwell.

Kahn, R. L., Wolfe, D. M., Quinn, R. P., Snoek, J. D., & Rosenthal, R. A. (1964). *Organizational stress: Studies in role conflict and ambiguity.* New York, NY: John Wiley & Sons.

Kaiser, A. E. (1989). A chronology of the theoretical developments in organizational behavior. In J. S. Ott (ed.), *Classic readings in organizational behavior* (pp. 10–26). Pacific Grove, CA: Brooks/Cole.

Kanigel, R. (1997). *The one best way: Frederick Taylor and the enigma of efficiency.* New York, NY: Viking.

Kamin, L. J. (1975). Reply to Samelson. *Social Research, 42*, 488–492.

Katz, D., & Kahn, R. L. (1966). *The social psychology of organizations*. New York, NY: John Wiley & Sons.

Katzell, R. A. (1957). Industrial psychology. In P. R. Farnsworth & Q. McNemar (eds.), *Annual review of psychology* (pp. 237–268). Palo Alto, CA: Annual Reviews, Inc.

Katzell, R. A. (1992). History of early I-O doctoral programs. *The Industrial-Organizational Psychologist, 28,* 51.

Katzell, R. A., & Austin, J. T. (1992). From then to now: The development of industrial-organizational psychology in the United States. *Journal of Applied Psychology, 77,* 803–835.

Kelly, B. N. (1981). Inventing psychology's past: E. G. Boring's historiography in relation to the psychology of his time. *Journal of Mind and Behavior, 2,* 229–241B.

Kelly, R. M., & Kelly, V. P. (1990). Lillian Moller Gilbreth. In A. N. O'Connell & N. F. Russo (eds.), *Women in psychology: A bio-bibliographic sourcebook* (pp. 117–124). New York, NY: Greenwood Press.

Kenagy, H. G., & Yoakum, C. S. (1925). *Selection and training of salesmen.* New York, NY: McGraw-Hill.

Kendall, W. E. (1956). Industrial psychology. In P. R. Farnsworth & Q. McNemar (eds.), *Annual review of psychology* (pp. 197–232). Stanford CA: Annual Reviews.

Kerlinger, F. N. & Lee, H. B. (2000). *Foundations of behavioral research* (4th ed.). Fort Worth, TX: Harcourt College Publishers.

Kevles, D. J. (1968). Testing the Army's intelligence: Psychologists and the military in World War I. *The Journal of American History, 55,* 565–581.

Kingsbury, F. A. (1923). Applying psychology to business. *Annals of the American Academy of Political and Social Science, 110,* 2–12.

Kirihara, S. H. (1959). Industrial psychology in Japan. *Reports of the Institute for the Science of Labour, 55,* 1–19.

Kirkpatrick, D. L. (1959). Techniques for evaluating training programs. *Journal of the ASTD, 13,* 3–9.

Kitson, H. D. (1921a). *The mind of the buyer: The psychology of selling.* New York, NY: Macmillan.

Kitson, H. D. (1921b). Industrial psychology in Europe. *Journal of Applied Psychology, 5,* 287–290.

Kitson, H. D. (1922a). A shift in emphasis needed in personnel research. *Journal of Applied Psychology, 6,* 141–148.

Kitson, H. D. (1922b). Second International Conference of Psychotechnics Applied to Vocational Guidance and to Scientific Management. *Journal of Applied Psychology, 6,* 418–424.

Kitson, H. D. (1922–23). Height and weight as factors in salesmanship. *Journal of Personnel Research, 1,* 289–294.

Klemm, O. (1936). Otto Klemm. In C. Murchison (ed.), *A history of psychology in autobiography* (Vol. 3, pp. 153–180). Worcester, MA: Clark University Press.

Knight, F. B., & Franzen, R. H. (1922). Pitfalls in rating schemes. *Journal of Educational Psychology, 13,* 204–213.

Koonce, J. M. (1984). A brief history of aviation psychology. *Human Factors, 26,* 499–508.

Koppes, L. L. (1997). American female pioneers of industrial and organizational psychology during the early years. *Journal of Applied Psychology, 82,* 500–515.

Koppes, L. L., & Bauer, A. M. (2006). Marion Almira Bills: Industrial psychology pioneer bridging science and practice. In D. A. Dewsbury, L. T. Benjamin, Jr., & M. Wertheimer (eds.), *Portraits of pioneers in psychology* (Vol. 6, pp. 103–116). Washington, DC: American Psychological Association & Mahwah, NJ: Lawrence Erlbaum.

Koppes, L. L., Landy, F. J., & Perkins, K. N. (1993). First American female applied psychologists. *The Industrial-Organizational Psychologist, 31,* 31–33.

Koppes, L. L. & Pickren, W. (2007). Industrial and organizational psychology: An evolving science and practice. In L. L. Koppes (ed.), *Historical perspectives in industrial and organizational psychology* (pp. 3–37). Mahwah, NJ: Lawrence Erlbaum Associates.

Koppes Bryan, L. L., & Vinchur, A. J. (2012). A history of industrial and organizational psychology. In S. Kozlowski (ed.), *Oxford handbook of organizational psychology* (pp. 22–75). New York, NY: Oxford University Press.

Kornhauser, A. W. (1922). The psychology of vocational selection. *Psychological Bulletin, 19,* 192–229.

Kornhauser, A. W. (1923–24). A statistical study of a group of specialized office workers. *Journal of Personnel Research, 2,* 103–123.

Kornhauser, A. W. (1929–30a). Industrial psychology in England, Germany, and the United States. *Personnel Journal, 8,* 421–434.

Kornhauser, A. W. (1929–30b). The study of work feelings. *Personnel Journal, 8,* 348–351.

Kornhauser, A. W. (1933). The technique of measuring employee attitudes. *Personnel, 9,* 99–110.

Kornhauser, A. W. (1946–47). Are public opinion polls fair to organized labor? *Public Opinion Quarterly, 10,* 484–500.

Kornhauser, A. W. (1947). Industrial psychology as management technique and as social science. *American Psychologist, 11,* 224–229.

Kornhauser, A. W. (1965). *Mental health of the industrial worker.* New York, NY: John Wiley & Sons.

Kornhauser, A. W., & Jackson, A. W. (1922). A note on the extent to which systems of character analysis are used in the business world. *Journal of Applied Psychology, 6,* 302.

Kornhauser, A. W., & Kingsbury, F. A. (1924). *Psychological tests in business.* Chicago, IL: University of Chicago Press.

Kornhauser, A. W., & Sharp, A. A. (1931–32). Employee attitudes: Suggestions from a study in a factory. *Personnel Journal, 10,* 393–404.

Kozlowski, S. W. J., Chen, G., & Salas, E. (2017). One hundred years of the *Journal of Applied Psychology*: Background, evolution, and scientific trends. *Journal of Applied Psychology, 102,* 237–253.

Kraiger, K., & Ford, J. K. (2007). The expanding role of workplace training: Themes and trends influencing training research and practice. In L. L. Koppes (ed.), *Historical perspectives in industrial and organizational psychology* (pp. 281–309). Mahwah, NJ: Lawrence Erlbaum Associates.

Kuder, G. F., & Richardson, M. W. (1937). A theory of estimation of test reliability. *Psychometrika, 2*, 151–156.

Kuhn, T. S. (1962). *The structure of scientific revolutions.* Chicago, IL: University of Chicago Press.

Kuna, D. P. (1979). Early advertising applications of the Gale-Cattell order-of-merit method. *Journal of the History of the Behavioral Sciences, 15*, 38–46.

Lachman, S. J. (1998). Ross Stagner (1909–1997). *American Psychologist, 53*, 482–483.

Laird, D. A. (1925a). Detecting abnormal behavior. *Journal of Abnormal and Social Psychology, 20*, 128–141.

Laird, D. A. (1925b). *The psychology of selecting men.* New York, NY: McGraw-Hill.

Lamiell, J. T. (1996). William Stern: More than "the IQ guy." In G. A. Kimble, C. A. Boneau, & M. Wertheimer (eds.), *Portraits of pioneers in psychology* (Vol. 2, pp. 73–85). Washington, DC: APA & Mahwah, NJ: Lawrence Erlbaum.

Lamiell, J. T. (2003). *Beyond individual and group differences: Human individuality, scientific psychology, and William Stern's critical personalism.* Thousand Oaks, CA: Sage.

Landauer, A. A., & Cross, M. J. (1971). The forgotten Australian: Muscio's contribution to industrial psychology. *Australian Journal of Psychology, 23*, 235–240.

Landy, F. J. (1989). *Psychology of work behavior* (4th ed.). Pacific Grove, CA: Brooks/Cole.

Landy, F. J. (1991). A conversation with Harold Burtt. *The Industrial-Organizational Psychologist, 28*, 73–75.

Landy, F. J. (1992). Hugo Münsterberg: Victim or visionary. *Journal of Applied Psychology, 77*, 787–802.

Landy, F. J. (1997). Early influences on the development of industrial and organizational psychology. *Journal of Applied Psychology, 82*, 467–477.

Landy, F. J., & Conte, S. M. (2016). *Work in the 21st century: An introduction to industrial and organizational psychology* (5th ed.). Hoboken, NJ: John Wiley & Sons.

Landy, F. J., & Farr, J. L. (1980). Performance rating. *Psychological Bulletin, 87*, 72–107.

Lane, S. C. (2007). A historical view of human factors in the United States. In L. L. Koppes (ed.), *Historical perspectives in industrial and organizational psychology* (pp. 243–263). Mahwah, NJ: Lawrence Erlbaum Associates.

Latham, G. P., & Budworth, M-H. (2007). The study of work motivation in the 20th century. In L. L. Koppes (ed.), *Historical perspectives in industrial and organizational psychology* (pp. 353–381). Mahwah, NJ: Lawrence Erlbaum Associates.

Latham, G. P., & Wexley, K. N. (1977). Behavioral observation scales for performance appraisal purposes. *Personnel Psychology*, *30*, 225–268.

Lawrence, P. R. (1987). Historical development of organizational behavior. In J. W. Lorsch (ed.), *Handbook of organizational behavior* (pp. 1–9). Englewood Cliffs, NJ: Prentice-Hall.

Leahey, T. H. (1979). Something old, something new: Attention in Wundt and modern cognitive psychology. *Journal of the History of the Behavioral Sciences*, *15*, 242–252.

Leahey, T. H. (2002). History without the past. In W. E. Pickren & D. A. Dewsbury (eds.), *Evolving perspectives in the history of psychology* (pp. 15–20). Washington, DC: American Psychological Association.

Leonard, T. C. (2016). *Illiberal reformers: Race, eugenics & American economics in the progressive era*. Princeton, NJ: Princeton University Press.

Levy, P. E. (2017). *Industrial/organizational psychology: Understanding the workplace* (5th ed.). New York, NY: Worth Publishers.

Lewin, K. (1947). Frontiers in group dynamics. *Human Relations*, *1*, 2–38.

Lewin, K., Lippitt, R., & White, R.K. (1939). Patterns of aggressive behavior in experimentally created social climates. *Journal of Social Psychology*, *10*, 271–301.

Likert, R. (1932). A technique for the measurement of attitudes. *Archives of Psychology*, *22*, 1–55.

Likert, R. (1961). *New patterns of management*. New York, NY: McGraw-Hill.

Link, H. C. (1918). An experiment in employment psychology. *Psychological Review*, *25*, 116–127.

Link, H. C. (1919). *Employment psychology: The application of scientific methods to the selection, training, and grading of employees*. New York, NY: Macmillan.

Link, H. C. (1920). The applications of psychology to industry. *Psychological Bulletin*, *17*, 335–346.

Link, H. C. (1921). A new journal of practical psychology and a translation of its introductory article. *Journal of Applied Psychology*, *5*, 85–88.

Link, H. C. (1923a). *Education and industry*. New York, NY: Macmillan.

Link, H. C. (1923b). What is intelligence? *The Atlantic Monthly*, *132*, 374–385.

Lipmann, O. (1926–27). Industrial psychology in Germany. *Journal of Personnel Research*, *5*, 97–99.

Lipmann, O. (1928–29). The human factor in production. *Personnel Journal*, *7*, 87–95.

Locke, E. A. (1968). Toward a theory of task motivation and incentives. *Organizational Behavior and Human Decision Processes*, *3*, 157–189.

Locke, E. A. (1982). The ideas of Frederick W. Taylor: An Evaluation. *Academy of Management Review*, *7*, 14–24.

Lofquist, I. H., & Dawis, R. V. (1969). *Adjustment to work: A psychological view of man's problems in a work-oriented society*. New York, NY: Appleton-Century-Crofts.

Lohman, D. F. (1997). The history of intelligence testing in context: The impact of personal, religious, and scientific beliefs on the development of theories and tests of human abilities. In R. F. Dillon (ed.), *Handbook on testing* (pp. 82–106). Westport, CT: Greenwood Press.

Longstaff, H. P. (1947). A note of popular pseudo-psychological beliefs in 1923 and 1946. *Journal of Applied Psychology, 31,* 91–93.

Lovett, B. J. (2006). The new history of psychology: A review and critique. *History of Psychology, 9,* 17–37.

Lovett, B. J. (2017). For balance in the historiography of psychology: Reply to Brock (2017). *History of Psychology, 20,* 218–224.

Lowe, K. B., & Gardner, W. L. (2000). Ten years of *Leadership Quarterly*: Contributions and challenges for the future. *Leadership Quarterly, 11,* 459–514.

Lowman, R. L., Kantor, J., & Perloff, R. (2007). A history of I-O psychology educational programs in the United States. In L. L. Koppes (ed.), *Historical perspectives in industrial and organizational psychology* (pp. 111–137). Mahwah, NJ: Lawrence Erlbaum Associates.

Magnusson, M. (ed.) (1990). *Chambers Biographical Dictionary*. Edinburgh: Chambers Harrap Publishers, Ltd.

Manson, G. E. (1925a). Group differences in intelligence tests: The relative difficulty of types of questions. *Journal of Applied Psychology, 9,* 156–175.

Manson, G. E. (1925b). Personality differences in intelligence test performance. *Journal of Applied Psychology, 9,* 230–255.

Manson, G. E. (1925–26a). What can the application blank tell? Evaluation of items in personal history records of four thousand life insurance salesmen. *Journal of Personnel Research, 4,* 73–99.

Manson, G. E. (1925–26b). Bibliography on psychological tests and other objective measures in industrial personnel. *Journal of Personnel Research, 4,* 301–328.

Manson, G. E. (1931). Occupational interests and personality requirements of women in business and in the professions. *Michigan Business Studies, 3(3).*

Marbe, K. (1936). Karl Marbe. In C. Murchison (ed.), *A history of psychology in autobiography* (Vol. 3, pp. 181–213). Worcester, MA: Clark University Press.

March, J. G., & Simon, H. A. (1958). *Organizations*. New York, NY: John Wiley & Sons.

Marrow, A. J. (1969). *The practical theorist: The life and work of Kurt Lewin*. New York, NY: Basic Books.

Maslow, A. H. (1943). A theory of human motivation. *Psychological Review, 50,* 370–396.

Maynard, D. C., Geberth, K. L., & Joseph, T. A. (2002). Coverage of industrial/organizational psychology in introductory textbooks: An update. *Teaching of Psychology, 29,* 154–157.

Mayo, E. (1923). The irrational factor in human behavior. *Annals of the American Academy of Political and Social Sciences, 110,* 117–121.

Mayo, E. (1924). The basis of industrial psychology. *Bulletin of the Taylor Society, 9,* 249–259.

Mayo, E. (1924–25). Revery and industrial fatigue. *Journal of Personnel Research, 3,* 273–281.

Mayo, E. (1933). *The human problems of an industrial civilization.* New York, NY: Viking.

McCollom, I. N. (1959). Psychologists in industry in the United States. *American Psychologist, 14*, 704–708.

McCollom, I. N. (1968). Industrial psychology around the world: Part one: America and Western Europe. Part Two: Eastern Europe, Africa, Asia, and Australasia. *International Review of Applied Psychology, 17*, 3–19; 137–148.

McComas, H. (1914). Some tests for efficiency in telephone operators. *Journal of Philosophy, Psychology, and Scientific Methods, 11*, 293–294.

McCormick, E. J. (1979). *Job analysis: Methods and applications.* New York, NY: AMACOM.

McCormick, E. J., Jeanneret, P. R., & Mecham, R. C. (1972). A study of job characteristics and job dimensions as based on the Position Analysis Questionnaire (PAQ). *Journal of Applied Psychology, 56*, 347–368.

McDougall, W. (1928). *An outline of psychology* (4th ed.). London: Methuen.

McGehee, W., & Thayer, P. (1961). *Training in business and industry.* New York, NY: McGraw-Hill.

McGovern, T. V., & Brewer, C. L. (2013). Undergraduate education in psychology. In D. K. Freedheim & I. B. Weiner (eds.), *Handbook of psychology Volume 1: History of psychology* (pp. 507–529). Hoboken, NJ: John Wiley & Sons.

McGregor, D. M. (1957). The human side of enterprise. *Management Review, 46*, 22–28.

McGregor, D. M. (1960). *The human side of enterprise.* New York, NY: McGraw-Hill.

McLeish, J. (1975). *Soviet psychology: History, theory, content.* London: Methuen & Co.

McReynolds, P. (1997). Lightner Witmer: The first clinical psychologist. In W. G. Bringmann, H. E. Lück, R. Miller, & C. E. Early (eds.), *A pictorial history of psychology* (pp. 465–470). Chicago, IL: Quintessence Publishing.

Meehl, P. E. (1954). *Clinical vs. statistical prediction.* Minneapolis: University of Minnesota Press.

Meine, F. (1923). Job analysis for employment purposes. *Annals of the American Academy of Political and Social Science, 110*, 22–31.

Meriam, J. L. (1906). *Normal school education and efficiency in teaching.* Teachers College Contributions to Education, *152*. New York, NY: Columbia University.

Merrill, H. F. (ed.) (1960). *Classics in management.* New York, NY: American Management Association.

Meskill, D. (2015). Psychological testing and the German labor market, 1925–1965. *History of Psychology, 18*, 353–366.

Meyer, H. H. (2007). The influence of formal and informal organizations on the development of I-O psychology. In L. L. Koppes (ed.), *Historical perspectives in industrial and organizational psychology* (pp. 139–168). Mahwah, NJ: Erlbaum.

Meyer, H. H., Kay, E., & French, J. R. P., Jr. (1965). Split roles in performance appraisal. *Harvard Business Review, 43*, 123–129.

Miller, R. (1997). Martha Muchow's concept of lifespace. In W. G. Bringmann, H. E. Lück, R. Miller, & C. E. Early (eds.), *A pictorial history of psychology* (pp. 337–341). Chicago, IL: Quintessence Publishing.

Miner, J. B. [James] (1922). An aid to the analysis of vocational interests. *Journal of Educational Research*, 5, 311–323.

Miner, J. B. [John] (2002). *Organizational behavior: Foundations, theories, and analyses*. New York, NY: Oxford University Press.

Miner, J. B. [John] (2006). *Organizational behavior 2: Essential theories of process and structure*. Armonk, NY: M. E. Sharpe.

Minton, H. L. (1997). Lewis M. Terman: Architect for a psychologically stratified society. In W. G. Bringmann, H. E. Lück, R. Miller, & C. E. Early (eds.), *A pictorial history of psychology* (pp. 329–336). Chicago, IL: Quintessence Publishing.

Mitchell, B. R. (1980). *European historical statistics, 1750–1975* (2nd ed.). New York, NY: Facts on File.

Moore, B. V. (1921). Personnel selection of graduate engineers: The differentiation of apprentice engineers for training as salesmen, designers, and executives of production. *Psychological Monographs, 30*(138).

Moore, B. V. (1962). Some beginnings of industrial psychology. In B. V. Gilmer (ed.), *Walter Van Dyke Bingham: Memorial Program/March 23, 1961* (pp. 1–5). Pittsburgh, PA: Carnegie Institute of Technology.

Moore, B. V., & Hartmann, G. W. (eds.) (1931). *Readings in industrial psychology*. New York, NY: Appleton-Century.

Moore, H. (1939). *Psychology for business and industry*. New York, NY: McGraw-Hill.

Moss, F. A. (1931). Scholastic aptitude tests for medical students. *Journal of the Association of American Medical Colleges*, 6, 1–16.

Muchinsky, P. M., & Culbertson, S. S. (2016). *Psychology applied to work* (11th Ed). Summerfield, NC: Hypergraphic Press.

Muhs, W. F. (1986). The Emerson Engineers: A look at one of the first management consulting firms in the U.S. In J. Pearce & R. Robinson (eds.), *Academy of Management best paper proceedings* (pp. 123–127). New York, NY: Academy of Management.

Münsterberg, H. (1913). *Psychology and industrial efficiency*. Boston, MA: Houghton Mifflin.

Münsterberg, H. (1914). *Psychology: General and applied*. New York and London: Appleton.

Münsterberg, H. (1918). *Business psychology*. Chicago, IL: LaSalle Extension University.

Murchison, C. (1929). *The psychological register* (Vol. 2). Worcester, MA: Clark University Press.

Murphy, G. (1929). *An historical introduction to modern psychology*. New York, NY: Harcourt Brace.

Murphy, G. (1930). *A historical introduction to modern psychology* (2nd ed.). London: Harcourt, Brace, & Co.

Murray, H. A. (1938). *Explorations in personality: A clinical and experimental study of fifty men of college age.* New York, NY: Oxford University Press.

Muscio, B. A. (1917). *Lectures on industrial psychology.* Sydney: Angus & Robertson.

Muscio, B. (1920). *Lectures on industrial psychology* (2nd ed.). London: Routledge.

Myers, C. S. (1911). *An introduction to experimental psychology.* Cambridge, England: Cambridge University Press.

Myers, C. S. (1920). Psychology and industry. *The British Journal of Psychology, 10,* 177–182.

Myers, C. S. (1925). *Industrial psychology.* New York, NY: People's Institute Publishing Company.

Myers, C. S. (1926). *Industrial psychology in Great Britain.* London: Cape.

Myers, C. S. (1929). *Industrial psychology.* London: Thornton Butterworth Ltd.

Myers, C. S. (1936). Charles Samuel Myers. In C. Murchison (ed.), *A history of psychology in autobiography* (Vol. 3, pp. 215–230). Worcester, MA: Clark University Press.

Nance, R. D. (1962). Current practices in teaching the history of psychology. *American Psychologist, 17,* 250–252.

Napoli, D. S. (1981). *Architects of adjustment: The history of the psychological profession in the United States.* Port Washington, NY: Kennibat Press.

Nelson, D. (1975). *Managers and workers: Origins of the new factory system in the United States 1880–1920.* Madison: University of Wisconsin Press.

News and Comment (1922a). *Journal of Applied Psychology, 6,* 81.

News and Comment (1922b). *Journal of Applied Psychology, 6,* 417.

News Notes (1922–23). *Journal of Personnel Research, 1,* 37–41.

*New York Times* (1936, March 8). Notes of the New York Schools. N9.

*New York Times* (1960, April 19). Beardsley Ruml obituary. 1, 37.

Norcross, J. C., Hailstorks, R., Aiken, L. S., Pfund, R. A., Stamm, K. E., & Christidis, P. (2016). Undergraduate study in psychology: Curriculum and assessment. *American Psychologist, 71,* 89–101.

Notes and News (1925). *Journal of Applied Psychology, 9,* 204.

Notes and News (1927). *Journal of Applied Psychology, 11,* 81.

O'Donnell, J. M. (1979). The crisis of experimentalism in the 1920s: E. G. Boring and his uses of history. *American Psychologist, 34,* 289–295.

O'Neil, W. M. (1986). Muscio, Bernard (1887–1926). *Australian Dictionary of Biography.* Retrieved from http://adb.anu.edu.au/biography/muscio-benard-7714/text13511.

Oschrin, E. (1918). Vocational tests for retail saleswomen. *Journal of Applied Psychology, 2,* 148–155.

Osterhammel, J. (2014). *The transformation of the world: A global history of the nineteenth century* (Patrick Camiller, trans.). Princeton, NJ: Princeton University Press.

Otis, A. S. (1920). The selection of mill workers by mental tests. *Journal of Applied Psychology, 4,* 339–341.

Ott, J. S. (ed.) (1989). *Classic readings in organizational behavior.* Pacific Grove, CA: Brooks/Cole.

Owen, R. (1825/1960). To the superintendents of manufactories, and to those individuals generally, who, by given employment to an aggregated population, may easily adopt the means to form the sentiments and manners of such a population. In H. F. Merrill (ed.), *Classics in management* (pp. 21–25). New York, NY: American Management Association.

Owens, W. A. (1976). Background data. In M. D. Dunnette (ed.), *Handbook of industrial and organizational psychology* (pp. 609–644). Chicago, IL: Rand McNally.

Parot, F. (2012). France. In D. B. Baker (ed.), *The Oxford handbook of the history of psychology: Global perspectives* (pp. 228–254). New York, NY: Oxford University Press.

Parsons, F. (1909). *Choosing a vocation*. Boston, MA: Houghton-Mifflin.

Paterson, D. G. (1922–23). The Scott Company's File Clerk Test. *Journal of Personnel Research, 1*, 547–561.

Paterson, D. G., & Ludgate, K. E. (1922–23). Blond and brunette traits: A quantitative study. *Journal of Personnel Research, 1*, 122–127.

Patterson (sic.), D. G. (1923). A note on popular pseudo-psychological beliefs. *Journal of Applied Psychology, 7*, 101–102.

Paulík, K. (2004). The history of psychology of work and organization in Czech and Slovak industry. *European Psychologist, 9*, 170–179.

Payne, S. C., & Pariyothorn, M. M. (2007). I-O psychology in introductory textbooks: A survey of authors. Retrieved from http://siop.org/tip/April07/07 payne.aspx. on April 5, 2015.

Pear, T H. (1948). Industrial psychology as I have seen it. *Occupational Psychology, 22*, 107–117.

Peirce, C. S., & Jastrow, J. (1885). On small differences of sensation. *Memoirs of the National Academy of Sciences for 1884, 3*, 75–83.

Perloff, R., & Naman, J. L. (1996). Lillian Gilbreth: Tireless advocate for a general psychology. In G. A. Kimble, C. A. Boneau, & M. Wertheimer (eds.), *Portraits of pioneers in psychology* (Vol. 2, pp. 106–116). Washington, DC: American Psychological Association.

Perrow, C. (1986). The short and glorious history of organizational theory. In F. J. Landy (ed.), *Readings in industrial and organizational psychology* (pp. 321–331). Chicago, IL: Dorsey.

Person, H. S. (1924). Industrial psychology: A layman considers its status and problems. *Bulletin of the Taylor Society, 9*, 163–171.

Person, H. S. (1947/1972). Foreword. In F. W. Taylor, *Scientific management: Comprising shop management, the principles of scientific management, testimony before the Special House Committee* (pp. v–xvi). Westport, CT: Greenwood Press.

Pickren, W. E., & Fowler, R. D. (2013). Professional organizations. In Freedheim, D. K. (ed.) & I. B. Weiner (ed.-in-Chief), *Handbook of psychology Vol. 1: History of psychology* (2nd ed., pp. 597–617). Hoboken, NJ: John Wiley & Sons.

Pickren, W. E., & Rutherford, A. (2010). *A history of modern psychology in context*. Hoboken, NJ: John Wiley & Sons.

Pillsbury, W. B. (1929). *The history of psychology*. New York, NY: Norton.

Pillsbury, W. B. (1941). Edouard Claparède 1873–1940. *Psychological Review, 48,* 271–278.

Pillsbury, W. B. (1946). Clarence Stone Yoakum 1879–1945. *Psychological Review, 53,* 195–198.

Pintner, R. (1923). *Intelligence testing: Methods and results*. New York, NY: Henry Holt and Company.

Poffenberger, A. T. (1925). *Psychology in advertising*. Chicago, IL: Shaw.

Poffenberger, A. T. (1927). *Applied psychology: Its principles and methods*. New York, NY: Appleton.

Poffenberger, A. T. (1933). Report on supply and demand for psychologists presented by the Committee on the Ph.D. in Psychology, Proceedings of the forty-first annual meeting of the American Psychological Association, Incorporated, Chicago, Illinois, September 7, 8, 9, 11, 12, 13, 1933. *Psychological Bulletin, 30,* 648–654.

Pond, M. (1926–27). Selective placement of metal workers I. Preliminary studies. II. Development of scales for placement. III. Selection of toolmaking apprentices. *Journal of Personnel Research, 5,* 345–368; 405–417; 452–466.

Porter, L. W. (1966). Personnel management. In P. R. Farnsworth, O. McNemar, & Q. McNemar (eds.), *Annual review of psychology* (pp. 395–422). Palo Alto, CA: Annual Reviews, Inc.

Pressey, S. L., & Pressey, L. W. (1919). "Cross-out" tests with suggestions as to a group scale of the emotions. *Journal of Applied Psychology, 3,* 138–150.

Prien, E. P. (1991). The Division of Applied Psychology at the Carnegie Institute of Technology. *Industrial-Organizational Psychologist, 29,* 41–45.

Prien, E. P., & Ronan, W. W. (1971). Job analysis: Review of research findings. *Personnel Psychology, 24,* 371–396.

Prien, E. P., Schippmann, J. S., & Prien, K. O. (2003). *Individual assessment: As practiced in industry and consulting*. Mahwah NJ: Lawrence Erlbaum Associates.

Primoff, E. S., & Fine, S. A. (1988). A history of job analysis. In S. Gael (ed.), *The job analysis handbook for business, industry, and government* (Vol. 1, pp. 14–29). New York, NY: John Wiley & Sons.

Putnam, M. L. (1929–30). Improving employee relations: A plan which uses data obtained from employees. *Personnel Journal, 8,* 314–325.

Ream, M. J. (1922). Group will-temperament tests. *Journal of Educational Psychology, 13,* 7–16.

Ream, M. J. (1924). *Ability to sell*. Baltimore, MD: Williams and Wilkins.

Renwick, W. (2013). Beeby, Clarence Edward. In *The dictionary of New Zealand biography. Te Ara – The encyclopedia of New Zealand* (updated June 5, 2013). Retrieved from www.TeAra.gov.nz/en/biographies/5b17/beeby-clarence -edward.

Rice, S. A. (1926–27). "Stereotypes": A source of error in judging human character. *Journal of Personnel Research, 5,* 267–276.

Roback, A. A. (1917). The moral issues involved in applied psychology. *Journal of Applied Psychology, 1*, 232–243.

Rodger, A. (1971). C. S. Myers in retrospect. *Bulletin of the British Psychological Society, 24*, 177–184.

Rodgers, D. T. (1998). *Atlantic crossings: Social politics in a Progressive age.* Cambridge, MA: Belknap Press of Harvard University Press.

Roethlisberger, F. J. (1941). *Management and morale.* Cambridge, MA: Harvard University Press.

Roethlisberger, F. J., & Dickson, W. J. (1939). *Management and the worker: An account of a research program conducted by the Western Electric Company, Hawthorne Works, Chicago.* Cambridge, MA: Harvard University Press.

Rogers, H. W. (1917). Psychological tests for stenographers and typewriters. *Journal of Applied Psychology, 1*, 268–274.

Rogers, H. W. (1946). *Biographical information.* Lafayette College Archives, Easton, PA.

Rogers, T. B. (1995). *The psychological testing enterprise: An introduction.* Pacific Grove, CA: Brooks/Cole.

Ross, D. (1969). The "Zeitgeist" and American psychology. *Journal of the History of the Behavioral Sciences, 5*, 256–262.

Ross, D. (1972). *G. Stanley Hall: The psychologist as prophet.* Chicago, IL: University of Chicago Press.

Rozin, P. (2006). Domain denigration and process preference in academic psychology. *Perspectives on Psychological Science, 1*, 365–376.

Ruse, M. (2015). Myth 12: That Wallace's and Darwin's explanations of evolution were virtually the same. In R. L. Numbers & K. Kampourakis (eds.), *Newton's apple and other myths about science* (pp. 96–102). Cambridge, MA: Harvard University Press.

Russell, C. J. (1991). A conversation with Morris S. Viteles. *The Industrial-Organizational Psychologist, 28*, 69–71.

Ryan, T. A., & Smith, P. C. (1954). *Principles of industrial psychology.* New York, NY: Ronald Press.

Salas, E., Priest, H. A., Stagl, K. C., Sims, D. E., & Burke, C. S. (2007). Work teams in organizations: A historical reflection and lessons learned. In L. L. Koppes (ed.), *Historical perspectives in industrial and organizational psychology* (pp. 407–438). Mahwah, NJ: Erlbaum.

Salgado, J. F. (2001). Some landmarks of 100 years of scientific personnel selection at the beginning of the new century. *International Journal of Selection and Assessment, 9*, 3–8.

Salgado, J. F. (2007). History of industrial/organizational psychology in Europe and the United Kingdom. In S. G. Rogelberg (ed.), *Encyclopedia of industrial and organizational psychology* (Vol. 1, pp. 309–312). Thousand Oaks, CA: Sage.

Salgado, J. F., Anderson, N. R., & Hülsheger, U. R. (2010). Employee selection in Europe: Psychotechnics and the forgotten history of modern scientific employee selection. In J. L. Farr & N. T. Tippins (eds.), *Handbook of employee selection* (pp. 921–941). New York, NY: Routledge.

Samelson, F. (1977). World War I intelligence testing and the development of psychology. *Journal of the History of the Behavioral Sciences, 13*, 274–282.

Samelson, F. (1980). E. G. Boring and his *History of experimental psychology. American Psychologist, 35*, 467–470.

Sarton, G. (1936/1957). *The study of the history of science.* Reprinted in *The study of the history of mathematics and the study of the history of science: Two volumes bound as one.* New York, NY: Dover Publications.

Sarup, G. (1978). Historical antecedents of psychology: The recurrent issue of old wine in new bottles. *American Psychologist, 33*, 478–485.

Savickas, M. L., & Baker, D. B. (2005). The history of vocational psychology: Antecedents, origin, and early development. In W. B. Walsh & M. L. Savickas (eds.), *Handbook of vocational psychology: Theory, practice, research:* (3rd ed., pp. 15–50). Mahwah, NJ: Lawrence Erlbaum Associates.

Schein, E. (1985). *Organizational culture and leadership: A dynamic view.* San Francisco: Jossey-Bass.

Schlueter, P., & Schlueter, J. (eds.) (2005). *Francis A. March: Selected writings of the first professor of English.* Easton, PA: Friends of Skillman Library, Lafayette College.

Schmidt, F. L. (1992). What do data really mean? Research findings, meta-analysis, and cumulative knowledge in psychology. *American Psychologist, 47*, 1173–1181.

Schmidt, F. L., & Hunter, J. E. (1977). Development of a general solution to the problem of validity generalization. *Journal of Applied Psychology, 62*, 529–540.

Schmidt, F. L., & Hunter, J. E. (1998). The validity and utility of selection methods in personnel psychology: Practical and theoretical implications of 85 years of research findings. *Psychological Bulletin, 124*, 262–274.

Schmidt, F. L., Hunter, J. E., McKenzie, R. C., & Muldrow, T. W. (1979). Impact of valid selection procedures on workforce productivity. *Journal of Applied Psychology, 64*, 609–626.

Schmidt, F.L., Ones, D. S., & Hunter, J. E. (1992). Personnel selection. In M. R. Rosenzweig & L. W. Porter (eds.), *Annual review of psychology* (pp. 627–670). Palo Alto, CA: Annual Reviews, Inc.

Schmidt, W. (1997). William Stern. In W. G. Bringmann, H. E. Lück, R. Miller, & C. E. Early (eds.), *A pictorial history of psychology* (pp. 322–325). Chicago, IL: Quintessence Publishing.

Schultz, D. P., & Schultz, S. E. (2004). *A history of modern psychology* (8th ed.). Belmont, CA: Thomson Wadsworth.

Schumann, D. W., & Davidson, E. (2007). Early influences of applied psychologists on consumer response: 1895–1925. In L. L. Koppes (ed.), *Historical Perspectives in industrial and organizational psychology* (pp. 265–280). Mahwah, NJ: Erlbaum.

Scott Company announcement (n.d.). Ferguson Collection. Carnegie Mellon University, Pittsburgh, PA.

Scott, W. D. (1903). *Theory of advertising.* Boston, MA: Small, Maynard.

Scott, W. D. (1908). *The psychology of advertising.* Boston, MA: Small, Maynard.

Scott, W. D. (1911). *Increasing human efficiency in business*. New York, NY: Macmillan.

Scott, W. D. (1915, October). The scientific selection of salesmen. *Advertising & Selling, 5–6*, 94–96.

Scott, W. D. (1916a). Selection of employees by means of quantitative determinations. *Annals of the American Political and Social Sciences, 65*, 182–193.

Scott, W. D. (1916b). *Aids in the selection of salesmen*. Pittsburgh, PA: Carnegie Institute of Technology.

Scott, W. D. (1917). A fourth method of checking results in vocational selection. *Journal of Applied Psychology, 1*, 61–66.

Scott, W. D. (1920). Changes in some of our conceptions and practices of personnel. *Psychological Review, 27*, 81–94.

Scott, W. D., Bingham, W. V., & Whipple, G. M. (1916). Scientific selection of salesmen. *Salesmanship, 4*, 106–108.

Scott, W. D., & Clothier, R. C. (1923). *Personnel Management*. Chicago, IL: Shaw.

Scott, W. D., & Hayes, M. H. S. (1921). *Science and common sense in working with men*. New York, NY: Ronald.

Scovill Manufacturing Company Employment Tests. (1928–29). *Personnel Journal, 7*, 143–145.

Scripture, E. W. (1895). *Thinking, feeling, doing*. New York, NY: Flood & Vincent.

Scudder, K. J. (1929). The predictive value of general intelligence tests in the selection of junior accountants and book-keepers. *Journal of Applied Psychology, 13*, 1–8.

Sells, S. B. (1964). Personnel management. In P. R. Farnsworth, O. McNemar, & Q. McNemar (eds.), *Annual review of psychology* (pp. 399–420). Palo Alto, CA: Annual Reviews, Inc.

Selznick, P. (1949). *TVA and the grass roots*. Berkley, CA: University of California Press.

Shafritz, J. M., & Ott, J. S. (eds.) (1996). *Classics of organization theory* (4th ed.). Belmont, CA: Wadsworth.

Sheldon, W. H. (1927–28). Social traits and morphologic types. *Personnel Journal, 6*, 47–55.

Shellow, S. M. (1925–26). Research in selection of motormen in Milwaukee. *Journal of Personnel Research, 4*, 222–237.

Shellow, S. M. (1926–27a). Selection of motormen: Further data on the value of tests in Milwaukee. *Journal of Personnel Research, 5*, 183–188.

Shellow, S. M. (1926–27b). An intelligence test for stenographers. *Journal of Personnel Research, 5*, 306–308.

Shore, R. P. (1982). Servants of Power revisited. *American Psychologist, 37*, 334–335.

*Shorter Oxford English Dictionary*, 5th ed. (2002). Oxford: Oxford University Press.

Simon, H. A. (1947). *Administrative behavior: A study of decision-making processes in administrative organizations*. New York, NY: Free Press.

Sirotkina, I., & Smith, R. (2012). Russian Federation. In D. B. Baker (ed.), *The Oxford handbook of the history of psychology: Global perspectives* (pp. 412–441). New York, NY: Oxford University Press.

Smith, A. (1776/1925). *An inquiry into the nature and causes of the wealth of nations* (4th ed.; 2nd vol.). London: Methuen & Co.

Smith, P. C., & Kendall, L. M. (1963). Retranslation of expectations: An approach to the construction of unambiguous anchors for rating scales. *Journal of Applied Psychology, 47*, 149–155.

Smith, P. C. Kendall, & Hulin, C. L. (1969). *Measurement of satisfaction in work and retirement.* Chicago, IL: Rand McNally.

Smith, R. (2007). Why history matters. *Revista de Historia de la Psicología, 28*, 125–146.

Snow, A. J. (1923). Labor turnover and mental alertness test scores. *Journal of Applied Psychology, 7*, 285–290.

Sokal, M. M. (1971). The unpublished autobiography of James McKeen Cattell. *American Psychologist, 26*, 626–635.

Sokal, M. M. (1981). The origins of the Psychological Corporation. *Journal of the History of the Behavioral Sciences, 17*, 54–67.

Sokal, M. M. (1984). James McKeen Cattell and American psychology in the 1920s. In J. Brozek (ed.), *Explorations in the history of psychology in the United States* (pp. 273–323). Lewisburg, PA: Bucknell University Press.

Sokal, M. M. (1987). James McKeen Cattell and mental anthropometry: Nineteenth century science and reform and the origins of psychological testing. In M. M. Sokal (ed.), *Psychological testing and American society 1890–1930* (pp. 21–45). New Brunswick, NJ: Rutgers University Press.

Sokal, M. M. (1992). Origins and early years of the American Psychological Association. *American Psychologist, 47*, 111–122.

Sokal, M. M. (1995). Stargazing: James McKeen Cattell, American men of science, and the reward structure of the scientific community. In F. Kessel (ed.), *Psychology, science, and human affairs: Essays in honor of William Bevan* (pp. 64–86). Boulder, CO: Westview.

Sokal, M. M. (2009). James McKeen Cattell, Nicholas Murray Butler, and academic freedom at Columbia University, 1902–1923. *History of Psychology, 12*, 87–122.

Spearman, C. (1904). General intelligence, objectively determined and measured. *American Journal of Psychology, 15*, 201–293.

Spearman, C. (1927). *The abilities of man: Their nature and measurement.* New York, NY: Macmillan.

Spector, P. E. (2016). *Industrial and organizational psychology: Research and practice* (7th ed.). Hoboken, NJ: John Wiley & Sons.

Spillmann, J., & Spillmann L. (1993). The rise and fall of Hugo Münsterberg. *Journal of the History of the Behavioral Sciences, 29*, 322–338.

Sporer, S. L. (1997). The origins of the psychology of testimony. In W. G. Bringmann, H. E. Lück, R. Miller, & C. E. Early (eds.), *A pictorial history of psychology* (pp. 476–479). Chicago, IL: Quintessence Publishing.

Sprung, L., & Sprung, H. (2001). History of modern psychology in Germany in 19th and 20th century thought and society. *International Journal of Psychology, 36*, 364–376.

Stagner, R. (1982). Reply to Shore. *American Psychologist, 37*, 335.

Starch, D. (1910). *Principles of advertising.* Madison, WI: University Cooperative Co.

Starch, D. (1915). The measurement of efficiency in reading. *Journal of Educational Psychology, 6*, 1–24.

Stern, W. (1923). Psychological science in Germany. *Scandinavian Scientific Review: Contributions to Philosophy, Psychology, and the Science of Education by Northern Scientists, 2*, 225–229.

Stern, W. (1934). Otto Lipmann: 1880–1933. *American Journal of Psychology, 46*, 152–154.

Stevens G., & Gardner, S. (1982). *The women of psychology, Vol. 1: Pioneers and innovators.* Cambridge, MA: Schenkman.

Stevens, S. S. (1973). *Edwin Garrigues Boring 1886–1968.* Washington, DC: National Academy of Sciences.

Stigler, S. M. (1999). *Statistics on the table: The history of statistical concepts and methods.* Cambridge, MA: Harvard University Press.

Stocking, G. (1965). On the limits of 'presentism' and 'historicism' in the historiography of the behavioral sciences. *Journal of the History of the Behavioral Sciences, 1*, 211–219.

Sturdevant, C. R. (1918). Training course of the American Steel & Wire Company. *Journal of Applied Psychology, 2*, 140–147.

Strelau, J. (1998). *Temperament: A psychological perspective.* New York, NY: Plenum Press.

Strong, E. K., Jr. (1911). *The relative merit of advertisements: A psychological and statistical study.* Dissertation. Columbia University. *Archives of Psychology, 17; Columbia Contributions to Philosophy and Psychology,* 19(3).

Strong, E. K., Jr. (1918). Work of the Committee of Classification of Personnel. *Journal of Applied Psychology, 2*, 130–139.

Strong, E. K., Jr. (1927). Vocational interest test. *Educational Record, 8*, 107–121.

Strong, E. K., Jr., & Uhrbrock, R. S. (1923). *Job analysis and the curriculum.* Baltimore, MD: Williams & Wilkins Co.

Summerscales, W. (1970). *Affirmation and dissent: Columbia's response to the crisis in World War I.* New York, NY: Teachers College Press.

Sward, K. (1935). Patterns of Jewish temperament. *Journal of Applied Psychology, 19*, 410–425.

Tagg, M. (1925). Industrial psychology in Russia. *Journal of the Institute of Industrial Psychology, 2*, 359–364.

Takasuna, M. (2012). Japan. In D. B. Baker (ed.), *The Oxford handbook of the history of psychology: Global perspectives* (pp. 347–365). New York, NY: Oxford University Press.

Taylor, F. W. (1903/1972). *Shop management.* Reprint of the 1947 compilation *Scientific management.* Westport, CT: Greenwood Press.

Taylor, F. W. (1911). *Principles of scientific management*. New York, NY: Harper.

Taylor, F. W. (1911/1972). *Principles of scientific management*. Reprint of the 1947 compilation *Scientific management*. Westport, CT: Greenwood Press.

Taylor, F. W. (1912/1972). *Taylor's testimony before the Special House Committee*. Reprint of the 1947 compilation *Scientific management*. Westport, CT: Greenwood Press.

Taylor, E. K., & Nevis, E. C. (1961). Personnel selection. In P. R. Farnsworth, O. McNemar, & Q. McNemar (eds.), *Annual review of psychology* (pp. 389–412). Palo Alto, CA: Annual Reviews.

Taylor, H. C., & Russell, J. T. (1939). The relationship of validity coefficients to the practical effectiveness of tests in selection. *Journal of Applied Psychology*, *23*, 565–578.

Tenopyr, M. L., & Oeltjen, P. D. (1982). Personnel selection and classification. In M. R. Rosenzweig & L. W. Porter (eds.), *Annual review of psychology* (581–618). Palo Alto, CA: Annual Reviews.

Terman, L. M. (1921). The status of applied psychology in the United States. *Journal of Applied Psychology*, *1*, 1–4.

Terman, L. M. (1922). The psychological determinist; or democracy and the I.Q. *Journal of Educational Research*, *6*, 57–62.

Thayer, P. W., & Austin, J. T. (1992). Harold E. Burtt (1890–1991). *American Psychologist*, *47*, 1677.

Thomas, K. (1999). Introduction. In K. Thomas (ed.), *The Oxford book of work* (pp. xiii–xxiii). Oxford: Oxford University Press.

Thompson, A. S. (1992). Doctoral training in I/O psychology at the University of Pennsylvania: History and characteristics. *The Industrial-Organizational Psychologist*, *30*, 15–18.

Thompson, A. S. (1998). Morris S. Viteles. *American Psychologist*, *53*, 1153–1154.

Thomson, G. H. (1916). A hierarchy without a general factor. *British Journal of Psychology*, *8*, 271–281.

Thomson, G. H. (1952). Godfrey Thomson. In E. G. Boring, H. S. Langfeld, H. Werner, & R. M. Yerkes (eds.), *A history of psychology in autobiography* (Vol. 4, pp. 279–294). New York, NY: Russell & Russell.

Thorndike, E. L. (1904). *Introduction to a theory of mental and social measurement*. New York, NY: Science.

Thorndike, E. L. (1918). Fundamental theorems in judging men. *Journal of Applied Psychology*, *2*, 67–76.

Thorndike, E. L. (1919). Scientific personnel work in the Army. *Science*, *49*, 53–61.

Thorndike, E. L. (1920). A constant error in psychological ratings. *Journal of Applied Psychology*, *4*, 25–29.

Thorndike, E. L. (1922). *The elements of psychology* (2nd ed.). New York, NY: Seiler.

Thorndike, R. L. (1949). *Personnel selection: Test and measurement techniques*. New York, NY: John Wiley & Sons.

Thorndike, R. L. (1991). Edward L Thorndike: A professional and personal appreciation. In G. A. Kimble, M. Wertheimer, & C. L. White (eds.),

*Portraits of pioneers in psychology* (pp. 139–151). Washington, DC: American Psychological Association and Hillsdale, NJ: Lawrence Erlbaum Associates.

Thurs, D. P. (2015). Myth 26: That the scientific method accurately reflects what scientists actually do. In R. L. Numbers & K. Kampourakis (eds.), *Newton's apple and other myths about science* (pp. 210–218). Cambridge, MA: Harvard University Press.

Thurstone, L. L. (1919a). Mental tests for prospective telegraphers; A study of the diagnostic value of mental tests for predicting ability to learn telegraphy. *Journal of Applied Psychology, 3,* 110–117.

Thurstone, L. L. (1919b). A standardized test for office clerks. *Journal of Applied Psychology, 3,* 248–251.

Thurstone, L. L. (1923). Psychology in the Civil Service. *Annals of the Academy of Political and Social Science, 110,* 194–199.

Thurstone, L. L. (1924–25). What is personnel research? *Journal of Personnel Research, 3,* 52–56.

Thurstone, L. L. (1927). Law of comparative judgment. *Psychological Review, 34,* 278–286.

Thurstone, L. L. (1928). Attitudes can be measured. *American Journal of Sociology, 33,* 529–554.

Thurstone, L. L. (1929). Theory of attitude measurement. *Psychological Review, 36,* 222–241.

Thurstone, L. L. (1931). Multiple factor analysis. *Psychological Review, 38,* 406–427.

Thurstone, L. L. (1935). *The vectors of mind.* Chicago, IL: University of Chicago Press.

Thurstone, L. L. (1938). *Primary mental abilities.* Chicago, IL: University of Chicago Press.

Thurstone, L. L. (1947). *Multiple factor analysis.* Chicago, IL: University of Chicago Press.

Thurstone, L. L. (1952). L. L. Thurstone. In E. G. Boring, H. S. Langfeld, H. Werner, & R. M. Yerkes (eds.), *A history of psychology in autobiography* (Vol. 4, pp. 295–231). New York, NY: Russell & Russell.

Thurstone, L. L., & Chave, E. J. (1929). *The measurement of attitude.* Chicago, IL: University of Chicago Press.

Thurstone, L. L., & Thurstone, T. G. (1930). A neurotic inventory. *Journal of Social Psychology, 1,* 3–30.

Titchener, E. B. (1898). The postulates of a structural psychology. *Philosophical Review, 7,* 449–465.

Titchener, E. B. (1909). The psychophysics of climate. *American Journal of Psychology, 20,* 1–14.

Tinker, M. A. (1932). Wundt's doctorate students and their theses: 1875–1920. *American Journal of Psychology, 44,* 630–637.

Tonn, J. C. (2003). *Mary P. Follett: Creating democracy, transforming management.* New Haven, CT: Yale University Press.

Trahair, R. S. C. (1984). *The humanist temper: the life and work of Elton Mayo.* New Brunswick, NJ: Transaction Books.

Triandis, H. C., Dunnette, M. D., & Hough, L. M. (eds.) (1994). *Handbook of industrial and organizational psychology* (Vol. 4, 2nd ed.). Palo Alto, CA: Consulting Psychologists Press.

Trist, E. L., & Bamforth, K. W. (1951). Some social and technical consequences of the long-wall method of coal-getting. *Human Relations, 4*, 6–38.

Trist, E. L., Emory, F., Murray, H., & Trist, B. (1997). *The social engagement of social science: A Tavistock anthology: The socio-ecological perspective*. Philadelphia, PA: University of Pennsylvania Press.

Twitmyer, E. B. (1902/1974). A study of the knee jerk. *Journal of Experimental Psychology, 103*, 1047–1066 [Reprint of Twitmyer's 1902 dissertation].

Uhrbrock, R. S. (1922). The history of job analysis. *Administration, 3*, 164–168.

US Bureau of the Census (1976). *The statistical history of the United States: From colonial times to the present* (Introduction and User Guide by B. J. Wattenberg). New York, NY: Basic Books.

US Employment Service (1939). *Dictionary of occupational titles*. Washington, DC: US Government Printing Office.

Van De Water, T. J. (1997). Psychology's entrepreneurs and the marketing of industrial psychology. *Journal of Applied Psychology, 82*, 486–499.

van Drunen, P. (1997). Psychotechnics. In W. G. Bringmann, H. E. Lück, R. Miller, & C. E. Early (eds.), *A pictorial history of psychology* (pp. 480–484). Chicago, IL: Quintessence Publishing.

van Strien, P. J. (1998a). Early applied psychology between essentialism and pragmatism: The dynamics of theory, tools, and clients. *History of Psychology, 1*, 205–234.

van Strien, P. J. (1998b). Psychotechnics in the Netherlands. *Revista de Historia de la Psicologia, 19*. 121–141.

Vaughn-Blount, K., Rutherford, A., Baker, D., & Johnson, D. (2009). History's mysteries demystified: Becoming a psychologist-historian. *American Journal of Psychology, 122*, 117–129.

Vecchio, R. P. (1995). *Organizational Behavior* (3rd ed.). Fort Worth, TX: Dryden.

Vernon, P. E. (1947). Research on employee selection in the Royal Navy and British Army. *American Psychologist, 2*, 35–51.

Vinchur, A. J. (2005). Charles Samuel Myers and Otto Lipmann: Early contributors to industrial psychology. *Industrial-Organizational Psychologist, 43*, 31–35.

Vinchur, A. J. (2007). A history of psychology applied to employee selection. In L. L. Koppes (ed.), *Historical perspectives in industrial and organizational psychology* (193–218). Mahwah, NJ: Lawrence Erlbaum Associates.

Vinchur, A. J., & Koppes, L. L. (2007). Early contributors to the science and practice of industrial psychology. In L. L. Koppes (ed.), *Historical perspectives in industrial and organizational psychology* (37–58). Mahwah, NJ: Lawrence Erlbaum Associates.

Vinchur, A. J., & Koppes Bryan, L. L. (2012). A history of personnel selection and assessment. In N. Schmitt (ed.), *Oxford handbook of personnel assessment and selection*. New York, NY: Oxford University Press.

Viteles, M. S. (1921). Tests in industry. *Journal of Applied Psychology, 5*, 57–63.

Viteles, M. S. (1922). Job specifications and diagnostic tests of job competency designed for the auditing division of a street railway company. *Psychological Clinic, 14*, 83–105.

Viteles, M. S. (1923). Psychology in business – In England, France, and Germany. *Annals of the Academy of Political and Social Science, 110*, 207–220.

Viteles, M. S. (1925). The clinical viewpoint in vocational selection. *Journal of Applied Psychology, 9*, 131–138.

Viteles, M. S. (1925–26a). Research in selection of motormen: Part I. Survey of the literature. *Journal of Personnel Research, 4*, 110–115.

Viteles, M. S. (1925–26b). Standards of accomplishment: Criteria of vocational selection. *Journal of Personnel Research, 4*, 483–486.

Viteles, M. S. (1926). Psychology in industry. *Psychological Bulletin, 23*, 631–680.

Viteles, M. S. (1928a). The mental status of the Negro. *Annals of the American Academy of Political and Social Sciences, 140*, 166–177.

Viteles, M. S. (1928b). Psychology in industry, *Psychological Bulletin, 25*, 309–340.

Viteles, M. S. (1932). *Industrial psychology*. New York, NY: Norton.

Viteles, M. S. (1947). Charles Samuel Myers 1873–1946. *Psychological Review, 54*, 177–181.

Viteles, M. S. (1953). *Motivation and morale in industry*. New York, NY: Norton.

Viteles, M. S. (1959). Fundamentalism in industrial psychology. *Occupational Psychology, 33*, 98–110.

Viteles, M. S. (1967). Morris S. Viteles. In E. G. Boring & G. Lindzey (eds.), *A history of psychology in autobiography* (Vol. 5, pp. 415–449). New York, NY: Appleton-Century-Crofts.

Viteles, M. S. (1974). Industrial psychology: Reminiscences of an academic moon-lighter. In T. S. Krawiec (ed.), *The psychologists* (Vol. 2, pp. 440–500). New York, NY: Oxford University Press.

Vobořil, D., Květon, P., & Jelínek, M. (2014). *Psychological machinery: Experimental devices in early psychological laboratories*. Frankfurt am Main: Peter Lang.

von Mayrhauser, R. (1987). The manager, the medic, and the mediator: The clash of professional psychological styles and the wartime origins of group mental testing. In M. M. Sokal (ed.), *Psychological testing and American society* (pp. 128–157). New Brunswick, NJ: Rutgers University Press.

von Mayrhauser, R. (1989). Making intelligence functional: Walter Dill Scott and applied psychological testing in World War I. *Journal of the History of the Behavioral Sciences, 25*, 60–72.

von Mayrhauser, R. (1992). The mental testing community and validity: A prehistory. *American Psychologist, 47*, 244–253.

Vroom, V. H. (1964). *Work and motivation*. New York, NY: John Wiley & Sons.

Wagner, R. (1949). The employment interview: A critical summary. *Personnel Psychology, 2*, 17–46.

Wallace, S. R., & Weitz, J. (1955). Industrial psychology. In C. P. Stone & Q. McNemar (eds.), *Annual review of psychology* (pp. 217–250). Stanford CA: Annual Reviews.

Wang, Z-M. (1994). Culture, economic reform, and the role of industrial and organizational psychology in China. In H. C. Triandis, M. D. Dunnette, & L. M. Hough (eds.), *Handbook of industrial and organizational psychology* (Vol. 4, pp. 689–725). Palo Alto, CA: Consulting Psychologists Press.

Warr, P. (2007). Some historical developments in I-O psychology outside the United States. In L. L. Koppes (ed.), *Historical perspectives in industrial and organizational psychology* (pp. 81–107). Mahwah, NJ: Lawrence Erlbaum Associates.

Watson, J. B. (1913). Psychology as the behaviorist views it. *Psychological Review*, *20*, 158–177.

Watson, R. I. (1960). The history of psychology: A neglected area. *American Psychologist*, *15*, 251–255.

Weber, C. O., & Leslie, M. (1926). Clerical tests agree with employer's ratings. *Industrial Psychology*, *1*, 708–711.

Weber, M. (1922/1946). *From Max Weber: Essays in Sociology*. Oxford: Oxford University Press [Original published in 1922].

Weber, M. (1947). *The theory of social and economic organizations*. New York, NY: Free Press.

Weidman, N. (2016). Overcoming our mutual isolation: How historians and psychologists can work together. *History of Psychology*, *19*, 248–253.

Weiss, H. M. (2014). Working as human nature. In J. K. Ford, J. R. Hollenbeck, & A. M. Ryan (eds.), *The nature of work: Advances in psychological theory, methods, and practice* (pp. 35–47). Washington, DC: American Psychological Association.

Welch, H. J., & Myers, C. S. (1932). *Ten years of industrial psychology: An account of the first decade of the National Institute of Industrial Psychology*. Oxford, UK: Sir I. Pitman & Son.

Wells, F. L., (1944). James McKeen Cattell 1860–1944). *American Journal of Psychology*, *57*, 270–275.

Wembridge, H. A. (1925). Discussion [of Experimental psychology in personnel problems by C. S. Yoakum]. *Bulletin of the Taylor Society*, *10*, 162–163.

Wenzel, B. M. (1979). Albert Theodore Poffenberger (1885–1977). *American Psychologist*, *34*, 88–90.

Wernimont, P. F., & Campbell, J. P. (1968). Signs, samples, and criteria. *Journal of Applied Psychology*, *52*, 372–376.

Wherry, R. J. (1983). Appendix: Wherry's theory of rating. In F. J. Landy & J. L. Farr (eds.), *The measurement of work performance* (pp. 283–303). New York, NY: Academic Press.

Wherry, R. J., & Bartlett, C. J. (1982). The control of bias in ratings: A theory of rating. *Personnel Psychology*, *35*, 521–551.

White, M. M. (1943). James Burt Miner 1873–1943. *Psychological Review*, *50*, 632–634.

Whyte, W. H. (1954, September). The fallacies of "personality" testing. *Fortune*, pp. 117–121. Reprinted in A. LaFarge (ed.), *The essential William H. Whyte* (pp. 43–66). New York, NY: Fordham University Press.

Wiendieck, G. (1997). Industrial psychology. In W. G. Bringmann, H. E. Lück, R. Miller, & C. E. Early (eds.), *A pictorial history of psychology* (pp. 510–513). Chicago, IL: Quintessence Publishing.

Wiener, N. (1948). *Cybernetics of control and communication in the animal and in the machine.* New York, NY: John Wiley & Sons.

Wiesner, W. H., & Cronshaw, S. F. (1988). A meta-analytic investigation of the impact of the interview format and degree of structure on the validity of the employment interview. *Journal of Occupational Psychology, 61,* 275–290.

Williams, W. (1925). *Mainsprings of men.* New York, NY: Charles Scribner.

Wilson, M. A. (2007). A history of job analysis. In L. L. Koppes (ed.), *Historical perspectives in industrial and organizational psychology* (pp. 219–241). Mahwah, NJ: Lawrence Erlbaum Associates.

Winston, A. S. (1996). "As his name indicates": R. S. Woodworth's letters of reference and employment for Jewish psychologists in the 1930s. *Journal of the History of the Behavioral Sciences, 32,* 30–43.

Winston, A. S. (1998). "The defects of his race": E. G. Boring and anti-Semitism in American psychology, 1923–1953. *History of Psychology, 1,* 27–51.

Wissler, (1901). The correlation of mental and physical tests. *Psychological Review, 3,* 1–63.

Woodward, J. (1958). *Management and technology.* London: Her Majesty's Stationery Office.

Woodworth, R. S. (1919). Examination of emotional fitness for warfare (Proceedings of the twenty-seventh annual meeting of the American Psychological Association, Baltimore, December 27 and 28, 1918). *Psychological Bulletin, 16,* 59–60.

Woodworth, R. S. (1929). *Psychology* (Rev. ed.). New York, NY: Henry Holt.

Woodworth, R. S. (1932). Robert S. Woodworth. In C. Murchison (ed.), *A history of psychology in autobiography* (Vol. 2, pp. 359–380). Worcester, MA: Clark University Press.

Woodworth, R. S. (1944). James McKeen Cattell 1860–1944. *Psychological Review, 51,* 201–209.

Wren, D. A., & Bedeian, A. G. (2009). *The evolution of management thought (6th ed.).* Hoboken, NJ: John Wiley & Sons.

Wright, T. A. (2006). The emergence of job satisfaction in organizational behavior. *Journal of Management History, 12,* 262–277.

Yates, D. H. (1946). Pseudopsychology. In *Encyclopedia of psychology.* New York, NY: Philosophical Library.

Yellowitz, I. (1991). Child labor. In E. Foner & J. A. Garraty (eds.), *The reader's companion to American history* (pp. 166–167). Boston, MA: Houghton Mifflin Company.

Yerkes, R. M. (ed.) (1921). *Psychological examining in the United States Army.* Memoirs of the National Academy of Science, Vol. 15. Washington, DC: Government Printing Office.

Yerkes, R. M. (1932). Robert Mearns Yerkes. In C. Murchison (ed.), *A history of psychology in autobiography* (Vol. 2, pp. 381–407). Worcester, MA: Clark University Press.

Yoakum, C. S. (1925). Experimental psychology in personnel problems: Emphasizing the need of additional quantitative analysis in such problems as learning curve and wages, individual differences, employment, and turnover. *Bulletin of the Taylor Society, 10,* 154–160.

Yoakum, C. S., & Yerkes, R. M. (1920). *Army mental tests.* Oxford, England: Holt.

Young, K. (1923). The history of mental testing. *Pedagogical Seminary, 31,* 1–48.

Zickar, M. J. (2001). Using personality inventories to identify thugs and agitators: Applied psychology's contribution to the war against labor. *Journal of Vocational Behavior, 59,* 149–164.

Zickar, M. J. (2003). Remembering Arthur Kornhauser: Industrial psychology's advocate for worker well-being. *Journal of Applied Psychology, 88,* 363–369.

Zickar, M. J. (2004). An analysis of applied psychology's indifference to labor unions in the United States. *Human Relations, 57,* 145–167.

Zickar, M. J. (2015). Digging through dust: Historiography for the organizational sciences. *Journal of Business Psychology, 30,* 1–14.

Zickar, M. J., & Gibby, R. E. (2007). Four persistent themes throughout the history of I-O psychology in the United States. In L. L. Koppes (ed.), *Historical perspectives in industrial and organizational psychology* (61–80). Mahwah, NJ: Lawrence Erlbaum Associates.

Zionchenko, V., & Munipov, V. (2005). Fundamentals of ergonomics. In N. Moray (ed.), *Ergonomics: Major writings. Volume 1: The history and scope of human factors* (pp. 17–37). London: Taylor & Francis.

Zusne, L. (1984). *Biographical dictionary of psychology.* Westport, CT: Greenwood.

# Name Index

# Subject Index